MW00570088

CHILD AND ADOLESCENT PSYCHIATRIC CLINICS OF NORTH AMERICA

Juvenile Justice

GUEST EDITORS
Robert Vermeiren, MD, PhD, and
Vladislav Ruchkin, MD, PhD

CONSULTING EDITOR
Andrés Martin, MD, MPH

April 2006 • Volume 15 • Number 2

SAUNDERS

An Imprint of Elsevier, Inc.
PHILADELPHIA LONDON TORONTO MONTREAL SYDNEY TOKYO

W.B. SAUNDERS COMPANY
A Division of Elsevier Inc.

Elsevier Inc. • 1600 John F. Kennedy Boulevard • Suite 1800 • Philadelphia, Pennsylvania 19103-2899

http://www.childpsych.theclinics.com

CHILD AND ADOLESCENT PSYCHIATRIC CLINICS OF NORTH AMERICA
Volume 15, Number 2
April 2006
ISSN 1056-4993
Editor: Sarah E. Barth
ISBN 1-4160-3511-7

Reprints: For copies of 100 or more, of articles in this publication, please contact the Commercial Reprints Department, Elsevier Inc., 360 Park Avenue South, New York, New York 10010-1710. Tel. (212) 633-3813; Fax: (212) 462-1935; email: reprints@elsevier.com.

Child and Adolescent Psychiatric Clinics of North America (ISSN 1056-4993) is published quarterly by W.B. Saunders, 360 Park Avenue South, New York, NY 10010-1710. Months of publication are January, April, July, and October. Business and Editorial Offices: 1600 John F. Kennedy Boulevard, Suite 1800, Philadelphia, PA 19103-2899. Accounting and Circulation Offices: 6277 Sea Harbor Drive, Orlando, FL 32887-4800. Periodicals postage paid at New York, NY and additional mailing offices. Subscription prices are $185.00 per year (US individuals), $280.00 per year (US institutions), $95.00 per year (US students), $210.00 per year (Canadian individuals), $330.00 per year (Canadian institutions), $115.00 per year (Canadian students), $235.00 per year (international individuals), $330.00 per year (international institutions), and $115.00 per year (international students). International air speed delivery is included in all *Clinics* subscription prices. All prices are subject to change without notice. **POSTMASTER:** Send address changes to *Child and Adolescent Psychiatric Clinics of North America*, Elsevier Periodicals Customer Service, 6277 Sea Harbor Drive, Orlando, FL 32887–4800. **Customer Service: 1-800-654-2452 (US). From outside of the US, call 1-407-345-4000.**

Child and Adolescent Psychiatric Clinics of North America is covered in *Index Medicus, ISI, SSCI, Research Alert, Social Search, Current Contents,* and *EMBASE/Excerpta Medica.*

Printed in the United States of America.

CONSULTING EDITOR

ANDRÉS MARTIN, MD, MPH, Associate Professor of Child Psychiatry and Psychiatry, Yale Child Study Center, Yale University School of Medicine; and Medical Director, Children's Psychiatric Inpatient Service, Yale-New Haven Children's Hospital, New Haven, Connecticut

CONSULTING EDITOR EMERITUS

MELVIN LEWIS, MBBS, FRCPsych, DCH, Professor Emeritus, Senior Research Scientist, Yale Child Study Center, Yale University School of Medicine, New Haven, Connecticut

GUEST EDITORS

VLADISLAV RUCHKIN, MD, PhD, Research Fellow, Center for Violence Prevention, Karolinska Institute, Stockholm; Director of Research and Psychiatrist, Skonviks Psychiatric Clinic, Center for Forensic Psychiatry, Säter, Sweden; and Assistant Professor Adjunct, Child Study Center, Yale University School of Medicine, New Haven, Connecticut

ROBERT VERMEIREN, MD, PhD, Professor of Forensic Psychiatry, VU University Medical Center/Leiden University, Duivendrecht, The Netherlands

CONTRIBUTORS

SUSAN BAILEY, MD, PhD, Professor of Child and Adolescent Forensic Mental Health, University of Central Lancashire, Lancashire, United Kingdom

JOHN F. CHAPMAN, PsyD, Clinical Superintendent, State of Connecticut–Judicial Branch, Court Support Services Division, Wethersfield, Connecticut

RANI A. DESAI, PhD, MPH, Associate Professor, Department of Psychiatry, Yale University School of Medicine, VA Connecticut Health System, West Haven, Connecticut

THEO DORELEIJERS, MD, PhD, Department of Child Psychiatry, VU University Medical Center, Amsterdam, The Netherlands

CRAIG DOWDEN, PhD, Carleton University, Ottawa, Ontario, Canada

PAUL R. FALZER, PhD, Clinical Assistant Professor, Department of Psychiatry, Yale University School of Medicine, VA Connecticut Health System, West Haven, Connecticut

PAUL J. FRICK, PhD, Research Professor, Department of Psychology, University of New Orleans, New Orleans, Louisiana

ELENA L. GRIGORENKO, PhD, Associate Professor of Child Studies and Psychology, Child Study Center, Yale Medical School; PACE Center, Department of Psychology, Yale University, New Haven, Connecticut; and Department of Psychology, Moscow State University, Moscow, Russia

INE JESPERS, Center for Mental Health VAGGA, Antwerp, Belgium

KRISTINA KAHILA, RN, Ward Manager, Psychiatric Treatment and Research Unit for Adolescent Intensive Care (EVA), Tampere University Hospital, Tampere, Finland

RIITTAKERTTU KALTIALA-HEINO, MD, DrMedSci, Docent, Chief Psychiatrist, Psychiatric Treatment and Research Unit for Adolescent Intensive Care (EVA), Tampere University Hospital, Tampere, Finland

NIRANJAN S. KARNIK, MD, PhD, Fellow in Child and Adolescent Psychiatry, Division of Child and Adolescent Psychiatry, Stanford University School of Medicine, Palo Alto; and Adjunct Instructor in Anthropology, History, and Social Medicine, University of California School of Medicine, San Francisco, California

PAMELA KNIGHT, MA, Doctoral student in Counselor Education and Supervision, Regent University, School of Psychology and Counseling, Virginia Beach, Virginia

JEFF LATIMER, Doctoral candidate, Principal Statistician, Research and Statistics Division, Department of Justice, Ottawa, Ontario, Canada

TERRIE MOFFITT, PhD, Professor, Institute of Psychiatry, King's College London, London, United Kingdom

ARNE POPMA, MD, PhD candidate, Department of Child and Adolescent Psychiatry, VU University Medical Center, Amsterdam, The Netherlands

ADRIAN RAINE, DPhil, Professor, Department of Psychology, University of Southern California, Los Angeles, California

VLADISLAV RUCHKIN, MD, PhD, Research Fellow, Center for Violence Prevention, Karolinska Institute, Stockholm; Director of Research and Psychiatrist, Skonviks Psychiatric Clinic, Center for Forensic Psychiatry, Säter, Sweden; and Assistant Professor Adjunct, Child Study Center, Yale University School of Medicine, New Haven, Connecticut

MARIE V. SOLLER, BA, Medical student, Stanford University School of Medicine, Palo Alto, California

HANS STEINER, Dr. med. univ., FAPA, FAACAP, FAPM, Professor of Psychiatry and Behavioral Sciences; Director of Education, Division of Child and Adolescent Psychiatry; and Co-Director, Center for Psychiatry and the Law, Stanford University School of Medicine, Palo Alto, California

DENIS G. SUKHODOLSKY, PhD, Associate Research Scientist, Child Study Center, Yale University School of Medicine, New Haven, Connecticut

PAUL TARBUCK, PhD, Gardener Unit, Bolton, Salford, and Trafford Mental Health National Health Service Trust, Prestwich, Manchester, United Kingdom

CHRISTOPHER R. THOMAS, MD, Professor, Department of Psychiatry and Behavioral Sciences, University of Texas Medical Branch at Galveston, Galveston, Texas

LEE A. UNDERWOOD, PsyD, Assistant Professor of Psychology and Counseling, Regent University, School of Psychology and Counseling, Virginia Beach, Virginia; and Senior Program Consultant, National Center for Mental Health and Juvenile Justice, Delmar, New York

ROBERT VERMEIREN, MD, PhD, Professor of Forensic Psychiatry, VU University Medical Center/Leiden University, Duivendrecht, The Netherlands

GINA M. VINCENT, PhD, Assistant Professor of Psychiatry (Psychology), Center for Mental Health Services Research, Law and Psychiatry Program, Department of Psychiatry, University of Massachusetts Medical School, Worcester, Massachusetts

STEPHEN A. ZERBY, MD, Assistant Professor, Western Psychiatric Institute and Clinic, University of Pittsburgh Medical Center, Pittsburgh, Pennsylvania

Cover art courtesy of Socorro Rivera, Mexico City, Mexico.

CONTENTS

FORTHCOMING ISSUES

July 2006

Pediatric Palliative Medicine
John P. Glazer, MD,
Joanne M. Hilden, MD, and
Dunya Yaldoo Poltorak, PhD, *Guest Editors*

October 2006

Depression
Gil Zalsman, MD, and
David Brent, MD, *Guest Editors*

January 2007

Training
Chris Varley, MD, *Guest Editor*

RECENT ISSUES

January 2006

Psychopharmacology
Andrés Martin, MD, MPH, and
Jeff Q. Bostic, MD, EdD, *Guest Editors*

October 2005

Anxiety
Susan E. Swedo, MD, and
Daniel S. Pine, MD, *Guest Editors*

July 2005

Child Psychiatry and the Media
Eugene V. Beresin, MD, and
Cheryl K. Olson, SD, *Guest Editors*

Child Adolesc Psychiatric Clin N Am
15 (2006) xiii

CHILD AND
ADOLESCENT
PSYCHIATRIC CLINICS
OF NORTH AMERICA

Dedication

Donald J. Cohen (1940–2001)

He has achieved success who has lived well, laughed often and loved much; who has gained the respect of intelligent men and the love of little children; who has filled his niche and accomplished his task; who has left the world better than he found it, whether by an improved poppy, a perfect poem, or a rescued soul; who has never lacked appreciation of earth's beauty or failed to express it; who has always looked for the best in others and given them the best he had; whose life was an inspiration; whose memory a benediction.

—Bessie Stanley; published in the *Lincoln (Kansas) Sentinel*, November 30, 1905

This issue is dedicated to the memory of our dear teacher, mentor, and friend.

RV
VR

1056-4993/06/$ – see front matter
doi:10.1016/j.chc.2005.12.006

ELSEVIER
SAUNDERS

Child Adolesc Psychiatric Clin N Am
15 (2006) xv–xvii

CHILD AND
ADOLESCENT
PSYCHIATRIC CLINICS
OF NORTH AMERICA

Foreword

Busted!

> There is no greater crime than leaving.
> In friends, what do you count on? Not on what they do.
> You never can tell what they will do. Not on what they are. That
> May change. Only on this: their not leaving.
>
> —Bertold Brecht

Well over 2 million children and adolescents under the age of 18 are enmeshed in the juvenile justice system in the United States alone. Compounding this stark figure is the disproportionate representation by individuals with mental illness and by members of ethnic or racial minorities: whereas these groups each represent some 15% of the general underage population, they each account for approximately two thirds of those in trouble with the law. Moreover, types of psychopathology are not equally distributed across the detention perimeter. Although it makes intuitive sense for conduct disorder and substance abuse to be concentrated within these populations, it is sobering to recognize the consistent documentation of unusually high rates of internalizing and language disorders, as well as of physical or sexual abuse.

By the time juveniles come to the attention of the legal authorities, mental health problems have been overlooked more often than not—an unfortunate state of affairs given that psychopathology can be an antecedent or root cause for their legal involvement in the first place. And beyond the controversy of putative causal links between mental illness and criminality, the fact remains that juvenile justice settings are all too frequently the locations where psychopathology is first identified, if not addressed. Through their sheer size and reach, public service gateways such as schools, primary health, child welfare and juvenile justice settings may be optimally positioned to recognize and target the mental health needs of children and adolescents. However, few of those points of entry were originally designed with behavioral health goals in mind, making for a progressively widening gap between service need and provision. When community resources dwindle or fail, it is these institutions in general, and juvenile justice

1056-4993/06/$ – see front matter
doi:10.1016/j.chc.2006.01.001 ***childpsych.theclinics.com***

settings in particular, that may come to be the de facto providers of mental health care for some of our neediest youth—a situation arrived at much less by proactive design than by sad default.

Addressing the mental health needs of juvenile offenders requires a concerted effort at all stages of their legal involvement: from first contact with the police, through detention, processing, adjudication, sentencing and disposition, to community re-entry. Furthermore, it should encompass early identification of psychopathology; access to appropriate therapeutic, vocational, social, and remedial services; proactive and aggressive involvement of caregivers and family members; efficient interagency coordination; and, eventually, optimal reintegration into the community. The proposed continuum is no small feat, and in the context of a political environment that places a premium on fiscal responsibility over service provision, an unlikely one. Underlying tensions such as this are nothing new: a softer, "child guidance" approach, initially formalized in the American juvenile justice court founded in Cook County, Illinois, in 1899, has historically favored understanding links with psychopathology and ensuring rehabilitation, yet long been at odds with a harsher, "law and order" philosophy relying on punishment and the absolute protection of society. Exemplifying the latter school of thought as early as 1857, Morel likened the rising tide of juvenile offenders to "a danger comparable to that of the invasion of the Barbarians in ancient times" [1]. Off with their heads, were policy decisions left to the intellectual heirs of Monsieur Morel.

In the United States, the pendulum has once again swung in the harsher direction: even in the face of reductions in violent crimes committed by juvenile offenders, more children and adolescents are entering juvenile justice facilities each year; more youngsters are incarcerated and more of them are serving in adult facilities; and the age of majority has decreased nationally to a median of 16 years at which adolescents can be tried as adults. These trends, and

> [t]his national shift toward punishment and accountability, [have left] juvenile justice systems unprepared, ill-equipped and under-funded to handle the increasing influx of children with serious and complex behavioral health problems [2].

In my native Connecticut, it has sometimes taken tragic events to spur action: for example, the completed suicide of a teenager while in detention and the ensuing *Tabitha B.* case (1998) paved the way for more timely and efficient mental health screening and assessment of incarcerated youths.

This issue of the *Clinics*, the first in the series devoted to juvenile justice, demonstrates that proactive planning and effective action within existing legal, financial, and logistic constraints are possible and can be articulated in an organized manner, rather than just as a response to the latest crisis or change in political winds or funding streams. Although the issue places special emphasis on psychopathology and on large-throughput mental health screening of detainees with subsequent in-depth assessment of those identified as at risk, it also offers solutions in a series of intervention-focused articles.

Even as my introductory comments are framed within the particulars of a United States that I am fortunate to live in, juvenile justice concerns are international in scope and pose challenges that we would do well to address jointly as an international community of scholars. It is in this spirit that the "*North America*" part of the series' title seems a misnomer, particularly given the international cast of expert contributors represented in this issue. I am indebted to my dear friends and colleagues Robert Vermeiren, now commuting daily between Antwerp and Amsterdam, and Vlad Ruchkin, in his new Swedish reincarnation, for taking the baton with as much vision and determination. Speaking as their friend, I celebrate and salute their changes, moves, and ever-exciting new projects, while appreciating the fact that they have never *really* left. And as one of their many students in all things forensic, medico-legal, and juvenile justice–related, I have this to add:

These youngsters are vulnerable, scared and in need; they have been through much and face challenges the likes of which we would be presumptuous even to imagine. These children face darkness on a daily basis, and need as much light as we as a community can shed. This issue is a testament to the fact that while they may indeed be in deep trouble, they will not be ignored. A concerted effort to think on behalf of the lives and well-being of these children, this issue proves that guest editors and contributors have not left them in the lurch:

Busted they may have been, but they are not forgotten.

Andrés Martin, MD, MPH
Consulting Editor
Yale Child Study Center
Yale University School of Medicine
230 South Frontage Road
New Haven, CT 06520-7900, USA
E-mail address: andres.martin@yale.edu

References

[1] Morel BA. Traité des dégénérescences physiques, intellectuelles et morales de l'espèce humaine et des causes qui produisent ces variétés maladives. Paris: J.B. Baillière; 1857 [in French].

[2] Connecticut Center for Effective Practices of the Child Health and Development Institute of Connecticut. Not just child's play: the role of behavioral health screening and assessment in the Connecticut juvenile justice system. Available at: http://www.chdi.org. Accessed December 18, 2005.

ELSEVIER
SAUNDERS

Child Adolesc Psychiatric Clin N Am
15 (2006) xix–xxii

CHILD AND
ADOLESCENT
PSYCHIATRIC CLINICS
OF NORTH AMERICA

Preface

Juvenile Justice

> As long as the conditions which produce the offender remain he will continue to offend, and as long as Penal law shuts its eyes to this transparent fact it is doomed to impotence as a weapon against crime.
>
> —W. Douglas Morrison [1]

This issue of the *Child and Adolescent Psychiatry Clinics of North America* reviews issues relevant to the mental health of children and adolescents involved with the juvenile justice system. Its relevance is predicated by an increasing awareness of the extent of mental health problems in juvenile offenders, and by the methodologically sound implementation of several psychosocial interventions to address them. To our knowledge, this is one of the first attempts to provide an overview of mental health issues relevant to the juvenile justice system, rather than to review broader aspects of work with juvenile delinquents. We focus our perspective on a more complex group of youth: those who often have more severe criminal behavior and suffer from a wider range of comorbid psychiatric disorders, and thus represent a greater challenge to the system in terms of providing adequate care. In addition, we focus on types of interventions specifically relevant and applicable within the juvenile justice system.

Although society has been struggling with "youth problem behavior" for centuries, the concept of juvenile delinquency is relatively new, dating back to the early 1800s. This does not mean that young people before the nineteenth century were law-abiding, but rather that adolescent criminal behavior was not differentiated from that of the adults from the "dangerous classes." As a result, juvenile delinquency was not perceived as developmentally unique, nor requiring a different treatment approach [2]. The juvenile justice system has from its inception struggled to balance the duty to protect the young and correct their behavior with the demand to punish them and to protect society. Consequently, it has been conjectured that inconsistencies and controversies in the decisions regarding

doi:10.1016/j.chc.2005.12.005

juvenile offenders underscore the general ambivalence of adults toward the nature of adolescence and the application of mechanisms of social control to youths who are nearing adulthood [3].

Keeping the balance between the needs for rehabilitation and retribution seemed especially challenging in the past decade. The United States and many other countries had experienced a clear upsurge in punitiveness directed at delinquent youth, which grew substantially during the late 1980s and peaked in 1994, but has since decreased for 9 consecutive years [4]. Yet for the past decade, over 2 million youth have been arrested, more than 100,000 of whom were placed in correctional facilities each year [5]. In 2003, law enforcement agencies in the United States made an estimated 2.2 million arrests of persons under age 18 [4], suggesting that the numbers remain painfully high. At the same time, we currently have more knowledge than ever about the factors associated with persistent antisocial involvement, which provide us with a strong guide for interventions. Although juvenile justice has traditionally focused on prevention of criminal behavior, recent findings on the overwhelming rates of mental health problems in the juveniles it serves strongly emphasize the need for interventions during the time of juvenile justice involvement. Because the juvenile justice system may be the only source of mental health services for many youth with serious emotional and behavioral disturbance [6], it is critical that these settings be able to adequately recognize and address serious psychopathology. This issue provides a concerted attempt to overview the mental health issues that seem most pressing within juvenile justice settings today. Recent research findings are covered in the three sections, as briefly outlined below.

First, decades of research on juvenile delinquency have yielded considerable progress in our understanding of the phenomenon of adolescent offending. In the context of transformation and search for identity, adolescent risk behavior has been construed both as an adaptive process, central to the normative tasks of adolescence, but also as problematic and representative of unconventional attitudes, values and perceptions of the other [7]. Although for many youths involvement in mild risk-taking behaviors represents a "normative" developmental step, for others it may be related to adjustment problems and higher levels of psychopathology (eg, anxiety, depression). It has long been recognized that persistent delinquency is associated with a number of individual and social factors [8]. There is substantial evidence, for example, that children with early and persistent conduct problems may differ from other children with regard to a number of specific characteristics (eg, fearless temperament, lack of empathy, lack of emotional expression), which can potentially offer an opportunity for early prevention and intervention efforts. There is also an increasing recognition that many juvenile offenders suffer from a wide range of psychiatric or academic problems, which may impact not only initiation of problem behaviors in youth, but also their long-term prognosis in terms of poor psychosocial adjustment and recidivism. The growing insight regarding factors associated with juvenile offending provides opportunities for individualized intervention and the development of specific treatment programs for antisocial juveniles.

Second, mental health services within the judicial system became essential for the adequate management of psychiatric problems and the provision of continuity of services (the "custodial treatment obligation" [9]). Because of the large number of juveniles entering the juvenile justice system, more and more emphasis is being put on the careful identification of youth in need of intervention, and on the prediction of long-term risks in juvenile offenders. Surprisingly, only a handful of instruments have been developed for juvenile justice youth, either for screening of mental health problems or for risk assessment. Efforts to determine the accuracy of current means to predict persistent criminal involvement may further benefit from recent advances in neurodevelopmental science. In light of recent research, neurobiologic factors relevant to antisocial behavior have become a topic of substantial scientific and clinical scrutiny. Although a welcome and exciting development, it is not one without danger—mere decades ago, biologic "evidence" was put to malevolent political purposes, as in the extinction of unwanted populations during the Nazi occupation and the development of sterilization programs in postwar Scandinavia. At the same time, the potential dangers of misuse refer not only to neurobiologic parameters, but to a broader range of risk predictors, including psychologic and social factors. With a juvenile justice system that has been increasingly focused on punitiveness, retribution, and toughness on crime, the potential for abuse of such scientific evidence cannot be underestimated. For example, in The Netherlands, a number of long-term facilities are being built for the permanent housing of (adult) offenders who are deemed "incurable." Similarly, some may wish to identify younger "superpredators" and send them off to places from where release may not be possible.

Finally, it has been suggested that the recent shift in policy focus from a rehabilitative ideology to one based on retribution occurred mostly in response to disillusionment with our capacity to rehabilitate, and the inability of the existing treatment strategies to control the behavior of unruly teenagers [3]. However, recent research suggests that, if anything, the punitive attitude toward juvenile delinquents that we as a society have adopted appears to be hardening the association between conduct problems and social maladjustment. In contrast, research has convincingly demonstrated that there are effective psychosocial treatments for juvenile offenders, including those with chronic, serious or violent antisocial behavior. Therefore, the final section in this issue is devoted to a review of existing and promising interventions for juvenile offenders. Considering the substantial lag between research findings and the everyday realities in health care settings, there is a pressing need for the identification and implementation of such effective and evidence-based practices. In addition to rolling out manualized treatment programs, attention should also focus on the specific conditions surrounding such programs, including physical environment, staffing, and management of services where treatments are organized. With this issue of the *Child and Adolescent Psychiatry Clinics of North America*, we have attempted to address the growing need for information regarding mental health issues in the juvenile justice realm, and hope that it may help to address aspects of clinical relevance, both in terms of judicial handling and therapeutic intervention.

Vladislav Ruchkin, MD, PhD
Center for Violence Prevention
Karolinska Institute
Stockholm, Sweden

Skonviks Psychiatric Clinic
Center for Forensic Psychiatry
Box 350
78327 Säter, Sweden
E-mail address: vladislav.ruchkin@yale.edu

Robert Vermeiren, MD, PhD
VU University Medical Center/
Leiden University
P/a De Bascule
Postbus 303
1115 ZG Duivendrecht, The Netherlands
E-mail address: robert@vermeiren.name

References

[1] Morrison WD. Introduction. In: Lombroso C, editor. The female offender. New York: D. Appleton & Company; 1915. p. xiv.

[2] Mason T. A history of delinquency? Available at: http://www.timothyjpmason.com/WebPages/Deviance/Deviance8.htm. Accessed December 6, 2005.

[3] Harris PW, Welsh WN, Butler F. A century of juvenile justice. In: LaFree G, editor. Criminal justice 2000, volume I: the nature of crime: continuity and change. Washington (DC): National Institute of Justice; 2000. p. 359–425.

[4] Snyder HN. Juvenile arrests 2003. Juvenile Justice Bulletin. Washington (DC): US Department of Justice, Office of Juvenile Justice and Delinquency Preventio; 2005. Available at: http://www.ncjrs.gov/pdffiles1/ojjdp/209735.pdf. Accessed December 6, 2005.

[5] Cocozza J. Identifying the needs of juveniles with co-occurring disorders. Corrections Today 1997;59:147–9.

[6] Burns BJ, Costello EJ, Angold A, et al. Children's mental health service use across service sectors. Health Aff (Millwood) 1995;14:147–59.

[7] Hockaday C, Crase SJ, Shelley 2nd MC, Stockdale DF. A prospective study of adolescent pregnancy. J Adolesc 2000;23:423–38.

[8] Glueck S, Glueck E. Unraveling juvenile delinquency. Cambridge (MA): Harvard University Press; 1950.

[9] Grisso T, Zimring FE. Double jeopardy: adolescents offenders with mental disorders. Chicago: University of Chicago Press; 2004.

ELSEVIER
SAUNDERS

Child Adolesc Psychiatric Clin N Am
15 (2006) 311–331

CHILD AND
ADOLESCENT
PSYCHIATRIC CLINICS
OF NORTH AMERICA

Developmental Pathways to Conduct Disorder

Paul J. Frick, PhD

Department of Psychology, University of New Orleans, 2001 Geology and Psychology Building, New Orleans, LA 70148, USA

Conduct disorder (CD) is defined as a repetitive and persistent pattern of behavior which violates the rights of others (eg, aggression, vandalism, theft) or which violates major age-appropriate societal norms or rules (eg, deceitfulness, truancy, running away from home) [1]. Depending on the exact definition of CD, between 3% and 5% of preadolescent boys and between 6% and 8% of adolescent boys meet criteria for the disorder, with boys outnumbering girls by about 4:1 before adolescence and by about 2:1 in adolescence [2]. Most youth who commit serious illegal and delinquent acts, especially violent acts, show a history of antisocial and aggressive behavior that precedes their serious delinquency, and they either have been diagnosed with CD or would have been diagnosed with this disorder had they been referred for mental health treatment [3]. Serious and violent adult offenders often show histories of antisocial and aggressive behavior dating back to early childhood [4]. As a result, understanding the development of CD is critical for understanding the causes of criminal and violent behavior.

Criminal behavior is only one, albeit a serious one, of the many consequences associated with CD. Children who have CD can cause significant disruptions to families who are trying to manage the behavior of an antisocial and aggressive child [5]. Children who have CD can victimize peers with their aggressive acts, and such victimization can have serious physical and emotional consequences [6]. Further, the behavioral problems associated with CD can disrupt the school environment in a way that detracts from the educational experience of all students and that leads to significant costs involved in trying to provide students who have CD with appropriate educational resources while ensuring the safety of students and teachers [7]. Further, children who have CD often experience a number

E-mail address: pfrick@uno.edu

doi:10.1016/j.chc.2005.11.003 ***childpsych.theclinics.com***

of psychosocial impairments related to their behavioral disturbance, including poor school performance, peer rejection, high rates of anxiety, high rates of depression and suicide, and early and serious substance use [3].

Multiple causal factors: a developmental pathways approach

Given these many serious and costly effects of CD, it is not surprising that it is one of the leading reasons that children and adolescents are referred to mental health clinics for services, and it is one of the most extensively studied of all childhood disorders [8]. A number of comprehensive reviews of this extensive body of research have documented a large number of risk factors for CD [3,8–11]. These risk factors are remarkable for the sheer number of variables that have been associated with CD and by their great diversity. These risk factors include neurochemical (eg, low serotonin) and autonomic (eg, low resting heart rate) irregularities, neurocognitive deficits (eg, deficits in executive functioning), deficits in the processing of social information (eg, a hostile attributional bias), temperamental vulnerabilities (eg, poor emotional regulation), and personality predispositions (eg, impulsivity). In addition to these dispositional factors, at least as many contextual risk factors have been associated with CD; these risk factors, are also notable for both their number and diversity. They include factors within the child's prenatal (eg, exposure to toxins), early child-care (eg, poor-quality child care), family (eg, ineffective discipline), peer (eg, association with deviant peers), and neighborhood (eg, high levels of exposure to violence) environments.

Given such a large and diverse array of risk factors, it has been difficult to determine the best method for studying them and for integrating them into comprehensive causal models to explain the development of CD. Some studies have focused on the influence of one or a few risk factors in isolation from others [12], whereas others have attempted to compare the relative effects of different factors to isolate those that seem most important [13]. One recent trend in research on CD is the use of a cumulative-risk perspective for understanding the potential effect of multiple risk factors. In the cumulative-risk perspective, the type of risk factor is not as important as the number of factors that are present for a child. For example, Stouthamer-Loeber and colleagues [14] reported that, in a high-risk sample of urban youth, the number of risk factors showed a linear association with risk for serious and persistent delinquency. Specifically, 2% of youth who had no childhood risk factor showed serious and persistent delinquency in adolescence, compared with 71% of youth who had risk factors from five different domains. Further, there is evidence that the cumulative effects of multiple risk factors may sometimes be interactive rather than additive. For example, Raine and colleagues [15] reported that, in a birth cohort of 4269 males born in Denmark, neither birth complications nor maternal rejection alone increased a child's risk for violent offending at age 18 years but the combination of the two domains led to substantial increases in risk.

The cumulative-risk perspective is critical for demonstrating that research focusing on only one risk factor or even on one domain of risk is likely to explain only a modest amount of the variance in measures of antisocial and aggressive behaviors. There are two notable limitations in this perspective, however. First, this perspective assumes that the same causal process is operating for all children who have CD, although this causal process may involve different combinations of risk factors across individuals. As a result, the cumulative-risk perspective does not explicitly recognize that distinct causal mechanisms may underlie the antisocial and aggressive behavior of subgroups of youth who have CD [16,17]. Second, the cumulative-risk perspective does not specify the developmental processes that may be disrupted by the dispositional or contextual risk factors and that predispose the child to act in an aggressive and antisocial manner. For example, knowledge that a child experienced birth complications and a rejecting home environment does not indicate what developmental mechanism(s) might be disrupted by this combination of risk factors. Furthermore, other combinations of risk factors might lead to the same developmental disruptions.

Focusing on the mechanisms through which the various risk factors can lead to the development of CD could be crucial for defining a few important routes or pathways that may put a child at risk for acting in an antisocial and aggressive manner. In addition, such a focus could be critical for treatment. Specifically, eliminating risk factors, such as improving prenatal care to reduce the risk of birth complications, is an important public health approach for reducing the incidence of CD [18]. Also understanding how birth complications may have placed the child at risk for CD would allow the implementation of interventions that could enhance the development of children who were not reached by such prenatal programs or who still experience birth complications despite the intervention.

Because of these limitations in the cumulative-risk perspective for understanding the etiology of CD, recent research has begun to use a developmental-pathways approach that attempts to overcome these limitations. The developmental-pathways approach can be defined by two important features. First, this approach explicitly recognizes that there are likely to be a number of different causal processes, each involving a distinct combination of risk factors, operating in the development of CD. Second, this approach integrates research on normal developmental processes with research on the correlates of antisocial and aggressive behavior in an attempt to specify clearly what effects these risk factors may have in putting the developing child at risk for showing CD. One example of such an approach to understanding the development of CD is the distinction that has been made between childhood-onset and adolescent-onset forms of CD.

Childhood-onset and adolescent-onset conduct disorder

A number of reviews of the literature have summarized research supporting the distinction between children who begin showing severe conduct problems in childhood versus those in whom the onset of severe antisocial behavior coincides with the onset of puberty [19,20]. Children in the childhood-onset group often begin showing mild conduct problems as early as preschool or early elementary school, and their behavioral problems tend to increase in rate and severity throughout childhood and into adolescence [21]. In contrast, the adolescent-onset group does not show significant behavioral problems in childhood, but they begin exhibiting significant antisocial and delinquent behavior coinciding with the onset of adolescence [19]. In addition to the different patterns of onset, the childhood-onset group is more likely to show aggressive behaviors in childhood and adolescence and is more likely to continue to show antisocial and criminal behavior into adulthood. For example, Moffitt and colleagues [22] reported on a birth cohort of 539 males born in New Zealand in 1972 and 1973 and followed through the age of 26 years. Within this cohort, the 45 men who had displayed significant conduct problems before adolescence were more likely to have had a criminal conviction (55%) and had more convictions (mean, 6.9; SD, 11.5) as adults than the 121 men who showed significant conduct problems starting in adolescence (34%; mean, 3.5; SD, 10.8), and both groups differed from controls that did not have histories of conduct problems (17%; mean, 0.6; SD, 3.1). The difference was more dramatic when the focus was on convictions for violent offenses, for which adults in the early-onset group (38%) were much more likely to be convicted than adults from either the adolescent-onset (14%) or control (5%) groups.

A number of longitudinal studies have supported the different outcomes between the two groups [23], and this difference is one of the primary reasons the distinction between childhood-onset and adolescent-onset CD has been adopted by many official diagnostic classification systems used to define CD [1]. More relevant to causal theory, however, is research demonstrating that the two groups also differ in a number of the dispositional and contextual risk factors for CD. Specifically, most of the dispositional (eg, temperamental risk, low intelligence) and contextual (eg, family dysfunction; poverty) correlates are more strongly associated with the childhood-onset subtype of CD [22]. In contrast, any difference between the adolescent-onset group and children who do not have CD seems to manifest primarily in a greater affiliation with delinquent peers and higher levels of rebelliousness and authority conflict [24].

The different outcomes and risk factors for the two subtypes of CD have led to theoretical models that propose very different causal mechanisms operating across the two groups. For example, Moffitt [19,24] has proposed that children in the childhood-onset group develop their problem behavior through a transactional process involving a difficult and vulnerable child (eg, impulsive, with verbal deficits) who experiences an inadequate rearing environment (eg, poor parental supervision, poor-quality schools). This dysfunctional transactional process disrupts the child's socialization, leading to poor social relations with persons both inside (eg, parents and siblings) and outside the family (eg, peers and teachers). These disruptions lead to enduring vulnerabilities that can negatively affect the child's psychosocial adjustment across multiple developmental stages.

In contrast, Moffitt [19,24] has proposed a very different causal model to explain the development of conduct problems in children in the adolescent-onset pathway. Because children in this group are more likely to have their problems limited to adolescence, and because they show fewer risk factors, this group is conceptualized as showing an exaggeration of the normative process of adolescent rebellion. That is, all adolescents show some level of rebelliousness to parents and other authority figures [19]. This rebelliousness is part of a process by which the adolescent begins to develop an autonomous sense of self and a unique identity. According to Moffitt, the child in the adolescent-onset group engages in antisocial and delinquent behaviors as a misguided attempt to obtain a subjective sense of maturity and adult status in a way that is maladaptive (eg, breaking societal norms) but encouraged by an antisocial peer group. Given that their behavior is viewed as an exaggeration of a process specific to adolescence and not caused by an enduring vulnerability, their antisocial behavior is less likely to persist beyond adolescence. They may, however, have impairments that persist into adulthood because of the consequences of their adolescent antisocial behavior (eg, a criminal record, dropping out of school, substance abuse).

Although the distinction between childhood-onset and adolescent-onset trajectories has been useful for explaining two pathways through which children may develop CD, it is important to note that clear differences in risk factors between the two groups have not always been found [25], and the applicability of this model to girls requires further testing [26]. The distinction, however, clearly illustrates that there are likely to be subgroups of children who have CD who show different risk factors reflective of different causal mechanisms operating across groups. Research has begun extending this conceptualization by exploring whether additional distinctions can be made within childhood-onset CD. This group seems to show the most severe, chronic, and aggressive pattern of behavior and more dispositional and contextual risk factors that probably result in an enduring vulnerability. Growing evidence suggests that a further distinction can be made that defines different types of vulnerabilities that may be present within this group of youth. This distinction is based on the presence of a callous and unemotional interpersonal style and is similar to the distinction made within samples of antisocial adults using the construct of psychopathy [27].

Callous-unemotional traits and developmental models of conduct disorder

Childhood-onset conduct disorder in children who have callous-unemotional traits

In samples of both clinic-referred and nonreferred youth, factor analyses have isolated a personality dimension characterized by a lack of guilt, lack of empathy, and lack of emotional expression that has been labeled callous-unemotional (CU) traits [28]. Table 1 lists examples of traits that comprise this dimension. These

Table 1
Items assessing callous-unemotional traits in children and the emotional detachment dimension of psychopathy in adults

Callous-unemotional traits	Emotional detachment
Is unconcerned about the feelings of others	Callous/lacks empathy for others
Does not feel bad or guilty	Lacks remorse or guilt
Is unconcerned about schoolwork	Fails to accept responsibility for own actions
Does not show emotions	Shallow affect
Fails to keep promises	
Does not keep the same friends	

Data from Frick PJ, Bodin SD, Barry CT. Psychopathic traits and conduct problems in community and clinic-referred samples of children: further development of the Psychopathy Screening Device. Psychol Assess 2000;12:382–93; and Cooke DJ, Mitchie C. Refining the construct of psychopathy: towards a hierarchical model. Psychol Assess 2001;13:171–88.

CU traits are similar to those comprising the emotional detachment component of psychopathy in adult forensic samples, which are included in Table 1 for comparison [29]. Importantly, CU traits have been reliably assessed in samples as young as age 4 years [30], and they seem to designate a stable dimension of personality, at least in later childhood and adolescence. For example, in a high-risk sample of older children (mean age, 10.65 years; SD, 1.60), parent ratings of CU traits were quite stable over 4 years as the sample transitioned into adolescence [31].

More importantly for designating a unique pathway to CD, fairly substantial evidence suggests that the presence of CU traits is associated with more severe, more aggressive, and more stable patterns of antisocial behavior in youth. Specifically, in samples of adjudicated adolescent, the presence of CU traits has been associated with more serious offending [32,33], more severe violence [34], and more behavioral infractions and poorer treatment progress while adjudicated [35]. In these samples, CU traits have also been associated with an earlier onset of offending, supporting its link to the childhood-onset subtype of CD [33,36]. Similar findings have been reported in high-risk [37] and community [38] samples of adolescents in which the presence of CU traits has been associated with more severe and earlier onset of antisocial behavior. The link between CU traits and severity of conduct problems has been documented in preadolescent samples as well. In both clinic-referred [39] and community samples [30,40], children who have CU traits and conduct problems exhibit more severe and more aggressive antisocial behavior than other children who have conduct problems. Further, the association between CU traits and aggression has been documented for both boys and girls [41]. Finally, similar to the findings in adjudicated youth, CU traits have predicted poorer treatment outcome in boys who have conduct problems [42].

In addition to these cross-sectional studies, a number of longitudinal studies have indicated that the presence of CU traits predicts later antisocial and aggressive behavior. For example, several studies of adjudicated adolescents have indicated that the presence of CU traits predicts reoffending, especially violent reoffending, and a shorter length of time to reoffending when youth are released from institutions [43–45]. Similarly, CU traits predicted increases in conduct problems over a 1-year period in a community sample (n = 1359) of children between the ages of 4 and 9 years [30]. Importantly, these prospective studies have generally included fairly limited follow-up periods of 1 to 2 years. In a more extended study of the predictive utility of CU traits, Frick and colleagues [46] reported that nonreferred children who had conduct problems and who also showed CU traits exhibited the highest rates of conduct problems, self-reported delinquency, and police contacts across a 4-year study period.

These studies suggest that, in youth who show conduct problems or delinquency, the presence of CU traits designates a particularly severe, aggressive, and chronic group. These studies, however, do not provide any data as to whether the causal processes that may lead to the behavioral problems are different for this group of antisocial youth. One of the strongest pieces of evidence for differences in causal processes across the two groups comes from a study of 3165 7-year-old twin pairs [47]. In this study, children scoring in the top 10% of the sample on a measure of conduct problems were further divided into those who had (n = 359) or did not have (n = 333) significant levels of CU traits, thus forming two subgroups of children who had childhood-onset conduct problems. Estimates of the genetic and environmental effects on variations in conduct problems were very different for the two groups. Specifically, the group heritability estimate for children scoring high on both conduct problems and CU traits was more than twice that for the group scoring low on CU traits. Although this twin study suggests that genetic factors may play a larger role in the development of conduct problems for children who have CU traits, it does not provide clues as to the mechanisms through which heredity may exert its effects. Understanding how genetics may play a role in the development of CU traits is important, because the fact that a trait has a strong genetic component does not mean that it is unchangeable [47].

One potentially important line of research has documented that children who have conduct problems and CU traits exhibit a distinct temperamental style. Specifically, in forensic [48], mental health [49] and community [50] samples, children and adolescents who have conduct problems and who also show CU traits exhibit a preference for novel, exciting, and dangerous activities. Further, children who have CU traits and conduct problems, but not other children who have conduct problems, show response perseveration on computer tasks in which a reward-oriented response set is primed [50–52]. That is, on tasks in which responding leads to a high rate of rewards initially but later leads to a high rate of punishment (eg, loss of points), children who have conduct problems and CU traits continue to respond despite the increasing rate of punishment. This reward-dominant cognitive style appears not only in computerized laboratory tests but also in social situations: youth who have CU traits emphasize the positive aspects (eg, obtaining rewards, gaining dominance) of solving peer conflicts with aggression and minimize the negative aspects (eg, getting punished) [48].

Perhaps one of the most consistent findings concerning temperamental differences in children who have CU traits is the finding that this group of children shows important differences in their response to emotional stimuli. For example, antisocial adolescents [48] and children who have conduct problems [49] and who also show CU traits seem to be less distressed by the effects of their behavior on others. Further, children who have CU traits and conduct problems show poorer recognition of visual depictions of emotional stimuli [53,54] and are less reactive to various types of negative emotional stimuli [50,55–59]. For example, in a sample of adolescents referred to a diversion program for delinquent behavior, youth with high levels of CU traits showed reduced emotional reactivity to words with negative emotional content (eg, gun, blood) compared with emotionally neutral words (eg, chair, table) using a lexical decision task that compared their response time for recognizing words with emotional or neutral content [58]. Similarly, in a sample of nonreferred children between the ages of 6 and 13 years, children who had conduct problems and CU traits showed evidence for reduced reactivity to pictures involving distressing emotional content (eg, a child in pain, a hurt animal) using a dot-probe task that compared the speed at which the location of a dot was detected in pictures with emotional or neutral content [57]. Both these tasks involved indirect assessments of emotional reactivity by assessing differences in a cognitive-orienting response to emotional and nonemotional stimuli. Similar deficits in emotional responding have been found in studies directly assessing the physiologic responses to emotional stimuli of children who have CU traits [55,56]. Also, these studies have consistently indicated that the deficit in emotional processing found in children who have CU traits is not a global deficit that is consistent across all types of emotional stimuli but is specific to negative emotional stimuli [57,58] and may even be specific to stimuli involving distress or pain in others [56,57].

Callous-unemotional traits and conscience development

Taken together, these findings suggest that CU traits designate a group of children who have CD and who show a distinct temperamental style, characterized by a preference for dangerous and novel stimuli, a reward-oriented response style, and a lack of reactivity to certain types of negative emotional stimuli. This temperamental style has been variously labeled as low fearfulness [60], low behavioral inhibition [61], low harm avoidance [62], or high daring [63]. Several studies of normally developing children have linked this temperamental style with lower scores on measures of conscience development in both concurrent [64,65] and prospective studies [66]. These findings have led to a number of theories as to how this temperament may be involved in conscience development (see [67] for a more extended review).

For example, some theories suggest that internalization of parental and societal norms is partly dependent on the negative arousal evoked by potential punishment for misbehavior, and that the guilt and anxiety associated with actual or anticipated wrongdoing can be impaired if the child has a temperament in which the negative arousal to cues of punishment is attenuated [68]. This temperament could make the child more difficult to socialize because he or she does not respond in the same way as other children to typical discipline strategies. In support of this possibility, Kochanska [69,70] reported that relatively fearful toddlers, but not fearless toddlers, showed enhanced scores on measures of conscience development later in childhood if they experienced gentle, consistent, and non–power-assertive parenting.

In addition to making the child more difficult to socialize, a temperament characterized by low levels of emotional reactivity could also negatively affect the development of empathetic concern in response to the distress in others. Specifically, some theories of empathy development in early childhood suggest that negative emotional arousal to the distress of others becomes conditioned to behaviors on the part of the child that prompted the distress [71]. As a result of this conditioning, the child learns to inhibit such behaviors as a means of avoiding this negative arousal. This learning process can facilitate the development of the child's ability to take the perspective of others by encouraging the child to anticipate which behaviors may lead to distress in others. This process through which avoidance learning fosters perspective taking can be impaired by a temperamental deficit in emotional arousal to the distress of others.

Thus, there are several developmental theories linking a temperament characterized by low levels of fearful inhibitions with impairments in conscience development. These theories are consistent with many of the characteristics of antisocial youth who have CU traits. Specifically, children who have conduct problems and CU traits seem to be less responsive to typical parental socialization practices [72,73], and they are more impaired in their moral reasoning [48,52,55]. Therefore, the use of CU traits to designate a distinct subgroup of youth within the childhood-onset pattern of CD could be important for linking research on antisocial and delinquent behavior with theories of conscience development. In addition, defining a group of youth with this distinct causal process could help in developing causal models for other youth who have childhood-onset CD but who do not show CU traits. Specifically, a high level of CU traits seems to be present in only about one third of clinic-referred children who have childhood-onset conduct problems [39]. The studies comparing the characteristics of antisocial youth who have or do not have CU traits provide some clues about the processes that may be operating in the development of the conduct problems in this latter group.

Childhood-onset conduct disorder in children who do not have callous-unemotional traits

Children who have childhood-onset CD seem to show higher levels impulsivity and higher rates of attention deficit hyperactivity disorder (ADHD) than children who do not have conduct problems and children who have adolescent-onset CD [19,24]. Within the childhood-onset group, children who have high and low levels of CU traits do not differ in their levels of impulsivity

[50] or rates of ADHD [39]. Second, children who have childhood-onset CD but who do not have elevated CU traits are less aggressive than children who have high levels of CU traits. When they do act aggressively, they are likely to confine their actions to reactive forms of aggression [34,40] in response to real or perceived provocation by others [50]. Third, children who have childhood-onset CD but who do not have CU traits are more likely to show intellectual deficits, especially deficits in verbal intelligence [74]. Fourth, the conduct problems of the low CU group seem to be more strongly related to ineffective parenting practices, such as poor monitoring and supervision by the parents or the use of harsh and inconsistent discipline [72,73]. Fifth, antisocial youth who do not have CU traits seem to have problems regulating their emotions. They exhibit high levels of self-reported anxiety [49,50], they are more reactive to the distress of others in social situations [48], and they are highly reactive to negative emotional stimuli [57,58].

Thus, children who have childhood-onset CD but do not have CU traits show a number of important dispositional (eg, impulsivity, low verbal intelligence, poor emotional regulation) and contextual (eg, higher rates of family dysfunction) risk factors, consistent with a characterological disturbance that is likely to lead to problems at multiple developmental stages. These risk factors are very different from those found in children who have high levels of CU traits. Further, the many different types of risk factors that are found in this group of youth make it likely that a number of different causal processes can lead to the impulsive and antisocial behavior they demonstrate. For example, the deficits in verbal dysfunction could be related to problems in executive functioning that make it difficult for the child to delay gratification and lead to deficits in the child's ability to anticipate the consequences of his or her behavior [75]. Further, given the strong association with ineffective parenting practices, it is also quite possible that children in this group are not socialized adequately and, as a result, do not learn to regulate their behavior appropriately in response to environmental contingencies [19]. Problems in regulating emotions seems to be the risk factor that most clearly distinguishes this group from children who have CU traits, who, as noted previously, show too little emotional arousal in many situations. As result, problems in emotional regulation have been the focus of one of the few causal theories developed specifically for this group of youth.

Specifically, it is quite likely that many children who have childhood-onset CD who do not show CU traits have a temperament characterized by strong emotional reactivity, a deficit in the skills needed to regulate their emotional reactivity adequately, or both [67]. These problems in emotional regulation can result in the child's committing impulsive and unplanned aggressive and antisocial acts for which he or she may be remorseful afterwards but still have difficulty controlling in the future [48]. Further, the problems in emotional regulation can also make a child particularly susceptible to becoming angry because of perceived provocations from peers, leading to aggressive acts within the context of high emotional arousal, such as in arguments and fights with teachers and classmates [58]. In addition, the problems in emotional regulation can disrupt socialization attempts by both parents and teachers. For example, Patterson and colleagues [20,76] have proposed that antisocial and aggressive youth often are involved in coercive cycles with their parents in which parent and child attempt to control each other through increasingly aversive behaviors (eg, harsh parental discipline, child's display of anger and hostility toward the parent). A child who has problems in emotional regulation can be more likely to elicit and maintain such coercive cycles in parent–child interactions and to generalize this pattern of behavior to other settings, such as at school and with peers [77].

Developmental pathways to conduct disorder: summary and implications for research

The available research suggests that a number of distinct causal pathways can lead children to act in a severely antisocial and aggressive manner and be diagnosed as having CD. Each pathway involves somewhat distinct patterns of risk factors that seem to lead to different disruptions in normative developmental processes. The research reviewed in this article has uncovered several such pathways, distinguishing first between adolescent-onset and childhood-onset CD, with the former being viewed as an exaggeration of the normal process of identity formation in adolescence that leads to high rates of rebelliousness and the latter involving more enduring vulnerabilities that lead to more pervasive problems across multiple developmental stages. Further, research suggests that an important distinction can be made within childhood-onset CD between those who have and those who do not have CU traits, with these two groups showing different types of enduring vulnerabilities. Those who have CU traits seem to show a temperament characterized by a lack of emotional reactivity to certain negative stimuli that could place the child at risk for problems in the development of empathy, guilt, and other aspects of conscience. In contrast, children who have childhood-onset CD but do not have CU traits show emotional (eg, problems regulating emotions), cognitive (eg, verbal deficits), and contextual (eg, poor rearing environments) risk factors that lead to problems in the regulation of emotions and behaviors, resulting in impulsive and reactively aggressive behaviors that are present across multiple developmental stages. Much more research is needed to refine the knowledge of these pathways and to determine if there might be other important distinctions or better methods of distinguishing among subgroups within the diagnostic category of CD. This research highlights the potential importance of using a developmental-pathways approach for understanding how the many risk factors associated with CD may be causally related to the development of CD. Further, this approach has several important implications for guiding future research in this area.

First, the developmental-pathways model suggests that research can no longer focus simply on documenting which risk factors are associated with CD or delinquency or even which risk factors account for the most or the most unique variance in measures of antisocial behavior, aggression, or delinquency. Such methods assume that CD is a unitary outcome. Specifically, a variable may be related to a measure of CD or differentiate between children who have or do not have CD in the overall sample. This overall association, however, may obscure the fact that it is related only to the behavior of a subgroup of youth who have CD (see [78] for a more extended discussion of this issue). For example, in a sample (n = 166) of preadolescent children (aged 6–13 years), a measure of dysfunctional parenting showed a moderate, but significant, relation to a measure of conduct problems after controlling for such demographic variables as age, gender, ethnicity, socioeconomic status, and intellectual level of the child [73]. This overall association, however, obscured very different associations within subgroups of children who had conduct problems: the association between ineffective parenting and conduct problems was quite strong among children who were low on CU traits but was negative and nonsignificant among children who were high on CU traits.

This differential association was detected through testing an interaction between a measure of parenting practices and a measure of CU traits in predicting conduct problems using multiple regression analysis. Sometimes, however, the effects of having distinct subgroups of children who have conduct problems do not emerge as interactions but lead to suppressor effects in correlational analyses. For example, in a sample of clinic-referred children, conduct problems were significantly associated with anxiety ($r = .30$; $P < .001$), but this association increased (partial $r = .41$; $P < .001$) when the level of CU traits was controlled [49]. Further, there was a nonsignificant negative correlation between CU traits and anxiety ($r = -.12$; $P =$ not significant) that became significant after controlling for conduct problems (partial $r = -31$; $P < .001$). This suppressor effect was replicated in a community sample of children [50] and in a sample of adjudicated adolescents [79]. This pattern of relations suggest that children who have conduct problems, with or without CU traits, display high levels of anxiety that may be secondary to their behavioral problems and a result of the many psychosocial impairments associated with their conduct problems. When the level of conduct problem severity is controlled, however, children with high levels of CU traits show lower levels of anxiety, suggesting that they are less distressed by the effects of their behavior, given a similar level of impairment.

These interactive and suppressor effects are just two examples of some of the complex multivariate associations that can result from the heterogeneous nature of CD and that are often ignored in research that focuses only on the univariate or main effects of risk factors. Because of the difficulty in detecting and interpreting these complex multivariate associations, some researchers have recommended greater use of person-centered analyses [80] that explicitly divide children into theoretically meaningful subgroups, such as childhood-onset and adolescent-onset groups [22] or groups with or without CU traits [39,50]. Such analyses are more consistent with the theoretical view of CD being a heterogeneous outcome and allow direct comparison of subgroups within this diagnostic category on variables of theoretical interest (eg, emotional reactivity) or practical importance (eg, risk for violence).

A second implication of the developmental-pathways approach for studying CD is the importance of integrating research on abnormal development, in this case research on severe antisocial and aggressive behavior, with research and theory on normal development. Unfortunately, the two bodies of research are largely conducted in isolation from each other with little integration of the theories and methods across the two areas [81]. Research on the normal processes involved in identity formation in adolescence could provide important clues about why some children show an exaggeration of this normative process resulting in adolescent-onset CD. Similarly, research on the normal processes involved in conscience development could be quite important for understanding how these processes may go awry in children who have CU traits. Finally, the growing body of research on how children develop strategies to regulate their emotions could be quite influential in explaining how some children who have childhood-onset CD develop their conduct problems secondary to their problems regulating their emotions [67].

This integration of research on normal development with research on antisocial and aggressive behavior leads to a third implication of a developmental-pathways approach for research on CD. By defining the processes earlier in development that can place a child at risk for developing CD (eg, lack of emotional reactivity, deficits in conscience development), this approach allows research into protective factors that might deflect children from these deviant pathways. Specifically, it is quite likely that a substantial portion of children who have a temperament characterized by low fearful inhibitions would, despite this temperamental risk factor, develop sufficient levels of empathy and guilt to inhibit serious antisocial and aggressive behaviors. Further, emerging developmental research is investigating certain parenting practices that might promote conscience development in relatively fearless children. For example, some research suggests that the use of parenting practices that do not rely solely on punishment-related arousal for internalization of parental norms but instead focus on the positive qualities of the parent–child relationship are more effective in promoting conscience development in relatively fearless children [82]. Alternatively, in a sample of preschool children (mean age, 4.39 years; SD, .51), fearless and behaviorally uninhibited children who experienced consistent and very strong rule-oriented (ie, authoritarian) parenting show enhanced conscience development (Cornell AH, Frick PJ. The contribution of parenting styles and behavioral inhibition to the development of conscience in preschool children; manuscript submitted for publication). These examples illustrate the importance of going beyond documenting patterns of risk in deviant samples and testing potential protective factors that can enhance development in children who may show some of the temperamental risk factors for CD.

Further, these last examples illustrate the need for more research focusing on the role of contextual factors in the development of CU traits and in the tendency of children who have these traits to show severe patterns of antisocial and aggressive behavior. As reviewed previously, much of the research that has been conducted in this group of youth has focused on cognitive and emotional risk factors that may be involved in the etiology of the conduct problems displayed by this group. Little research has investigated contextual factors that may interact with the child's temperament to enhance or to decrease the child's risk for CU traits and subsequent severe antisocial and aggressive behavior. For example, one study that did focus on the child's peer context reported that young adolescent youth who had CU traits showed very high rates of deviant peer affiliation that could play an important role in the level and severity of their antisocial behavior [83]. Further, in one of the few studies to investigate the stability of CU traits across an extended follow-up period (ie, 4 years), the presence of fewer contextual risk factors (eg, higher socioeconomic status and less family dysfunction) was associated with reductions in the level of CU traits over time [31].

Developmental pathways to conduct disorder: implications for assessment and intervention

Although the past decade has led to a number of advances in the understanding of the different developmental pathways that can lead to CD, only recently have there been attempts to focus on the applied implications of this research for assessment and treatment. One key implication of this approach is an emphasis on prevention. As noted previously, the most serious and violent offenders often show childhood-onset CD, and thus they have a history of behavior problems that often precedes their serious delinquency by many years. Further, a number of interventions have proven effective in treating CD in preschool and early school-age children; however, their effectiveness decreases greatly in older children and adolescents [84,85]. Thus, intervening early in the developmental trajectory of childhood-onset CD, when the behaviors seem to be more malleable, is an important goal for preventing later serious delinquency. Even these interventions, however, require a child to have already shown serious and impairing problem behavior, albeit at an early age. Focusing on the early developmental processes that can precede even these early conduct problems would open the possibility of prevention programs that promote optimal development in children who have certain risk factors (eg, a fearless temperament, poor emotional regulation) even before the behavioral problems emerge.

A second implication of the developmental approach outlined here is that interventions, whether they are implemented as prevention or treatment programs, need to be comprehensive and target multiple risk factors. Each of the pathways leading to CD involves multiple interacting factors. Thus, it is not surprising that some of the most effective interventions for CD are those that involve multiple components rather than targeting only a single risk factor. For example, the Families and Schools Together (FAST Track) program is a multicomponent intervention designed to intervene early for children who have conduct problems. Its effectiveness has been documented in a large, multisite trial [86]. The FAST Track intervention was community based (ie, implemented largely in schools) and involved several treatment components including (1) a parenting intervention that focused on teaching parents more appropriate behavior management skills, (2) a cognitive behavior intervention that focused on helping children develop anger control and social problem-solving skills, (3) a classroom intervention that helped teachers implement more effective behavior management skills, (4) academic tutoring, and (5) a case-management component involving home visits to support family functioning.

A third implication of the developmental-pathways approach is that interventions not only need to be comprehensive, like the FAST Track program, but also need to be individualized. Because the causal processes leading to CD may be different across subgroups of children who have the disorder, it is quite likely that treatments will need to be different across these groups as well. The only direct test of this assumption to date is a study testing the effectiveness of a parenting intervention for boys ages 4 to 9 years referred to a mental health clinic for conduct problems [42]. These authors reported that children who had CU traits showed a less positive overall response to this treatment than other children who had conduct problems. This differential effectiveness was not found consistently across all phases of the treatment, however. That is, children who did or did not have CU traits seemed to respond equally well to the first part of the intervention that focused on teaching parents methods of using positive reinforcement to encourage prosocial behavior. In contrast, only the group that did not have CU traits showed added improvement with the second part of the intervention that focused on teaching parents more effective discipline strategies. This outcome would be consistent with the reward-oriented response style that, as reviewed previously, seems to be characteristic of children who have CU traits.

These findings suggest that interventions may be more effective if they are more specifically tailored to the unique needs of children within the different developmental pathways. This focus on a comprehensive and individualized approach to treatment may be particularly important for enhancing the effectiveness of existing treatments for older children and adolescents who show severe antisocial and delinquency behavior. For example, a recent study group commissioned by the Office of Juvenile Justice and Delinquency Prevention of the United States Department of Justice reviewed four juvenile justice programs that provided individualized and comprehensive services to adjudicated youth under the age of 13 years [87]. This summary outlined several features of such comprehensive models that seemed to be critical to their success. One critical feature was that a system existed for ensuring that an array of mental health, medical, child welfare, and educational services were available to adjudicated youth. Another critical feature was the existence of a system for providing a comprehensive assessment to determine the specific needs of the adjudicated youth and of a strong case-management system for ensuring that services were provided in an integrated and coherent manner. A similar model of individualized interventions has proven to be effective for older adjudicated youth. Multisystemic therapy uses an individualized approach to intervention that has proven effective for reducing recidivism in a number of adjudicated adolescent samples [88]. Multisystemic therapy starts with a comprehensive assessment of the various individual and contextual risk factors that may have contributed to the child's or adolescent's antisocial behavior. This assessment is used to guide an individualized treatment plan tailored to each child's specific developmental needs. The treatment is closely supervised and monitored to ensure that it is implemented in a rigorous and coordinated manner.

Research on the various developmental pathways leading to CD could be important for guiding these comprehensive and individualized approaches to treatment. Knowledge of the different developmental processes that may be operating in the various subgroups of youth who have CD could help in determining the most effective combination of services for an individual child [89]. For example, interventions that focus on enhancing identity development in adolescents and increasing their contact with prosocial peers, such mentoring programs [90,91] or programs that provide structured after-school activities [92] may be particularly effective for children within the adolescent-onset pathway. Interventions that focus on anger control [93] or parental supervision and discipline [94] may be more effective for children within the childhood-onset pathway who do not exhibit CU traits. Further, interventions that intervene early in the parent–child relationship to teach parents ways to foster empathic concern in their young child or that help the child develop cognitive perspective-taking skills may be more effective for children who have CU traits [95]. Later in development, interventions that emphasize the reward-oriented response style of this group and attempt to motivate children by appealing to their self-interest, rather than interventions that focus solely on punishment-oriented strategies, may be more effective for this group of youth who have CD [89].

Using research on developmental pathways and implementing an individualized approach to treatment requires a comprehensive assessment that goes well beyond simply assessing the diagnostic criteria for CD. As summarized by McMahon and Frick [96], the developmental-pathways approach for understanding CD suggests that assessments must accomplish several important goals. First, the evaluation must assess the wide variations in onset, type, and severity of antisocial and aggressive behavior that are present across the different developmental pathways. This assessment is important for helping determine which pathway might best describe the individual child and for determining the intensity of and the most appropriate setting for treatment. It provides important information on the child's level of risk of harm to others. Second, given that children in the different developmental pathways are likely to show a number of problems in adjustment that may require intervention [3], in addition to their behavioral problems, it is important to assess some of the most common co-occurring problems with CD, such as impulsivity, anxiety, peer rejection, substance abuse, and cognitive deficits. Third, it is important to assess for the most common risk factors that can be associated with the different pathways to CD, which again helps in determining the pathway that may best describe the child and also uncovers important targets of intervention. Fourth, it is important to assess for other characteristics, like the presence of CU traits, that can help determine the pathway that best describes the child and explain the development of the problem behavior.

With respect to this last recommendation, it is important to note that there are significant limitations in the assessment tools that are available for assessing CU traits. The two most widely used and the only commercially available tools for assessing these traits at present are the Antisocial Process Screening Device (APSD; [97]) and the Psychopathy Checklist -Youth Version (PCL-YV; [98]). The APSD involves parent and teacher ratings to assess CU traits in preadolescent children. In contrast, the PCL-YV requires a highly trained clinician to complete a semistructured interview and collect collateral information (eg,institutional charts) to score a checklist that includes CU traits. The PCL-YV has primarily been used in samples of adjudicated older adolescents. Although they are not commercially available, a number of self-report inventories have been developed for use in samples of both adjudicated and nonadjudicated adolescents [37,38,58]. Also, some studies have used combinations of items from existing ratings scales to assess CU traits in child samples [30,47]. Thus, although the evidence for the importance of assessing CU traits in samples of antisocial youth is growing, and a number of different measures are available for research purposes, there is a clear need for more systematic development of measures of CU traits that have proven adequate reliability and validity to guide evaluations in applied settings.

In conclusion, the developmental-pathway perspective for understanding the causes of CD has important implications for both research and practice. Because children who have CD are served in schools, in mental health clinics, and in juvenile justice settings, this research is relevant for professionals working in a number of different settings. Although it is important not to overstate the available support for this model of CD, it does offer substantial hope that significant advances in the understanding of serious criminal and violent behavior are on the horizon. Most importantly, there has been the view in the past that many of the most severely antisocial and delinquent youth are "untreatable" [99]. It may be, instead, that existing treatments have not been the most appropriate for certain groups of antisocial youth. By understanding how the causal processes leading to CD may vary across groups, and by clearly articulating the developmental mechanisms that are involved, this research could provide a firm basis for enhancing prevention and treatment programs for groups of antisocial youth who have not heretofore responded to existing treatments.

References

[1] American Psychiatric Association. Diagnostic and statistical manual of mental disorders. 4th edition, text revised. Washington (DC): American Psychiatric Press; 2000.

[2] Loeber R, Burke JD, Lahey BB, et al. Oppositional defiant and conduct disorder: a review of the past 10 years, part I. J Am Acad Child Adolesc Psychiatry 2000;39:1468–82.

[3] Vermeiren R. Psychopathology and delinquency in adolescents: a descriptive and developmental perspective. Clin Psychol Rev 2003;23:277–318.

[4] Marshall L, Cooke DJ. The childhood experiences of psychopaths: a retrospective study of familial and societal factors. J Personal Disord 1999;13:211–25.
[5] Lytton H. Child and parent effects in boys' conduct disorder: a reinterpretation. Dev Psychol 1990;26:683–97.
[6] Hanish LD, Guerra NG. A longitudinal analysis of patterns of adjustment following peer victimization. Dev Psychopathol 2002;14:69–89.
[7] Frick PJ. Developmental pathways to conduct disorder: implications for serving youth who show severe aggressive and antisocial behavior. Psychol Sch 2004;41:823–34.
[8] Frick PJ. Conduct disorders and severe antisocial behavior. New York: Plenum; 1998.
[9] Dodge KA, Pettit GS. A biopsychosocial model of the development of chronic conduct problems in adolescence. Dev Psychol 2003;39:349–71.
[10] Loeber R, Farrington DP. Young children who commit crime: epidemiology, developmental origins, risk factors, and early interventions, and policy implications. Dev Psychopathol 2000;12: 737–62.
[11] Raine A. Biosocial studies of antisocial and violent behavior in children and adults: a review. J Abnorm Child Psychol 2002;30:311–26.
[12] Herpertz SC, Mueller B, Qunaib M, et al. Response to emotional stimuli in boys with conduct disorder. Am J Psychiatry 2005;162:1100–7.
[13] Sameroff AJ, Peck SC, Eccles JS. Changing ecological determinants of conduct problems from early adolescence to early adulthood. Dev Psychopathol 2004;16:873–96.
[14] Stouthamer-Loeber M, Loeber R, Wei E, et al. Risk and promotive effects in the explanation of persistent serious delinquency in boys. J Consult Clin Psychol 2002;70:111–23.
[15] Raine A, Brennan P, Mednick SA. Birth, complications combined with early maternal rejection in at age 1 year predispose to violent crime at age 18 years. Arch Gen Psychiatry 1994;51: 984–8.
[16] Frick PJ, Ellis ML. Callous-unemotional traits and subtypes of conduct disorder. Clin Child Fam Psychol Rev 1999;2:149–68.
[17] Frick PJ, Marsee MA. Psychopathy and developmental pathways to antisocial behavior in youth. In: Patrick CJ, editor. Handbook of psychopathy. New York: Guilford; 2006. p. 355–74.
[18] Olds D, Henderson CR, Cole R, et al. Long-term effects of nurse home visitation on children's criminal and antisocial behavior: 15-year follow-up of a randomized controlled trial. JAMA 1998;280:1238–44.
[19] Moffitt TE. Adolescence-limited and life-course persistent antisocial behavior: a developmental taxonomy. Psychol Rev 1993;100:674–701.
[20] Patterson GR. Performance models for antisocial boys. Am Psychol 1996;41:432–44.
[21] Lahey BB, Loeber R. Framework for a developmental model of oppositional defiant disorder and conduct disorder. In: Routh DK, editor. Disruptive behavior disorders in childhood. New York: Plenum; 1994. p. 139–80.
[22] Moffitt TE, Caspi A, Harrington H, et al. Males on the life-course persistent and adolescence-limited pathways: follow-up at age 26 years. Dev Psychopathol 2002;14:179–207.
[23] Frick PJ, Loney BR. Outcomes of children and adolescents with conduct disorder and oppositional defiant disorder. In: Quay HC, Hogan A, editors. Handbook of disruptive behavior disorders. New York: Plenum; 1999. p. 507–24.
[24] Moffitt TE. Life-course persistent and adolescence-limited antisocial behavior: a 10-year research review and research agenda. In: Lahey BB, Moffitt TE, Caspi A, editors. Causes of conduct disorder and juvenile delinquency. New York: Guilford; 2003. p. 49–75.
[25] Lahey BB, Schwab-Stone M, Goodman SH, et al. Age and gender differences in oppositional behavior and conduct problems: a cross-sectional household study of middle childhood and adolescence. J Abnorm Psychol 2000;109:488–503.
[26] Silverthorn P, Frick PJ. Developmental pathways to antisocial behavior: the delayed-onset pathway in girls. Dev Psychopathol 1999;11:101–26.
[27] Patrick CJ, editor. Handbook of psychopathy. New York: Guilford; 2006.
[28] Frick PJ, Bodin SD, Barry CT. Psychopathic traits and conduct problems in community and

clinic-referred samples of children: further development of the Psychopathy Screening Device. Psychol Assess 2000;12:382–93.

[29] Cooke DJ, Michie C. Refining the construct of psychopathy: towards a hierarchical model. Psychol Assess 2001;13:171–88.

[30] Dadds MR, Fraser J, Frost A, et al. Disentangling the underlying dimensions of psychopathy and conduct problems in childhood: a community study. J Consult Clin Psychol 2005;73:400–10.

[31] Frick PJ, Kimonis ER, Dandreaux DM, et al. The four-year stability of psychopathic traits in non-referred youth. Behav Sci Law 2003;21:713–36.

[32] Caputo AA, Frick PJ, Brodsky SL. Family violence and juvenile sex offending: potential mediating roles of psychopathic traits and negative attitudes toward women. Crim Justice Behav 1999;26:338–56.

[33] Salekin RT, Neumann CS, Leistico AR, et al. Psychopathy and co-morbidity in a young offender sample: taking a closer look at psychopathy's potential importance over disruptive behavior disorders. J Abnorm Psychol 2004;113:416–22.

[34] Kruh IP, Frick PJ, Clements CB. Historical and personality correlates to the violence patterns of juveniles tried as adults. Crim Justice Behav 2005;32:69–96.

[35] Spain SE, Douglas KS, Poythress NG, et al. The relationship between psychopathic features, violence, and treatment outcome: the comparison of three youth measures of psychopathic features. Behav Sci Law 2004;21:85–102.

[36] Silverthorn P, Frick PJ, Reynolds R. Timing of onset and correlates of severe conduct problems in adjudicated girls and boys. Journal of Psychopathology and Behavioral Assessment 2001;23:171–81.

[37] Lynam DR. Pursuing the psychopath: capturing the fledgling psychopath in a nomological net. J Abnorm Psychol 1997;106:425–38.

[38] Andershed HA, Gustafson SB, Kerr M, et al. The usefulness of self-reported psychopathy-like traits in the study of antisocial behaviour among non-referred adolescents. European Journal of Personality 2002;16:383–402.

[39] Christian RE, Frick PJ, Hill NL, et al. Psychopathy and conduct problems in children: II. Implications for subtyping children with conduct problems. J Am Acad Child Adolesc Psychiatry 1997;36:233–41.

[40] Frick PJ, Cornell AH, Barry CT, et al. Callous-unemotional traits and conduct problems in the prediction of conduct problem severity, aggression, and self-report of delinquency. J Abnorm Child Psychol 2003;31:457–70.

[41] Marsee MA, Silverthorn P, Frick PJ. The association of psychopathic traits with aggression and delinquency in non-referred boys and girls. Behav Sci Law, in press.

[42] Hawes DJ, Dadds MR. The treatment of conduct problems in children with callous-unemotional traits. J Consult Clin Psychology 2005;73:1–5.

[43] Brandt JR, Kennedy WA, Patrick CJ, et al. Assessment of psychopathy in a population of incarcerated adolescent offenders. Psychol Assess 1997;9:429–35.

[44] Forth AE, Hart SD, Hare RD. Assessment of psychopathy in male young offenders. Psychol Assess 1990;2:342–4.

[45] Toupin J, Mercier H, Dery M, et al. Validity of the PCL-R for adolescents. Issues in Criminological and Legal Psychology 1995;24:143–5.

[46] Frick PJ, Stickle TR, Dandreaux DM, et al. Callous-unemotional traits in predicting the severity and stability of conduct problems and delinquency. J Abnorm Child Psychol 2005; 33:471–87.

[47] Viding E, Blair RJR, Moffitt TE, et al. Evidence for substantial genetic risk for psychopathy in 7-year-olds. J Child Psychol Psychiatry 2005;46:592–7.

[48] Pardini DA, Lochman JE, Frick PJ. Callous-unemotional traits and social cognitive processes in adjudicated youth: exploring the schema of juveniles with psychopathic traits. J Am Acad Child Adolesc Psychiatry 2003;42:364–71.

[49] Frick PJ, Lilienfeld SO, Ellis ML, et al. The association between anxiety and psychopathy dimensions in children. J Abnorm Child Psychol 1999;27:381–90.

[50] Frick PJ, Cornell AH, Bodin SD, et al. Callous-unemotional traits and developmental pathways to severe aggressive and antisocial behavior. Dev Psychol 2003;39:246–60.
[51] Barry CT, Frick PJ, Grooms T, et al. The importance of callous-unemotional traits for extending the concept of psychopathy to children. J Abnorm Psychol 2000;109:335–40.
[52] Fisher L, Blair RJR. Cognitive impairment and its relationship to psychopathic tendencies in children with emotional and behavioral difficulties. J Abnorm Child Psychol 1998;26:511–9.
[53] Blair RJR, Colledge E, Murray L, et al. A selective impairment in the processing of sad and fearful expressions in children with psychopathic tendencies. J Abnorm Child Psychol 2001;29: 491–8.
[54] Stevens D, Charman T, Blair RJR. Recognition of emotion in facial expressions and vocal tones in children with psychopathic tendencies. J Genet Psychol 2001;16:201–11.
[55] Blair RJR. Responsiveness to distress cues in the child with psychopathic tendencies. Pers Individ Dif 1999;27:135–45.
[56] Blair RJR, Jones L, Clark F, et al. The psychopathic individual: a lack of responsiveness to distress cues? Psychophysiology 1997;34:192–8.
[57] Kimonis ER, Frick PJ, Fazekas H, et al. Psychopathy, aggression, and the processing of emotional stimuli in non-referred boys and girls. Behav Sci Law, in press.
[58] Loney BR, Frick PJ, Clements CB, et al. Emotional reactivity and callous unemotional traits in adolescents. J Clin Child Adolesc Psychol 2003;32:66–80.
[59] Fung MT, Raine D, Loeber R, et al. Reduced electrodermal activity in psychopathy-prone adolescents. J Abnorm Psychol 2005;114:187–96.
[60] Rothbart MK, Bates JE. Temperament. In: Damon W, editor. Handbook of child psychology, vol. 3. social, emotional, and personality development. New York: Wiley; 1998. p. 105–76.
[61] Kagan J, Snidman N. Temperamental factors in human development. Am Psychol 1991;46: 856–62.
[62] Cloninger CR. A systematic method for clinical description and classification of personality variants. Arch Gen Psychiatry 1987;44:573–88.
[63] Lahey BB, Waldman ID. A developmental propensity model of the origins of conduct problems during childhood and adolescence. In: Lahey BB, Moffitt TE, Caspi A, editors. Causes of conduct disorder and juvenile delinquency. New York: Guilford; 2003. p. 76–117.
[64] Asendorf JB, Nunner-Winkler G. Children's moral motive strength and temperamental inhibition reduce their egoistic behavior in real moral conflicts. Child Dev 1992;63:1223–35.
[65] Kochanska G, Gross JN, Lin MH, et al. Guilt in young children: development, determinants, and relations with a broader system of standards. Child Dev 2002;73:461–82.
[66] Rothbart MK, Ahadi SA, Hershey K. Temperament and social behavior in childhood. Merrill Palmer Q 1994;40:21–39.
[67] Frick PJ, Morris AS. Temperament and developmental pathways to conduct problems. J Clin Child Adolesc Psychol 2004;33:54–68.
[68] Kochanska G. Toward a synthesis of parental socialization and child temperament in early development of conscience. Child Dev 1993;64:325–47.
[69] Kochanska G. Children's temperament, mothers' discipline, and security of attachment: multiple pathways to emerging internalization. Child Dev 1995;66:597–615.
[70] Kochanska G. Multiple pathways to conscience for children with different temperaments: from toddlerhood to age 5. Dev Psychol 1997;33:228–40.
[71] Blair RJR. A cognitive developmental approach to morality: investigating the psychopath. Cognition 1995;57:1–29.
[72] Oxford M, Cavell TA, Hughes JN. Callous-unemotional traits moderate the relation between ineffective parenting and child externalizing problems: a partial replication and extension. J Clin Child Adolesc Psychol 2003;32:577–85.
[73] Wootton JM, Frick PJ, Shelton KK, et al. Ineffective parenting and childhood conduct problems: the moderating role of callous-unemotional traits. J Consult Clin Psychol 1997;65:301–8.
[74] Loney BR, Frick PJ, Ellis M, et al. Intelligence, psychopathy, and antisocial behavior. Journal of Psychopathology and Behavioral Assessment 1998;20:231–47.

[75] Raine A, Moffitt TE, Caspi A, et al. Neurocognitive impairments in boys on the life-course persistent antisocial path. J Abnorm Psychol 2005;114:38–49.
[76] Patterson GR, Reid JB, Dishion TJ. Antisocial boys. Eugene (OR): Castilia; 1992.
[77] Gauvain M, Fagot BI. Child temperament as a mediator of mother-toddler problem-solving. Social Dev 1995;4:257–76.
[78] Richters JE. The Hubble hypothesis and the developmentalist's dilemna. Dev Psychopathol 1997; 9:193–230.
[79] Frick PJ, Lilienfeld SO, Edens JF, et al. The association between anxiety and antisocial behavior. Primary Psychiatry 2000;7:52–7.
[80] Bergman LR, Magnusson D. A person-oriented approach in research on developmental psychopathology. Dev Psychopathol 1997;9:291–319.
[81] Frick PJ. Integrating research on temperament and childhood psychopathology. Its pitfalls and promise. J Clin Child Adolesc Psychol 2004;33:2–7.
[82] Kochanska G, Murray KT. Mother-child mutually responsive orientation and conscience development: from toddler to early school age. Child Dev 2000;71:417–31.
[83] Kimonis ER, Frick PJ, Barry CT. Callous-unemotional traits and delinquent peer affiliation. J Consult Clin Psychol 2004;72:956–66.
[84] Brestan EV, Eyberg SM. Effective psychosocial treatments for conduct disordered children and adolescents. J Clin Child Psychol 1998;27:180–9.
[85] Kazdin AE. Conduct disorders in childhood and adolescence. 2nd edition. Thousand Oaks (CA): Sage; 1995.
[86] Conduct Problems Prevention Research Group. The effects of the FAST Track Program on serious problem outcomes at the end of elementary school. J Clin Child Adolesc Psychol 2004;33:650–61.
[87] Burns B, Howell JC, Wiig JK, et al. Treatment, services, and intervention programs for child delinquents. Office of Juvenile Justice and Delinquency Child Delinquency Bulletin Series 2003;March:1–15.
[88] Henggeler SW, Schoenwald SK, Borduin CM, et al. Multisystemic treatment of antisocial behavior in children and adolescents. New York: Guilford; 1998.
[89] Frick PJ. Effective interventions for children and adolescents with conduct disorder. Can J Psychiatry 2001;46:26–37.
[90] Grossman JB, Tierney JP. Does mentoring work? An impact study of the Big Brothers/Big Sisters program. Eval Rev 1998;22:403–26.
[91] Jackson Y. Mentoring for delinquency children: an outcome study with young adolescent children. J Youth Adolesc 2002;31:115–22.
[92] Mahoney JL, Stattin H. Leisure activities and adolescent antisocial behavior: the role of structure and social context. J Adolesc 2000;23:113–27.
[93] Larson J, Lochman JE. Helping schoolchildren cope with anger. New York: Guilford; 2003.
[94] Patterson GR, Forgatch MS. Parents and adolescents living together. Eugene (OR): Castalia; 1987.
[95] Chi-Ming K, Greenberg MT, Walls CT. Examining the role of implementation quality in school-based prevention using the PATH curriculum. Prev Sci 2003;4:55–63.
[96] McMahon RJ, Frick PJ. Evidence-based assessment of conduct problems in children and adolescents. J Clin Child Adolesc Psychol 2005;34:477–505.
[97] Frick PJ, Hare RD. The Antisocial Process Screening Device. Toronto (Ontariio, Canada): Multi-Health Systems; 2001.
[98] Forth AE, Kosson D, Hare RD. Hare psychopathy checklist: youth version. Toronto, (Ontario, Canada): Multi-Health Systems; 2004.
[99] Salekin RT. Psychopathy and therapeutic pessimism: clinical lore or clinical reality? Clin Psychol Rev 2002;22:79–112.

ELSEVIER
SAUNDERS

Child Adolesc Psychiatric Clin N Am
15 (2006) 333–351

CHILD AND
ADOLESCENT
PSYCHIATRIC CLINICS
OF NORTH AMERICA

Mental Health Problems in Juvenile Justice Populations

Robert Vermeiren, MD, PhD[a,*], Ine Jespers[b], Terrie Moffitt, PhD[c]

[a] *VU University Medical Center/Leiden University, P/a De Bascule, Postbus 303, 1115 ZG Duivendrecht, The Netherlands*
[b] *Center for Mental Health VAGGA, Antwerp, Belgium*
[c] *Institute of Psychiatry, King's College London, London, UK*

Decades of scientific research on the phenomenon of adolescent delinquency have resulted in the recognition of a large number of environmental and individual risk factors [1]. Until recently, research on psychiatric pathology as risk factor for delinquency has not received much attention and has therefore remained a subject of ongoing scientific debate [2]. Over the past years, interest in the subject seems to have grown, because several sound prevalence studies have been conducted on psychiatric disorders in juvenile justice populations [3–10]. Because current research has consistently shown high rates of disorders, the debate is slowly shifting toward aspects of clinical relevance (ie, for judicial handling and therapeutic intervention). For specific disorders with overall low prevalence, such as autism spectrum disorders and psychosis, research is still on the epidemiologic level. Therefore, this article summarizes the existing knowledge about the overlap between delinquency and psychiatric pathology, with specific focus on disorders that have been less studied in juvenile justice populations.

Recently, Grisso and Zimring [11] have listed three principal reasons for concern regarding mental disorders in youthful offenders: (1) the custodial treatment obligation (ie, the obligation to respond to mental health needs), (2) assurance of due process in adjudicative proceedings, and (3) public safety (ie, to the extent that there is a relation between an adolescent's mental health status and future violent behavior, the obligation to offer specific provisions). Too

* Corresponding author.
E-mail address: robert@vermeiren.name (R. Vermeiren).

doi:10.1016/j.chc.2005.11.008 ***childpsych.theclinics.com***

often, mental health treatment within the juvenile justice system is lacking for those in need. A study by Domalanta and colleagues [12] showed that only about 20% of depressed incarcerated youth and only 10% of adolescents with other disorders were receiving treatment. Fewer than half of incarcerated youth who required treatment because of substance use disorder (SUD) received intervention [13]. For those reasons, it is necessary to conduct further research not only on the prevalence of mental health disorders but also on the related needs for intervention.

For several reasons, high rates of mental disorders may be expected in youth in contact with juvenile justice. First, prevalence rates of psychiatric disorders in community samples were shown to be around 15% [14]. Also, severe delinquency is common in the adolescent population, with about 5% showing an early-onset and persistent pattern of antisocial behavior [15]. A substantial number of adolescents will show offending behavior and will have a mental health disorder simply because of coincidental overlap between both conditions. Second, because delinquent and antisocial behavior reaches high levels among juvenile justice populations, a diagnosis of conduct disorder (CD) will often be made. Because CD shows high comorbidity rates with several other psychiatric disorders [16], increased levels of many types of disorders may be expected. Third, risk factors for youthful offending overlap substantially with those for several types of nondisruptive child psychiatric disorders. Therefore, identical risk factors may underlie both antisocial behavior and emotional or developmental problems. Finally, selection processes may play a role. Disorders for which mental health intervention is provided, such as SUDs, may also lead to judicial involvement. Also, because of the prevalence of complex comorbidity, treatment in a regular mental health care program may be intricate and often is not possible, thus increasing the likelihood of judicial involvement. In addition, severely disordered persons may be less likely to have the personal capability and have adequate resources to defend themselves and to avoid more drastic legal interventions.

The findings in this article are presented in three parts. First is an overview of the existing literature and the reported general prevalence rates. Next, specific disorders are discussed, further subdivided as internalizing disorders, externalizing disorders, and psychosis and developmental disorders. A third section discusses findings related to the longitudinal course and the predictive power of psychiatric disorders in young offenders.

General findings

Research on the prevalence of mental disorders in juvenile justice youth has increased steadily during the past years but remains limited compared with similar research in adults. In 2002, a review on psychiatric disorders in representative samples of imprisoned adults was published [17]. When only studies that used validated instruments for clinical diagnosis were included, 62 studies could be identified, totaling 23,000 individuals. For minors, only 16 studies can be included, totaling 4495 individuals. Furthermore, six of those studies (3118 participants) were published since 2002, after the adult review appeared. For that reason, it may be concluded that research on psychopathology in juvenile delinquents is still in its infancy and that prevalence studies should continue to receive attention.

The paucity of research on mental health disorders in juvenile justice populations may have several explanations. First, child psychiatry has long been controversial within the forensic field because of concern that the child psychiatrist may overemphasize the role of individual factors. Although this reservation may seem to arise because of the focus on disorders, current insights acknowledge that disorders are determined by both (early) environmental and biologic antecedents. In addition, child psychiatrists themselves have long neglected forensic mental health issues, and attention to the topic is currently still limited. Second, limited research has been conducted on specific mental health interventions in juvenile justice populations (see the article by Chapman elsewhere in this issue), and such interventions have long been considered ineffective. Therefore, psychiatric prevalence studies may not have received much attention. Third, youth in juvenile justice constitute an extremely difficult group to investigate. Many youthful offenders do not accept child psychiatry or mental health services because of their fear of stigmatization, previous experiences, and aggression [18]. In general, these youths are more likely to express toughness than sickness [19]. Therefore, although a large number of youthful offenders may experience emotional or relationship problems, only some express a wish to receive mental health intervention [18]. In addition, parents are usually very difficult to reach [8], while obtaining information from parents is considered an essential part of child psychiatric assessment. Because juvenile justice youth are difficult to interest in research, the few studies on mental health characteristics of this population have focused almost exclusively on youth in detention and not on the broader group of youth within the juvenile justice system. Therefore, this article focuses predominantly on detained populations, although attempts are made to focus on other juvenile justice youth as well.

Prevalence rates and comorbidity

Although research consistently reveals high levels of psychiatric disorders among detained juveniles, rates vary widely by study, ranging from more than 50% to 100% [3–10,20–22]. CD and SUDs carry highest prevalence rates, but other mental disorders also present commonly in this population [8]. Because CD criteria overlap with offending behavior, some authors have provided rates of mental disorder excluding this disorder. Still, more than half of these adolescents are diagnosed with at least one other psychiatric diagnosis [8]. Only a few studies have focused on nondetained juvenile justice subgroups, such as adjudicated nondetained adolescents [23,24] and adolescents on parole [25]. Although rates are lower in these groups than in detained groups, the number of psychiatric disorders in these populations was still much higher than would be expected in the general population. Youth at a pre–juvenile justice level, namely those in contact with police, have been studied in two cross-national samples (United States and Belgium) by means of self-report questionnaires, and it was found that arrested youth had higher levels of both internalizing and externalizing pathology than seen in compared with nonarrested youth [26]. Hence, although the number of studies is still limited, substantial mental health needs seem characteristic for juveniles at all levels of the juvenile justice system.

Comorbidity, defined as the presence of more than one disorder, has consistently been described in more than half of delinquent youths [2,8,9], a finding that underscores the complexity of psychiatric problems in these youth. Not surprisingly, the mean number of psychiatric disorders is high, between 2.7 and 3.1 as reported in two studies [5,20]. SUDs may be particularly important in this respect, because multiple substance use is the rule rather than an exception, and co-occurrence of substance use and other disorders is frequent [27,28]. Although a long history of mental health problems is characteristic for youthful offenders [8], it has been shown that early problem behavior (eg, an onset of CD before age 10 years) is related to high comorbidity rates [7]. Comorbidity may pose a particular problem in detained girls, because a recent study [3] has shown that 93% of the investigated females were carrying more than one disorder, and 78% had three or more disorders. Because many studies have concentrated on only a limited number of disorders, current comorbidity figures may still be incomplete. For example, posttraumatic stress disorder (PTSD) has been investigated in only some studies, but some authors have reported high rates of this condition in detained groups [29,30].

Of clinical importance is the comorbidity with other risk-taking behaviors, such as sexual risk and risk of AIDS [31], because the high levels of severe risk-taking behaviors in juvenile justice youth may further complicate the diagnostic picture and, of course, possible intervention. SUDs in particular may be associated with such increased risk, because more than half of substance users were reported to have had multiple partners and unprotected vaginal sex during the last month [31].

Limitations of current research

Although there is a fair amount of research on the mental health problems of delinquent youths, current findings are diverse and hard to interpret, for several possible reasons.

First, the type and nature of the psychiatric interviews (structured or semi-structured) and of the diagnostic classifications (use of different *Diagnostic and Statistical Manual* [*DSM*] versions) varied by study. Because inconsistent results were also obtained in studies using similar instruments, it is questionable whether the nature of the interview explains much of the variance.

Second, the moment of investigation and the period of diagnostic assessment also differed by study. Some studies focused on youth shortly after detention [8], whereas others investigated youth in the postadjudication phase [9,10]. The moment of assessment may have relevance, because detention itself may influence the psychologic condition (eg, by exacerbating depressive symptoms) [2]. With respect to psychiatric diagnosis, different time frames (eg, point prevalence versus prevalence over a specific period) were often used. Although this difference may well have influenced the findings, it is questionable whether this disordered population is able to reflect over longer periods, and hence, to what extent this difference has truly influenced findings. Similar considerations may relate to the self-reported degree of impairment associated with a psychiatric diagnosis, because such self-assessment may not be reliable [32].

Third, enormous differences exist among studies on relevant sociodemographic and criminological characteristics, such as age, gender, ethnicity, family structure, socioeconomic status, and the nature of criminal behavior. Ethnic differences may be particularly important, because several studies have shown lower levels of mental health problems in minority groups [4,8]. Other confounders of substantial influence may not have been mentioned until now, such as the impact of urban living and related exposure to community violence or the availability of substances. Unfortunately, information on relevant factors is too often lacking or vague, making adequate comparison of study findings difficult.

Fourth, studies were conducted in different countries and, for those in the United States, in different states. State-specific differences were shown by Wasserman and colleagues [10], demonstrating different prevalences of some psychiatric disorders in detention samples from Illinois and New Jersey. Such differences may bear different grounds, such as jurisdiction-specific judicial handling of youths or the allocation of offenders to specific institutions. In addition, because almost all studies were conducted in incarcerated youths, the psychopathologic profile of an extreme group is described. Because most studies only provide limited information on type and severity of offenses and no information on local judicial procedures, comparison of these aspects is not possible at present.

Fifth, some studies investigated antisocial youths referred specifically for psychiatric assessment. Although this population may give an overall impression of the types of psychopathology typically present in the delinquent youths referred for clinical services, the epidemiologic value of such information is limited, and generalization toward the whole delinquent population is unjustified. Future studies should avoid such bias, because previously described unavoidable selection processes may already create inherent methodologic problems hampering adequate interpretation of results.

Last, because information from parents is largely unavailable, almost all current prevalence studies have relied uniquely on the youths themselves as informants. Although this reliance is understandable given the difficulties in finding parents willing to be interviewed, it may hamper reliability of findings. This problem may be particularly relevant for disorders requiring investigation of the age of onset, such as attention deficit hyperactivity disorder (ADHD). Research in clinical samples has shown that inconsistency between adolescents and parents in reporting mental health disorders is a general problem, because denial of problems by one of the informants ranges from 12% to 97% [33]. A recent study of parent information in 120 of 569 detained adolescents suggests otherwise: parent information was shown to reveal potentially new information in only about 30% of cases [32]. Although youth reported higher rates of disorder, disagreement between youth and parents was most obvious with respect to disorder-related impairment. Disagreement could be attributed to different understanding of questions, lack of awareness of parents of the adolescent's behavior, and differences in thresholds for problem behavior. For those reasons, issues of assessment and consistency of reporting should be further investigated. A further argument for focusing on third-party information in future studies is the finding that external information may increase the long-term predictive validity [22].

Specific disorders

Internalizing disorders

Depression and suicide

Recent studies in incarcerated samples found prevalence rates of depressive disorder between 2% and 13% for males [4,6–10,30] and between 14% and 36% for females [3,5,6,8]. Studies reporting on gender differences all described higher rates of depression in delinquent girls than in delinquent boys, although this difference was not always significant [34]. In addition, a recent paper-and-pencil self-report study did not find gender differences in depression [12]. Interestingly, the number of males scoring above the clinical cut-off in this study was higher than interview-based prevalence rates of other studies and was within the range of girls. Although clinical *DSM* diagnoses cannot be generated by means of self-report questionnaires, these findings may bear methodologic consequences, in particular with regard to the usefulness of interview methods in male delinquents [35].

According to Pliszka and colleagues [36], depressed individuals were shown to have higher levels of substance use than nondepressed juvenile delinquents [34,35], and positive correlations were found between depressive symptoms and severity of substance abuse [37]. Because depression did not disappear, even after weeks of abstinence, it was suggested that depression is not merely secondary to drug abuse and dependence [38].

The high comorbidity between antisocial behavior and depression may be explained largely by the presence of common risk factors [39], such as traumatization and familial disadvantage. Additionally, the consequences of antisocial behavior, such as adjudication or incarceration, may exacerbate the onset of depression [40].

Because of the oft-reported association between violent antisocial behavior and suicidality, it is not surprising that high prevalence rates of current suicidal ideation were found in incarcerated youths (10%–9%) [10,41] and that lifetime rates as high as 34% have been reported [42–44]. In one study by Morris and colleagues [42], the rate of suicidal ideation was found to be comparable between detained youths and school students, but delinquents scored higher on the number of actual attempts committed and the injury rate. Similarly, Penn and colleagues [45] have shown that incarcerated youth are more likely to use violent methods when attempting suicide, a finding of high clinical relevance. Gender differences may also be of importance, because studies have consistently reported higher rates of suicidality in detained girls than in detained boys. Although there is no doubt about the clinical relevance of suicidality in detained youth, a problem in summarizing current scientific reports relates to the variability in terminology used. Therefore, in addition to studies of clinical predictors and possibilities for intervention, prevalence studies should be conducted as well.

For many years, depression has been considered the predominant risk factor for suicidal behavior. Recent findings in nonforensic populations have shown that other conditions, such as disruptive behavior, may independently increase suicide risk, especially when comorbid substance abuse is present [46]. For that reason, clinical predictors of suicidality may differ for forensic populations as compared with the general population. This possibility is supported by the results of a recent school-based sample of adolescents showing that adolescents who exhibited combined suicidal and violent behavior scored substantially worse than only-suicidal adolescents on measures of overt aggression, sensation seeking, perception of risk, and substance use [47].

Studies in juvenile justice populations have similarly demonstrated that clinical predictors of suicide may present differently than in community or clinical samples, although studies comparing forensic populations with control groups are scarce. Until now, most studies have directly compared suicidal and nonsuicidal youth within forensic populations. Findings of those studies are inconsistent, probably because of the diversity in the selection and composition of detained populations. Also, factors related to stress resulting from involvement with juvenile justice, and in particular incarceration, may also increase suicide risk. In incarcerated youth, Ruchkin and colleagues [44] have shown that depression did not independently predict lifetime suicidal behavior, but separation anxiety, ADHD, and a number of personality- and parenting-related variables did. Similar results were obtained in a study in juvenile detainees and adolescent inpatients, showing that impulsivity and substance use were independent predictors of suicide risk in detained juveniles but not in inpatients [48]. Still others have shown predictive validity of affective symptoms [45,49], a finding that should stimulate further research, particularly because suicide risk in this population poses a substantial clinical problem. To rule out inconsistency of findings arising from methodologic differences, multisite studies should be conducted, preferably using identical instruments as part of similar research designs.

Posttraumatic stress disorder and abuse

Although earlier reports have described a relationship between traumatic experiences and antisocial behavior in juveniles, studies of PTSD in juvenile justice populations are scarce. In some earlier studies, 16% to 32% of detained boys were found to experience PTSD [29,50], and an additional 20% were found to exhibit partial criteria [29]. Because three quarters of the participants in one of these studies were referred specifically for psychiatric examination, however, selection bias may have prevailed [29]. More recent studies found much lower PTSD rates, between 2% and 11% [6,10,51], with only one exception finding PTSD in 24% [30]. In girls, much higher rates of current PTSD may prevail, ranging from 33% to 55% [3,5,50,52], with 65% reporting lifetime PTSD and an additional 12% partial PTSD [52]. Interestingly, one recent study found PTSD in only 7% of a female detention group [6]. Steiner and colleagues [29] argued that because PTSD subjects often may feel afraid to disclose the presence of PTSD symptoms, a more diligent investigation of this issue could optimize willingness to report these problems. This suggestion may be relevant, especially in boys, and such a diagnostic approach should be considered in future research.

The importance of recognizing PTSD in delinquents is further underscored by personality assessments showing an association between PTSD and impulsivity, aggression, and negative emotions (eg, anxiety and depression) [29,52]. Of clinical interest is the finding in boys [29] that PTSD-positive delinquents are clearly the most troubled in terms of impulse control and control of aggression, an observation that may have prognostic implications. The presence of high levels of dissociative disorder (28.3%) and dissociative disorder not otherwise specified (20%) in delinquents of both genders [53] further supports the observation that traumatized delinquents are severely troubled youths in need of adequate intervention.

Bipolar disorder

Although some studies reported relatively high levels of *DSM-IV* manic disorder in detained youth (20%) [36], more recent reports found mania in only 1.5% to 3.0% of this group [8,10,30,54]. With regard to manic disorder, methodologic considerations are warranted, because some diagnostic instruments may overdiagnose mania and diagnose mania in adolescents who do not have clinical hypomania. Historically, it may be of interest that Pinel used the term "manie sans delire" (mania without delirium) in the early nineteenth century when referring to antisocial persons who did not have noticeable psychosis [55]. Hence, before further elaborating on the prevalence and significance of manic disorder within a conduct-disordered or a delinquent population, the diagnostic validity and reliability of currently used instruments should be determined.

Anxiety disorder

Studies of anxiety disorder in incarcerated youths indicated rates ranging from 20% to 21% in males and from 31% to 59% in females [5,8,10]. A lower rate (9%) was found in one study in detained Dutch adolescents [9]. Ulzen and

Hamilton [56] suggested that the presence of anxiety disorders in delinquents might be a function of the state of incarceration itself and the result of the numerous out-of-home placements that typically precede a youth's incarceration. Interestingly, a recent school-based study in three cross-cultural samples did not show an association between anxiety and subtypes of antisocial behavior [57], a finding that may support the idea that anxiety represents a consequence of legal involvement. To date, the significance of anxiety symptoms in relation to delinquent development is still largely unknown and should be further studied. In this research, the role of callous and unemotional characteristics should receive particular attention, because such psychopathic traits were found to be negatively associated with anxiety (see the article by Frick elsewhere in this issue).

Externalizing disorders

Conduct disorder

Not surprisingly, literature has demonstrated that the absolute majority of adolescent delinquents may receive a diagnosis of CD [2,8]. Indeed, it is rather remarkable that between one quarter and two thirds of delinquent adolescents do not carry a CD diagnosis [4,6,8–10,30]. The absence of a formal CD diagnosis in delinquent adolescents may have reasonable explanations, however, even in delinquent youth who were adjudicated or incarcerated on criminal grounds. First, an individual may face incarceration for a single major offense, such as person-related aggression or rape, without having committed other antisocial acts. Such offense may be severe enough to warrant secure detention and close supervision but not adequate for a diagnosis of CD. This consideration provides some justification for criticizing the categorical approach of the *DSM*, because a person who steals once, who bullies, and who has destroyed someone's property once during the last couple of months will receive a diagnosis of CD. Second, adolescents may get in trouble for behaviors not listed in *DSM*, such as drug dealing. Finally, most studies in delinquents have relied exclusively on information provided by the youth themselves, and it is to be expected that delinquents—and incarcerated persons in particular—would be reluctant to report voluntarily on officially unknown severe antisocial acts, even when confidentiality is assured. Detained youths are often suspicious and even paranoid toward investigators, and their attitudes may contribute to the lower-than-expected prevalence of CD. Hence, an underreporting of antisocial behavior and an underestimation of the true prevalence of CD in this population is likely, particularly in youth in the preadjudication phase.

Based on the developmental taxonomic model of Moffitt [15], the *DSM-IV* has adopted an age-of-onset approach, differentiating an early-onset from a late-onset CD subtype. Although relevant, a practical weakness of the age-of-onset subtyping is its limited usefulness in clinical settings, because it has been reported that multi-informant retrospective reports on the age of onset of antisocial behavior do not enhance the prediction of future behavior problems in clinical populations [58]. Furthermore, it has been demonstrated that both the adolescence-limited and life-course–persistent subgroups show similar levels of antisocial behavior and arrest during adolescence (although there are slightly more convictions for violent behavior in life-course–persistent CD) [59]. Because some have reported positively on the discriminative validity of the age-of-onset subtyping, more research on this issue is needed [7,60].

Attention deficit/hyperactivity disorder

The rate of actual ADHD reported in detained adolescents is diverse, ranging from 1% to 18% in boys and from 6% to 34% in girls [3–6,8–10,30]. Although these percentages may give the impression that ADHD is more prevalent in female than in male delinquents, studies that have directly compared genders have not been consistent [6,8].

Although the impact of ADHD on the onset of early conduct problems has been established, the role of ADHD for the continuation or deterioration of antisocial behavior in delinquent adolescents remains unclear. Because several evidence-based psychotherapeutic and psychopharmacologic treatments for ADHD are available, further research is needed on this association. In addition, a number of issues need attention in such studies. First, diagnostic reliability is an issue of particular importance in forensic populations. The lack of information from third-party informants all too often hampers the evaluation of development-related criteria. Richards [61] explained his findings of the low prevalence of ADHD (4%) in detained youth as a result of the lack of developmental data and of difficulties in delineating this disorder when antisocial behavior is present. Although this explanation is acceptable, it remains unclear why several other studies, most of which faced the same shortcomings, found much higher rates of ADHD. Second, differentiating the features of ADHD from the diagnostic symptoms of other disorders may be particularly complex in delinquent youth characterized by high comorbidity rates. Such diagnostic complexity may be particularly present with regard to CD and PTSD. Particularly in girls, differentiating ADHD from PTSD may be complex, and the high rates of ADHD may well be a trauma-related phenomenon. Third, there is an ongoing debate whether ADHD should be perceived as one categorical syndrome (with categorical subtypes) or as a dimension of characteristics related to attention, hyperactivity, and impulsivity. Clinically, a dimensional approach may be most relevant, because it may facilitate the evaluation of intervention outcomes. Finally, the relationship between ADHD and neurocognitive deficits needs further study. The presence of cognitive verbal deficits is one of the strongest risk factors for the development and continuation of antisocial behavior [15,62,63], and ADHD may be intrinsically related to cognitive dysfunction. Insight into these aspects is of great scientific as well as clinical interest, because it may allow adequate subtyping and the individualization and optimization of treatment.

Substance use disorder

SUDs have been investigated widely in juvenile justice populations, and it is no surprise that such problems occur at alarmingly high rates. Recent studies have shown SUDs of any kind in one third to more than half of detained youth [6,8,10,64], with more than one fifth of the whole population abusing more than one substance [27,64]. In adjudicated, mainly nonincarcerated, youths lower rates were found, although numbers were still higher than would be expected in the normal population [23]. Importantly, it has been stated that studies of SUDs may underestimate true prevalence rates, because youth themselves may not report accurately on impairment issues [27].

Non–diagnosis-based self-report studies have confirmed the pervasive use of legal, semilegal, and illegal substances among detained youths. In a study of 1801 detained adolescents, alcohol use was found to occur almost universally by age 15 years, and one fourth reported repeated binge drinking [42]. Marijuana use was reported by more than 70%, whereas 40% mentioned having used marijuana more than 40 times. About one quarter had used cocaine by age 14 years, and more than 30% had used cocaine at least once. Several studies have reported less frequent substance use by ethnic minority youth, in particular African Americans [27,42]. Differences in prevalence by minority status were also found in a Belgian sample by Vermeiren and colleagues [65], who reported less substance abuse in adjudicated minority youths (predominantly of northern-African origin). Findings on gender differences in substance use among delinquent youths have proven inconsistent. For example, one study found higher rates of alcohol use in delinquent girls than in boys [50], but other studies demonstrated similar levels of use [8,42].

Although current findings have consistently shown that substance use among youth in juvenile justice is a substantial problem, some issues remain. First, differences in terminology with regard to substance use or abuse hamper interpretation, and cross-cultural and time-related differences in substance use may make direct comparison of findings difficult. Second, the decision to impose incarceration may be influenced by the presence of substance abuse, which may at least partly explain the higher rates of substance use in this population. Those reasons may well explain the current inconsistency with regard to the overlap between SUDs and other externalizing problems. Although positive relationships between substance abuse/dependence in delinquents and severity of antisocial behavior [35], violent offending [66], and levels of comorbid psychopathology [67] have been reported, a more recent study demonstrated a negative association with violence [64]. Although this finding may be relevant scientifically and clinically, a more crucial problem may be the unavailability of treatment programs, because it was shown that the services needed for treatment for detainees upon release are mostly unavailable [27].

Psychosis and developmental disorders

In contrast to the numerous reports on schizophrenia and psychosis in adult criminals, sound investigations of psychotic disorders in juvenile delinquents are rare. The few existing studies on psychotic disorders/schizophrenia in adolescent delinquents have provided prevalence rates ranging from 1% to 2% [4,8,61,68].

Psychotic symptomatology has more often been subject of study in detained youths, and rates as high as 25% to 75% have been reported [8,20,50,69]. Based on the psychosis screen of the Diagnostic Interview Schedule for Children, Vreugdenhil and colleagues [69] found that 25% of detained boys had at least one pathognomonic symptom for schizophrenia. When the presence of at least three nonpathognomonic symptoms was required for diagnosis, another 9% met criteria for an atypical psychotic disorder. With the same instrument, psychotic symptoms were also found frequently (49%) in a community control group [50]. Therefore, methodologic considerations are warranted, because most clinicians working with juvenile offenders may not agree that clinical psychotic disorder occurs frequently in these youths.

Related to the discussion on the overlap between schizophrenia and criminality are the sparse reports on the development of behavioral problems as prodromata of schizophrenia [70,71]. Through study of offspring of psychiatric patients and controls, Amminger and colleagues [70] found that future schizophrenics had a higher number of conduct problems than controls, and, surprisingly, that non–substance-abusing future schizophrenics were characterized by a higher level of antisocial behavior than seen in substance-abusing schizophrenics. Because these studies assessed behavioral problems of minor severity, the possible relationship between early antisocial behavior and the prodromata of schizophrenia remains largely unexplored. These findings should, however, encourage further elaboration of this topic.

Although the high number of psychotic symptoms described in incarcerated delinquent youths is quite remarkable, the significance of these symptoms remains unclear. Because early psychotic symptoms were shown to be predictive for violence in future schizophreniform persons [71], further research is warranted. Instead of representing a psychotic disorder, the enumerated psychotic symptoms may well be related to other types of psychopathology, such as PTSD or personality disorders. Current research lends partial support to this possibility, because psychotic symptomatology was found to occur more often in traumatized than in nontraumatized detainees [69]. The nature of the most frequently described symptoms, suspiciousness and superstitious thinking, may support this possibility.

Autism-related disorders

The possible relationship between delinquency and autism spectrum disorders has become an issue of particular interest over the past years. Systematic research on this issue is almost nonexistent: scientific contributions are limited to case reports and theoretical opinions [72–74]. One of the largest studies to date is a retrospective study of individuals referred for forensic psychiatric investigation [75]. Interestingly, although 15% were found to have ADHD and 15% were found to have pervasive developmental disorder (PDD) (12% PDD not otherwise specified and 3% Asperger disorder), in only a few cases were these neuropsychiatric disorders diagnosed during the forensic assessment itself. Therefore, the authors concluded that the contribution of constitutional problems to later criminal development may be underestimated. Repetitive and subtle forms of delinquency may, however, be limited to specific subgroups of autistic individuals, such as persons who have Asperger's disorder or high-functioning autistic individuals. Because of the severity of their handicap, core autistic individuals may lack the ability to organize delinquent acts in a way that they remain undetected afterwards [74], although less disturbed autistic individuals may not have this inability.

With regard to overall comorbidity, individuals who have a PDD have been reported to be at risk for a wide array of psychiatric disturbances, including aggression and antisocial behavior [76]. The presence of comorbid psychopathology may therefore provide a valuable argument for an association between autism spectrum disorders and delinquency [72]. In addition, specific disorders linked to a greater risk for offending, such as ADHD, also occur at a higher rate in autistic individuals. Autism itself may also be considered a risk factor for delinquency. When other conditions, such as adverse family conditions are present, individuals who have a PDD may be at particular risk for developing conditions that enhance vulnerability for delinquency. Underlying mechanisms may also play a role. Gilour and colleagues [77] have reported that two thirds of clinically referred children who have CD show pragmatic language impairments and other features similar to those of individuals with autism. Therefore, higher rates of autism related disorders may be found in juvenile justice populations.

The discussion on the overlap between autism spectrum disorders and delinquency often focuses on specific groups of severe violent or sexual offenders [73,74]. Based on an analysis of the literature, Silva [74] has postulated a relationship between autism spectrum disorder and serial homicidal behavior. With regard to sexually inappropriate behaviors in general, a number of reports have suggested autistic individuals to be at particular risk [73]. Because these studies have focused on specific groups of autistic individuals or offenders, most including only a limited number of participants, the extent to which these findings apply to the broader group of autistic individuals remains unknown. Indirect evidence for a relationship between PDD and offending comes from studies in adults. Ahlmeyer and colleagues [78] found that sex offenders were more often schizoid, avoidant, depressive, dependent, self-defeating, and schizotypal than general inmates, whereas general inmates were more often narcissistic, antisocial, and sadistic.

A most controversial issue is the possible overlap between autism spectrum disorders and psychopathy, both of which are characterized by deficient empathy. Several reports have focused on the issue, and it has been stated that vast qualitative differences exist between the two conditions [79]. Because methodologically sound comparative studies are lacking, however, clear evidence for such opinion cannot be provided. Recently, Soderstrom and colleagues [80] have shown relationships between autism-related disorders/ADHD, and factor 2 (unemotional) and factor 3 (behavioral dyscontrol) of the Hare's Psychopathy Checklist, whereas no association existed with factor 1 (interpersonal). Although they provide some evidence, a major problem in these studies is the dearth of valid and reliable diagnostic instruments for either autistic disorder or psychopathy. Also, as mentioned previously, a specific and crucial diagnostic problem is the lack of reliable information from parents, which does not allow systematic assessment of early development. Therefore, whether it will ever be possible to differentiate autism from psychopathy by means of traditional diagnostic instruments remains unknown. At present, the need for neurobiologic measurements for this purpose cannot be excluded.

Longitudinal studies

Existing longitudinal studies in juvenile justice populations have mainly investigated the role of sociodemographic and criminological predictors, leaving the predictors of future mental health in these populations relatively under-investigated. Apart from predicting recidivism, investigating the long-term development of psychiatric problems may have relevance, because former juvenile justice youths may need to rely heavily on mental health services [81]. For example, a recent follow-up study in previously adjudicated individuals (mean follow-up of 8 years) has demonstrated that more than 10% of males and 20% of females had committed at least one suicide attempt by early adulthood, and one fifth of males and one third of females reported psychologic consultation [82]. In addition, 5% had undergone a psychiatric hospitalization (4.5% of males and 7.1% of females), and 12% had followed a drug addiction program/therapy (similar rates for both genders). Conversely, when investigating the antecedents of adult psychiatric patients, child and adolescent psychiatric disorders can be found frequently. Of all such early disorders, disruptive behavior disorders are the most frequent [83].

Considering the detrimental psychosocial outcome of previously detained youth, it is not surprising that many delinquents are prone to future offending. Notwithstanding sparse research, a number of mental health conditions have shown predictive validity for future offending, such as a diagnosis of CD, ADHD, a history of abuse or neglect, and the presence of substance abuse [22,84,85]. In Vermeiren and colleagues' [22] sample, however, substance abuse did not differentiate nonrecidivists from recidivists, and Putnins [86] described only a limited 6-month predictive validity of self-reported substance use for recidivism. In yet another longitudinal study [87], desistors were compared with persistors; apart from differences in rates of delinquency, desistors were also characterized by better social capacities [87]. In adulthood, desistors were described as having a better feeling of support, higher job satisfaction, fewer psychiatric problems, and closer social relationships.

Although higher levels of externalizing problems and substance use may be perceived as risk factors, internalizing problems may indicate a better outcome. Nonrecidivism has been related to higher levels of psychologic distress, lower levels of restraint [88,89], and the presence of a *DSM* diagnosis of depression [22]. Similarly, in substance-abusing adolescents following day treatment, a better initial adherence, a more regular attendance, and a longer length of treatment was predicted by self-reported symptoms of anxiousness and depression [90]. Although those studies suggest that more distressed or internalizing individuals re-offend less often and develop better, these findings should be addressed with caution and need replication, because the number of individuals in those studies is low, and the assessment of internalizing problems is diverse.

Summary

Over the past years, research on the prevalence of mental health problems in juvenile justice populations has increased steadily, although the absolute number of studies still remains limited compared with similar work in adults. The positive effect of existing initiatives is an increased awareness of the problem among clinicians, scientists, and policy makers. For that reason, it is to be expected that more studies will be conducted and published in the near future and may help future policy making and clinical forensic work. Of course, much still needs to be done. First, diagnostic issues remain (eg, with regard to the development of reliable and valid instruments for forensic populations). When parents are unavailable as informants, diagnostic work may be intricate, particularly in diagnoses for which developmental information is needed. In other conditions (eg, psychosis and mania), also, current instruments may lack validity. Differentiating between different disorders may often prove complicated in this multiply disordered population. Second, although several studies have demonstrated different rates of psychiatric disorders for specific ethnic subgroups, diagnostic issues have not been investigated in this respect. Such issues may be relevant, because of the almost consistent finding of lower psychiatric pathology in African Americans compared with other groups [8] in contrast to the finding that African Americans may have the greatest level of needs and are most at risk for having underserved mental health needs [91]. Third, diagnostic studies have until now focused on the subgroup of incarcerated youth. Other subgroups within the field of juvenile justice, or specific delinquent subgroups (eg, sexual offenders) have not been investigated systematically. Because differences in mental health profiles may be expected, further investigation is warranted. Fourth, the role of less-prevalent disorders (ie, autism-related disorders) has remained underinvestigated, although current reports suggest this disorder is related to at least some forms of antisocial behavior. Finally, a number of therapeutic issues need attention. A crucial next step is the translation of current diagnostic findings to guidelines for prevention and intervention. As described previously, therapeutic guidelines have been developed for a number of psychiatric conditions that occur frequently in juvenile justice populations. Studies on the effectiveness of these programs in juvenile justice populations are scarce, however. Also, although several intervention programs (eg, multisystem therapy, functional family therapy) have been demonstrated to be effective in these populations, the influence of individual characteristics, such as mental health conditions, on outcome has remained poorly investigated.

Overall, further studies are warranted. Because substantial continuity of psychiatric dysfunction from childhood to adulthood has been demonstrated, with CD being the childhood disorder in most cases [83], youth in juvenile justice should be given high priority. Identification and treatment of early disorders is a necessity and should be targeted at disrupting the path toward problem behaviors and psychiatric dysfunction in later life.

References

[1] Rutter M, Giller H, Hagell A. Antisocial behavior by young people. New York: Cambridge University Press; 1998.

[2] Vermeiren R. Psychopathology and delinquency in adolescents: a descriptive and developmental perspective. Clin Psychol Rev 2003;23:277–318.

[3] Dixon A, Howie P, Starling J. Psychopathology in female juvenile offenders. J Child Psychol Psychiatry 2004;45:1150–8.

[4] Gosden NP, Kramp P, Gabrielsen G, et al. Prevalence of mental disorders among 15–17-year-old male adolescent remand prisoners in Denmark. Acta Psychiatr Scand 2003;107:102–10.

[5] Lederman CS, Dakof GA, Larrea MA, et al. Characteristics of adolescent females in juvenile detention. Int J Law Psychiatry 2004;27:321–37.

[6] McCabe KM, Lansing AE, Garland A, et al. Gender differences in psychopathology, functional impairment, and familial risk factors among adjudicated delinquents. J Am Acad Child Adolesc Psychiatry 2002;41:860–7.

[7] Ruchkin V, Koposov R, Vermeiren R, et al. Psychopathology and age at onset of conduct problems in juvenile delinquents. J Clin Psychiatry 2003;64:913–20.

[8] Teplin LA, Abram KM, McClelland GM, et al. Psychiatric disorders in youth in juvenile detention. Arch Gen Psychiatry 2002;59:1133–43.

[9] Vreugdenhil C, Doreleijers TA, Vermeiren R, et al. Psychiatric disorders in a representative sample of incarcerated boys in the Netherlands. J Am Acad Child Adolesc Psychiatry 2004; 43:97–104.

[10] Wasserman GA, McReynolds LS, Lucas CP, et al. The voice DISC-IV with incarcerated male youths: prevalence of disorder. J Am Acad Child Adolesc Psychiatry 2002;41:314–21.

[11] Grisso T, Zimring FE. Double jeopardy: adolescents offenders with mental disorders. Chicago: University of Chicago Press; 2004.

[12] Domalanta DD, Risser WL, Roberts RE, et al. Prevalence of depression and other psychiatric disorders among incarcerated youths. J Am Acad Child Adolesc Psychiatry 2003;42:477–84.

[13] Johnson TP, Cho YI, Fendrich M, et al. Treatment need and utilization among youth entering the juvenile corrections system. J Subst Abuse Treat 2004;26:117–28.

[14] Roberts RE, Attkisson CC, Rosenblatt A. Prevalence of psychopathology among children and adolescents. Am J Psychiatry 1998;155:715–25.

[15] Moffitt TE. Adolescence-limited and life-course-persistent antisocial behavior: a developmental taxonomy. Psychol Rev 1993;100:674–701.

[16] Angold A, Costello EJ, Erkanli A. Comorbidity. J Child Psychol Psychiatry 1999;40:57–87.

[17] Fazel S, Danesh J. Serious mental disorder in 23000 prisoners: a systematic review of 62 surveys. Lancet 2002;359:545–50.

[18] Anderson L, Vostanis P, Spencer N. Health needs of young offenders. J Child Health Care 2004;8:149–64.

[19] Shelton D. Experiences of detained young offenders in need of mental health care. J Nurs Scholarsh 2004;36:129–33.

[20] Atkins D, Pumariega AJ, Rogers K, et al. Mental health and incarcerated youth. I: Prevalence and nature of psychopathology. J Child Fam Stud 1999;8:193–204.
[21] Shelton D. Emotional disorders in young offenders. J Nurs Scholarsh 2001;33:259–63.
[22] Vermeiren R, Schwab-Stone M, Ruchkin V, et al. Predicting recidivism in delinquent adolescents from psychological and psychiatric assessment. Compr Psychiatry 2002;43:142–9.
[23] Doreleijers T, Moser F, Thijs P, et al. Forensic assessment of juvenile delinquents: prevalence of psychopathology and decision-making at court in the Netherlands. J Adolesc 2000;23: 263–75.
[24] Vermeiren R, de Clippele A, Deboutte D. Eight month follow-up of delinquent adolescents: predictors of short-term outcome. Eur Arch Psychiatry Clin Neurosci 2000;250:133–8.
[25] Andrade RC, Silva VA, Assumpcao Jr FB. Preliminary data on the prevalence of psychiatric disorders in Brazilian male and female juvenile delinquents. Braz J Med Biol Res 2004; 37:1155–60.
[26] Vermeiren R, Jones SM, Ruchkin V, et al. Juvenile arrest: a cross-cultural comparison. J Child Psychol Psychiatry 2004;45:567–76.
[27] McClelland GM, Elkington KS, Teplin LA, et al. Multiple substance use disorders in juvenile detainees. J Am Acad Child Adolesc Psychiatry 2004;43:1215–24.
[28] Robertson AA, Dill PL, Husain J, et al. Prevalence of mental illness and substance abuse disorders among incarcerated juvenile offenders in Mississippi. Child Psychiatry Hum Dev 2004;35:55–74.
[29] Steiner H, Garcia IG, Matthews Z. Posttraumatic stress disorder in incarcerated juvenile delinquents. J Am Acad Child Adolesc Psychiatry 1997;36:357–65.
[30] Ruchkin VV, Schwab-Stone M, Koposov R, et al. Violence exposure, posttraumatic stress, and personality in juvenile delinquents. J Am Acad Child Adolesc Psychiatry 2002;41:322–9.
[31] Teplin LA, Elkington KS, McClelland GM, et al. Major mental disorders, substance use disorders, comorbidity, and HIV-AIDS risk behaviors in juvenile detainees. Psychiatr Serv 2005; 56:823–8.
[32] Ko SJ, Wasserman GA, McReynolds LS, et al. Contribution of parent report to voice DISC-IV diagnosis among incarcerated youths. J Am Acad Child Adolesc Psychiatry 2004;43: 868–77.
[33] Kramer TL, Phillips SD, Hargis MB, et al. Disagreement between parent and adolescent reports of functional impairment. J Child Psychol Psychiatry 2004;45:248–59.
[34] Chiles JA, Miller ML, Cox GB. Depression in an adolescent delinquent population. Arch Gen Psychiatry 1980;37:1179–84.
[35] McManus M, Alessi NE, Grapentine WL, et al. Psychiatric disturbance in serious delinquents. J Am Acad Child Psychiatry 1984;23:602–15.
[36] Pliszka SR, Sherman JO, Barrow MV, et al. Affective disorder in juvenile offenders: a preliminary study. Am J Psychiatry 2000;157:130–2.
[37] Neighbors B, Kempton T, Forehand R. Co-occurrence of substance abuse with conduct, anxiety, and depression disorders in juvenile delinquents. Add Behav 1992;17:379–86.
[38] Riggs PD, Baker S, Mikulich SK, et al. Depression in substance-dependent delinquents. J Am Acad Child Adolesc Psychiatry 1995;34:764–71.
[39] Fergusson DM, Lynskey MT, Horwood LJ. Comorbidity between depressive disorders and nicotine dependence in a cohort of 16-year-olds. Arch Gen Psychiatry 1996;53:1043–7.
[40] Kashani JH, Manning GW, McKnew DH, et al. Depression among incarcerated delinquents. Psychiatry Res 1980;3:185–91.
[41] Battle AO, Battle MV, Tolley EA. Potential for suicide and aggression in delinquents at juvenile court in a southern city. Suicide Life Threat Behav 1993;23:230–44.
[42] Morris RE, Harrison EA, Knox GW, et al. Health risk behavioral survey from 39 juvenile correctional facilities in the United States. J Adolesc Health 1995;17:334–44.
[43] Rohde P, Seeley JR, Mace DE. Correlates of suicidal behavior in a juvenile detention population. Suicide Life Threat Behav 1997;27:164–75.
[44] Ruchkin VV, Schwab-Stone M, Koposov RA, et al. Suicidal ideations and attempts in juvenile delinquents. J Child Psychol Psychiatry 2003;44:1058–66.

[45] Penn JV, Esposito CL, Schaeffer LE, et al. Suicide attempts and self-mutilative behavior in a juvenile correctional facility. J Am Acad Child Adolesc Psychiatry 2003;42:762–9.
[46] Brent DA, Baugher M, Bridge J, et al. Age- and sex-related risk factors for adolescent suicide. J Am Acad Child Adolesc Psychiatry 1999;38:1497–505.
[47] Vermeiren R, Schwab-Stone M, Ruchkin VV, et al. Suicidal behavior and violence in male adolescents: a school-based study. J Am Acad Child Adolesc Psychiatry 2003;42:41–8.
[48] Sanislow CA, Grilo CM, Fehon DC, et al. Correlates of suicide risk in juvenile detainees and adolescent inpatients. J Am Acad Child Adolesc Psychiatry 2003;42:234–40.
[49] Howard J, Lennings CJ, Copeland J. Suicidal behavior in a young offender population. Crisis 2003;24:98–104.
[50] Ulzen TP, Hamilton H. The nature and characteristics of psychiatric comorbidity in incarcerated adolescents. Can J Psychiatry 1998;43:57–63.
[51] Abram KM, Teplin LA, Charles DR, et al. Posttraumatic stress disorder and trauma in youth in juvenile detention. Arch Gen Psychiatry 2004;61:403–10.
[52] Cauffman E, Feldman SS, Waterman J, et al. Posttraumatic stress disorder among female juvenile offenders. J Am Acad Child Adolesc Psychiatry 1998;37:1209–16.
[53] Carrion VG, Steiner H. Trauma and dissociation in delinquent adolescents. J Am Acad Child Adolesc Psychiatry 2000;39:353–9.
[54] Garland AF, Hough RL, McCabe KM, et al. Prevalence of psychiatric disorders in youths across five sectors of care. J Am Acad Child Adolesc Psychiatry 2001;40:409–18.
[55] Maughs S. Concept of psychopathy and psychopathic personality: its evolution and historical development. J Crim Psychopathol 1941;2:239.
[56] Ulzen TPM, Hamilton H. The nature and characteristics of psychiatric comorbidity in incarcerated adolescents. Can J Psychiatry 1998;43:57–63.
[57] Vermeiren R, Deboutte D, Ruchkin V, et al. Antisocial behaviour and mental health findings from three communities. Eur Child Adolesc Psychiatry 2002;11:168–75.
[58] Sanford M, Boyle MH, Szatmari P, et al. Age-of-onset classification of conduct disorder: reliability and validity in a prospective cohort study. J Am Acad Child Adolesc Psychiatry 1999;38:992–9.
[59] Moffitt TE, Caspi A, Dickson N, Silva P, et al. Childhood-onset versus adolescent-onset antisocial conduct problems in males: Natural history from ages 3 to 18 years. Dev Psychopathol 1996;8:399–424.
[60] Lahey BB, Loeber R, Quay HC, et al. Validity of DSM-IV subtypes of conduct disorder based on age of onset. J Am Acad Child Adolesc Psychiatry 1998;37:435–42.
[61] Richards I. Psychiatric disorder among adolescents in custody. Aust N Z J Psychiatry 1996;30: 788–93.
[62] Beitchman JH, Wilson B, Johnson CJ, et al. Fourteen-year follow-up of speech/language-impaired and control children: psychiatric outcome. J Am Acad Child Adolesc Psychiatry 2001;40:75–82.
[63] Vermeiren R, De Clippele A, Schwab-Stone M, et al. Neuropsychological characteristics of three subgroups of Flemish delinquent adolescents. Neuropsychology 2002;16:49–55.
[64] Vreugdenhil C, Van Den Brink W, Wouters LF, et al. Substance use, substance use disorders, and comorbidity patterns in a representative sample of incarcerated male Dutch adolescents. J Nerv Ment Dis 2003;191:372–8.
[65] Vermeiren R, De Clippele A, Deboutte D. A descriptive survey of Flemish delinquent adolescents. J Adolesc 2000;23:277–85.
[66] Haapasalo J, Hamalainen T. Childhood family problems and current psychiatric problems among young violent and property offenders. J Am Acad Child Adolesc Psychiatry 1996;35: 1394–401.
[67] Milin R, Halikas JA, Meller JE, et al. Psychopathology among substance abusing juvenile offenders. J Am Acad Child Adolesc Psychiatry 1991;30:569–74.
[68] Hollander HE, Turner FD. Characteristics of incarcerated delinquents: relationship between development disorders, environmental and family factors, and patterns of offense and recidivism. J Am Acad Child Psychiatry 1985;24:221–6.

[69] Vreugdenhil C, Vermeiren R, Wouters LF, et al. Psychotic symptoms among male adolescent detainees in The Netherlands. Schizophr Bull 2004;30:73–86.
[70] Amminger GP, Pape S, Rock D, et al. Relationship between childhood behavioral disturbance and later schizophrenia in the New York High-Risk Project. Am J Psychiatry 1999;156:525–30.
[71] Arseneault L, Cannon M, Murray R, et al. Childhood origins of violent behaviour in adults with schizophreniform disorder dagger. Br J Psychiatry 2003;183:520–5.
[72] Palermo MT. Pervasive developmental disorders, psychiatric comorbidities, and the law. Int J Offender Ther Comp Criminol 2004;48:40–8.
[73] Hellemans H, Colson K, Verbraeken C, et al. Sexual behavior in high-functioning male adolescents and young adults with autism spectrum disorder. J Autism Dev Disord, in press.
[74] Silva JA, Leong GB, Ferrari MM. A neuropsychiatric developmental model of serial homicidal behavior. Behav Sci Law 2004;22:787–99.
[75] Siponmaa L, Kristiansson M, Jonson C, et al. Juvenile and young adult mentally disordered offenders: the role of child neuropsychiatric disorders. J Am Acad Psychiatry Law 2001;29:420–6.
[76] Sverd J. Psychiatric disorders in individuals with pervasive developmental disorder. J Psychiatr Pract 2003;9:111–27.
[77] Gilmour J, Hill B, Place M, et al. Social communication deficits in conduct disorder: a clinical and community survey. J Child Psychol Psychiatry 2004;45:967–78.
[78] Ahlmeyer S, Kleinsasser D, Stoner J, et al. Psychopathology of incarcerated sex offenders. J Personal Disord 2003;17:306–18.
[79] Soderstrom H. Psychopathy as a disorder of empathy. Eur Child Adolesc Psychiatry 2003;12:249–52.
[80] Soderstrom H, Nilsson T, Sjodin AK, et al. The childhood-onset neuropsychiatric background to adulthood psychopathic traits and personality disorders. Compr Psychiatry 2005;46:111–6.
[81] Lewis DO, Yeager CA, Lovely R, et al. A clinical follow-up of delinquent males: ignored vulnerabilities, unmet needs, and the perpetuation of violence. J Am Acad Child Adolesc Psychiatry 1994;33:518–28.
[82] Corneau M, Lanctot N. Mental health outcomes of adjudicated males and females: the aftermath of juvenile delinquency and problem behaviour. Crim Behav Ment Health 2004;14:251–62.
[83] Kim-Cohen J, Caspi A, Moffitt TE, et al. Prior juvenile diagnoses in adults with mental disorder: developmental follow-back of a prospective-longitudinal cohort. Arch Gen Psychiatry 2003;60:709–17.
[84] Dembo R, Williams L, Schmeidler J, et al. Recidivism among high risk youths: a 2 1/2-year follow-up of a cohort of juvenile detainees. Int J Addict 1991;26:1197–221.
[85] Dembo R, Turner G, Sue CC, et al. Predictors of recidivism to a juvenile assessment center. Int J Addict 1995;30:1425–52.
[86] Putnins A. Substance use and the prediction of young offender recidivism. Drug Alcohol Rev 2003;22:401–8.
[87] Clingempeel WG, Henggeler SW. Aggressive juvenile offenders transitioning into emerging adulthood: factors discriminating persistors and desistors. Am J Orthopsychiatry 2003;73:310–23.
[88] Duncan RD, Kennedy WA, Patrick CJ. Four-factor model of recidivism in male juvenile offenders. J Clin Child Psychol 1995;24:250–7.
[89] Steiner H, Cauffman E, Duxbury E. Personality traits in juvenile delinquents: relation to criminal behavior and recidivism. J Am Acad Child Adolesc Psychiatry 1999;38:256–62.
[90] Pagnin D, de Queiroz V, Saggese EG. Predictors of attrition from day treatment of adolescents with substance-related disorders. Addict Behav 2005;30:1065–9.
[91] Rawal P, Romansky J, Jenuwine M, et al. Racial differences in the mental health needs and service utilization of youth in the juvenile justice system. J Behav Health Serv Res 2004;31:242–54.

ELSEVIER
SAUNDERS

Child Adolesc Psychiatric Clin N Am
15 (2006) 353–371

CHILD AND ADOLESCENT PSYCHIATRIC CLINICS OF NORTH AMERICA

Learning Disabilities in Juvenile Offenders

Elena L. Grigorenko, PhD[a,b,c,*]

[a]Child Study Center, Yale Medical School, New Haven, CT, USA
[b]PACE Center, Department of Psychology, Yale University, New Haven, CT, USA
[c]Department of Psychology, Moscow State University, Moscow, Russia

According to 2005 indicators from the National Center for Educational Statistics [1], the temporary decline of juvenile crime and victimization that was registered between 1999 and 2001 has ended. Juvenile crime is on the rise again. Specifically, in 2004, approximately 16% of all arrests were of individuals younger than 18 years of age [2]. Although the level of juvenile crime was never satisfactorily low, this increase raises questions of why the social and cultural systems in the United States, one of the richest countries of the world, cannot protect young people from committing, participating in, and being victims of crime.

As a group, arrested adolescents seem to differ from other adolescents in a number of important ways. Although no nationwide data for the United States are available, various research studies indicate that one of the most pronounced characteristics of these adolescents is a low level of academic achievements.[1] Specifically, these teenagers score lower on a variety of academic measures than do nondelinquent teenagers [3–5], and individuals committing more serious aggressive crimes (eg, assault, battery, manslaughter, rape, arson) show lower aca-

Preparation of this article was supported by a grant from the American Psychological Foundation and by a grant under the Javits Act Program (Grant No. R206R00001) as administered by the Institute for Educational Sciences, US Department of Education.

* 230 South Frontage Road, New Haven, CT 06510.

E-mail address: elena.grigorenko@yale.edu

[1] Here the terms "learning disabilities," "learning difficulties," "academic difficulties," "low [academic] achievement/performance," and "academic failure" are used interchangeably. The basis for this generalization of concepts is that the relevant literature uses all of these terms, and, for the purposes of this review, the fine-grain distinctions between these concepts are not crucial. It is important to note, however, that NONE of these concepts are viewed as synonymous with IQ. Thus, nowhere here is it assumed that learning difficulties are equitable with low IQ or mental retardation. When the terms "intelligence," "IQ," or "general cognitive ability" are used, their connotation is assumed to be different from the terms descriptive of learning difficulties.

doi:10.1016/j.chc.2005.11.001

demic achievement profiles than individuals committing property crimes (eg, misdemeanors and status offenses) [6]. Moreover, individuals who have learning disabilities (LDs) seem to be arrested [7] and placed in correctional institutions [8] more often than individuals who do not have LDs. Finally, a link has been reported between low academic achievement and recidivism [9–11], whereas effective remediation of academic difficulties has been linked to reduced rates of recidivism and more prosocial behavior [11–13].

For unselected samples, voluminous literature points to an association between low academic performance and conduct problems. In fact, academic failure is one of the most substantial predictors of behavior and social maladaptation [14].

Typically, research on the link between LDs/academic difficulties and juvenile delinquency/behavior problems focuses on the following five areas:

1. Comparative analyses of academic achievement of detained or adjudicated juveniles with the general population of clinical samples
2. Investigation of the prevalence rates (co-manifestation) of LDs and academic problems in detention and prison settings
3. Comparative analyses of academic achievement of children who have behavior problems and typically developing children
4. Studies of the prevalence rates of LDs and academic problems in children who have behavior problems
5. Studies of prevalence rates of behavior problems in children who have LDs

A smaller body of research focuses on specific links between particular types of disabilities (eg, dyslexia, dyscalculia) and particular types of behavior problems (eg, conduct disorder).

This article provides a capsule overview of this literature, but a few initial notes are important. The roots of this literature are in studies of reading problems (specific reading retardation, as it was referred to almost 3 decades ago) and antisocial behaviors, but the body of the literature that has accumulated since the first seminal studies of Rutter and colleagues [15] convincingly attests to the presence of an association between antisocial behavior and difficulties in many academic domains. This article, unless specified otherwise, generalizes the findings with regard to reading problems to academic problems in general. In addition, this overview does not attempt to represent the literature comprehensively. The goal is to bring to the reader's attention the themes that seem to be most important in the context of this special issue. Thus, this article does not claim to discuss all or even most details of the reviewed research.

The review is organized into three parts. First, it briefly reviews the literature concerning estimates of the prevalence of learning deficiencies among criminal offenders. Second, it summarizes a number of relevant points from studies of the association between low academic achievement and conduct problems in nonincarcerated samples. Third, it discusses studies of postrelease academic profiles of juvenile offenders. It concludes with a comment on possible future directions for this research.

Learning deficiencies in criminal offenders

Learning and intellectual deficiencies have been viewed as a prime factor in criminality for centuries [16]. This view became especially prevalent in the nineteenth century, when schooling was viewed as a solution to many social problems and universal education was expected to eliminate criminal behavior. The extreme version of these beliefs was expressed by Lewis Terman [17], a proponent of intelligence testing for educational purposes and an adapter and developer of the Binet intelligence scales in the United States. Terman wrote, "There is no investigator who denies the fearful role of mental deficiency in the production of vice, crime and delinquency... Not all criminals are feeble-minded but all feeble-minded are at least potential criminals." Early in the twentieth century, using mostly observations and clinical reports, Goddard [18] and Sutherland [19] independently concluded that approximately 50% of delinquents in prison were mentally deficient. With limited or no quantitative data, criminal behavior and learning and intellectual deficiencies were tightly linked in the minds of the public and its servants throughout most of the nineteenth and twentieth century [20], whether in Nazi Germany [21] or in Vermont [22].

The penetration and expansion of quantitative methodologies in psychology resulted in, among many other things, the development of a massive body of literature attesting to the presence of a robust link between adult and juvenile offending, on the one hand, and low levels of IQ and schooling, on the other. Although there is a substantial body of literature investigating the links between IQ and criminality, the focus of this article is on the link between learning difficulties and criminality.[2]

Numerous studies have attested to the overall at-risk neuropsychological profiles of cognitive functioning in adolescents who have criminal records. It has been shown that these teenagers tend to have lower levels of IQ [11,23–26] and especially of verbal intelligence [11,23], to show deficient communication skills [3], and to display high levels of hyperactivity [27] as well as deficits in attention modulation [28], impulse control [29], and executive functioning [30,31]. In addition, incarcerated juvenile offenders show a complex pattern of multiple, often comorbid, psychiatric disturbances [26,32].

Similarly, there are multiple reports of elevated frequency (25%–97%) of learning problems among juvenile delinquents [33–38] and adult prison inmates [27,34,39–42]. For example, in the United States, Meltzer and colleagues [38] compared rates of academic difficulties (in reading, writing, spelling, and mathematics) in age-matched male groups of 53 juvenile delinquent youth and 51 high school students. In the group of offenders, 51% performed at a level at least 1 year behind their actual grade level in all academic domains tested, as compared

[2] It is important to acknowledge the high level of correlations between IQ and academic achievement. However, the role of IQ in the link between academic achievement and criminality has not been investigated systematically and will not be the central point of discussion here.

with 21% of the control group. In a study of Scottish juvenile offenders, researchers screened 50 inmates and diagnosed dyslexia in 50% of them [35]. The diagnosis in this study was based on a computerized self-assessment screening test for dyslexia. With regard to adult offenders, Jensen and colleagues [39] evaluated the prevalence of dyslexia among 63 Swedish prison inmates; the estimated rate was reported at 41%. These authors used tests of achievement and intelligence and interviews with inmates to make informed clinical decisions with regard to diagnosis of specific reading disorder as delineated in the *Diagnostic and Statistical Manual-III-revised*. As a group, individuals who had dyslexia performed at either lower or comparable levels on a number of indicators of intellectual, cognitive, and neuropsychologic functioning, as compared with individuals who did not have dyslexia. Another Swedish study [42] reported the rate of dyslexia at 31% in a group of 61 inmates. These researchers used interviews with inmates about their reading and writing habits, their school background, and their avoidance of or breaking off from studies because of reading and writing difficulties.

Different studies of academic deficiencies use different methods of diagnosing LDs. Specifically, in the reviewed articles, the diagnostic schemes included the discrepancy criterion [36,39] (referring to reading performance below that predicted by individual's grade and age [38,41]), self-reported problems with reading, writing, and spelling [35], and phonological[3] deficit [43,44]. There is no doubt that such inconsistency and imprecision in establishing diagnosis of learning (eg, reading or mathematics) difficulties contributes to the heterogeneous picture of the prevalence of learning and intellectual deficiencies among offenders. For example, in an attempt to evaluate the frequency of reading problems among offenders, Moody and colleagues [41] evaluated single-word reading in 253 prisoners selected at random from the population of Texas prison inmates. They reported that 47.8% of their sample showed a level of performance below the twenty-fifth percentile on the Woodcock Reading Mastery Test. In addition, the sample scored poorly on the measure of reading comprehension. Clearly, with this strategy of estimating rates of reading difficulties by imposing a categorical threshold on a continuous measure, the prevalence estimates will vary depending on where the threshold is established. For example, in the field of LDs, the consensus threshold is typically established at the fifteenth percentile. Correspondingly, if Moody and colleagues [41] lowered the threshold they applied to the Woodcock Reading Mastery Test scores to dichotomize the performance in their sample, the rates of reading deficiencies would have been lower than the obtained 47.8%.

Recently, evidence regarding the substantially elevated rates of reading-related problems in delinquent and imprisoned individuals has been at least partially reevaluated. The basis for this reevaluation is the field's lack of un-

[3] A number of studies utilize modern cognitive theories of learning disabilities. For example, with regard to assessing dyslexia, studies often use measures of phonemic processing, under the assumption that deficient phonemic processing is central to the manifestation of dyslexia.

derstanding of the causality underlying this observed association. The issue is that IQ and school underachievement, on the one hand, and offending behavior, on the other, both correlate with multiple factors that are considered to be risk factors for both intellectual/learning and social/behavior maladjustment. For example, it was stated that poverty is overrepresented in the population of inmates and thus can be a confounding variable that artificially inflates the rates of these deficiencies, because these rates are higher among persons at the lower levels of socioeconomic status.

To control for such confounding effects, researchers now typically include in their models indicators of socioeconomic status, ethnicity, and other possible family-based risk factors (eg, criminal histories of parents and other relatives). More recent studies report prevalence estimates of learning deficiencies among inmates that are about two to three times lower than those presented previously (eg, 11% [43,44] and 19.4%–25% [36]). In one study, when detained crime suspects with self-reported LDs were matched by age, sex, and IQ to a sample from the general population, there were no differences on multiple measures of reading performance [45].

For example, in a carefully designed study, Samuelsson and colleagues [46] compared reading-related indicators collected from inmates with those collected from two control groups (a group of adults equated on educational level, reading habits, and socioeconomic status, and a reading-level–matched group of students 13–15 years old). Perhaps surprisingly, the results indicated that prison inmates and adult controls did not differ on indicators of reading and writing skills. In addition, depending on the diagnostic scheme, the prevalence of dyslexia among the inmates varied between 6.1% and 14.6% and thus was comparable with that in the general population. In addition, the inmates did not differ from or performed better than the group of reading-level–matched control adolescents. Fewer than 10% of the inmates exhibited phonological deficits, considered to be the hallmark deficiency in individuals with reading disorders.

Similarly, in another Swedish study, Svensson and colleagues [44] used reading achievement tests (word reading, spelling, and comprehension) to evaluate 163 juvenile detainees (mean age, 15.5 years). The results indicated that 70% of the participants had some academic difficulties, but these difficulties were serious enough to be of serious concern (ie, reading below fourth grade level) in only 11% of the sample.

Although the prevalence of learning disorders among offenders might be lower than initially thought, the presence of LD is still considered a risk factor for maladaptive outcomes after release. For example, the postrelease adaptation of incarcerated youth who had special LDs was reported to be poorer than that of incarcerated youth who did not have LDs. Specifically, after release, juvenile offenders who had LDs were less engaged with community and were approximately 2.3 times more likely to return to the juvenile correctional system [47].

In summary, a rather diverse set of studies has investigated the strength of the link between learning difficulties in various academic domains and criminality.

Most researchers in the field acknowledge the presence of the association, but the reported magnitude of this association varies widely. There are multiple explanations for this diversity of results:

1. Differences in sampling strategies, whereby some researchers worked with temporarily detained suspects and others worked with convicted criminals
2. Differences in assessment instruments, ranging from self-reports on school difficulties to scores on standardized achievement tests
3. Differences in diagnostic criteria used to differentiate groups of individuals who had LDs from other offenders
4. The lack of control for the impact of other important factors that are associated with both antisocial behaviors and poor academic performance, such as low socioeconomic status, minority or immigrant status, comorbid psychopathology, and familial predisposition to these conditions

These reasons, individually and collectively, contribute to the variable and inconsistent patterns of results. These inconsistencies can and should be resolved with large-scale, careful, and systematic studies of performance of offenders in academic domains, controlling for the possible impact of confounding variables. Without such studies, the importance and magnitude of the association between learning problems and criminality is difficult to assess. In the absence of such studies, it is useful to turn to the relevant evidence accumulated in the framework of research on this association in samples of nonincarcerated individuals.

Link between academic problems and conduct problems in nonincarcerated samples

It was reported that, in both community and clinical samples, academic problems and disruptive behavior disorder co-manifest more often than would be expected by chance [48]. Specifically, studies suggest substantially higher rates of antisocial behaviors in children who have academic (eg, reading) problems than in children who do not have such problems [15,49–52].

Conversely, other studies have indicated heightened risk of academic difficulties in children who have conduct problems [53–55]. Specifically, it has been reported that children served under the IDEA[4] category of emotional and behavior disorders (E/BD[5]) have elevated frequencies of academic failure [56,57], although specific estimates of the frequency range widely (33%–81% [58]). Moreover, as a group, these children show more achievement problems

[4] The Individuals with Disabilities Education Act is the chief public law under which children with special educational needs are served in the United States.

[5] This is the category of IDEA under which children with conduct and oppositional defiant disorder are typically served.

[59,60], perform substantially worse than their disorder-free peers [61] (1–2 years below grade level at younger ages [62], falling further behind their same-age peers [61,63]), and have lower high school graduation rates [64] and lower enrollment rates in postsecondary institutions [65].

In this context, the results of the National Adolescent and Child Treatment Study are illustrative [56]. In this study, researchers followed up a group of 812 children by means of annual interviews. These children were diagnosed as having serious E/BDs and were served under the IDEA for a duration of 7 years. The sample was recruited from six states: Alabama, Mississippi, Florida, Colorado, New Jersey, and Wisconsin. In general, the results showed that the children had a number of serious problems in all domains of functioning at entry in the study and showed a relatively small amount of improvement throughout the years of follow-up. The information was collected through multiple sources and included data on demographic characteristics, psychological functioning (assessed through direct evaluations and indirect reports), received services, and life-course outcomes (eg, academic achievement and criminal and law enforcement records). At study entry, the participants were 8 to 18 years old (mean age, 13.89 years; SD, 2.35). The distribution of primary diagnostic categories was conduct disorder (66.9%), anxiety disorder (18.5%), attention deficit hyperactivity disorder (ADHD) (11.7%), and schizophrenic disorder (4.7%); 41% of the sample had multiple diagnoses. Fifty-eight percent of the sample was below grade level in reading, and 93% was below grade level in mathematics. The IQ level was low-average (mean, 85.5, SD, 17.1). The sample scored at the 97.5th percentile for behavior problems (as assessed by the Child Behavior Check List) and at the sixth percentile for adaptive behaviors (as assessed by the Vineland Adaptive Behavior Scales). At the completion of the study, the participants' academic performance remained very weak. Specifically, 80.25% of participants whose IQs were at or over 70 were below grade level in reading, and 95.6% were below grade level in mathematics. Of those who were 18 years of age or older, only 25.1% had obtained a high school diploma, and 17.4% received a General Educational Development degree. Only 3.7% had completed at least 1 year of college. On average, their scores on the Child Behavior Check List improved, but scores on the Vineland Adaptive Behavior Scales declined to the third percentile. In addition, across the duration of the study, approximately 66.5% of the sample had a least one contact with police in which the participant was believed to be the perpetrator of a crime. In essence, this study presented a very worrisome picture of a group of children on a long-term path toward severe maladaptation in their society. As in studies of criminal offenders, the evidence attests to a link between poor academic performance, learning difficulties, and maladaptive social behaviors. The causes for this overlap are unclear, however [48]. When this link is considered longitudinally, the literature is inconsistent concerning the causal interpretation of the co-manifestation. There are four possible explanations of this observed overlap. The first hypothesis assumes that behavior problems cause academic problems. The second hypothesis suggests reversed causality: academic problems cause behavior problems. The third hypothesis suggests reciprocal causation. The fourth explanation hypothesizes the presence of a shared etiological factor responsible for the observed overlap.

In the context of existing findings, all four hypotheses seem to be plausible, although the amounts of data supporting each of them are different. In some studies, after adjustment for intelligence and socioeconomic status, early behavior problems seem to exhibit temporal precedence over academic difficulties [66–70]. The prevalence rates of academic problems in children who have E/BD are high and remain stable [57] or worsen over time [56,57,71].

Other studies that suggest that poorer academic performance (eg, early reading difficulties) is causally associated with increased risk for conduct problems in middle childhood [72], but some researchers have not found any elevation of behavioral problems among children who have learning difficulties [73]. Other researchers have proposed that learning (reading) difficulties do not cause but rather exacerbate already existing behavior problems [66]. Of interest is evidence that maladaptive psychopathologic symptoms are less stable and are more modifiable in boys whose reading performance improves in first grade than in boys whose reading skills do not improve or worsen [74].

Smart and colleagues [67] have investigated the causal connection between learning (reading) levels and behavior problems. They followed public school children from grade 2 to grade 4. They found no evidence to support the claims that learning problems lead to the development of behavior problems or that behavior problems lead to the development of learning problems. The researchers, however, did find that children who have both reading and behavior problems had, as a group, the worst reading outcomes at the follow-up. They interpreted these findings as evidence that behavior problems, especially ADHD, seem to exacerbate reading problems.

The third hypothesis suggests reciprocal causation for conduct and academic behaviors. This model assumes that behavior problems at a preceding time will be the best predictor of academic performance at a given time, and that academic performance at a given time will be the best predictor of behavior problems in the future time. Although this model has not been comprehensively tested in the literature, there is some evidence supporting it [70]. For example, some studies suggest that LDs (eg, dyslexia) might exacerbate preexisting conduct problems [75].

The fourth hypothesis assumes the presence of shared etiological mechanisms that contribute to the manifestation of either disorder or of both disorders. One study supporting this hypothesis was a large-scale study of children from Dunedin, New Zealand. These children (n = 925) were initially studied at the age of 3 years and then were reevaluated every year until they reached their fifteenth year, at which time information on delinquent behavior was collected from the police and the youths' self-reports. For each child an index of family adversity was derived from indicators of socioeconomic status, family size, and parental marital status and relationships. When it became possible developmentally, the sample was stratified so that groups of typical, dyslexic, and borderline readers were identified. The dyslexic and borderline readers displayed a higher degree of behavior problems than the normal readers but also had a significantly higher rate of family adversity.

When family adversity was taken into account, the differences between the groups of typical readers and those with reading disabilities either disappeared or were lessened. McGee and colleagues [66] interpreted this finding as showing that family adversity is an etiological factor common to both academic and behavioral difficulties. Clearly, family adversity is not the only possible contributor to the etiological overlap between learning difficulties and delinquency; there are many good candidates for this role, including genetic factors. It is possible that variation in certain genes (eg, the dopaminergic or serotonergic genes) might contribute causally to variations in both maladaptive learning and behavior. Finally, it is possible that LD and delinquency are linked through epiphenomenologic causality [76], that is, the statistical association between disorders A and B is attributable to the substantive associations both share with disorder C. ADHD is a good candidate for such a causal agent linking LD and delinquency.

Attempting to understand the complex pattern of associations between low academic achievement and conduct problems, researchers have considered that other variables might exist [77]; that is, that intermediate factor(s) could have either moderating or mediating effects on the link between low achievement and antisocial behavior. Three observations in the literature are important to mention here.

First, it seems that, the association between academic and conduct problems might be explained, at lease partially, by an overlap between reading and conduct disorders and ADHD [50,53,78], especially inattentiveness [55,79]. Recently, there has been a growing body of research indicative of the presence of etiological overlap between ADHD and dyslexia [80]. In fact, it appears that there are shared genes that contribute to the manifestation of both disorders [81]. Similarly, there are reports of engagement of the same genes (eg, the dopamine receptor 4, DRD4) with both ADHD and conduct problems [82]. Thus, it is possible that ADHD, at least through some of its etiological factors, accounts for the observed overlap in the two disorders.

Second, a number of important factors that can influence the association between academic performance and conduct problems were considered. For example, Anderson and colleagues [83], employing secondary analysis of an existing dataset, investigated differences in academic progress of 42 students who had E/BD and 61 students who had LD over a time period of 5 years of elementary schooling. Trying to understand what these variables might be, the investigators considered such factors as school attendance, behavior discipline referrals, early retention, school mobility, and type of special education settings.

Four important findings emerged from this study. First, the LD students demonstrated significant gains in both mathematics and reading scores over time, whereas the E/BD students showed no or little change, even though their starting points were substantially higher than those of the LD students. In other words, students who had E/BD performed significantly better than those with LDs in the domains of mathematics and reading in kindergarten and first grade, but this difference diminished by middle school. Grade retention was associated with lower academic performance over time. Second, LD students, on average, received lesser levels of full-time services in special education than students who had E/BD. Indicators of school attendance, behavior offenses, and school mobility did not act as meaningful predictors of academic progress over time. Third, multiple insights were generated by the research on the so-called Walker sample [84], a longitudinal study from grade 4 to grade 11 of two samples of males who, at entry in grade 4, displayed either a high risk (n = 39) or a lower risk (n = 41) for antisocial behavior patterns. The grouping was based on extensive data collected by different methods aimed at representating an "antisocial construct" [84]. Longitudinal measures of propensity for engaging in antisocial behavior across a number of different domains of functioning were considered for the two groups. The criterion variable was the number of cumulative arrests and resulting court dispositions of offenses. The most general finding of this study was that individuals who were considered to be at risk for antisocial behavior early in life tended to become antisocial. These data attest to the durability of antisocial behavior [85]. The best single predictor of the criterion was the academic skill construct, followed by socially focused constructs of antisociality, delinquency, and engagement with deviant peers.

In short, early indices of delinquent behaviors should be treated seriously. Educational interventions should be delivered to these high-risk children, because their engagement in schooling and levels of academic performance seem to play an important mediating role in the manifestation and realization of the early risk.

The researchers also consider the influence of important moderating effects, such as gender, on the achievement–behavior association. It was also reported that the association between reading difficulties and externalizing symptoms is stronger in males than in females [67,78], although this finding has been disputed by results suggesting an elevated but not gender-preferential risk of attention and conduct problems in children who have reading problems [55].

There is also some limited evidence that some specific academic problems seem to be more characteristic than others of certain behavior deficits. For example, the results of early British epidemiological studies suggested an association between antisocial behavior and reading problems [15]. These findings resulted in a hypothesis linking antisocial behavior specifically with IQ-discrepant underachievement. The results of the Dunedin study, however, pointed out a broader connection between externalizing problems, hyperactivity, and inattention, on the one hand, and IQ and academic problems, on the other [66,86]. It has also been suggested that children diagnosed as having E/BD perform worse in mathematics than in reading [87,88]. Other studies, on the contrary, have shown that the most severe deficits in academic performance in these children are in the area of written language [57]. A recent meta-analysis of academic profile of students who have E/BD [61] suggests that E/BD students overall perform significantly lower than do students without disabilities (effect size, −0.69), with the largest deficiencies present in mathematics (−0.81) and spelling (−0.81). Thus, the academic deficit, at least in the group of students served under the E/BD paragraph of the IDEA, seems to be general and to penetrate all domains of academic functioning. Needed are multifactorial accounts of the association between LDs and delinquency in which this association is viewed as a consequence of interactions between specific aspects of learning and specific psychosocial aspects of delinquency [89].

To summarize, studies of community and clinical samples contribute valuable information about the structure and etiology of the overlap between learning disorders and conduct disorders. These studies are easier to design and carry out than studies of incarcerated youth. It is possible that the first testable model of this overlap will be developed in the context of these studies and then transferred to studies of incarcerated juveniles.

Effects of arrest on education

The two preceding sections of this article briefly reviewed the literature on the link between LDs and conduct problems in incarcerated and nonincarcerated individuals. This section considers how society's punitive attitude toward juvenile delinquents seems to strengthen the association.

The escalation of the number and magnitude of crimes committed by youth has generated a variety of attitudes toward and explanations of this phenomenon [90,91]. For example, this increase has been referred to as a public health epidemic [92–95]. The predominant response, however, is sentencing and mandatory incarceration with the intent of punishing youth who commit crimes and preventing recidivism [96]. Because juvenile offenders are increasingly tried as adults [97,98] and because their sentences are becoming more punitive [99], one would assume that there are data supporting the effectiveness of these decisions.

There is, however, relatively little research on the impact of disciplining children with disabilities and on the postincarceration adjustment and developmental trajectories of juvenile delinquents. These lines of research are especially scarce in the domain of juveniles' cognitive adaptation and schooling [83,100]. However, it appears that, from a sociological lens, at least in the United States, the collateral damage caused by incarceration, specifically, the damage to educational pathways and schooling, outweighs its benefits [101]. In addition, such research is difficult to do because of the nature of the population of interest. It is even more difficult to do now: under the pressure of the No Child Left Behind Act, underachieving youth who have behavioral problems are often cut off from schooling because of school officials' fears that their scores will reduce the overall school score and result in sanctions toward the school.

Archwamety and Katsivannis [11] examined records of 505 delinquent 12- to 18-year-old males committed to Nebraska's correctional facilities from 1991 through 1997. Among these males, the researchers identified three groups: (1) those who received remedial teaching in reading; (2) those who received remedial teaching in mathematics; and (3) those who did not need remedial teaching. The remedial services were delivered if a youth was at least one grade level behind and his performance in the assigned area (reading or mathematics) was below the fiftieth percentile. A person could be assigned to only one group at a time, to ensure the completion of remediation. In addition, for most individuals, the data from an achievement test (the Peabody Individual Achievement Test) and an IQ test (the Wechsler Intelligence Test Revised) were available. Both remedial groups were significantly worse off than the nonremedial group on all measures, and the mathematics remedial group was worse than the reading remedial group in mathematics, verbal, performance, and full-scale IQ. There were no differences in reading and writing performance between the two remedial groups. The groups were compared on a number of outcome variables, including parole violation and recidivism. The researchers reported that members of both remedial groups committed more parole violations ($P < .01$) and more repeated crimes ($P < .05$) than did the members of control groups. (There were no differences between the two remedial groups.) Thus, it seems that among incarcerated youngsters the prognosis is worse for those individuals who need remediation on basic academic skills (reading and mathematics). This study is impressive in terms of the number of examined records, and it contributes to a field where the evidence is scarce. It suffers from a number of important methodologic difficulties, however. Specifically, the group analyses indicated that the level of performance in the recidivist group was lower than that of the nonrecidivist group on Peabody Individual Achievement Test writing and mathematics (but not reading) and verbal and full-scale IQ (but not performance). It is unclear how much reading and mathematics performance (and, correspondingly, remediation) were associated with general intellectual functioning. Clearly, a better statistical or experimental control is needed to produce clearly interpretable data on intellectual and behavioral differences between the remedial and nonremedial groups. Finally, given the minimal detail on the facility in the article, it is difficult to evaluate whether the sample is representative of the population of juveniles in Nebraska or in the United States as a whole. Therefore the level of generalizability of these findings is difficult to judge.

The Transition Research on Adjudicated Youth in Community Settings project followed a sample of 531 youths who had been incarcerated in the Oregon Youth Authority, the state of Oregon juvenile correctional system [102]. For 4 years the researchers conducted postrelease interviews every 6 months with each youth and, when available, with a family member. The project was aimed at documenting the youth's educational, personal, and criminal histories and the services and treatment they received while in the juvenile correctional system. Approximately 60% of the youth in this study returned to the juvenile or adult correctional system [47]. Re-entry took place most commonly within the first 12 months after exit; if a person did not return to the system in the year following release, it was almost certain that he or she would not return to the system [103]. Only half of the youth engaged in schooling, work, or both within the first year after release; individuals who had disabilities (primarily E/BD or LD) were about twice less likely to engage in such activities. Such engagement was associated with an approximately 200% decrease in the likelihood of the youth's returning to the correctional system. Another factor reported to be important in reducing the risk of returning to the correctional system was the receipt of mental health and community-based services.

Of particular interest for this discussion is a comparative evaluation of adaptation in youth who either had or did not have a disability diagnosis. A number of findings obtained within the Transition Research on Adjudicated Youth in Community Settings study are relevant. First, 57.7% of the sample (n = 305) had a diagnosed disability. The most prevalent disability was E/BD (52% of all disabilities), followed by LD (39% of all disabilities); these disabilities were observed in 53% of the total sample. A handful of individuals (5%) had hearing impairment/deafness. The rest had a variety of diagnoses (eg, speech and language impairment, mental retardation), each of which represented less than 1% of the disabilities in the sample. Thus, the data from this study support the hypothesis that individuals who have special educational needs, especially those diagnosed as having E/BD and LD, are overrepresented among incarcerated youth. Second, although the researchers investigated a number of potentially important variables (eg, gender, ethnicity, family socioeconomic status, adopted or foster/biologic parentage, having a child, criminality in family, history of running away, obtaining a high school diploma before release, ADHD, psychiatric diagnosis, record of prior treatment for alcohol or substance abuse, or grade retention at school before commitment), little evidence was found for differentiation of the groups with and without disabilities on these variables. Thus, it seems that, as a group, youth who have disabilities do not possess more "other" risk factors than the group of youth who do not have disabilities. Third, the group of incarcerated youth who had disabilities performed much worse (eg, were more likely to fail a grade while in school) than a comparable group of nonincarcerated youth who had disabilities [104]. Thus, the impact of disability seems to be more noticeable in incarcerated youth than in nonincarcerated youth.

An increasing body of evidence suggests that sanctioning itself might be a hindering factor for reinstating the pattern of adequate schooling after release [101]. Specifically, it has been shown that a first arrest has no major effect on mathematics and reading achievement test scores during seventh and eighth grade but does increase the odds of repeating eighth grade. For students entering ninth grade, the same study found that being arrested dramatically increases the risk of dropping out of school and substantially lowers attendance and grades. The consequences of arrest are very pronounced and increase for youth sentenced to stay in detention. In other words, the act of arrest seems to make schooling, which is already difficult for this population, even more difficult and often impossible.

According to a qualitative study by Todis and colleagues [105] of juvenile youth transitioning from youth correctional facilities back into their communities, the goal of continued schooling seemed to differentiate those who successfully adapted to the community from those who reoffended. In support of this observation, studies suggest that successful schooling (ie, going to school and progressing as abilities permit) is an important factor in predicting nonrecidivism

[106]. Also, academic success is associated with a decrease in problem behavior [107]. School graduation incentives are the most cost-effective strategy for preventing the commission of serious crimes by delinquent youth [108].

This section has presented studies illustrating the importance of sustaining schooling in detention and continuing it after release. Today, under the pressure of the No Child Left Behind Act and the zero-tolerance atmosphere of public schools, returning to schooling after release is an extremely challenging task. Continuing education, however, seems to be one of the best predictors of an individual's not returning to the correctional system. If juvenile delinquency is a public health problem, then schooling of juvenile delinquents and providing special educational services to those who are in need of them is an effective way to limit the epidemic of juvenile crime.

Summary

Students who drop out of school are 3.5 times more likely to be arrested than those who graduate [109,110]. Dropout rates are much higher among students who have special educational needs than for typical students. It has been estimated that half of all students who have E/BD and almost a third of students who have LD drop out of school [111]. It has further been reported that 82% of prisoners have been high school dropouts [109,110]. The link between schooling experiences, academic achievement, and delinquency is strong. It is important to understand this association for preventive and remediational purposes. As Pollard and colleagues [112] pointed out, "Adjudicated youths have a history of frustrating educational experiences and academic failures." Minimizing this school-related frustration might go far in preventing the manifestation of antisocial behaviors.

In addition, given their special educational profile and academic skills, many juvenile delinquents may be unable to understand factual information about trials [113], its legal language [114], and Miranda rights [115].

Finally, understanding the link between academic achievement and antisociality as it exists in juvenile offenders will provide rich material for further work in developmental psychology on understanding variability and similarity in developmental trajectories across the life-course.

References

[1] National Center for Education Statistics. Available at: http://nces.ed.gov/pubs2005/2005050.pdf. Accessed December 28, 2005.

[2] Federal Bureau of Investigations. Available at: http://www.fbi.gov/ucr/cius_04/persons_arrested/table_38-43.html. Accessed December 28, 2005.

[3] Davis AD, Sanger DD, Morris-Friehe M. Language skills of delinquent and nondelinquent adolescent males. J Commun Disord 1991;24:251–66.

[4] Finn GD, Stott MW, Zarichny KT. School performance of adolescents in juvenile court. Urban Education 1988;23:150–61.

[5] Lawrence R. School performance, containment therapy, and delinquent behavior. Youth Soc 1985;17:69–95.

[6] Beebe MC, Mueller F. Categorical offenses of juvenile delinquents and the relationship to achievement. Journal of Correctional Education 1993;44:193–8.

[7] Leon P, Rutherford R, Nelson C. Special education in juvenile corrections. Reston, (VA): The Council for Exceptional Children; 1991.

[8] Wagner M, D'Amico R, Marder C, et al. What happens next? Trends in post school outcomes of youth with disabilities. The second comprehensive report from the National Longitudinal Transition Study of Special Education Students. Menlo Park (CA): SRI International; 1992.

[9] Archwamety T, Katsryannis A. Factors related to recidivism among delinquent females in a state correctional facility. J Child Fam Stud 1998;7:59–67.

[10] Katsiyannis A, Zhang D, Barrett DE, et al. Background and psychosocial variables associated with recidivism among adolescent males: a 3-year investigation. Journal of Emotional and Behavioral Disorders 2004;12:23–9.

[11] Archwamety T, Katsiyannis A. Academic remediation, parole violations, and recidivism rates among delinquent youths. Remedial and Special Education 2000;21:161–70.

[12] Leschield AW, Coolman M, Jaffe P, et al. The role of the family court clinic in the assessment of school-related disorders with young offenders. Guidance and Counseling 1986;1:19–24.

[13] Spellacy FJ, Brown WG. Prediction of recidivism in young offenders after brief institutionalization. J Clin Psychol 1984;40:1070–4.

[14] Morrison GM, D'Incau B. The web of zero-tolerance: characteristics of students who are recommended for expulsion from school. Education & Treatment of Children 1997;20:316–35.

[15] Rutter M, Yule W. Reading retardation and antisocial behavior: the nature of the association. In: Rutter M, Tizard J, Whitmore K, editors. Education health and behavior. London: Longmans; 1970. p. 240–55.

[16] Lindsay WL, Taylor JL, Sturmey P, editors. Offenders with developmental disabilities. New York: John Wiley & Sons; 2004.

[17] Terman LM. The measurement of intelligence. Boston: Houghton Mifflin; 1911.

[18] Goddard HH. Juvenile delinquency. New York: Dodd, Mead and Company; 1921.

[19] Sutherland EH. The professional thief. Chicago: Chicago University Press; 1937.

[20] Scheerenberger RC. A history of mental retardation. London: Brooks; 1983.

[21] Burleigh M, Wippermann W. The racial state: Germany, 1933–1945. Cambridge (UK): Cambridge University Press; 1991.

[22] Gallager NL. Breeding better Vermonters. Hanover (NH): Unviersity of New England Press; 1999.

[23] Elmund A, Melin L, von Knorring A-L, et al. Cognitive and neuropsychological functioning in transnationally adopted juvenile delinquents. Acta Paediatr 2004;93:1507–13.

[24] Lynam D, Moffitt TE, Stouthamer-Loeber M. Explaining the relation between IQ and delinquency: class, race, test motivation, school failure, or self-control? J Abnorm Psychol 1993; 102:187–96.

[25] Chae PK, Jung H-O, Noh K-S. Attention deficit hyperactivity disorder in Korean juvenile delinquents. Adolescence 2001;36:707–25.

[26] Kroll L, Rothwell J, Bradley D, et al. Mental health needs of boys in secure care for serious or persistent offending: a prospective, longitudinal study. Lancet 2002;359:1975–9.

[27] Rasmussen K, Almvik R, Levander S. Attention deficit hyperactivity disorder, reading disability, and personality disorders in a prison population. J Am Acad Psychiatry Law 2001;29: 186–93.

[28] Newman JP. Reaction to punishment in extroverts and psychopaths. Implications for the impulsive behavior of disinhibited individuals. J Res Pers 1987;21:464–80.

[29] White JL, Moffitt TE, Caspi A, et al. Measuring impulsivity and examining its relationship to delinquency. J Abnorm Psychol 1991;103:192–205.

[30] Seguin JR, Pihl RO, Harden PW, et al. Cognitive and neuropsychological characteristics of physically aggressive boys. J Abnorm Psychol 1995;104:614–24.
[31] Kelly T, Richardson G, Hunter R, et al. Attention and executive function deficits in adolescent sex offenders. Child Neuropsychology 2002;8:138–43.
[32] Mostafa SR, el-Zeiny NA. Assessment of level of intellectual functioning among juvenile boy delinquents in Alexandria and its relation to behavioral deviance. J Egypt Public Health Assoc 1992;67:623–37.
[33] Dalteg A, Levander S. Twelve thousand crimes by 75 boys: a 20-year follow-up study of childhood activity. Journal of Forensic Psychiatry 1998;9:39–57.
[34] Underwood R. Learning disability as a predisposing cause of criminality. Can Ment Health 1976;24:11–6.
[35] Kirk J, Reid G. An examination of the relationship between dyslexia and offending in young people and the implications for the training system. Dyslexia: the Journal of the British Dyslexia Association 2001;7:77–84.
[36] Snowling MJ, Adams JW, Bowyer-Crane C, et al. Levels of literacy among juvenile offenders: the incidence of specific reading difficulties. Crim Behav Ment Health 2000;10:229–41.
[37] Critchley EM. Reading retardation, dyslexia and delinquency. Br J Psychiatry 1968;114: 1537–47.
[38] Meltzer LJ, Levine MD, Karniski W, et al. An analysis of the learning styles of adolescent delinquents. J Learn Disabil 1984;17:600–8.
[39] Jensen J, Lindgren M, Meurling AW, et al. Dyslexia among Swedish prison inmates in relation to neuropsychology and personality. J Int Neuropsychol Soc 1999;5:452–61.
[40] Daderman AM, Lindgren M, Lidberg L. The prevalence of dyslexia and AD/HD in a sample of forensic psychiatric rapists. Nord J Psychiatry 2004;58:371–81.
[41] Moody KC, Holzer CE, Roman MJ, et al. Prevalence of dyslexia among Texas prison inmates. Tex Med 2000;96:69–75.
[42] Alm J, Andersson J. A study of literacy in prisons in Uppsala. Dyslexia: the Journal of the British Dyslexia Association 1997;3:245–6.
[43] Samuelsson S, Gustavsson A, Herkner B, et al. Is the frequency of dyslexic problems among prison inmates higher than in a normal population? Reading and Writing 2000;13: 297–312.
[44] Svensson I, Lundberg I, Jacobson C. The prevalence of reading and spelling difficulties among inmates of institutions for compulsory care of juvenile delinquents. Dyslexia: the Journal of the British Dyslexia Association 2001;7:62–76.
[45] Winter N, Holland AJ, Collins S. Factors predisposing to suspected offending by adults with self-reported learning disabilities. Psychol Med 1997;27:595–607.
[46] Samuelsson S, Herkner B, Lundberg I. Reading and writing difficulties among prison inmates: a matter of experiential factors rather than dyslexic problems. Scientific Studies of Reading 2003;7:53–73.
[47] Bullis M, Yovanoff P, Havel E. The importance of getting started right: further examination of the facility-to-community transition of formerly incarcerated youth. J Spec Educ 2004;38: 80–94.
[48] Hinshaw SP. Externalizing behavior problems and academic underachievement in childhood and adolescence: causal relationships and underlying mechanisms. Psychol Bull 1992;111: 127–55.
[49] Sturge C. Reading retardation and antisocial behaviour. J Child Psychol Psychiatry 1982;23: 21–31.
[50] Maughan B, Gray G, Rutter M. Reading retardation and antisocial behaviour: a follow-up into employment. J Child Psychol Psychiatry 1985;26:741–58.
[51] Beitchman JH, Young AR. Learning disorders with a special emphasis on reading disorders: a review of the past 10 years. J Am Acad Child Adolesc Psychiatry 1997;36:1020–32.
[52] Virkkunen M, Nuutila A. Specific reading retardation, hyperactive child syndrome, and juvenile delinquency. Acta Psychiatr Scand 1976;54:25–8.

[53] Frick PJ, Kamphaus RW, Lahey BB, et al. Academic underachievement and the disruptive behavior disorders. J Consult Clin Psychol 1991;59:289–94.
[54] Hawkins J, Lishner D. Schooling and delinquency. In: Johnson EH, editor. Handbook of crime and delinquency prevention. New York: Guilford Press; 1987. p. 179–221.
[55] Carroll JM, Maughan B, Goodman R, et al. Literacy difficulties and psychiatric disorders: evidence for comorbidity. J Child Psychol Psychiatry 2005;46:524–32.
[56] Greenbaum PE, Dedrick RF, Friedman RM, et al. National Adolescent and Child Treatment Study (NACTS): outcomes for children with serious emotional and behavioral disturbance. Journal of Emotional and Behavioral Disorders 1996;4:130–46.
[57] Mattison RE, Hooper SR, Glassberg LA. Three-year course of learning disorders in special education students classified as behavioral disorder. J Am Acad Child Adolesc Psychiatry 2002;41:1454–61.
[58] Ruhl KL, Berlinghoff DH. Research on improving behaviorally disordered students' academic performance: a review of the literature. Behavioral Disorders 1992;17:178–90.
[59] Scruggs TE, Mastropieri MA. Academic characteristics of behaviorally disordered and learning disabled students. Behavioral Disorders 1986;11:184–90.
[60] Walker HM, Colvin G, Ramsey E. Antisocial behavior in school: strategies and best practices. Belmont (CA): Brooks/Cole Publishing Co; 1995.
[61] Reid R, Gonzalez JE, Nordness PD, et al. A meta-analysis of the academic status of students with emotional/behavioral disturbance. J Spec Educ 2004;38:130–43.
[62] Trout AL, Nordness PD, Pierce CD, et al. Research on the academic status of children with emotional and behavioral disorders: a review of the literature from 1961 to 2000. Journal of Emotional and Behavioral Disorders 2003;11:198–210.
[63] Coutinho MJ. Reading achievement of students identified as behaviorally disordered at the secondary level. Behavioral Disorders 1986;11:200–7.
[64] Ensminger ME, Juon HS. Transition to adulthood among high-risk youth. In: Jessor R, editor. New perspectives on adolescent risk behavior. New York: Cambridge University Press; 1998. p. 365–91.
[65] Bullis M, Fredericks HD, editors. Vocational and transitional services for adolescents with emotional and behavioral disorders: strategies and best practices. Champaign (IL): Research Press; 2002.
[66] McGee R, Williams S, Share DL, et al. The relationship between specific reading retardation, general reading backwardness and behavioural problems in a large sample of Dunedin boys: a longitudinal study from five to eleven years. J Child Psychol Psychiatry 1986;27:597–610.
[67] Smart D, Sanson A, Prior M. Connections between reading disability and behavior problems: testing temporal and causal hypotheses. J Abnorm Child Psychol 1996;24:363–83.
[68] Sanson A, Prior M, Smart D. Reading disabilities with and without behaviour problems at 7–8 years: prediction from longitudinal data from infancy to 6 years. J Child Psychol Psychiatry 1996;37:529–41.
[69] Prior M, Smart D, Sanson A, et al. Relationships between learning difficulties and psychological problems in preadolescent children from a longitudinal sample. J Am Acad Child Adolesc Psychiatry 1999;38:429–36.
[70] Fergusson DM, Lynskey MT. Early reading difficulties and later conduct problems. J Child Psychol Psychiatry 1997;38:899–907.
[71] Nelson JR, Benner GJ, Lane K, et al. Academic achievement of K-12 students with emotional and behavioral disorders. Except Child 2004;71:59–73.
[72] Bennett KJ, Brown KS, Boyle M, et al. Does low reading achievement at school entry cause conduct problems? Soc Sci Med 2003;56:2443–8.
[73] Jorm AF, Share DL, Matthews R, et al. Behaviour problems in specific reading retarded and general reading backward children: a longitudinal study. J Child Psychol Psychiatry 1986; 27:33–43.
[74] Kellam SG, Rebok GW, Ialongo N, et al. The course and malleability of aggressive behavior

from early first grade into middle school: results of a developmental epidemiologically-based preventive trial. J Child Psychol Psychiatry 1994;35:259–81.
[75] Cornwall A, Bawden HN. Reading disabilities and aggression: a critical review. J Learn Disabil 1992;25:281–8.
[76] Angold A, Costello EJ, Erkanli A. Comorbidity. J Child Psychol Psychiatry 1999;40:57–87.
[77] Gellert A, Elbro C. Reading disabilities, behaviour problems and delinquency: a review. Scandinavian Journal of Educational Research 1999;43:131–55.
[78] Willcutt EG, Pennington BF. Psychiatric comorbidity in children and adolescents with reading disability. J Child Psychol Psychiatry 2000;41:1039–48.
[79] Maughan B, Pickles A, Hagell A, et al. Reading problems and antisocial behaviour: developmental trends in comorbidity. J Child Psychol Psychiatry 1996;37:405–18.
[80] Willcutt EG, Pennington BF, Olson RK, et al. Neuropsychological analyses of comorbidity between reading disability and attention deficit hyperactivity disorder: in search of the common deficit. Dev Neuropsychol 2005;27:35–78.
[81] Willcutt EG, Pennington BF, Smith SD, et al. Quantitative trait locus for reading disability on chromosome 6p is pleiotropic for attention-deficit/hyperactivity disorder. Am J Med Genet 2002;114:260–8.
[82] Holmes J, Payton A, Barrett J, et al. Association of DRD4 in children with ADHD and comorbid conduct problems. Am J Med Genet 2002;114:150–3.
[83] Anderson JA, Kutash K, Duchnowski AJ. A comparison of the academic progress of students with EBD and students with LD. Journal of Emotional and Behavioral Disorders 2001; 9:106–15.
[84] Walker HM, Stieber S, Bullis M. Longitudinal correlates of arrest status among at-risk males. J Child Fam Stud 1997;6:289–309.
[85] Kazdin AE. Conduct disorder in childhood and adolescence. London: Sage; 1987.
[86] McGee R, Share DL. Attention deficit disorder-hyperactivity and academic failure: which comes first and what should be treated? J Am Acad Child Adolesc Psychiatry 1988;27:318–25.
[87] Stone FB, Rowley VN. Educational disability in emotionally disturbed children. Except Child 1964;30:423–6.
[88] Schroeder LB. A study of the relationships between five descriptive categories of emotional disturbance and reading and arithmetic achievement. Except Child 1965;32:111–2.
[89] Brier N. The relationship between learning disability and delinquency: a review and reappraisal. J Learn Disabil 1989;22:546–53.
[90] Costanzo M, Oskamp S, editors. Violence and the law. Thousand Oaks (CA): Sage; 1994.
[91] Kalogerakis MG. Adolescent violence in America: a historical perspective. In: Flaherty LT, editor. Adolescent psychiatry: developmental and clinical studies. Hillsdale (NJ): Analytic Press, Inc.; 2003. p. 15–26.
[92] Prothrow-Stith DB. The epidemic of youth violence in America: using public health prevention strategies to prevent violence. J Health Care Poor Underserved 1995;6:95–101.
[93] Hutton M. Violence in America. Reaching epidemic proportions. J Fla Med Assoc 1995; 82:667–8.
[94] Fontanarosa PB. The unrelenting epidemic of violence in America. Truths and consequences. JAMA 1995;273:1792–3.
[95] Koop CE, Lundberg GB. Violence in America: a public health emergency. Time to bite the bullet back. JAMA 1992;267:3075–6.
[96] MacKenzie DL, Hebert E, editors. Correctional boot camps: a tough intermediate sanction. Washington (DC): US Department of Justice, National Institute of Justice; 1996.
[97] Moseley-Braun C. Yes: send a message to young criminals. Am Bar Assoc J 1994;80:525–46.
[98] Sickmund M. How juveniles get to criminal court. Washington (DC): US Department of Justice; 1994.
[99] Schwartz I, editor. Juvenile justice and public policy toward a national agenda. New York: Lexington; 1992.
[100] Katsiyannis A, Smith CR. Disciplining students with disabilities: legal trends and the issue of interim alternative education settings. Behavioral Disorders 2003;28:410–8.

[101] Hirschfield P. The impact of juvenile justice involvement on educational outcomes [PhD thesis]. Evanston (IL): Department of Sociology, Northwestern University; 2004.
[102] Bullis M, Yovanoff P, Mueller G, et al. Life on the "outs"—examination of the facility-to-community transition of incarcerated youth. Except Child 2002;69:7–22.
[103] Bullis M, Fredericks HD. Providing effective vocational transition services to adolescents with emotional and behavioral disorders. Champaign-Urbana (IL): Research Press; 2002.
[104] Wagner M. Dropouts with disabilities: what do we know? Menlo Park (CA): SRI International; 1991.
[105] Todis B, Bullis M, Waintrup M, et al. Overcoming the odds: qualitative examination of resilience among formerly incarcerated adolescents. Except Child 2001;68:119–39.
[106] Bullis M, Walker HM, Stieber S. The influence of peer and educational variables on arrest status among at-risk males. Journal of Emotional and Behavioral Disorders 1998;6:141–52.
[107] Gottfredson DC, Gottfredson GD, Skroban S. A multimodel school-based prevention demonstration. J Adolesc Res 1996;11:97–115.
[108] Greenwood PW, Model KE, Rydell CP, et al. Diverting children from a life of crime. Santa Monica (CA): RAND Corporation; 1996.
[109] US Department of Education. Mini-digest of educational statistics, 1994. Washington (DC): National Center for Educational Statistics; 1994.
[110] US Department of Education. Dropout rates in the United States: 1994. Washington, (DC): National Center for Educational Statistics; 1996.
[111] Wagner M. Outcomes for youth with serious emotional disturbance in secondary school and early adulthood. Future Child 1995;5:90–112.
[112] Pollard RR, Pollard CJ, Meers GD. A sociological, psychological, and educational profile of adjudicated youth with disabilities. Journal for Vocational Special Needs Education 1995;17: 56–61.
[113] Cooper DK. Juveniles' understanding of trial-related information: are they competent defendants? Behav Sci Law 1997;15:167–80.
[114] Smith TF. Law talk: Juveniles' understanding of legal language. J Crim Justice 1985;13: 339–53.
[115] Goldstein NES, Condie LO, Kalbeitzer R, et al. Juvenile offenders' Miranda rights comprehension and self-reported likelihood of offering false confessions. Assessment 2003;10: 359–69.

ELSEVIER
SAUNDERS

Child Adolesc Psychiatric Clin N Am
15 (2006) 373–390

CHILD AND
ADOLESCENT
PSYCHIATRIC CLINICS
OF NORTH AMERICA

Legal Issues, Rights, and Ethics for Mental Health in Juvenile Justice

Stephen A. Zerby, MD[a], Christopher R. Thomas, MD[b,*]

[a]Western Psychiatric Institute and Clinic, University of Pittsburgh Medical Center, Pittsburgh, PA, USA
[b]Department of Psychiatry and Behavioral Sciences, University of Texas Medical Branch at Galveston, 301 University Boulevard, Galveston, TX 77555, USA

The legal issues, rights, and ethics of working with minors, the mentally ill, and those involved in the justice system are among the most demanding areas for health professionals. Providing consultation and treatment for mentally ill youth in the juvenile justice system involves and confronts all of these concerns. Mental health professionals must be aware of the legal and ethical expectations and constraints in this area to provide appropriate and competent service. The American Academy of Child and Adolescent Psychiatry emphasized the importance of clinician awareness of legal and ethical matters in the Practice Parameter for the Assessment and Treatment of Youth in Juvenile Detention and Correctional Facilities [1]. There have been extensive changes in the procedures for handling youth charged with offenses in the past 2 decades as a result of legislation and judicial decisions. Many of these changes were prompted by the dramatic increase in youth violence and juvenile arrests beginning in the 1980s. Although juvenile arrest rates began to decline in 1994, the number of youth in detention increased 46% and the number of delinquents committed to facilities increased 51% from 1991 to 1999 [2]. Recent epidemiologic studies indicate that the majority of youth held in the juvenile justice system have mental disorders [3,4]. To meet their needs, mental health professionals must be aware of the legal and ethical issues involved.

* Corresponding author.
E-mail address: crthomas@utmb.edu (C.R. Thomas).

doi:10.1016/j.chc.2005.11.006

childpsych.theclinics.com

Legal issues

Criminal responsibility/diminished capacity

Since ancient times, societies have recognized the importance of development and maturity in assigning criminal responsibility. Roman law held that children under age 7 years were not culpable. By the seventeenth century the concept was expanded for courts to presume those above age 14 years as fully responsible and those between ages 7 and 14 years as lacking capacity but open to question, with the burden on the state to demonstrate criminal responsibility in court. The creation of the juvenile justice system in the United States was intended to provide rehabilitation over punishment for youth who have a questionable degree of criminal responsibility. It rested in part on the concept of *parens patriae,* or the right of the state to protect citizens lacking full legal capacity. States vary in their defined purpose for the juvenile court, with some following the best interests of the child and state as defined by the 1959 Standard Juvenile Court Act and others using the principles of protecting both child and community interests and constitutional rights as outlined in the Legislative Guide for Drafting Family and Juvenile Court Acts. In the 1990s, 17 states modified their juvenile court purpose to include concepts of balanced and restorative justice, emphasizing accountability and community safety [5]. Developmental research on criminal decision making supports the concept of differing expectations and culpability for youth. Adolescent offenders exhibit age-related differences in temporal perspective, resistance to peer influence, and risk perception that may contribute to their delinquent behavior [6].

States differ as to the earliest age of criminal responsibility. Sixteen states have statutes setting a minimum age for juvenile court jurisdiction: one at age 6 years, three at age 7 years, one at age 8 years, and 11 at age 10 years. States also differ on the upper age limit of juvenile court jurisdiction, with four setting it at age 15 years, ten at age 16 years, and the remaining at age 17 years. In response to rising rates of youth violence and arrests, three states lowered the upper age limit in the 1990s: Wyoming from 18 to 17 years, and New Hampshire and Wisconsin from 17 to 16 years. Many states set higher age limits for juvenile court jurisdiction over status offenses and dependency matters, usually age 20 years. Most states also provide juvenile courts with means for extended authority over adjudicated delinquents to provide sanctions and services beyond the upper age limit of original jurisdiction, usually age 20 years. Although the intent of juvenile courts in addressing criminal responsibility of youth is similar across states, the differences in age limits and stated purpose create important variations of which clinicians should be aware.

Waiver or transfer to adult criminal court

All states have means of transferring defendants from juvenile to adult criminal court. There are several methods by which cases can be transferred, including judicial waivers, prosecutor discretion, and statutory exclusion. Judicial waiver is accomplished by three means: discretionary, presumptive, and mandatory. Discretionary judicial waiver permits the judge to transfer the case after certain criteria have been satisfied. In most cases, the prosecutor initiates this process and bears the burden of proof. The criteria usually include consideration of the juvenile's maturity, current charges, history of prior offenses, chance for rehabilitation, and public safety, established by *Kent v United States 1966* [7]. Waiver hearings usually involve a mental health evaluation of the juvenile, and in some states this evaluation is required by statute. Clinicians may be asked to assess the youth's level of maturity, amenability to rehabilitation, and likelihood of future violence and offense in addition to the presence and role of any mental disorder [8]. Presumptive judicial transfer represents a major modification that shifts the burden of proof from the prosecutor to the juvenile. In other words, the defense must prove why a judge should not have the case transferred to criminal court and that the youth would best be handled in the juvenile court. Mandatory judicial waiver removes any opportunity to argue the merits of transfer, requiring the judge only to determine if the case meets criteria set by law for waiver. Concurrent jurisdiction (also referred to as "prosecutor discretion" or "direct file") is another means by which the prosecutor is allowed to decide whether to file a case in juvenile or adult criminal court. Laws establish jurisdiction for certain types of offenses in both courts and permit the prosecutor to determine which court will try a specific case. Although concurrent jurisdiction is similar to mandatory judicial waiver, it removes judicial review from the transfer process. Statutory exclusion laws require juvenile defendants to be tried in adult criminal courts when charged with certain offenses. Most often, this transfer is for serious or violent offenses and will specify additional restrictions, such as age or prior offense record. In some states, reverse waiver laws allow the criminal court to transfer direct file or excluded cases back to juvenile court for adjudication or disposition, usually on a motion from the prosecutor. Although reverse waiver might offer the option of individual protection in excluded cases, there is no guarantee that it will be exercised, and even when used it will result in additional delays. Finally, some states have statutes that hold that if a juvenile has been previously transferred or waived to adult criminal court, all subsequent charges will be handled there, the "once an adult, always an adult" provision [9].

In the 1990s, all states except Nebraska enacted laws to facilitate transfer from juvenile to adult criminal courts in response to rising rates of youth violence and crime. This action was in part based on beliefs that juvenile courts did not work and that more serious and violent juvenile offenses would be better handled as adult cases in criminal courts [10]. These changes have contributed to an overall increase in the number of cases transferred, from 6800 in 1987 to 10,000 in 1996 [11], and the number of youth in adult prisons has doubled in the past decade [12]. Previously, most cases were transferred by judicial waiver; now most are transferred by statutory exclusion. Research on the impact of these changes indicates that they have not achieved their goals nor improved the handling of delinquents and that there are many unintended adverse consequences.

There is no evidence that adult criminal court waiver statutes have any deterrent effect. Several studies have found no change in rates of delinquency following enactment of such laws [13]. One extensive review of long-term outcome for youth tried in criminal courts compared with those tried in juvenile court found that transfer resulted in extensive delay of case processing without necessarily providing longer sentences [14]. A study on the impact of new transfer laws in Pennsylvania found that many cases that previously would have been handled in juvenile court (eg, younger offenders or ones with less serious offense histories) were now sent to criminal court. Half the cases targeted for exclusion were either returned to juvenile justice or dismissed, however. The result was that the change produced longer delays [15]. Mandatory transfers have resulted in some juveniles with no prior offenses or involvement in rehabilitative efforts being sent to adult criminal court for trial [16].

Independent of new transfer laws, the use of judicial waiver has changed. Studies have found that the use of judicial waiver has increased and that petitions for transfer are more likely to be granted [15]. Recent studies find that youth tried in adult criminal court have significantly higher rates of recidivism and are more likely to be victimized, physically and sexually, than youth tried in the juvenile justice system [17]. A 5-year study in Florida of 475 matched pairs of young offenders found that those handled by the criminal court had higher rates of felony recidivism and that the second offense was more serious than the first [18]. Transfer or waiver to criminal court can result in youth incarcerated in prison, with fewer services that address their developmental needs and exposure to adult criminals. Minority youth are disproportionately affected by transfer to criminal court. A California study found that minorities comprised 95% of youth transferred to criminal court and that minority youth were twice as likely as white youth to be transferred for violent offenses [19]. The same report found that among youth tried in criminal court, black and Asian youth were more likely than white youth to be imprisoned. There also seem to be regional differences within the same juvenile justice system: a study in Virginia found that rural youth are more likely to be waived or transferred to adult criminal court [20].

Alternatives to waiver or transfer do exist. Some states have provided judges with the option of using sentences from both the juvenile and criminal system. One method allows judges to select the system that is most appropriate for disposition based on the individual case. Another approach allows judges to impose concurrent or sequential sentences from both systems. Although these procedures preserve the flexibility and resources of the juvenile system, they are relatively new, and there is no information as to their use or impact.

Competency to stand trial

With hearings focusing on rehabilitation rather than trials concerned with setting punishment, the juvenile justice system in the past seldom considered issues of competency to stand trial [21]. Following the series of judicial decisions on due process in juvenile court and the increasing use of transfer or waiver to adult criminal court, the competency of youth to stand trial has emerged as an important legal issue during the past decade. As with adult competency to stand trial, the standards usually used to assess youth derive from *Dusky v United States 1960* [22], which defines that the defendant understands the nature of the court proceedings and is able to assist in the defense [23]. The Supreme Court delineated eight guidelines in determining competency to stand trial in *Wieter v Settle 1961* [24]. Since then, a number of competency measurements to assess defendants have been created based on these rulings [25]. Research with delinquents using these scales have consistently shown that competency to stand trial is related to age, with most preteens being incompetent [26–28]. Although these studies report that juveniles aged 15 years or older were usually competent, their scores were still lower than those of adults, especially in understanding plea bargaining. The most comprehensive research project to date, with four sites and 927 juveniles, the MacArthur Juvenile Adjudicative Competence Study also examined issues related to legal decision making and found that adolescents exhibited psychosocial immaturity and tended more often to make choices that reflected compliance with authority [28]. Besides age, features that distinguish competent from incompetent delinquents include intelligence, history of previous juvenile arrest [29], special education needs, and history of mental health problems [30]. One study addressed the complex interaction of age, mental illness, and cognitive ability in competency among juveniles, finding that although cognitive impairment combined with psychiatric symptoms accounted for most of the variance, age still played an important role in performance on the measures [31]. The importance of age in competency to stand trial is critical, because many states determine incompetence in adult criminal court only as a result of mental impairment and disability, not as a result of immaturity, and youth as young as age 10 years can face transfer to adult court in some states. Some states do require that a youth be found competent before transfer to adult criminal court, but this requirement is uncommon. The issue is further complicated in the juvenile justice system, with only 26 states having specific statutes concerning juvenile competency [32]. No state sets a minimum age as a threshold for competency, and many require that incompetence be a result of mental illness, as in the adult criminal court. In contrast to most states, Florida does allow a youth to be found incompetent on the basis of immaturity.

Even for juveniles considered to be competent to stand trial, questions have been raised as to their developmental ability to understand fully and work effectively with defense counsel [33]. One study used a hypothetical defense attorney–client vignette to compare the decision-making processes in 203 juveniles with those of 110 adults in pretrial detention [34]. The juveniles were more likely to consider denial of offense or refusal to talk and far less likely to consider honest communication as strategies in the scenario. They were also more likely to evaluate strategies by short-term gain, such as release to home, rather than long-term outcomes. The authors conclude that even competent juveniles exhibit significant age-related differences in decision making and developmental differences in psychosocial judgment that could adversely affect their ability to work with defense counsel. A separate study considered the issue of attorney–client trust in 163 detained or incarcerated males between ages 12 and 20 years but did not find any age-related differences [35].

There is even less research on the important area of juvenile competency restoration, which is a misnomer because youth found incompetent are unlikely ever to have been competent. In one study on the subject, 110 youth in placement for delinquency who scored below an accepted cut off in a modified competency measure were shown an instructional video tape and participated in a group discussion followed by retesting with the same competency measure [36]. Although the intervention resulted in significant improvement in scores on the posttest, only 12 youth scored above the acceptable cut-off level, and improvement in scores was unrelated to age. Similarly, a report on the Florida Competence Restoration program comparing staff determinations of restoration of competence for juveniles and adults found that there were no age-related differences [37].

There is also limited research in the area of juvenile preadjudicative competence, the understanding of Miranda rights, and offering confession. Studies have found that many arrested youth waive their rights, including the right to counsel [38,39]. As with competency to stand trial, age, intelligence, and history of special education are related to adolescents' comprehension of their Miranda rights [40,41]. This report also found that age predicted the likelihood of offering false confession. A separate study found that the ability to understand Miranda rights and competency to stand trial were strongly related and that suggestibility was predictive for both [42].

Mental health professionals asked to evaluate the competency of juveniles are challenged by a lack of legal precedent, vague and varied statutes, and limited research. It is also a rapidly changing area, as evident in the recent legal ruling by the Supreme Court of Indiana, *In Re K.G. 2004* [43], that decided the state's provisions on adult competency to stand trial did not pertain to juveniles, even though there was no specific statute on juvenile competency [44]. Standards for competency of adolescents and preadolescents have been proposed based on current research and legal procedures, including mandatory assessments based on age or before transfer and relaxed expectations for juvenile court understanding [28,45]. It is important for any clinician performing competency evaluations of juvenile defendants to be aware of these issues and new developments.

Legal issues of mental health services

It is important for clinicians working with the juvenile justice system to be aware of state laws regarding mental health services for minors that apply to youth in detention or correctional placement. In most cases, parental consent will be needed for treatment of youth below a certain age. Some states set a separate age of consent for mental health services that differs from the age of consent for other medical treatments, recognizing that a minor might not seek necessary treatment if parental consent is required. Although these laws allow youth to consent to treatment without parental permission, they may not also grant authority to refuse treatment if a parent consents. For example, a 16-year-old may be able to sign into a psychiatric unit, and the parents may also be able to sign in this youth, even if the youth refuses. States may also grant an individual authority to make treatment decisions as an emancipated minor. Court decree, marriage, or military service is usually specified in statutes as a requirement for emancipation. An important exception to obtaining consent is a health emergency, when attempting to obtain consent would delay treatment and threaten the life of the youth.

Ethics in juvenile justice

The boundaries between ethics, rights, professional guidelines, general practice, constitutional and statutory law, and case law remain blurred, because each dynamically influences the others, and overlap occurs in certain situations, such as when a specific ethical issue is also a legal issue. Each domain is intended to give guidance to professionals in the conduct of their work. Ethics is distinguished by the introduction of a moral dimension into analysis of a problem and subsequent decision making. Given the age of the patients and their vulnerable status, ethical concerns for juveniles have special significance [46]. Current concepts of rights arise from constitutional and statutory law as interpreted through the courts as case law, along with the guidance of professional guidelines and the opinions of professional organizations. Professional organizations have issued ethical guidelines for psychiatry, psychology, child and adolescent psychiatry, and forensic psychiatry over the years, but these guidelines have tended not to address directly the juvenile justice system and the youths within it [47].

Ethics applied to juvenile justice

Ethics can be defined as a body of knowledge and methodology with which to resolve dilemmas with a moral dimension arising out of clinical, forensic, or research situations. The presence of juveniles within the justice system presents professionals with a particularly challenging set of conditions for meeting the demands of ethical principles [48]. Given the correctional setting, there are two relevant sets of ethical principles to be considered, those of the clinician and those of the forensic evaluator [49–51].

Chief clinical ethical principals include autonomy (respecting the patient's decision making), nonmaleficence (avoiding harming the patient), beneficence (promoting the welfare of the patient), and justice (making fair decisions for both the patient and society). Autonomy is a complex issue for youths within the justice system, because parents or guardians may be more or less involved in decision making, and legal counsel may play an active role in guiding the youth's reasoning through its defined advocacy role. Because of their incarceration, the issue of coercion is pertinent, because a youth may cooperate with treatment as a means of pleasing the justice system to procure a lesser punishment. Non-maleficence is especially of concern when a professional assumes an advocacy role because of external pressures or personal motivation to help vulnerable youths. In certain situations the professional may overreach in a way that one's professional peers may feel is necessary but that, given the youth's circumstances, may cause harm (eg, advocating for a systemic change that might benefit a large number of youths in the system but is detrimental to the individual youth). Beneficence is a complex issue for youths involved with the juvenile justice system: as in the general clinical setting, one provides assessments and interventions, but doing so can be difficult in the juvenile justice setting because of the relative lack of resources [52,53].

These basic principles of ethics are more easily applied to clinical work in correctional settings and are more difficult to apply to what is defined more strictly as forensic work [49]. Chief forensic ethical principles include boundary issues, honesty and striving for objectivity, appropriate financial arrangements such as avoiding contingency fees [49], respect for persons; justice [50,51], confidentiality, and maintaining checks on countertransference to maintain the objectivity of the evaluation [54]. Major considerations when conducting forensic work in the juvenile justice setting are the role of the forensic examiner and the relationship with the juvenile examinee. The purpose of forensic work is to aid the court rather than the patient; there is no therapeutic relationship, and confidentiality is limited because the examiner reports to the court. The examinee should be informed of the agency of the examiner, the evaluation's purpose, and to whom the results will be divulged [47]. Justice plays a prominent role in youths involved with the justice system, because decisions must be made regarding what is fair to the youth, to the family or legal guardians, and to society. Often the needs of one party are in conflict with those of another, such as the youth's desire for freedom conflicting with society's desire for safety [51].

Given the two different roles which mental health professionals may assume in the juvenile justice setting, an inevitable ethical dilemma that arises is dual agency: a professional who participates as both a treating clinician and as a supposedly impartial expert witness becomes caught in the bind of competing interests, those of clinical duties toward the patient and family and duties toward the court [55]. The underlying problem in this situation is that a clinician with a therapeutic relationship with a patient may provide biased expert testimony to the court, and that testimony also may damage the therapeutic alliance. The general recommendation is to avoid this position if at all possible, depending on the specific situation, such as resource availability [54,56,57].

Special ethical concerns in the juvenile justice setting

The juvenile justice system, despite its mission of rehabilitation and treatment, differs from traditional mental health treatment by virtue of its correctional capacity, with functions of punishment, incapacitation, and deterrence in the interest of public safety. Mulvey and Phelps [48] argue that placing a youth in the juvenile justice system raises ethical questions, such as whether the youth becomes stigmatized and whether programming in such a coercive setting is beneficial. They describe two main ethical tensions in the juvenile justice setting: the juvenile's needs (paternalism) versus the juvenile's rights and treatment versus retribution. They propose that complex ethical problems be analyzed by focusing on these two sets of tensions, cautioning that ultimately there are no right or wrong answers but rather sets of principles that can be used for guidance. They caution that, like statutes, ethical guidelines are most useful as a limiting mechanism that help define certain actions as unacceptable, but they can rarely be applied affirmatively to direct decision making [48].

The ethics of advocacy

Advocacy ("giving aid to a cause") groups have been involved with and have guided the juvenile justice movement from its inception in the nineteenth century [58]. Today there exist groups that monitor the system and drive reforms, such as the Office of Juvenile Justice and Delinquency Prevention, the National Center for Juvenile Justice, and the Coalition for Juvenile Justice. It can be difficult for clinicians who work within the juvenile justice system to avoid contact with advocates or advocacy groups, which are not bound by the same ethical guidelines as mental health care providers but rather direct their efforts toward the furthering of social or political ideology. The mental health professional may face the additional pressure to shift from a clinical or forensic role to one of advocacy that constitutes the furtherance of a cause. The clinician must balance ethical principles (such as beneficence toward the youth) against the justice concept of furthering a broader cause (such as a sociopolitical ideology that may represent a "larger good") while avoiding allowing the youth's role to shift to being a means to advance that cause. The American Academy of Child and Adolescent Psychiatry Ethics Code Principle IV expresses a commitment to advocacy for children, adolescents, and their families: the psychiatrist is called upon to recognize a larger responsibility to them and to society [57]. The Committee on Adolescence of the American Academy of Pediatrics called on pediatricians to take active roles as advocates for the health care of juveniles within the justice system [59]. A 1995 paper called on health care providers within the juvenile justice setting to become advocates for the youths they serve [60]. Appelbaum [61] cautioned that the roles of forensic consultant and advocate are substantially different, because advocacy implies a loss of objectivity that would be detrimental to the role of impartial expert witness. This concept can be extended to the role of the clinician, who likewise needs to maintain a degree of objectivity within the therapeutic alliance. Caution may be the best course of action when advocacy issues arise, and one may argue against the mental health professional's assuming the role of advocate as a "third hat" to wear in addition to those of clinician and forensic evaluator. Perhaps this role is better relegated to outside work, in the more general sense of advocacy for youths in the juvenile justice system, rather than assumed in specific cases.

Ethics and consent to research and treatment

Although there is little in the literature regarding the ethics of research involving juveniles within the juvenile justice system, certain principles involving research with high-risk youth can be extrapolated to the juvenile justice setting. Youths within the juvenile justice setting are considered a vulnerable population because of their age, separation from family, and incarceration in a potentially coercive environment [53,62,63]. Vulnerability would be more pronounced should a mental illness, cognitive limitation, or developmental disorder also be present. Therefore great care must be taken to protect youths in the juvenile justice setting. When obtaining informed consent, the researcher should pay attention to any possible coercion to consent or assent to the study, because the incarcerated youth may believe that participation may lead to leniency in his or her legal situation. Autonomy to consent is an issue with such youths, and depending on their guardianship status, age and maturity, and the risks and benefits of the study or treatment, consideration may be given to self-consent for research and treatment [53]. Self-consent may be considered in situations in which it is not in the youth's best interest to involve a parent, such as in abuse and neglect situations. Given such youths' high-risk status, participation in research and treatment may be in their best interest, as well as in society's. Some argue that such research in high-risk youths is legally allowed and ethically is to be encouraged, with appropriate safeguards, such as informed consent and review by a research ethics panel [64]. Ethical and methodologic issues should be followed closely throughout the course of the study [65,66].

Roles and institutional abuse

An ethical problem arises when the professional is asked to approve or participate in procedures such as mechanical or chemical restraint and it is unclear whether the interventions are medical/therapeutic or disciplinary/administrative in nature. Institutional practices such as confinement and physical punishment can become abusive, and the professional in the juvenile justice setting may be faced with decisions regarding whether to ignore or condone these practices or to voice concern about disciplinary or administrative practices that may harm the juvenile's health ("institutional abuse") [52]. The two main indications for restraint and seclusion are therapeutic and administrative. An ethical problem arises for the professional when these interventions are used for nontherapeutic measures. The decision must be made whether to oppose, ignore, condone, or participate in such interventions, and the effects on the youths, institutional personnel, and families should be taken into account [67]. Nationwide the protocols for the use of restraint and seclusion are not uniform, and recommendations have been made to develop national policy regarding their use [68]. The role of health professionals in correctional settings may become blurred between care giving and correctional roles. Health professionals must be able to separate punitive considerations in assessing health and be able to practice without being compromised by security requirements [69]. There is a case to be made for including correctional officers in the treatment team, because the juveniles' relationships with correctional staff and information provided by them can be important in gaining an understanding of these youths. Effective treatment can be compromised when confidentiality dictates that medical, mental health, and security records remain separate [70].

Rights in juvenile justice

A brief history of the juvenile justice system

Moral principles and ethical concerns expressed by advocacy groups contributed to the birth of the juvenile justice system and likewise contributed to the evolution of concepts of juvenile's rights within the juvenile justice system. A brief history of the juvenile justice system will assist understanding the development of these rights. In the nineteenth century early juvenile justice settings were heavily influenced by the House of Refuge and Reformatory advocacy movements, which were characterized by the principle of *parens patriae* in which the state possessed the right to assume custody of children to prevent delinquency. This doctrine was upheld by the *Ex parte Crouse 1839* [71] decision, which rendered legitimacy to the reform movement and laid the groundwork for the doctrine that the state could deprive children of their liberty for rehabilitation. At the end of the nineteenth century the child-saving advocacy movement spurred the creation of juvenile courts with the intent of removing children from the adult criminal law system and providing them with interventions such as probation [58]. In 1899 the first juvenile court was created in Illinois for neglected, dependent, and delinquent children under age 16 years to handle minor offenses with the goal of rehabilitation instead of punishment. Juvenile courts then spread under a *parens patriae* doctrine that supported state intervention to protect both children and the community and to foster rehabilitation. Although immaturity shielded children from culpability, it also denied them the civil rights enjoyed by adults. By the 1950s there was criticism of juvenile courts, because youths were being incarcerated who probably would not have been sent to facilities if they had due process rights, and it was realized that the focus of these facilities was punishment, not rehabilitation as originally intended [72]. *Kent v United States* [7] challenged the state's *parens patriae* authority by requiring due process in the transfer of juveniles to criminal court. *In re Gault* [73] saw the end of the *parens patriae* authority of the juvenile court by requiring a notice of charges, the rights of confrontation and examination, a right to counsel, and privilege against self-incrimination, thus bringing adult proceedings into juvenile court [58,72] and asserting the right to due process of children charged with delinquency [74]. *In Re Winship* [75] required proof beyond a reasonable doubt for delinquency proceedings, further bringing juvenile court procedures closer to those of adult court. The further criminalization of juvenile court was halted by *McKeiver v Pennsylvania* [76], which denied the need for a jury trial in delinquency proceedings [58]. *McKeiver* [76] ruled that although criminal law procedural safeguards belonged in the juvenile courts, some of the informality of the juvenile courts was preserved, because juvenile courts were allowed to remain distinct in nature from adult courts [77].

Gault [73] led to legislative changes such as those in the Colorado Children's Code, the California Juvenile Code, and New Jersey legislation, and a transformation of juvenile court was transformed from a rehabilitative model to an adversarial model [78]. The American Bar Association Joint Commission on Juvenile Justice Standards (1971–1976) recommended drastic changes to the juvenile justice system, such as the abolition of the rehabilitation model, determinate rather than indeterminate sentencing, removal of status offenders from the juvenile justice system, guidelines to regulate disposition of cases, curtailment of the court's authority in abuse and neglect cases, and the phasing out of juvenile correctional facilities [79]. In parallel with the juvenile court's growing resemblance to adult criminal court, the focus on punishment over rehabilitation expanded [72]. A recent exception to this trend is the juvenile death penalty. Although in *Stanford v Kentucky* [80] the death penalty for crimes committed at ages younger than 18 years was allowed, in *Roper v Simmons* [81], the court decided otherwise, declaring capital punishment for juveniles unconstitutional.

Current ideas about the rights of juveniles

In general, children have been viewed as more vulnerable than adults, and a number of "protective" laws have been developed to protect them from their immaturity, lack of judgment, and their limited ability to make critical decisions in a mature manner [63]. These protective laws include child labor laws, protection laws, child support laws, mandatory education laws, safety laws, and child pornography laws. Concepts of children's rights are constantly changing, along with society [82]. Because of their vulnerabilities, and because of the involvement of their parents, the normal child or adolescent is not considered to have the same constitutional rights as adults [63], and this concept lends support to the existence of a separate justice system for juveniles.

Limitations of juvenile decision-making abilities

A rationale for establishing limitations of juveniles' rights can be found in studies of limitations of their decision-making abilities and comprehension of complex abstract legal concepts. Juveniles were found to be more vulnerable to coercion in interrogation settings [83]. Age-dependent factors that affected legally relevant decision-making processes were viewed as a potential threat to the attorney–client relationship and to juveniles' effective participation as trial defendants [84]. A study of students' appreciation of waiving Miranda rights found that although they were able to grasp factual information, their comprehension of the significance of the right to silence was compromised [85]. Emerging knowledge about cognitive and neurobiologic development supports the conclusion that juveniles should not be held to adult standards of criminal responsibility [86,87]. These findings therefore argue against the allocation to juveniles of the same rights as those of adults, because they support the concept that juveniles in the justice system should be afforded greater advocacy and assistance. Another factor that supports a greater degree of paternalism in the juvenile justice setting is comorbidity. A substantial body of literature supports the high prevalence of mental disorders [87–90], substance abuse [60,89–91], learning disorders [92], and medical problems [93] in juvenile justice populations. These comorbid conditions may impair the juvenile's ability to appreciate fully and exercise allotted rights. These findings also lend some support to the concept of a right to health care in juvenile justice settings.

Right to health care and educational programs in juvenile justice settings

Children confined in juvenile corrections institutions are considered to have the right to receive adequate health care, including mental health care. In 1984 the National Commission on Correctional Health Care developed the Standards for Health Services in Juvenile Correctional Facilities to suggest minimum standards to implement this right. The courts intervened to address the standards of care in these settings. *Gary H. v Hegstrom* [94] established the right to treatment for chemical dependency, prompt initial evaluation and monitoring for efficacy and side effects of medications, and adequate mental health resources. *Morales v Turman* [95] found incarcerated youths entitled to adequate infirmary facilities, access to medical staff, sufficient staffing, and freedom from unnecessary medication. *Inmates of Boys' Training School v Affleck* [96] outlined a comprehensive system of medical, psychiatric, and dental care. Juveniles' rights to minimally adequate health care are grounded in the Eighth Amendment's prohibition of cruel or unusual punishment and in the Fourteenth Amendment's prohibition against curtailing liberty without due process of law [52]. In 1989 the Committee on Adolescence of the American Academy of Pediatrics issued a position paper that called on pediatricians to become advocates for improved medical care for incarcerated youths. It further stated that all citizens, including incarcerated youths, have the right to appropriate health care and that such health care is essential to rehabilitation [59]. The right to care for injuries and illness acquired during incarceration was deemed mandatory on the basis of law and morality, and health care providers were called on to become advocates for detained youth [60]. In the 2001 Recommendations for Juvenile Justice Reform,

Hanson [97] argued that incarcerated youth are entitled to educational programs that facilitate their development, rehabilitation, and re-entry into the community.

Summary

Juveniles within the justice system are a vulnerable population with certain age-appropriate fundamental rights. The understanding and implementation of these rights has arisen from advocacy movements, which historically have used moral concepts that, when applied to delinquent youth, resulted in the creation of the juvenile justice system. Through continued practical implementation of moral theory, in the form of ethics, this system continues to develop and provide for the rehabilitation needs of youth and the safety needs of society. Although far from a perfect system, the mechanism for continued growth and development remains in place, in the form of correctional and health care professionals, advocacy organizations, the legal and judicial systems, legislatures, and the juveniles within the system. Law and ethics continue to guide to how these youths and society are served by this complex but useful system.

References

[1] Penn J, Thomas CR. Practice parameter for the assessment and treatment of youth in juvenile detention and correctional facilities. Washington (DC): American Academy of Child and Adolescent Psychiatry; 2005.

[2] Sickmund M. Juveniles in corrections. Juvenile offenders and victims national report series. Washington (DC): US Department of Justice, Office of Justice Programs, Office of Juvenile Justice and Delinquency Prevention; 2004.

[3] Teplin LA, Abram KM, McClelland GM, et al. Psychiatric disorders in youth in juvenile detention. Arch Gen Psychiatry 2002;59:1133–43.

[4] Vermeiren R. Psychopathology and delinquency in adolescents: a descriptive and developmental perspective. Clin Psych Rev 2003;23:277–318.

[5] Bazemore G, Umbreit M. Balanced and restorative justice: prospects for juvenile justice in the 21st century. In: Roberts AR, editor. Juvenile justice sourcebook: past, present, and future. New York: Oxford University Press; 2004. p. 467–509.

[6] Fried CS, Reppucci ND. Criminal decision making: the development of adolescent judgment, criminal responsibility, and culpability. Law Hum Behav 2001;25(1):45–61.

[7] *Kent v United States*, 383 US 541 (1966).

[8] Kruh IP, Brodsky SL. Clinical evaluations for transfer of juveniles to criminal court: current practices and future research. Behav Sci Law 1997;15:151–65.

[9] Griffin P, Torbet P, Szymanski L. Trying juveniles as adults in criminal court: an analysis of state transfer provisions. Washington (DC): US Department of Justice, Office of Justice Programs, Office of Juvenile Justice and Delinquency Prevention; 1998.

[10] Feld BC. Race, youth violence, and the changing jurisprudence of waiver. Behav Sci Law 2001;19:3–22.

[11] Stahl A. Delinquency cases waived to criminal court, 1987–1996. Washington (DC): US Department of Justice, Office of Justice Programs, Office of Juvenile Justice and Delinquency Prevention; 1999.

[12] Austin J, Johnson K, Gregoriou M. Juveniles in adult prisons and jails: a national assessment. Washington (DC): US Department of Justice, Office of Justice Programs, Office of Juvenile Justice and Delinquency Prevention; 2000.
[13] Singer S. Recriminalizing delinquency: violent juvenile crime and juvenile justice reform. Cambridge (UK): Cambridge University Press; 1996.
[14] Fagan J. The comparative advantage of juvenile versus criminal court sanctions on recidivism among adolescent felony offenders. Law Policy 1996;18:77–113.
[15] Snyder H, Sickmund M, Poe-Yamagata E. Juvenile transfers to criminal court in the 1990's: lessons learned from four studies. Washington (DC): US Department of Justice, Office of Justice Programs, Office of Juvenile Justice and Delinquency Prevention; 2000.
[16] Gillespie LK, Norman MD. Does certification mean prison: some preliminary findings from Utah. Juv Fam Court J 1984;35:23–35.
[17] Elliot D, Hatot N, Sirovatka P, editors. Youth violence: a report of the Surgeon General. Washington (DC): US Public Health Service; 2001.
[18] Florida Department of Juvenile Justice. A DJJ success story: trends in transfer of juveniles to adult criminal court. Tallahassee (FL): Florida Department of Juvenile Justice; 2002.
[19] Males M, Macallair D. The color of justice: an analysis of juvenile adult court transfers in California. Washington (DC): US Department of Justice, Office of Justice Programs; 2000.
[20] Poulos TM, Orchowsky S. Serious juvenile offenders: predicting the probability of transfer to criminal court. Crime Delinq 1994;40:3–17.
[21] Grisso T, Miller MO, Sales B. Competency to stand trial in juvenile court. Int J Law Psychiatry 1987;10:1–20.
[22] *Dusky v United States*, 362 US 402 (1960).
[23] Resnick PJ, Noffsinger S. Competency to stand trial and the insanity defense. In: Simon RI, Gold LH, editors. Textbook of forensic psychiatry. Arlington (VA): American Psychiatric Publishing, Inc.; 2004. p. 329–47.
[24] *Wieter v Settle*, 193 F. Supp. 318 (1961).
[25] Melton GB, Petrila J, Poythress NG, et al. Youth psychological evaluations for the courts, a handbook for mental health professionals and lawyers. 2nd edition. New York: Guilford; 1997.
[26] Savitsky JC, Karras D. Competency to stand trial among adolescents. Adolescence 1984; 19(74):349–58.
[27] McKee GR. Competency to stand trial in preadjudicatory juveniles and adults. J Am Acad Psychiatry Law 1998;26(1):89–99.
[28] Grisso T, Steinberg L, Woolard J, et al. Juveniles' competence to stand trial: a comparison of adolescents' and adults' capacities as trial defendants. Law Hum Behav 2003;27(4):333–63.
[29] McKee GR, Shea SJ. Competency to stand trial in family court: characteristics of competent and incompetent juveniles. J Am Acad Psychiatry Law 1999;27(1):65–73.
[30] Baerger DR, Griffin E, Lyons JS, et al. Competency to stand trial in preadjudicated and petitioned juvenile defendants. J Am Acad Psychiatry Law 2003;31:314–20.
[31] Warren JI, Aaron J, Ryan E, et al. Correlates of adjudicative competence among psychiatrically impaired juveniles. J Am Acad Psychiatry Law 2003;31:299–309.
[32] Redding RE, Frost LE. Adjudicative competence in the modern juvenile court. Va J Soc Policy Law 2001;9:353–410.
[33] Grisso T, Schwartz R, editors. On trial. Chicago (IL): University of Chicago Press; 2000.
[34] Schmidt MA, Reppucci ND, Woolard JL. Effectiveness of participation as a defendant: the attorney-juvenile client relationship. Behav Sci Law 2003;21:175–98.
[35] Pierce CS, Brodsky SL. Trust and understanding in the attorney-juvenile relationship. Behav Sci Law 2002;20:89–107.
[36] Cooper DK. Juveniles' understanding of trial-related information: are they competent defendants? Behav Sci Law 1997;15:167–80.
[37] McGaha A, Otto RK, McClaren MD, et al. Juveniles adjudicated incompetent to proceed: a descriptive study of Florida's competence restoration program. J Am Acad Psychiatry Law 2001;29(4):427–37.

[38] Grisso T, Pomicter C. Interrogation of juveniles: an empirical study of procedures, safeguards and rights waiver. Law Hum Behav 1977;1:321–42.
[39] Dodge DC. Due process advocacy. Washington (DC): US Department of Justice, Office of Justice Programs, Office of Juvenile Justice and Delinquency Prevention; 1997.
[40] Grisso T. Juveniles' waiver of rights: legal and psychological competence. New York: Plenum; 1981.
[41] Goldstein NE, Condie LO, Kalbeitzer R, et al. Juvenile offenders' Miranda rights comprehension and self-reported likelihood of offering false confessions. Assessment 2003;10(4):359–69.
[42] Redlich AD, Silverman M, Steiner H. Pre-adjudicative and adjudicative competence in juveniles and young adults. Behav Sci Law 2003;21:393–410.
[43] *In Re KG*, 808 N. E 2004;2d:631.
[44] Sirkin JW. Juvenile competence to stand trial. Legal Digest 2005;33(2):267–8.
[45] Oberlander LB, Goldstein NE, Ho CN. Preadolescent adjudicative competence: methodological considerations and recommendations for practice standards. Behav Sci Law 2001;19:545–63.
[46] Ratner RA. Ethics in child and adolescent forensic psychiatry. Child Adolesc Psychiatr Clin N Am 2002;11:887–904.
[47] Schetky DH. Forensic evaluations of children and adolescents. In: Krause L, Arroyo W, editors. Recommendations for juvenile justice reform. Washington (DC): American Academy of Child and Adolescent Psychiatry Task Force on Juvenile Justice Reform; 2001. p. 19–22.
[48] Mulvey EP, Phelps P. Ethical balances in juvenile justice research and practice. Am Psychol 1988;43(1):65–9.
[49] Wettstein RM. Ethics and forensic psychiatry. Psychiatr Clin North Am 2002;25:623–33.
[50] Appelbaum PS. The parable of the forensic psychiatrist: ethics and the problem of doing harm. Int J Law Psychiatry 1990;13:249–59.
[51] Appelbaum PS. A theory of ethics for forensic psychiatry. J Am Acad Psychiatry Law 1997; 25(3):233–47.
[52] Costello JC, Jameson EJ. Legal and ethical duties of health care professionals to incarcerated children. J Leg Med 1987;8(2):191–263.
[53] Meade MA, Slesnick N. Ethical considerations for research and treatment with runaway and homeless adolescents. J Psychol 2002;136(4):449–63.
[54] Schetky DH. Ethical issues in forensic child and adolescent psychiatry. J Am Acad Child Adolesc Psychiatry 1992;31(3):403–7.
[55] Strasburger LH, Gutheil TG, Brodsky A. On wearing two hats: role conflicts in serving as both psychotherapist and expert witness. Am J Psychiatry 1997;154(4):448–56.
[56] American Academy of Psychiatry and the Law. Ethical guidelines for the practice of forensic psychiatry. Available at: http://www.psych.org/psych_pract/ethics/ppaethics.cfm. Accessed December 15, 2005.
[57] American Academy of Child and Adolescent Psychiatry. Code of ethics. Available at: http://www.aacap.org/CodeOfEthics/CodeOfEthics.pdf. Accessed December 15, 2005.
[58] Fellmeth RC. Child rights and remedies: how the US legal system affects children. Atlanta (GA): Clarity Press; 2002.
[59] American Academy of Pediatrics Committee on Adolescence. Health care for children and adolescents in detention centers, jails, lock-ups, and other court-sponsored residential facilities. Pediatrics 1989;84(6):1118–20.
[60] Morris RE, Harrison EA, Knox GW, et al. Health risk behavioral survey from 39 juvenile correctional facilities in the United States. J Adolesc Health 1995;17:334–44.
[61] Appelbaum PS. In the wake of AKE: The ethics of expert testimony in an advocate's world. Bull Am Acad Psychiatry Law 1987;15(1):15–25.
[62] Scott ES, Repucci ND, Woolard JL. Evaluating adolescent decision making in legal contexts. Law Hum Behav 1995;19(3):221–44.
[63] Healey JM. The legal rights of minors in the health care process II. Conn Med 1982;43(11):751.
[64] Lynch A. Ethics of research involving children. Ann R Coll Physicians Surg Can 1992;25(6): 371–2.

[65] Claveirole A. Listening to young voices: challenges of research with adolescent mental health service users. J Psychiatr Ment Health Nurs 2004;11:253–60.
[66] Munir K, Earls F. Ethical principles governing research in child and adolescent psychiatry. J Am Acad Child Adolesc Psychiatry 1992;31(3):408–14.
[67] Crespi TD. Restraint and seclusion with institutionalized adolescents. Adolescence 1990; 25(100):825–9.
[68] Kraus L, Morris R. Seclusion and restraint standards in juvenile corrections. In: Krause L, Arroyo W, editors. Recommendations for juvenile justice reform. Washington (DC): American Academy of Child and Adolescent Psychiatry Task Force on Juvenile Justice Reform; 2001. p. 44–6.
[69] Gulotta KC. Factors affecting nursing practice in a correctional health care setting. J Prison Jail Health 1986–7;6(1):3–22.
[70] Holt C. The correctional officer's role in mental health treatment of youthful offenders. Issues Ment Health Nurs 2001;22:173–80.
[71] *Ex parte Crouse*, 4 Whart. 9 (PA 1839).
[72] Reppucci ND. Adolescent development and juvenile justice. Am J Community Psychol 1999; 27(3):307–26.
[73] *In re Gault*, 387 US 1 (1966).
[74] Polier JW. Prescriptions for reform—doing what we set out to do? Juvenile justice: changes in goals, procedures, and semantics. Bull Am Acad Psychiatry Law 1978;6(2):154–75.
[75] *In Re Winship*, 397 US 358 (1970).
[76] *McKeiver v Pennsylvania*, 403 US 528 (1971).
[77] Curran WJ. Public health and the law: due process, jury trials, and juvenile justice. Am J Public Health 1971;61(9):1901–2.
[78] Snyder PR, Lawrence H, Martin LH. Leaving the family out of family court: criminalizing the juvenile justice system. Am J Orthopsychiatry 1978;48(3):390–3.
[79] Mayo L, Isralowitz R. The American juvenile justice system: an evaluation of standards. Child Welfare 1980;59(3):131–44.
[80] *Stanford v Kentucky*, 492 US 361 (1989).
[81] *Roper v Simmons*, (03–633) 112 S. W. 3d 397 (2005).
[82] Horowitz R. Legal rights of children. Child Adolesc Psychiatr Clin N Am 2002;11:705–17.
[83] Peterson-Badali M, Abramovitch R, Koegl CJ, et al. Young people's experience of the Canadian Youth Justice System: interacting with police and legal counsel. Behav Sci Law 1999;17: 455–65.
[84] Schmidt MG, Reppucci ND, Woolard JL. Effectiveness of participation as a defendant: the attorney-juvenile client relationship. Behav Sci Law 2003;21:175–98.
[85] Wall SM, Furlong M. Comprehension of Miranda rights by urban adolescents with law-related education. Psychol Rep 1985;56:359–72.
[86] Steinberg L, Scott E. Less guilty by reason of adolescence: developmental immaturity, diminished responsibility, and the juvenile death penalty. Am Psychol 2003;58(12):1009–18.
[87] Lewis DO, Yeager CA, Blake P, et al. Ethics questions raised by the neuropsychiatric, neuropsychological, educational, developmental, and family characteristics of 18 juveniles awaiting execution in Texas. J Am Acad Psychiatry Law 2004;32:408–29.
[88] Kashani JK, Manning GW, McKnew DH, et al. Depression among incarcerated delinquents. Psychiatry Res 1980;3(2):185–91.
[89] Teplin LA, Abram KM, McLelland GM, et al. Psychiatric disorders in youth in juvenile detention. Arch Gen Psychiatry 2002;59:1133–43.
[90] Council on Scientific Affairs. Health status of detained and incarcerated youths. JAMA 1990; 263(7):987–91.
[91] Dembo R, Dertke M, Schmeidler J, et al. Prevalence, correlates, and consequences of alcohol and other drug use among youths in a juvenile detention center. J Prison Jail Health 1986–7;6(2): 97–127.
[92] Sikorski JB. Learning disorders and the juvenile justice system. Psychiatr Ann 1991;21(12): 742–7.

[93] Feinstein RA, Lampkin A, Lorish CD, et al. Medical status of adolescents at time of admission to a juvenile detention center. J Adolesc Health 1998;22:190–6.
[94] *Gary H. v Hegstrom*, 831 F.2d 1430 (9th Cir. 1987).
[95] *Morales v Turman*, 430 US 322 (1977).
[96] *Inmates of Boys' Training School v Affleck*, 346 F. Supp. 1354, 1374 (DRI 1972).
[97] Hansen G. Meeting the educational needs of incarcerated youth. In: Krause L, Arroyo W, editors. Recommendations for juvenile justice reform. Washington (DC): American Academy of Child and Adolescent Psychiatry Task Force on Juvenile Justice Reform; 2001. p. 47–51.

ELSEVIER
SAUNDERS

Child Adolesc Psychiatric Clin N Am
15 (2006) 391–406

CHILD AND
ADOLESCENT
PSYCHIATRIC CLINICS
OF NORTH AMERICA

Recent Developments in Mental Health Screening and Assessment in Juvenile Justice Systems

Susan Bailey, MD, PhD[a,*], Theo Doreleijers, MD, PhD[b], Paul Tarbuck, PhD[c]

[a]*University of Central Lancashire, Lancashire, UK*
[b]*Department of Child Psychiatry, VU University Medical Center, Amsterdam, The Netherlands*
[c]*Gardener Unit, Bolton, Salford, and Trafford Mental Health National Health Service Trust, Prestwich, Manchester, UK*

Developments within health care services for young offenders have traditionally lagged behind those for general child and adolescent populations [1]. Well-established fundamental underlying principles apply in screening, assessment, and case management of all young people who are experiencing mental illness or distress, wherever they may be. Given the transitional nature of adolescence, any assessment of mental health must involve a consideration of the presence or absence of illness or disorder and evaluation of various components of development. Formal systems of classification of psychiatric disorder are invaluable for both clinical practice and research purposes and are crucial to individual case management in an era of evidence-based clinical decision making. Both the International Classification of Diseases, tenth edition [2] and the *Diagnostic and Statistical Manual of Mental Disorders, fourth edition* [3] allow a multiaxial approach to classification, permitting different aspects of an adolescent's problems to be recorded separately without requiring an artificial judgment about the primacy of each. As described elsewhere in this volume, comorbidity occurs frequently.

Overall the domains of mental disorder most relevant to juvenile justice populations are the mood disorders, including major depression and bipolar dis-

* Corresponding author. Gardener Unit, Bolton, Salford, and Trafford Mental Health National Health Service Trust, Bury New Road, Prestwich, Manchester M25 3BL, UK.

E-mail address: Nathan.Whittle@gardener.bstmht.nhs.uk (S. Bailey).

doi:10.1016/j.chc.2005.12.004

orders; anxiety disorders and posttraumatic stress disorder; substance-related disorders; disruptive behavior disorders such as attention deficit hyperactivity disorder, oppositional defiant disorder, and conduct disorder; and psychoses such as schizophrenia (also including adolescent precursors of psychotic conditions that can include a prodromal stage featuring many of the symptoms of other disorders) [4].

The following section describes a developing range of screening and assessment tools for use in the specific field of child and adolescent forensic mental health.

Screening and assessment

Screening is the identification of unrecognized problems in apparently well persons through procedures that can be applied rapidly and inexpensively [5,6]. A screening test is essentially a filter system to identify individuals who require further detailed assessment. A good mental health screening program should identify recognized and important problems with a test that is simple, safe, acceptable, and low in cost to administer. Screening for mental health should be conducted in the context of adequate treatment facilities with recognized benefits to the individual. The screening process is similar to triage in a medical setting where incoming patients are individually classified according to the level of urgency. Like triage, screening is useful in systems that have limited resources.

Even the better instruments used to screen youth's mental disorders have major limitations if applied to routine screening of the young people who come into contact with the juvenile justice system. Many require specialist clinical skills, are lengthy to administer, or require extensive information from other informants such as parents or teachers. Other instruments fail to cover important relevant problems for this specific population (eg, substance abuse or suicide risk). One of the keys to developing a screening tool is to consider the most desirable psychometric properties. Ideally, a good screening test should have a high sensitivity (a measure of the true positives: correctly identifying disordered persons as disordered) and high specificity (a measure of true negatives: correctly identifying not-disordered persons as not disordered). In practice, however, there must be a trade off between an acceptable level of sensitivity and the numbers of false positives a system can deal with. Within this context it is important not to flood limited resources with a high number of false screen positives but it is also essential to keep the number of false negatives to a minimum, especially for youngsters who have serious conditions such as depressive disorders or suicidal intent.

Assessment strives to create a comprehensive individualized picture of the youngster to establish the presence or absence of mental illness or needs among screened young people to determine how disorders manifest in that individual and focus on recommendations for differential diagnosis or some specific intervention. Such assessments usually take more than 30 minutes to administer and are informed and supplemented with clinical interviews and past records from other agencies. Administration does not necessarily have to be performed by child mental health specialists, but anyone undertaking such assessment must have considerable training and expertise. Inevitably, increased costs are associated with the complexity and with greater depth and breadth of enquiry of tests used for assessment as compared with tools used for screening.

Screening and assessment instruments in clinical (nonforensic) settings

In generic child and adolescent mental health services, checklists, rating scales, questionnaires, and (semi-)structured interview schedules have been devised to improve the reliability and validity of information and observation used in diagnostic assessment. In general, adolescents report more reliably about internalizing disorders, including suicidal thoughts and gestures, whereas parents and caregivers report more reliably about externalizing disorders. In generic child and adolescent mental health services populations, a youngster's abnormal behavior can usually be recognized with sufficient accuracy for routine screening purposes by a brief symptom/behavioral checklist such as the Rutter A scale [7] or the Child Behavior Checklist [8]. The Strengths and Difficulties Questionnaire [9,10] is a newer instrument that has the merit of being shorter than the Child Behavior Checklist. More specific instruments such as the Conners' Parent and Teacher Questionnaires [11] have shown particular value in identifying attention deficit hyperactivity disorder and evaluating response to pharmacologic treatment of children and young adolescents who have attention deficit hyperactivity disorder.

Instruments for clinical diagnostic assessment include a number of highly structured interviews, such as the Diagnostic Interview for Children and Adolescents [12] and the Diagnostic Interview Schedule for Children [13], and semistructured instruments that require greater clinical interpretation and thus greater training to ensure reliability. The most widely used semistructured interview is the Schedule for Affective Disorders and Schizophrenia for School Age Children [14]. In addition, assessment of family relationships is important, as is the developmental anamnesis and, indicated when specific dysfunction exists, (neuro)psychologic tests. Detailed description of their construction and performance is outside the scope of this article. Readers are directed to Gowers [15].

Screening and assessment in forensic child and adolescent contexts

In the forensic clinical field where written communication between (often non–mental health) disciplines is common, a commonly understood language of reliable and valid diagnoses is important. In forensic settings, assessing adolescents who have a mental health problem is beset with obstacles. The fear for being sentenced on the basis of their own information can make suspected adolescents reticent. They may perceive forensic experts as part of the court process rather than as professionals who might be able to provide help. Similarly, they may view professionals in the same way they view other adults (eg, parents and teachers) with whom they have had difficulty in sustaining positive relationships. In any assessment, the interviewer needs to strike a balance between engagement and the need to elicit information. Another important aspect is the instability of adolescents' emotions from day to day, especially in the context of incarceration [16] where emotional reactions may be seen as a real expression of fear and helplessness.

In the United States and Europe, recent studies of young offenders have been performed using large samples across custody and community settings with clear definitions of mental disorders and reliable measures of adolescent psychopathology [16–21]. Developmental psychopathology [22,23] has enabled clinicians to understand better how mental disorders in adolescence emerge, evolve, and change in a developmental context. Grisso and colleagues [24] point to four conceptual aspects of mental disorders in the forensic adolescent population that should be taken into account when screening for and assessing disorders (and the subsequent trajectory of the disorders into adulthood, including links with violence, delinquency, and early onset psychosis). The concepts are age relativity, discontinuity, comorbidity, and demographic differences.

Age relativity

Developmental psychopathologists delineate symptoms of disorder if they deviate from average behaviors of children and youth at a particular developmental stage and, importantly, if they lead to psychosocial problems in the context of the developmental period [25,26]. In juvenile justice, age is a critical factor in establishing criminal responsibility and in the appropriate placement of young persons who are deemed to require incarceration. These factors vary from jurisdiction to jurisdiction. For example legal responsibility in The Netherlands starts at 12 years of age and in the United Kingdom at 10 years. This variety has implications for the design of instruments, applicability across countries, and comparability of samples.

Discontinuity

Cicchetti and Rogosch [25] use two concepts to iterate complex pathways in the development and remission of disorders during childhood and adolescence that must be considered in every forensic assessment. Equifinality means that disorders of different origins can lead to the same outcomes and is best exemplified in adolescents who have severe depression who may not necessarily have presented with the same problems in childhood but who have similar clinical presentations in their adolescent years. Multifinality refers to clinical presentations with similar starting points leading to different disorders [27]. Because the expression of symptoms and disorders may change over time, repetitive assessment is a requirement. Particularly in severe cases, carrying out diagnostic assessments at different important decision-points may be needed.

Comorbidity

Comorbidity means that youngsters meet criteria for more than one disorder. Comorbidity more common in delinquents than in the general population [19,28,29], with some disorders such as conduct disorder, depression, and substance misuse frequently co-occurring [18]. The complexity of comorbidity in youth in juvenile justice is discussed elsewhere in this issue.

Demographic differences

A complex range of factors influences the varying rates of mental disorders across communities and settings. Arrest patterns, for instance, vary from city to city, from neighborhood to neighborhood, and from decade to decade. Mental disorder is more prevalent in children and adolescents who live in poverty [30]. Differences in response related to cultural backgrounds (across ethnic backgrounds and also across the diverse range of adolescent subcultures) need much more investigation.

Prevalences of mental disorders among juvenile offenders may differ substantially at the different stages of their involvement with the juvenile justice system. Doreleijers [31] demonstrated that the rates of mental disorder in youth varied depending on the severity of their involvement with the juvenile justice system: 30% in arrested adolescents, 65% in adolescents brought before the court, 70% in adolescents having an assessment on request of the court, and 90% or in those who were sentenced to detention or forced treatment.

Pathways of care and the juvenile justice system

For the benefit of young persons in juvenile justice system, it is crucial to develop clear pathways of care. Juvenile justice is a high-volume system, which makes clear logistics necessary. Early identification of mental health needs may result in diversion from custody by using community services rather than adjudication and derive economic benefit by affording noncustodial disposal. Nonetheless a significant number of young persons progress to pretrial assessment, albeit from the home or a residential-care setting.

Preadjudication dispositions should be informed therefore by best available screening and assessment processes. In this context specific tools may be used to derive markers of psychopathology and of ongoing risk to self and others as well as to address medicolegal questions posed by the criminal judicial system including assessment on disposition, matters of public protection, treatment for mental disorders, and need for security and likelihood of recidivism.

For those detained in prison, a first-look screen must determine if urgent problems (such as suicidal intent or consequences of substance use) require immediate attention; a detailed diagnostic assessment of the young person may take a longer period of time and continue as the youngster moves from one institution to another. Later critical transitions, for which an additional screening may be useful, include re-entry into the community, assessment of readiness for re-entry, mental health planning for integrated continuing care postdetention as part of a multiagency re-entry strategy, and, where necessary, community residential programs monitoring emotion or reactions, especially where the young person is returning to stressful conditions such as a troublesome family.

Specific screening and assessment instruments for juvenile justice youth

In this section, four different instruments are discussed in detail. The first two instruments discussed are screening instruments employed in youth entering the juvenile justice system. The third is an interview-based first-line instrument administered to delinquent youth referred after arrest to the Dutch Child Protection Board (CPB). It is used for screening psychopathology and for writing a concise report for the juvenile court. The fourth is a new and promising avenue in forensic assessment, namely needs assessment, and provides detail on a recently developed needs-assessment instrument for use in adolescents.

Massachusetts Youth Screening Instrument–version 2

The Massachusetts Youth Screening Instrument–version 2 (MAYSI-2) was developed between 1994 and 2002. Continued work between 2003 and 2005 resulted in updated user's manuals and developed norms with regard to gender, age, and ethnicity. It is now used in the United States with data on outcomes for forensic youth mental health services [32–34]. The MAYSI-2 consists of a brief self-report inventory (52 questions) that can be administered to youths at entry or any transitional placement point in the juvenile justice system. It is designed to identify youths experiencing thoughts, feelings, or behaviors that may be indicative of mental disorders or acute emotional crises requiring immediate attention. Used with boys and girls aged 12 to 17 years, administration and scoring require about 10 to 15 minutes on yes/no responses. Items deal with the past few months on six of the scales and ever-in-the-whole-life for one scale. The seven scales include alcohol/drug use, anger/irritability, depressed/anxious mood, somatic complaints, suicidal ideation, thought disturbance, and traumatic experiences. Factor analyses performed on the evolving tool led to the thought disturbance scale for use with boys only; the factor analysis for girls did not produce a coherent factor of items that could be interpreted as indicators of thought disturbance [35].

Internal consistency reliability and validity has been established for MAYSI-2. Younger adolescents score the same or higher than older adolescents on most scales but score lower on alcohol/drug use [36]. Girls score higher than boys on most scales [36]. The instrument's initial reliability and internal consistency have been affirmed [37]. MAYSI-2 scores tended to be higher for white non-Hispanic youths than for youths of ethnic minority backgrounds [36,38]. These findings are consistent with reports of prevalence of mental health disorders in young offenders [19,39].

Reported benefits in surveys of nonspecialist users of MAYSI-2 include ease of administration, relevance of scale content, perceived meaningfulness of results, and low cost of the instrument. A commonly perceived limitation was the lack of an inbuilt mechanism for judging when young people may be under- or over-reporting their problems.

The Youth Justice Board Screening Questionnaire Interview for Adolescents

In 2003 the youth justice government agency in the United Kingdom, the Youth Justice Board, commissioned the development of a mental health screening tool to sit along side the extant comprehensive psychosocial and criminological baseline assessment tool, ASSETT, to be used with every young person aged 10 to 17 years having contact with the youth justice system. Therefore, the Youth Justice Board Screening Questionnaire Interview for Adolescents (SQIfA) was developed. The SQIfA consists of three brief sections: section A asks the young person direct questions in the areas of depressive symptoms, anxiety, reaction to severe trauma/stress, deliberate acts of self-harm, and alcohol and drug misuse; section B asks about direct contacts with child and adolescent mental health services and about past illness and interventions; section C is observational with questions to be answered by the interviewer concerning hyperactivity and possible psychotic symptoms. The SQIfA is designed to be repeatable as health needs change over time. Any positive score in the problem areas or previous contacts with psychiatric services would indicate a need of more extensive assessment. In a validity and reliability study, the psychometric properties of three brief screening tools were compared in an adolescent offending population against a diagnostic semistructured interview assessment of mental health needs, the Salford Needs Assessment Schedule for Adolescents [40]. The three tools used in the study were the Strengths and Difficulties Questionnaire [9,10]; the MAYSI-2 [32], and the new SQIfA [41]. Young people aged 10 to 18 years, on a variety of community- and custody-based orders encompassing the whole range of frequency and severity of offending, were included in the study; both males and females were recruited. The study showed that the Strengths and Difficulties Questionnaire exhibited low sensitivity and high specificity within this population, whereas the MAYSI-2 had a high sensitivity but low specificity. The SQIfA demonstrated both moderately good sensitivity and specificity. Therefore, it is now recommended that all young people who enter the British juvenile justice system should be screened using the SQIfA; those identified as being at risk will have a more detailed mental health assessment.

Basic Protection Board Examination

In The Netherlands, police officers who register minors because of serious delinquent behavior are legally obliged to refer them (except from referral to the public prosecutor's office) to the CPB, where social workers perform a psychosocial assessment. The role of these social workers is to inform the judicial authorities (public prosecutor's office and investigative magistrate) about the need for intervention and treatment and to make suggestions about judicial follow-up procedures. In the more severe cases, when the young person is detained at the police office (for a maximum of 3 days when over 12 years old, after which an initial hearing must take place), the assessment is conducted in the police station [42].

In the late 1990s, the lack of uniformity of the traditionally nonstructured psychosocial assessments by CPB workers was found to result too often in unfounded recommendations for intervention and in unspecific referral for a more detailed forensic examination. Therefore, the CPB management had an instrument developed that would standardize CPB assessments and improve their quality. This instrument is the Basis Raads Onderzoek (Basic Protection Board Examination, or BARO). The BARO aims at identifying psychopathology while also describing the living circumstances of the young offender. The BARO covers nine domains of problems and functioning, including:

1. Delinquent behavior
2. Physical development
3. Psychosocial development
4. Functioning within the family
5. School functioning
6. Leisure-time functioning
7. Externalizing problems
8. Internalizing problems
9. Environmental conditions

Each of these domains contains several questions that can be administered to the young person, the parents/caregivers, and, where possible, the teacher. Item responses on these questions are weighted to obtain an overall domain score ranging from "no concern" to "very much concern." For each domain, the assessor must indicate what information sources were used for making the weighted scores. In addition, the BARO provides a severity index (combined Y and P index) that is empirically based on five questions answered by the young offender (Y-index) and five questions answered by their parents (P-index).

The final page of the BARO contains a decision tree that allows the CPB workers to come to a conclusion in a standardized way. The BARO also proposes the format for the subsequent report (maximum of four pages). This format is now used in CPB reports across The Netherlands and was found to make the procedures for screening and assessment more transparent.

A validation study involving 295 young offenders showed that the BARO has good psychometric properties and that the discriminative validity is good-to-excellent for predicting the presence of psychopathology [43]. Information obtained from both the young person and the parents was found to be more reliable than information from the young person alone. Receiver operator curve estimation has shown that the two primary screening outcome scores (Y and

P index and domain score) have good validity for assessing the presence of psychopathology. The practical usefulness of the BARO has been examined through interviews with the CPB workers [44] who considered the BARO to be a valuable first-line screening/assessment instrument for young offenders. Recently, the BARO-R has been translated into English, Finnish, German, and Russian [45,46].

Needs assessment

Needs assessment may have advantages over more traditional ways of diagnosing disorders, mainly because this method also indicates whether specific conditions need attention and intervention. Especially in delinquent youth characterized by multiple problems, such an approach may carry substantial advantage. A health care need should be distinguished from a general need. One definition of a health care need is "the ability to benefit in some way from (health) care" [41]. Another is "a need is a cardinal (significant) problem that can benefit from an intervention that is not being offered" [47]. Other definitions focus on who makes the judgment of need. Researchers have refined both individual and population needs-assessment methods to take into account the different perspectives of clients, caregivers, and professionals [48–51].

Needs assessment and risk assessment are two separate but intertwined processes. Assessment of danger to others and the need to address this problem is at the center of legislative and policy decision making. The attention of the public and media are focused on this area. Risk assessment has a theory and methodology separate from needs assessment. It combines statistical data with clinical information in a way that integrates historical variables, current crucial variables, and the contextual or environmental factors. Some of these clinical and contextual factors are potential areas of need. Therefore needs assessment may both inform and be a response to the risk-assessment process [52,53]. The reciprocal process can be termed "risk management" when accurate information about the risk assessment, combined with recurrent needs assessment, leads to risk-management procedures. A recurrent needs-assessment and risk-assessment process should identify changes in problem areas, thus leading to monitoring or intervention as part of risk management. Core to this assessment are appropriate mental health screening tools and processes that are available to the young person at any point in the system.

Salford Needs Assessment Schedule for Adolescents

There is little specific literature about needs-assessment instruments for adolescent offenders [54–56]. Questionnaire-based instruments do not usually collect sufficient information to conduct a comprehensive needs assessment. Therefore, the initiative was taken to develop an interview-based instrument [40]. Because developing a new interview-based assessment instrument is a lengthy process, an adult needs-assessment instrument was adapted to construct the Salford Needs

Assessment Schedule for Adolescents [40]. It most closely follows the design of the Cardinal Needs Schedule [47], which is widely used with adult populations and has well-established reliability and validity. It covers areas of functioning relevant to adolescents; each area is independent and can be omitted if not relevant. The psychometric properties (test–retest and interrater reliability) were described as acceptable-to-good [40]. Content categories include:

1. Self-care skills
2. Cooking and dietary skills
3. Physical/health problems
4. Educational attendance
5. Educational performance
6. Weekday occupation
7. Social relations
8. Family difficulties
9. Cultural identity
10. Destructive behavior
11. Aggression to persons
12. Oppositional defiant behavior
13. Sexually inappropriate behavior
14. Substance/alcohol abuse
15. Depressed mood
16. Self-harm
17. Psychologic problems (anxiety, obsessions, eating/anorexia, hyperactivity/attention problems)
18. Hallucinations, paranoid ideation
19. Leisure activities
20. Living situation
21. Benefits, money

The process of rating need status is shown in Figs. 1 and 2, which outline the assessment, the algorithmic decision-making process, and the resulting need categories. A clinical version is available, as is a shortened form (including a screening questionnaire) developed for use by Youth Offending Teams (Kroll L, Woodham A, Rothwell J, et al, unpublished data, 2002).

Two recent studies in the United Kingdom have used the Salford Needs Assessment Schedule for Adolescents. One study adopted a cross-sectional design (Youth Justice Board Website [http://www.youth-justice-board.gov.uk]) [57], investigating 301 young offenders, 151 in custody and 150 in the community, in six geographically representative areas across England and Wales. Each young person was interviewed to obtain demographic information and mental health and social needs. Participants were found to have high levels of need in a number of different areas, including mental health (31%), education/work (48%), and social relationships (36%), but these needs often were unmet because they were not recognized. One in five young offenders were identified as having mental retardation (IQ<70).

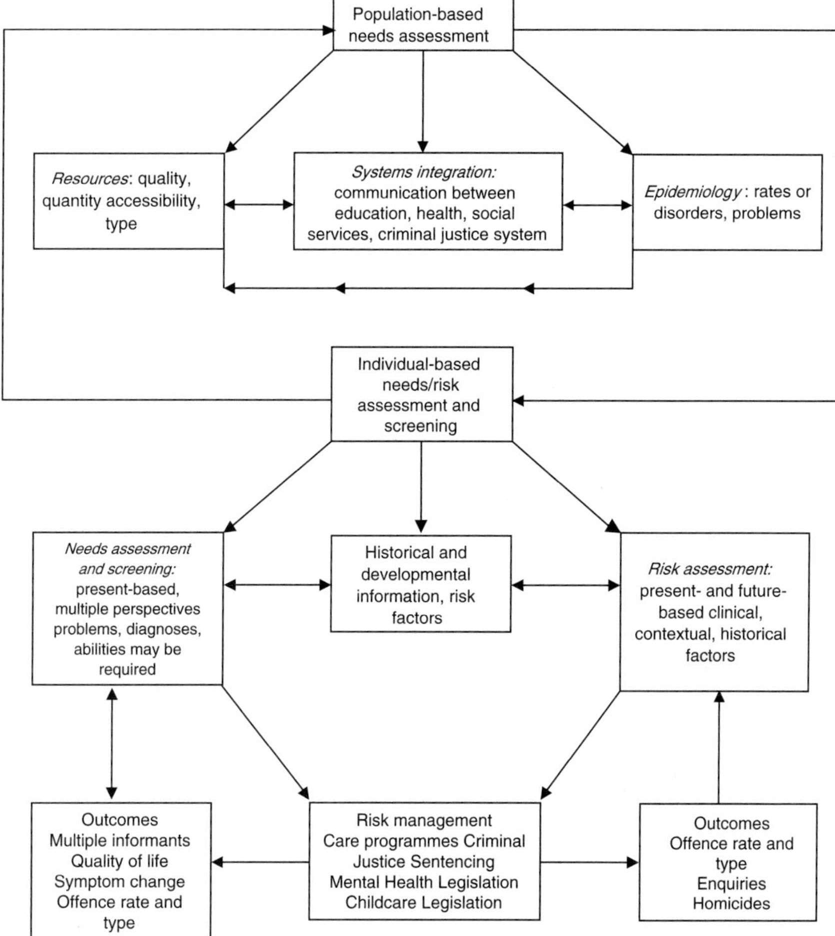

Fig. 1. Relationship between various screening, need assessment, risk assessment, and management approaches in juvenile justice systems. (*From* Kroll L. Needs assessment in adolescent offenders. In: Bailey S, Dolan M, editors. Adolescent forensic psychiatry. London: Arnold Publishing; 2004. p. 24; with permission.)

These findings emphasize the importance of structured needs assessment within custody and community settings as part of a care program approach that should improve continuity of care [57].

The second study was a longitudinal prospective study, now in its sixth year of follow-up, aimed at describing the psychosocial outcomes, including needs, of boys in secure detention and at establishing possible correlations with criminal outcomes. Although the average number of needs requiring an intervention at follow-up (mean, 3.4) was much lower than before admission to secure care (mean, 8.2), not all needs of the juveniles were met. Educational and occupational needs were particularly well dealt with, but often many mental health

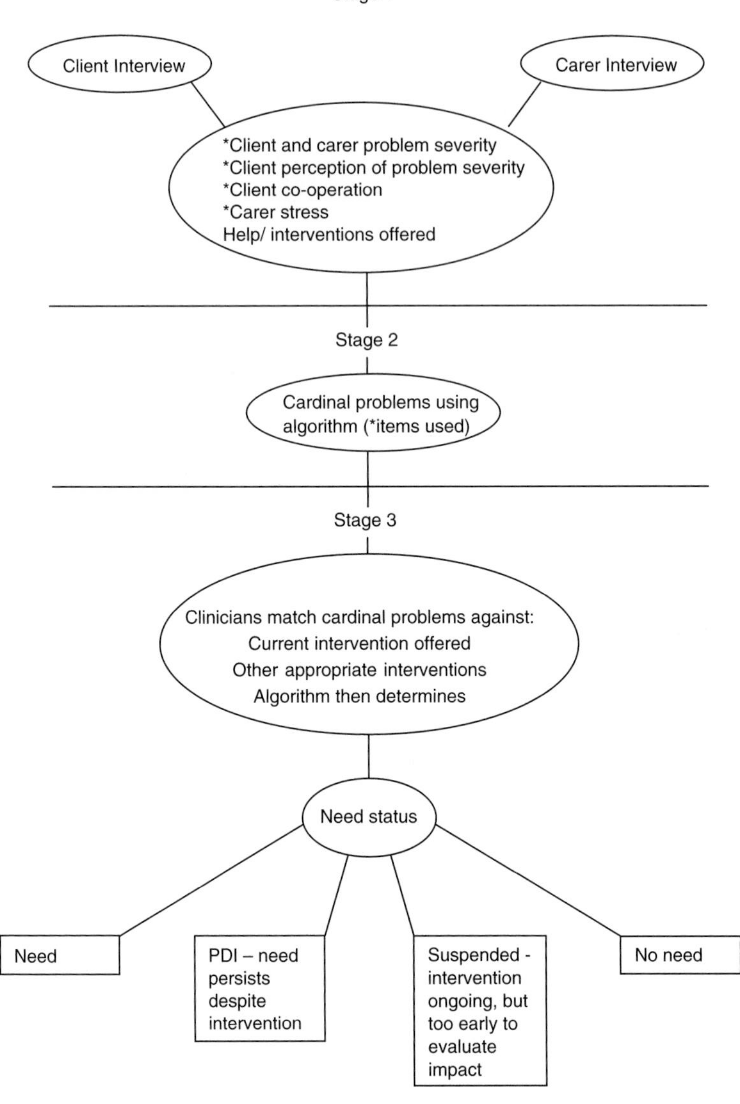

Fig. 2. The Salford Needs Assessment Schedule for adolescents. (*From* Kroll L. Needs assessment in adolescent offenders. In: Bailey S, Dolan M, editors. Adolescent forensic psychiatry. London: Arnold Publishing; 2004. p. 21; with permission.)

problems had persisted or worsened. For example, at follow-up 31% still had a need for treatment of substance abuse, a significant increase compared with when they were in secure care (21%). Although a high rate of mental health problems were present both initially and at follow-up, mental health problems did not predict criminal outcome. The mental health needs of this group were not static but changed over time and with changing circumstances. Therefore, it may be concluded that services need to be designed to meet these changing needs [16,18].

Summary and future directions for practice and research

Although developments within health care services for young offenders have traditionally lagged behind those for general child and adolescent populations, a better understanding of the characteristics of young offenders and their mental health problems is now emerging. This understanding is being accompanied by the development of dedicated screening and assessment instruments that have significant validity and reliability. Although as yet there are no internationally recognized definitions of concepts associated with screening and assessment, the sharing of information and studies is stimulating debate and understanding. Of particular note is work in The Netherlands, the United Kingdom, and United States. Further work is required to examine the needs of the juvenile justice population that may then guide appropriate investment in under-resourced services.

Poor outcome results of treatment studies on offenders across the United States and Europe has encouraged a culture of therapeutic nihilism that is changing only slowly. Using a needs approach could offer new approaches of investigating treatment effects by combining observational and intervention studies assessing services, treatments, and individual characteristics. To investigate the results, a combination of qualitative and quantitative research methods should be used [58]. This type of program and research has been proposed for use in violent adult offenders [59], particularly embedding psychologic treatments within the system being studied and collaborating closely with those involved directly with the offenders.

References

[1] Bailey S. Treatment of delinquents. In: Rutter M, Taylor E, editors. Child and adolescent psychiatry: modern approaches. 4th edition. Oxford (UK): Blackwell Scientific; 2002. p. 1019–37.
[2] World Health Organization. The ICD 10: classification of mental and behavioural disorders. Clinical descriptions and diagnostic guidelines. World Health Organization: Geneva (Switzerland): World Health Organization; 1992.
[3] American Psychiatric Association. Diagnostic and statistical manual of mental disorders. 4th edition. Washington (DC): American Psychiatric Association; 1994.
[4] Vreugdenhil C, Vermeiren R, Wouters CFJM, et al. Psychotic symptoms among male adolescent detainees in The Netherlands. Schizophr Bull 2004;30(1):73–86.
[5] Wasserman GA, Jensen PS, Ko SJ, et al. Mental health assessments in juvenile justice: report on the Consensus Conference. J Am Acad Child Adolesc Psychiatry 2003;42(7):752–61.
[6] Scholte EM, Doreleijers TAH. Screening of serious and violent juvenile offenders. Update. In: Tonry M, Bijleveld C, editors. Crime and justice. Chicago: Chicago University Press; 2005.
[7] Rutter M. A children's behaviour questionnaire for completion by teachers: preliminary findings. J Child Psychol Psychiatry 1967;8:1–11.

[8] Achenbach TM, Edeibrock CS. Manual for the Child Behaviour Checklist and Revised Child Behaviour Profile. Burlington (VT): University of Vermont; 1983.
[9] Goodman R. The Strength and Difficulties Questionnaire: a research note. J Child Psychol Psychiatry 1997;38:581–6.
[10] Bourdon KH, Goodman R, Rae DS, et al. The Strengths and Difficulties Questionnaire: US normative data and psychometric properties. J Am Acad Child Adolesc Psychiatry 2005;44(6): 557–64.
[11] Conners CK. Recent drug studies with children. J Learn Disabil 1971;4:467–83.
[12] Herjanic B, Reich IN. Development of a structured diagnostic interview for children: agreement between child and parent on individual symptoms. J Abnorm Child Psychol 1982;10:307–24.
[13] Costello EJ, Edeibrook C, Costello AJ. Validity of the NIMH Diagnostic Interview Schedule for Children: a comparison between psychiatric and paediatric referrals. J Abnorm Child Psychol 1985;13:579–95.
[14] Orvaschel H, Pulg-Antich J, Chambers W, et al. Retrospective assessment of pre-pubertal major depression with the Kiddie-SADS-E. J Am Acad Child Psychiatry 1982;21:695–707.
[15] Gowers SG. Assessing adolescent mental health. In: Bailey S, Dolan M, editors. Adolescent forensic psychiatry, vol. 1. London: Arnold Publishing; 2004. p. 3–13.
[16] Kroll L, Rothwell J, Bradley D, et al. Mental health needs of boys in secure care for serious or persistent offending: a prospective, longitudinal study. Lancet 2002;359(9322):1975–9.
[17] Kazdin AE. Adolescent development, mental disorders, and decision making of delinquent youths. In: Grisso T, Schwartz G, editors. Youth on trial: a developmental perspective on juvenile justice. Chicago: University of Chicago Press; 2000. p. 33–65.
[18] Harrington RC, Kroll L, Rothwell J, et al. Psychosocial needs of boys in secure care for serious or persistent offending. J Child Psychol Psychiatry 2005;46(8):859–66.
[19] Teplin LA, Abram KM, McClelland GM, et al. Psychiatric disorders in youth in juvenile detention. Arch Gen Psychiatry 2002;59(12):1133–43.
[20] Vermeiren R. Psychopathology and delinquency in adolescents: a descriptive and developmental perspective. Clin Psychol Rev 2003;23(2):277–318.
[21] Vreugdenhil C, Doreleijers TAH, Vermeiren R, et al. Psychiatric disorders in a representative sample of incarcerated boys in The Netherlands. J Am Acad Child Adolesc Psychiatry 2004; 43(1):97–104.
[22] Garmezy N, Rutter M. Stress, coping, and development in children. New York: McGraw-Hill; 1983.
[23] Cicchetti D. The emergence of developmental psychopathology. Child Dev 1984;55(1):1–7.
[24] Grisso T, Vincent G, Seagrave D. Mental health screening and assessment in juvenile justice. New York: Guilford Press; 2005.
[25] Cicchetti D, Rogosch FA. A developmental psychopathology perspective on adolescence. J Consult Clin Psychol 2002;70(1):6–20.
[26] Mash EJ, Dozois DJA. Child psychopathology: a developmental-systems perspective. In: Mash EJ, Barkley RA, editors. Child psychopathology. 2nd edition. New York: Guilford Press; 2003. p. 3–71.
[27] Coll GC, Kagan J, Resnick JS. Behavioural inhibition in young children. Child Dev 1984; 55:1005–19.
[28] Harrington RC, Bailey S. Prevention of antisocial personality disorder: mounting evidence on optimal timing and methods [editorial]. Crim Behav Ment Health 2004;14:75–81.
[29] Doreleijers TAH, Scholte EM, Vermeiren R. Co-occurrence of serious and violent delinquency with other problems. In: Tonry M, Bijleveld C, editors. Crime and justice. Chicago: Chicago University Press; 2006.
[30] Bailey S, Jasper A, Ross K. Social diversity. In: Bailey S, Dolan M, editors. Adolescent forensic psychiatry. London: Arnold Publishing; 2004. p. 181–201.
[31] Doreleijers TAH. Van justitialisering tot onderzoek naar effectiviteit van probleemgestuurde jeugdzorg [From 'justicialising' juvenile offenders to a more evidence based approach]. Tijdschrift voor Criminologie [Dutch Journal of Criminology] 2005;47:38–45.

[32] Grisso TJ, Barnum R. Massachusetts Youth Screening Instrument (MAYSI). Worchester (MA): University of Massachusetts Medical Center; 1998.
[33] Grisso T, Barnum R. Massachusetts Youth Screening Instrument–second version: users manual and technical report. Worcester (MA): University of Massachusetts Medical School; 2000.
[34] Grisso T, Barnum R. Massachusetts Youth Screening Instrument–version 2: user's manual and technical report. Sarasota (FL): Professional Resource Press; 2003.
[35] Grisso T, Barnum R, Fletcher K, et al. Massachusetts Youth Screening Instrument for mental health needs of juvenile justice youths. J Am Acad Child Adolesc Psychiatry 2001;40(5):541–8.
[36] Cauffman E. A statewide screening of mental health symptoms among juvenile offenders in detention. J Am Acad Child Adolesc Psychiatry 2004;43(4):430–9.
[37] Archer RP, Stredny RV, Mason JA. An examination and replication of the psychometric properties of the Massachusetts Youth Screening Instrument–version 2 (MAYSI-2) among adolescents in detention settings. Assessment 2004;11:1–13.
[38] Wasserman GA, McReynolds LS, Ko SJ, et al. Screening for emergent risk and service needs among incarcerated youth: comparing MAYSI-2 and voice DISC-IV. J Am Acad Child Adolesc Psychiatry 2004;43(5):629–39.
[39] Grisso T. Double jeopardy: adolescent offenders with mental disorders. Chicago: University of Chicago Press; 2004.
[40] Kroll L, Woodham A, Rothwell J, et al. Reliability of the Salford Needs Assessment Schedule for adolescents. Psychol Med 1999;29(4):891–902.
[41] Stevens A, Raftery J. Introduction: concepts of need. In: Stevens A, Raftery J, editors. Healthcare needs assessment, vol 1. Oxford (UK): Radcliffe Medical Press; 1994. p. 13–4.
[42] Doreleijers TAH, Spaander M. The development and implementation of the BARO: a new device to detect psychopathology in minors with first police contacts. In: Corrado RR, Roesch R, editors. Multi-problem violent youth. A foundation for comparative research on needs, interventions and outcomes. Washington (DC): IOS Press; 2002.
[43] Doreleijers TAH, Jäger M, van Wijk AP, et al. Screening und Diagnostik bei jugendlichen Sexualstraftätern in den Niederlanden. In: Schläfke D, Hässler F, Fegert JM, editors. Forensische Begutachtung, Diagnostik und Therapie press. Stuttgart (Germany): Schattauer GmbH; 2005. p. 86–95.
[44] van Heerwaarden Y, de Roy E, Slump GJ. Het Basis RaadsOnderzoek (BARO) in de praktijk: een kwaliteitsslag? [First examination by the Child Welfare Council in practice: a quality battle?]. Tijdschrift voor Orthopedagogiek, Kinderpsychiatrie en Klinische Kinderpsychologie 2004;29(1):18–29.
[45] Gutschner D, Doreleijers TAH. Das Screeninginstrument BARO.ch für sozial auffällige Jugendliche. Vierteljahresschrift für Heilpädagogik und ihre Nachbargebiete 2004;73:191–202.
[46] Gutschner D, Doreleijers TAH. Das Screeninginstrument BARO.ch zur Erstbeurteilung von jugendlichen Straftätern. Zeitschrift für Nervenheilkunde 2004;23:326–31.
[47] Marshall M, Hogg LI, Gath DH, et al. The Cardinal Needs Schedule: a modified version of the MRC Needs for Care assessment schedule. Psychol Med 1995;25:605–17.
[48] Marshall M. How should we measure need? Concept and practice in the development of a standardized assessment schedule. Philoso Psychiatr Psychol 1994;1(1):27–36.
[49] Brewin CR, Wing JK, Mangen SP, et al. Principles and practice of measuring needs in the long-term mentally ill: the MRC Needs for Care assessment. Psychol Med 1987;17:971–81.
[50] Phelan M, Slade M, Thornicroft G, et al. The Camberwell Assessment Need (CAN): the validity and reliability of an instrument to assess the needs of people with severe mental illness. Br J Psychiatry 1995;167:589–95.
[51] Kurtz Z, Thomas R, Bailey S. A study of the demand and needs for forensic child and adolescent mental health services in England and Wales, Mental Health Services of Salford. J Adolesc 1997;21:108–18.
[52] Bailey S, Dolan M. Violence. In: Bailey S, Dolan M, editors. Adolescent forensic psychiatry. London: Arnold Publishing; 2004. p. 16, 213–27.
[53] Bailey S. Violent children: a framework for assessment. Adv Psychiatr Treat 2002b;8:97–106.

[54] Towberman DB. National survey of juvenile needs assessment. Crime Delinq 1992;38(2): 230–8.
[55] McLaney MA, Del-Boca F, Babor T. A validation study of the Problem Oriented Screening Instrument for Teenagers (POSIT). J Ment Health 1994;3:363–76.
[56] Knight JR, Goodman E, Pulerwitz T, et al. Reliability of the Problem Oriented Screening Instrument for Teenagers (POSIT) in adolescent medical practice. J Adolesc Health 2001;29(2): 125–30.
[57] Chitsabesan P, Kroll L, Bailey S, et al. National Study of Mental Health Provision for Young Offenders: part I—The mental health needs of young offenders in custody and in the community. Br J Psychiatry, in press.
[58] Swales J. The National Health Service and the science of evaluation: two anniversaries. Health Trends 1998;38:230–8.
[59] Howells K, Watt B, Hall G, et al. Developing programmes for violent offenders. Leg Criminol Psychol 1997;2(1):117–28.

ELSEVIER
SAUNDERS

Child Adolesc Psychiatric Clin N Am
15 (2006) 407–428

CHILD AND
ADOLESCENT
PSYCHIATRIC CLINICS
OF NORTH AMERICA

Psychopathy and Violence Risk Assessment in Youth

Gina M. Vincent, PhD

Center for Mental Health Services Research, Law and Psychiatry Program, Department of Psychiatry, University of Massachusetts Medical School, 55 Lake Avenue North, WSH 8B-21, Worcester, MA 01655, USA

Clinicians are frequently asked to conduct assessments of delinquents' likelihood of future harm to others as a result of the juvenile justice system's obligation to protect public safety. As Grisso [1] explained, this obligation functions to protect society from the immediate risk of harm from dangerous youth and to reduce recidivism by providing interventions to youths involved with the juvenile justice system. Primarily, these assessments can be relevant for two forms of legal decisions. First, disposition decisions require the court to consider both the most appropriate sanctions and interventions with the best potential for reducing the likelihood of delinquent behaviors in the future. The most dangerous youths should receive the most punitive sanctions and most intensive interventions in the most secure facilities. Second, transfer decisions designed to waive juveniles to adult court generally require evidence about the youth's likelihood of being dangerous to others, treatment amenability, and level of maturity [2]. If a youth is likely to be dangerous and is likely to be resistant to rehabilitation within the juvenile justice system, transfer to adult court is nearly inevitable. The consistent considerations in both transfer and disposition decisions are a youth's danger to others and treatment needs. Thus, to assess the risk of violence, forensic risk evaluators require tools capable of assessing the likelihood of violence in the future, the presence of childhood psychopathology, and the relationship between violence and psychopathology.

Sound empirical evidence from a host of longitudinal studies has established that a small proportion (around 6%) of early male delinquents become chronically antisocial and proceed to commit more than 50% of all crime [3–5]. By

E-mail address: Gina.Vincent@umassmed.edu

doi:10.1016/j.chc.2005.12.001
childpsych.theclinics.com

conducting comprehensive literature reviews [6–8], meta-analyses [9], and longitudinal studies [4,10], researchers have directed considerable attention to the identifying factors that put children and adolescents at highest risk for violent and serious delinquent behavior. Admittedly, there is no absolute consensus regarding the most salient risk factors for violence and antisociality in youth, but in the last decade several risk-assessment and management tools have been developed that integrate the empirical evidence by systematic translation into risk factors [11,12].

Another approach to identifying factors that may influence delinquents' likelihood for aggressive and violent behavior has evolved from consideration of previously established models for assessing the risk of violence in adults; namely, psychopathic personality disorder. Substantial adult research, including meta-analytic and longitudinal studies [13–17], using the Psychopathy Checklist-revised (PCL-R) [17] or its screening version (PCL:SV) [18], has identified psychopathy as the best single predictor of violence available to clinicians today [19]. Adult male psychopaths have an average 5-year violent reoffense rate of approximately 50% compared with the average 20% to 30% violent reoffense rate of nonpsychopathic adult offenders. Indeed, the robust association between adult psychopathy and future acts of violence may compel the conclusion that failure to use the PCL in any assessment of violence risk in an adult male may be unreasonable or unethical [19]. There are concerns about the use of this construct with youth, however. The malleability of the presence and expression of symptoms of psychopathology across early stages of development makes it unclear whether personality disorders even exist before early adulthood [20,21].

This article discusses practices for clinical assessment of the risk of violence conducted to assist with legal decisions in the juvenile justice system. It begins by describing some special considerations for selecting instruments for assessing the risk of violence. The next section summarizes the advantages and disadvantages of the instruments designed for assessing psychopathic traits in youth by describing their development, application, and, to a lesser extent, psychometric properties. The next section summarizes empiric evidence for the association between psychopathic features (as measured by these tools) and serious delinquency and violence in child and adolescent populations. This review is followed by a discussion of the limitations of these instruments and recommendations for the use of indicators of psychopathy in assessing and managing the risk of violence. Finally, the article briefly reviews preferred risk-assessment tools for youth and concludes with some general suggestions for practitioners.

General considerations in assessment of the risk of violence

The goal of assessments of the risk of violence is to target those in highest need of rehabilitation efforts and risk monitoring. Generally, assessors want to use tools with known predictive validity that also are capable of guiding intervention and treatment planning and capturing changes in risk. To make an informed decision about the selection and use of risk-assessment tools for youth, familiarity with the prominent issues in this area, and specifically with approaches to decision making, the nature of risk factors, and developmental malleability, is critical.

The first issue concerns approaches to decision making: clinical or actuarial judgment. Clinical judgment generally refers to unstructured assessments in which risk variables are not necessarily explicit, may not be empirically validated, and demonstrate little value in the prediction of recidivism [22,23]. By contrast, actuarial assessments generally contain items selected empirically based on a known association with a given outcome (eg, reoccurrence of violence) and are scored according to some algorithm to produce a judgment about the likelihood of violence.

The second issue pertains to the nature of risk factors: circumstances or life events that increase an individual's likelihood of engaging in criminal activity. Risk factors and, consequently, items in risk-assessment tools, are either static (eg, past physical abuse) or dynamic (eg, peer group or school performance). Dynamic factors are variable and can be used to guide rehabilitative efforts by targeting influences on antisocial behavior and guiding interventions aimed at changing those factors. Static factors, on the other hand, generally are historical and are difficult if not impossible to change. Some assessment tools also include protective factors, positive circumstances or life events that are generally dynamic and reduce the likelihood of a youth committing crime.

A third approach to violence risk judgments, known as structured professional judgment (SPJ), was developed in response to the limitations of current practices. Structured professional risk-assessment tools are informed by the state of the discipline in clinical theory and empiric research to guide clinical decisions about risk and treatment planning [24]. The intent was to improve clinical judgment by adding structure and to improve actuarial decision making by adding clinical discretion. In this way, the SPJ model draws on the strengths of both the clinical and actuarial (formula-driven) approaches to decision making and attempts to minimize their respective drawbacks [25]. These instruments emphasize prevention rather than prediction. They typically contain both static and dynamic risk factors because they assume that risk is not entirely stable and can change as a result of various factors (eg, treatment quality and quantity, developmental factors, protective factors, and context). SPJ assessment tools are designed to guide clinicians in determining what level of risk management is needed, in which contexts, and at what points in time.

A crucial third issue for assessments of risk for violence and serious offending among youth is the impact of developmental factors on the time frame for which predictions remain accurate. A significant limitation in attempts to identify youth who will become chronic and violent offenders is the inevitably high false-positive rate. Many youth who engage in violent behavior at one stage of development do not continue to do so as their development proceeds. Indeed, at least 50% of children who exhibit pervasive and serious antisocial behavior before age 10 years do not develop into violent adolescents [26,27], and an even greater portion of adolescents committing serious offenses do not develop into antisocial adults [28]. The implication is, if current violent behavior is used as a simple predictor of violence in the future, the prediction will be wrong more often than it is right. For this reason, risk for violence/recidivism should be reassessed frequently, particularly for youth under age 16 years, and preference should be given to assessment tools that can measure changes in risk.

Assessment of youth psychopathy

Psychopathy is a personality disorder that involves distinct interpersonal, affective, and behavioral symptoms [17]. Personality disorder is a disturbance in relating to one's self, others, and the environment that is chronic in nature, typically evident by childhood or adolescence and persisting into middle or late adulthood. Symptoms of personality disorder are rigid, inflexible, and maladaptive ways of relating that are stable across time, situations, and interactions with different people. What distinguishes psychopathy from other personality disorders is its specific symptom pattern. Interpersonally, psychopathic individuals are arrogant, superficial, deceitful, and manipulative; affectively, their emotions are shallow and labile, they are unable to form strong emotional bonds with others, and they are lacking in empathy, anxiety, and guilt; behaviorally, they are irresponsible, impulsive, sensation seeking, and prone to delinquency and criminality [29–31].

For the past 3 decades, a version of the Hare PCL multi-item symptom construct rating scales has been used to inform the discipline about psychopathy in adults. Research using the Hare scales has generated remarkably consistent findings regarding prevalence of psychopathic symptoms and the association of these symptoms with antisocial behavior across samples from a variety of populations [17]. The PCL-R is the standard for clinical forensic assessments of psychopathy, and it is strongly predictive of violence. Because the Hare scales were designed for adult males, the shift in focus to children and adolescents required the development of new measures.

Several instruments have been developed to assess psychopathy or psychopathic traits in children or adolescents. The purpose of these tools varies. Some were designed for clinical use to assist with risk management or early intervention strategies, and others were designed for research purposes only, at least for the present. The assessment methods also vary. There are three main types: expert clinical rating scales, informant rating scales, and self-report scales. Expert clinical rating scales require qualified professionals to make judgments about the presence and severity of symptoms based on examinee interviews and extensive collateral information. Informant rating scales call for ratings of multiple characteristics of an examinee by persons (generally two) related to the examinee. Self-report measures ask examinees to rate their own characteristics using a series of questions. These youth psychopathy measures are reviewed briefly here.

Expert rating scales

Psychopathy Checklist: Youth Version

The Psychopathy Checklist: Youth Version (PCL:YV) [32] is a downward extension of the PCL-R used to provide a dimensional assessment of the prototypical psychopath among adolescents aged 12 to 18 years. Most of the research reported here was based on two previous modifications of the PCL-R for use with adolescents [33].

The PCL:YV should be used to identify "youth who represent a more serious management problem within institutions, who need intensive intervention, and who require more resources for risk management in the community" [32]. Like the PCL-R, the PCL:YV is an expert symptom-rating scale that defines psychopathy along interpersonal, affective, and behavioral symptom clusters. PCL:YV assessments are administered through a 60- to 90-minute semistructured interview and a thorough review of collateral information, including psychosocial histories, juvenile offense records, and institutional records, at a minimum. It comprises 20 items scored on a three-point scale (0 = item does not apply; 1 = item applies somewhat; 2 = item definitely applies) based on each symptom's pervasiveness, severity, and chronicity. For the most part, the item descriptions do not differ from those in the PCL-R, but a few were modified to reflect adolescent experiences and the greater influence of family, peers, and school on their lives. For example, the PCL-R item referring to number of short-term marriages was revised to reflect the stability in interpersonal relationships generally.

The PCL:YV normative sample ($n > 2000$) consisted largely of white males, primarily from secure custody settings or forensic psychiatric facilities, but also included African Americans and youths from probation settings. A small proportion of the sample came from community settings. Only about 12% of the sample was girls. PCL:YV total scores have high interrater reliability ($r = .90–.96$) and internal consistency regardless of the population tested (ie, institutional, probation, or community) [32]. Scores are dimensional, meaning that they represent the level or severity of psychopathic traits, and can be calculated for both total scores and symptom cluster scores. Results of confirmatory factor analytic (CFA) studies suggest the PCL:YV has two valid test structures: (1) the Hare 20-item, four-factor model comprised of interpersonal, affective, impulsive behavioral style and antisocial behavioral dimensions, and (2) a 13-item, three-factor model, which includes the same first three factors but eliminates seven items related to specific antisocial or criminogenic behavior (the antisocial behavior factor). The PCL:YV cannot be used to make categorical classifications of psychopathy or risk for violence based on cutoff scores.

Consistent with findings from adult psychopathy studies, PCL:YV studies have demonstrated strong associations with symptoms of disruptive behavior disorders [34,35], attention-deficit hyperactivity disorder [36], and substance abuse [37]. High-scoring adolescent offenders also seem to have some anomalies in executive functions related to impulsivity [38] and poor interpersonal relations and parental attachment [34].

Generally, few studies have evaluated use of the PCL:YV in female samples. Those that have included girls have not reported results separately by gender. In the PCL:YV test manual, Forth and colleagues [32] reported item and mean score comparisons between males and the approximately 250 girls in the normative sample from various datasets and did not find any differences. They concluded that PCL:YV scores did not seem to be unduly influenced by gender.

Informant rating scales

Antisocial Process Screening Device

The Antisocial Process Screening Device (APSD) [39] is a 20-item informant rating scale designed to detect antisocial processes in children aged 6 to 13 years so that preventative measures can be taken before tendencies lead to crime and other destructive behaviors. Given the questionable validity of children's self-reports, APSD ratings are provided by one parent and one teacher. Like the PCL:YV, the APSD was patterned after the PCL-R, containing 20-items rated on the same three-point scale. The authors adapted each PCL-R item into an analogous behavioral-rating item that was more applicable to children. Items are phrased as statements requiring informants to rate the presence of psychopathic traits, such as whether the child's emotions seem shallow and whether the child seems to keep the same friends. The APSD is a dimensional rating scale: items are scored by comparing parent and teacher ratings and using the higher score on each item.

CFA suggests the APSD fits two valid test structures: (1) a two-factor model comprising a callous-unemotional factor and a second factor reflecting narcissistic traits and conduct problems, and (2) a three-factor model that divides narcissistic traits and conduct problems into separate dimensions [40]. Like the PCL:YV, APSD scores represent the strengths of a child's traits and should not be used to make categorical diagnoses based on a cutoff score. Across studies, the factors have had fair-to-good internal consistency [39]. Correlations between parent and teacher ratings have ranged from .26 to .40 [41,42].

The APSD normative sample consisted of 1120 elementary school children from the third, fourth, sixth, and seventh grades. Recent validation studies have extended its use to children referred to outpatient mental health clinics, and some samples were 50% female [40,43]. There is some evidence that APSD scores do not differ significantly between gender groups [44] but may vary according to ethnicity [41]. In a prospective study of children, Frick and colleagues [45] discovered that callous-unemotional features were relatively stable during childhood, especially for children with callous-unemotional scores falling in the lowest or highest quartiles at age 6 years. APSD scores are associated with symptoms of behavioral disorders, attention deficit hyperactivity disorder [44,46], and impaired emotional processing characterized by hyporesponsiveness to distress cues [47,48]. The APSD may detect a subtype of children who have severe conduct disorder and low susceptibility to anxiety, and the factors have different correlates indicating assessments of distinct traits, the callous-unemotional factor being associated with cognitive and emotional deficits and the conduct problems factor being associated with behavioral dysregulation [49].

Modified Childhood Psychopathy Scale

The original Childhood Psychopathy Scale (CPS) [50] was an informant (parent) behavioral rating scale consisting of 41 items selected from the Childhood Behavior Checklist and the Common Language Version of the California Child Q-set. Lynam [50] selected the 41 items because they were face-valid measures of 13 psychopathic characteristics as defined by the PCL-R. Recently, the CPS was modified (mCPS) by deleting the criminogenic items and adding items pertaining to additional psychopathic characteristics, such as grandiosity and proneness to boredom [51]. Now all items are rated as yes/no, and there is a self-report version in addition to the informant-rater version completed by a caregiver. The mCPS is thought to have a two-factor structure similar to the PCL-R, with factor 1 representing interpersonal and affective characteristics and factor 2 representing behavioral characteristics.

Lynam and colleagues [51] found the factors to have good internal consistency for both the caregiver and self-report measures. The mCPS seems to have reasonable rater reliability, with correlations between parent and self-report ratings being relatively high for total and factor scores [52]. Research with both versions of the CPS scale suggests that the scales are associated in the expected direction, with several variables known to be correlated with psychopathy. For example, secondary analyses of community youths from the Pittsburgh Youth Study sample have reported the CPS to be correlated with tests of impulsivity and early delinquent behavior for 12.5-year-olds [50]. The mCPS seems to be associated with electrodermal hyporesponsivity in 16-year-olds [53] and with measures of the five-factor model of personality in both age cohorts [51].

Some confusion about use of the mCPS remains. One issue is that the composition of the mCPS is unclear because the test has changed across studies. For example, Fung and colleagues [53] defined the mCPS as a 55-item test, which they reduced to 44-items for a self-report version and to 48 items for a parent version. Lynam and colleagues' [51] parent version contained 41 items, and the self-report version contained 37 items. Another source of confusion is the age of the intended target group. The ages of study participants have ranged from middle childhood to late adolescence. Another concern is that the factor structure of the mCPS has not been validated using confirmatory analysis. Because of the changes in this scale from the original CPS, it cannot be assumed that the original factor structure identified by Lynam [50] is still valid.

Self-report inventories

Self-report Antisocial Process Screening Device

The self-report version of the APSD is a modification of the informant-rated APSD designed to assess psychopathic traits in adolescents. APSD items were rewritten in the first person for adolescents to rate their own behaviors [43]. According to CFA studies, the self-report APSD can be viewed as having three factors: narcissism, impulsivity, and callous-unemotional [54], each having fair internal consistency [52]. In their study of juveniles aged 11 to 17 years attending a diversion program, Falkenbach and colleagues [52] found that both the caregiver- and self-report versions of the APSD correlated highly with parallel versions of the mCPS, at least with respect to total test scores.

Studies of the self-report APSD primarily have used justice-involved adolescent samples with fairly equal numbers of boys and girls [55,56]. The self-report APSD has low diagnostic efficiency with respect to the PCL:YV [54,57] and is not correlated with PCL:YV scores among young adolescent offenders aged 14 to 16 years. Nonetheless, there is some evidence that the self-report APSD seems to identify a more serious type of juvenile offender with a high frequency of violent acts [58] and impaired emotional processing [59].

Psychopathy Content Scale

The Psychopathy Content Scale (PCS) [60] is a self-report measure designed to act as a screening device for juvenile psychopathy among adolescents. The PCS was derived from the Millon Adolescent Clinical Inventory [61], a 160-item yes/no self-report scale. The authors identified 25 items that were face-valid indicators of psychopathy. Five items were dropped to improve the internal consistency of the scale, resulting in a 20-item scale with an internal consistency of .87. PCS scores are obtained by summing the total number of items endorsed. Murrie and Cornell [62] provided some support for the concurrent validity of the PCS, finding a significant positive correlation with the PCL-R using a sample of adolescent civil psychiatric inpatients. A cutoff score of 11 correctly identified 85% of high PCL-R and 57% of low PCL-R scorers. Hierarchical regression analyses have found PCS scores to be positively related to instrumentality and negatively related to empathy among incarcerated young offenders [63].

Research with the PCS has been limited, but fortunately most studies have used incarcerated adolescent samples that included many girls. Murrie and Cornell [62] recommended the PCS be used only as a screening tool to identify youths who may be highly psychopathic and should be targeted for a more thorough assessment with the PCL:YV. However, even the best cutoff score identified in their study would miss 15% of those with high PCL scores because they would not meet the PCS cutoff. Generally, screening tools target a number of false positives (ie, identifying a youth as psychopathic when he or she is not), but a good screening tool should have few if any false negatives (ie, identifying a youth as not psychopathic when her or she is); that is, a good screening tool should screen in nearly all individuals having the psychopathology in question. Another potential limitation comes from CFA findings. The PCS seems to fit a two-factor structure with one factor that is strikingly similar to the PCL interpersonal/affective trait cluster. Unfortunately, the second factor (the behavioral factor) consists almost entirely of criminogenic items, in this case conduct problems such as substance use, rather than items reflecting impulsive or irresponsible lifestyles that are thought to be more indicative of an actual psychopathic syndrome [64].

Youth Psychopathic Traits Inventory

The Youth Psychopathic Traits Inventory (YPI) [65] is a self-report tool designed to measure psychopathic traits in community-based adolescents aged 12 years and older. It has 50 items (rated on a four-point scale) aggregated into 10 scales that load onto three factors (interpersonal, affective, and impulsive lifestyle). The YPI does not include items related to criminogenic behaviors to be consistent with Cooke and Michie's [66] view that psychopathy consists of three symptom dimensions related to personality deviance. Using a sample of adolescent offenders, Skeem and Cauffman [67] reported that YPI scores had good test–retest reliability, sound concurrent validity as indicated by correlations with PCL:YV scores and measures of anxiety, and predictive validity for self-reported institutional misbehaviors over a 1-month period. Because the YPI is in its infancy, little information is available on the psychometric properties, and currently its use is restricted to research.

Discussion

Youth psychopathy measures differ in their intended purpose and practical application. The preferred measures for clinical practice are the PCL:YV for adolescents and the APSD for younger children. Each of the tools defines psychopathy as a disorder comprising arrogant interpersonal, callous unemotional, and impulsive behavioral features and contains multiple symptom indicators related to these traits. With the exception of the PCS and PCL:YV (four-factor model only), the assessments deemphasize specific criminogenic behaviors. Most have been validated in youth samples that were reasonably distributed across ages and settings (eg, secure custody, community). The PCL:YV has high interrater reliability, and most other measures have fair item reliability and sound factor structures. Results of concurrent validity studies have been promising, albeit scarce for some tools (eg, mCPS, PCS, YPI).

Although the research is promising, these tools still suffer from a number of limitations to varying degrees. First, the extent to which the self-report measures can be used in practice remains unclear. In general, the use of self-report tools to assess psychopathy is problematic for a number of reasons, including an inability to incorporate collateral information, an inability to detect deceitfulness, and a slight dependency on the insight of examinees [68].

Second, there are several outstanding questions about the use of psychopathy assessments in girls. Most tools lack adequate norm samples for girls and the generalizability to girls has not been tested rigorously. Despite the PCL:YV authors' claim against gender influences on test scores, rigorous analyses of adult gender differences on PCL-R scores give cause for concern. Analyzes using item-response theory identified significant differences in the measurement of adult women and adult men within the PCL-R normative sample. Specifically, many of the behavioral items were less relevant indicators of psychopathy among women than men [69]. Until similar analyses have been reported for the PCL:YV, its generalizability to girls is tenuous.

Finally, the most significant concern with the application of psychopathy to youth is the questionable stability of personality traits. Aside from one prospective study using the APSD, the stability of psychopathic symptom ratings on these measures has not been tested. Scholars have raised a number of concerns about the assessment of psychopathy in youth because it is debatable whether personality, normal or abnormal, is crystallized during childhood and adolescence [70–72]. Childhood psychopathology is continuous with adult psychopathology for some, but not all, adult disorders [73], because disorders can arise early in life and remit altogether as a result of developmental processes [74]. A related issue is the malleability of symptom expression: Even if a stable psychopathy syndrome exists before adulthood, it may be difficult or even impossible to assess in a meaningful manner. Children may express symptoms indicative of psychopathology at some point in their development because of normal variations in functioning [75]. As researchers have argued, some characteristics of psychopathy (eg, impulsivity, irresponsibility, and need for stimulation) may be symptomatic of characterologic disorders when expressed in adults but merely indicative of developmental immaturity when expressed in young people [70,72]. Further, the reliability of symptom assessments in young people is complicated by heterotypic continuity (ie, symptoms rarely manifest consistently across time) [74,76].

In sum, cross-sectional research suggests it is possible to assess, with good interrater reliability, traits that are phenotypically similar to psychopathy in adults; however, there is no direct evidence that what is being measured is truly psychopathy, a stable personality disorder [77]. Youth psychopathy assessments are not diagnostic tools, and no tool has established valid cutoffs for making categorical ratings. Indeed, the authors of the PCL:YV stated explicitly, "It is inappropriate for clinicians or other professionals to label a youth as a psychopath" [32].

Psychopathic traits and serious crime and violence

In the last decade a number of publications have reported the course of psychopathy in adolescents and children. The best-studied area of psychopathy in youth is its association with conduct problems, criminality, and violence. To evaluate and interpret the results of recidivism studies, however, it is important to be familiar with some methodological considerations. Methods across recidivism studies can vary substantially, and some of the heterogeneity across findings is attributable to this variability [78].

Methodological considerations

Longitudinal studies can vary in the length of follow-up periods, definition of time at risk (the length of time one has an opportunity to reoffend), method, and definition of outcomes. Most importantly, the methods can be prospective, studying trends by recording data at one point in time and again during several points in time in the future (eg, risk factors at time 1 and recidivism at time 2), or retrospective, studying trends by recording data from various time periods simultaneously. Generally, retrospective findings need to be interpreted with the most caution. Aside from limitations arising from record keeping and recall, sampling procedures limit the generalizability of findings. For example, several studies have recorded current PCL-R scores and adolescent violence simultaneously for a cohort of incarcerated adults and found that psychopathy "postdicted" violence (the more psychopathic inmates had more violent histories as adolescents). It would be inaccurate to interpret these findings as meaning that violent youth in general are more likely to be psychopathic than nonviolent youth. A prospective study of adolescents could find that most of those who engage in violent behavior at some point have few psychopathic traits, desist by early adulthood, and are rarely incarcerated as adults. This issue is particularly important, because the most commonly used measures of psychopathy contain items related to past antisocial behavior. So for these measures simply correlating psychopathy with past violence spuriously inflates estimates of the relationship between psychopathy and crime and violence.

Recidivism studies vary widely in the operationalization of outcomes. Some make a distinction between general and violent recidivism, whereas others lump all recidivism together. Some define violence broadly to include verbal aggression, threats, and arson; in others, definitions are narrow, including only physical harm to a person. Some researchers define recidivism narrowly as postrelease community incidents only, whereas others include institutional misconduct and conditional release violations. Even among those recording postrelease incidents, some define recidivism as new convictions only, but others define recidivism as including any arrests. Most studies employ a single method for measuring recidivism, generally official criminal records, but a minority use multiple methods, supplementing official records with self-reported or collateral information. Added variability is found in the metric used to quantify recidivism [19]. This measure may include mere occurrence (any versus no recidivism), frequency (number of reoffenses during follow-up), nature (instrumental versus reactive violence), or imminence (time to reoffending).

As summarized by Hart [19] and Douglas and colleagues [78], broader definitions of violence and longer follow-up periods generally lead to higher base rates and more powerful statistical predictions. Further, self-report measures of violence generate significantly greater and ostensibly more accurate reports of violent incidents. Unless the follow-up period is fixed, it is particularly crucial that outcome measures incorporate time at risk before reoffending, using survival or Cox regression analyses, because of the wide variability within samples.

Generally, statistics using dichotomous outcomes underestimate predictive accuracy because these statistics ignore the complexity of the data.

Studies in adolescent offenders

Similar to findings in adults, there is good evidence that delinquents scoring high on the PCL:YV have a specific and severe pattern of offending, at least with respect to incarcerated adolescent males. Reviewing the findings of male adolescent offender samples only, cross-sectional research indicates that those with high PCL:YV scores are most likely to have histories of relatively frequent offending, violent offending beginning at an early age [79,80], and severe patterns of institutional misconduct [33,81]. Specifically, retrospective longitudinal studies have reported a high rate of past escape attempts [82], and prospective studies reported noncompliance with institutional programming [35] among those with high PCL:YV scores. There is evidence that the commission of violent crimes increases from early adolescence to early adulthood (age 19–21 years) for relatively psychopathic adolescents and decreases for less psychopathic adolescents [36]. This pattern does not hold for nonviolent crime. For both high and low PCL:YV scoring adolescent offenders, the rates of nonviolent crime increase from early adolescence to early adulthood.

Retrospective studies of adolescents spanning periods of 5 to 10 years generally have reported strong associations between PCL:YV scores and general and violent recidivism. In an average 5-year "retrospective follow-up" study of juvenile sex offenders, Gretton and colleagues [82] found that the highest third of PCL:YV (file-based) scorers were four times more likely to recidivate and were three times more likely to recidivate violently than the lowest third of PCL:YV scorers. Prospective studies spanning periods of 1 to 3 years generally have found a fairly strong prediction for violent recidivism [83,84] and occasionally for general recidivism [80,85,86]. These findings have been consistent with the self-report APSD and mCPS, both of which have significant correlations with the occurrence of any recidivism (measured by self-report and parent report) over a 1-year period [52]. The few longitudinal studies that quantified the time to recidivism consistently found that PCL:YV scores were negatively related to time to a reoffense. Put simply, the higher the PCL:YV score, the sooner after release an individual would reoffend [82,85], particularly for violent reoffending [84].

Studies in children

Although several studies have reported strong associations between the APSD and number of conduct problems, aggression, and delinquency [55,87,88], most of these studies have been cross-sectional. Put simply, conduct problems and other outcomes were measured based on past or current behaviors. Nonetheless, one value of these studies has been the discovery that patterns among children aged 6 to 13 years are similar to those of adolescents: those who have psychopathic traits in each dimension (ie, narcissistic interpersonal style, callous-unemotional affect, and conduct problems) of the antisocial behavior and impulsive lifestyle trait cluster tend to be more aggressive and severely conduct disordered than children who have the conduct-problem features of psychopathy alone. In other words, youths exhibiting all the features of psychopathy to some degree are distinct from youths who are merely impulsive and antisocial.

Few prospective studies have been conducted in children, but the findings have supported data from the retrospective studies mentioned previously. Using the APSD in a sample of children in the community and a 1 -year follow-up, Frick and colleagues [89] found that children who had both callous-unemotional traits and conduct problems had higher rates of self-reported delinquency and instrumental aggression than those who had conduct problems alone. In an extended follow-up study, self-reported delinquency (both general and violent), conduct problems, and parent-reported police contacts were recorded for the children in this sample once a year over 4 years [90]. Children who had both callous-unemotional traits and conduct problems had the highest rates of each of these antisocial outcomes in each year of the follow-up. The trajectories of delinquency were fairly stable for this group, and they accounted for the majority of police contacts in the sample. Although half of the sample was female, findings were not reported separately for girls. So again, little is known about the predictive validity of these measures in girls.

Discussion

Although the association between psychopathy and recidivism seems to generalize to youth, published prospective studies in adolescents have been rare, have used short follow-up periods averaging 12 to 27 months, and have yet to track recidivism systematically into adulthood, although some retrospective and prospective studies included early adult crime for older members of the baseline sample [82]. All of the retrospective studies and a few prospective studies used file-based ratings of the PCL:YV. Although the validity of this procedure with the PCL:YV is unknown, item-response theory studies of the PCL-R indicate that file-based–only ratings contain a fair amount of measurement bias [69].

Another issue is that measures of youth psychopathy rarely have been scrutinized rigorously by testing whether they provide incremental validity over other risk factors for youth violence (eg, age of onset, number of prior arrests). One exception found both the interpersonal/affective factor and behavioral factor of the PCL added to the prediction of any recidivism after several demographic, criminal history, and psychologic variables were taken into account [79]. The PCL:YV did not have incremental validity for violent reoffending specifically.

Few prospective studies have scrutinized the source of psychopathy's predictive validity by evaluating the unique contribution of individual symptom clusters. This point is crucial. If measures of psychopathy merely predict recidivism among youth based on dimensions related to antisocial or impulsive behavior, one must seriously question whether a coherent syndrome, or even its unique interpersonal and unemotional symptoms, operates for youth as in adults. A few studies can shed light on this issue. In one study using the original two-factor model and file-based PCL:YV scores, the PCL:YV's prediction of recidivism stemmed primarily from its behavioral factor, which included the antisocial behavior items [79].

Researchers using the three-factor model of the PCL:YV, which does not include any antisocial items, have reached different conclusions. Corrado and colleagues [85] used Cox regression to predict the days to a reoffense from interview-based PCL:YV three-factor scores and the interaction term between these factors, thought to be more representative of an underlying syndrome. They reported that the prediction of any form of recidivism, and violent recidivism specifically, could be attributed to the interaction of all three factors, thought to be more indicative of an overall psychopathy syndrome. Also using interview-based scores, Vincent and colleagues [84] found that a cluster of adolescent offenders scoring high on each of the interpersonal, affective, and lifestyle behavioral factors were much more likely to recidivate violently (50%), and did so sooner after release (average, 14 months), than adolescents who had behavioral features alone (27% recidivated after an average of 18 months).

Another limitation is the lack of research in females. The only published recidivism study in girls found that PCL:YV scores did not predict future offending in a sample of 62 adolescent female offenders after taking into account victimization experiences; however, the follow-up period for this study was only 3 months [91]. Indeed, the sparse research on violence prediction in adult women lends further support to the notion that the problems in the field are of such magnitude that psychopathy should not be used for predictive purposes in female samples [92].

Psychopathy and risk assessment/management with youth

Psychopathic traits in general, and PCL:YV and APSD scores in particular, are clearly linked to future violence and antisocial behavior among youth over short time periods and define one putative factor for risk for general and violent recidivism. Regarding the PCL:YV, Forth [93] stated, "Within the juvenile justice context, this information may be useful in identifying youth who represent a more serious management problem within institutions, who need intensive intervention, and who require more resources for risk management in the community." Generally, high PCL:YV or APSD scores in youth, like high PCL-R scores in adults [19], may compel a conclusion of high risk over short periods of time. Given that adolescence is a time of extreme developmental change, clinicians should reassess risk and psychopathic characteristics routinely in high-risk youth to determine if maturation attenuates risk.

These assessments are not to be used for decisions pertaining to transfer to adult court or for restricting access to treatment. As mentioned previously, these decisions are to be based not only on risk of violence but also on amenability to treatment and maturity. Few studies have reported the connection between psychopathic characteristics and amenability to treatment in young offenders, and most are not published (see [32] for a review of unpublished studies). Possibly the most consistent finding for adolescent offenders is that those who have psychopathic traits spend less time in treatment or are less likely to complete treatment than less psychopathic youths. This finding has been reported among adolescents in a residential treatment [34], a substance-abuse program [94], and sex offender treatment [82]. In general, psychopathy is related to noncompliance with treatment, dropping out, and disruptive behavior in treatment. In the short term, youth who have predominantly high antisocial lifestyle traits are at a greater likelihood of general and violent reoffending than youth who have few of these behavioral traits [84]. There is some evidence, however, that those who have only behavioral traits are more likely to desist than youth who have prominent psychopathic features. Psychopathic traits, as measured by the self-report APSD and the mCPS, also relate negatively to treatment progress and institutional misconduct [95].

For the purposes of treatment and risk management, assessors should consider the constellation of psychopathic traits and their impact on risk decisions and the suitability of treatment modalities. Because of the evidence of the relative stability of these traits [89] and conjecture that these features may be at the core of this disorder [96,97], those who have prominent callous/unemotional features may require innovative interventions designed specifically for offenders who have psychopathic traits. Youth who have psychopathic traits should be allotted intensive resources [98] to maximize the potential of altering the trajectory to long-term offending. Rogers and colleagues [99] demonstrated that even treatment designed for general mental health problems decreased psychopathic characteristics in juveniles.

Other tools for assessment of the risk of violence

Psychopathy assessments may provide one piece of the risk-assessment puzzle, but they are insufficient on their own. Psychopathy represents only one risk factor, not a comprehensive risk assessment, and should be used in conjunction with several environmental, individual, and familial variables and protective factors identified as contributing to the likelihood of youth violence. Some comprehensive risk-assessment tools for youth include psychopathic traits (eg, callous-unemotional) as a risk factor. Preferred psychological instruments are in circulation that were designed to assess the likelihood for future violence or recidivism in juvenile justice–involved youths. For example, the Risk-Sophistication-Treatment-Inventory [2] was designed to assess a youth offender's appropriateness for transfer to adult court. The most widely used assessment tools are reviewed briefly here. To learn more about these tools and other instruments, readers are directed to other comprehensive summaries of assessment and screening tools for youth [100].

The Structured Assessment of Violence Risk in Youth

The Structured Assessment of Violence Risk in Youth (SAVRY) [12] is based on the SPJ risk assessment framework and is designed for use with adolescents between the approximate ages of 12 and 18 years who have been detained or referred for an assessment of violence risk. Qualified trained evaluators conduct systematic assessments of predetermined risk factors that are empirically associated with violence, consider the applicability of each risk factor to a particular examinee, and classify each factor's severity. The ultimate determination of an examinee's overall level of violence risk (low, medium, or high) is based on the examiner's professional judgment as informed by a systematic appraisal of relevant factors. The SAVRY protocol is composed of six items defining protective factors and 24 items defining risk factors. Risk items are divided into three categories, historical, individual, and social/contextual, and include a risk factor related to psychopathic traits. Evaluators are also able to designate additional risk and protective factors, because the SAVRY is not exhaustive for any given individual. In the course of conducting a risk assessment or assessing patterns in past violent episodes, additional factors or situational variables may emerge that are important in understanding the potential for future violence. In such situations, the additional factors should be documented and weighed in final decisions of risk. The entire instrument is coded based on record review and an interview with the youth examinee. The time required for assessment varies with the complexity of each case.

The Early Assessment Risk Lists

The Early Assessment Risk List for Boys (EARL-20B) version 2 [11] and the Early Assessment Risk List for Girls (EARL-21G) version 1 [101] are risk-assessment devices, using the SPJ approach, for evaluating children under 12 years of age who are exhibiting disruptive behavior problems that may be indicative of future antisocial, aggressive, or violent conduct. According to the authors, the intended purpose of these instruments is to increase general understanding of early childhood risk factors for violence and antisociality, provide a structure for developing risk assessment schemas for individual children, and assist with risk management planning. The EARL-20B and EARL-21G contain 20 or 21 items, respectively, divided across three categories, family, child, and responsivity (the ability and willingness of the child and family to engage in and benefit from interventions). Like the SAVRY, these checklists are coded based on all available collateral information and interviews with examinees where possible. Risk factors related to psychopathic traits are included. Evaluators provide an overall decision about the child's level of risk (low, medium, or high) and appropriate interventions commensurate with the level of risk.

Youth Level of Service/Case Management Inventory

The Youth Level of Service/Case Management Inventory (YLS/CMI) [102] is a standardized inventory for assessing risk and needs factors in adolescent juvenile offenders and assisting in case management. The authors designed the YLS/CMI primarily to assist with pre- and postadjudication case planning, but it also can assist with other decisions, such as preadjudication diversion and detention, waivers to adult court and the mental health system, and postadjudication dispositions. This protocol uses an adjusted actuarial approach; that is, total scores are derived by objective ratings and summed to designate risk levels. This actuarially derived risk level can by overridden based on clinical judgment. The YLS/CMI contains 42 items divided across eight subscales (ie, prior and current offenses, parenting, education/employment, peer associations, substance abuse, personality, and attitudes). Like the SAVRY and EARLs, evaluators are able to consider additional risk factors not included in the checklist. The YLS/CMI can be administered and scored by front-line staff of juvenile justice and correctional agencies, although some initial training is required. The entire assessment takes 20 to 30 minutes.

Summary

The goals of assessment of the risk of violence are to target those at the highest risk of harming others and to inform clinicians how best to minimize this risk through supervision and intervention efforts. Generally, assessors want to use tools with known predictive validity that also are capable of guiding intervention and treatment planning and capturing changes in risk. Although actuarial judgments have demonstrated superior predictive validity, critics have documented the danger of overreliance on actuarial decisions [103–105]. First, actuarial tools have limited clinical utility because a consequence of the empirical test construction methods is that many risk factors make little sense theoretically or clinically. Consequently, assessment procedures are not tied to intervention strategies in a prescriptive manner. Second, actuarial measures are of little value for understanding the causes of antisocial behavior and violence because of overemphasis on the effect of variables rather than on the meaning of variables [106]. Finally, actuarial tools often make exclusive use of static variables, which, by definition, cannot measure changes in risk and provide little guidance with risk management. The inability to measure change in risk is a primary concern with assessments of psychopathy. Put simply, once a youth is labeled as psychopathic, it is unclear that even drastic changes through adolescence will permit the youth to be labeled as nonpsychopathic or as no longer psychopathic. These assessments may assist with evaluations of the risk of violence and with planning for intervention in children and adolescents, but the potential for misuse in forensic decision making cannot be ignored [72]. (Some research, however, indicates these concerns may not be as serious as suspected [107].)

In light of these concerns, scholars have produced a few risk-assessment schemes for youth using an SPJ or adjusted actuarial approach, namely, the SAVRY, EARL-20B and EARL-21G, and the YLS/CMI. Because of their design, one would expect these tools to be capable of assessing increases and reductions in risk as long as evaluators conduct periodic reassessments; however, the ability to measure change has yet to be demonstrated empirically. Another possible limitation is that, although findings from retrospective studies seem promising, the prospective predictive validity data for most of these measures are limited at this time [100]. Nonetheless, these tools provide a structured framework on which evaluators can base their conclusions about a youths' violence risk and the best practices for managing that risk. It is recommended these tools be used along with some assessment of psychopathic features; evaluators also should include specific considerations and limitations based on the current state of research.

References

[1] Grisso T. Double jeopardy. New York: Guilford Press; 2004.

[2] Salekin RT. Risk-Sophistication-Treatment-Inventory (RST-I): professional manual. Lutz (FL): Psychological Assessment Resources; 2004.

[3] Farrington DP. The twelfth Jack Tizard Memorial Lecture: the development of offending and antisocial behaviour from childhood: key findings from the Cambridge study in delinquent development. J Child Psychol Psychiatry 1995;36:929–64.

[4] Farrington DP, West DJ. Criminal, penal and life histories of chronic offenders: risk and protective factors and early identification. Crim Behav Ment Health 1993;3:492–523.

[5] Roberts BW, Caspi A, Moffitt TE. The kids are all right: growth and stability in personality development from adolescence to adulthood. J Pers Soc Psychol 2001;81:670–83.

[6] Hawkins DJ, Herrenkohl T, Farrington DP, et al. A review of predictors of youth violence. In: Loeber R, Farrington D, editors. Serious and violent juvenile offenders: risk factors and successful interventions. New York: Sage Publications; 2001. p. 106–46.

[7] Reppucci ND, Fried CS, Schmidt MG. Youth violence: risk and protective factors. In: Corrado RR, Roesch R, Hart SD, et al, editors. Multi-problem violent youth: a foundation for comparative research on needs, interventions, and outcomes. Amsterdam: IOS Press; 2002. p. 3–22.

[8] US Department of Health and Human Services. Youth violence: a report of the Surgeon General. Rockville (MD): US Department of Health and Human Services; 2001.

[9] Lipsey MW, Derzon JH. Predictors of violent or serious delinquency in adolescence and early adulthood: a synthesis of longitudinal research. In: Loeber R, Farrington D, editors. Serious and violent juvenile offenders: risk factors and successful interventions. New York: Sage; 1998. p. 86–105.

[10] Loeber R, Stouthamer-Loeber M, Van Kammen WB, et al. Initiation, escalation, and desistance in juvenile offending and their correlates. J Crim Law Criminol 1991;82:36–82.

[11] Augimeri LK, Koegl CJ, Webster CD, et al. Early Assessment Risk List for Boys (EARL-20B) (version 2). Toronto: Earlscourt Child and Family Centre; 2001.

[12] Borum R, Bartel P, Forth A. Manual for the Structured Assessment for Violence Risk in Youth (SAVRY) (version 1.1). Tampa (FL): University of South Florida; 2003.

[13] Hemphill JF, Hare RD, Wong S. Psychopathy and recidivism: a review. Leg Criminol Psychol 1998;3:141–72.

[14] Lipsey MW, Wilson DB. Practical meta-analysis. Applied social research methods series, vol. 49. Thousand Oaks (CA): Sage; 2003.
[15] Salekin RT, Rogers R, Sewell K. A review and meta-analysis of the psychopathy checklist and psychopathy checklist-revised: predictive validity of dangerousness. Clin Psychol Sci Pract 1996;3:203–15.
[16] Steadman HJ, Silver E, Monahan J, Appelbaum PS, et al. A classification tree approach to the development of actuarial violence risk assessment tools. Law Hum Beh 2000;25:173–80.
[17] Hare RD. The Hare PCL-R. 2nd edition. Toronto: Multi-Health Systems; 2003.
[18] Hart SD, Cox DN, Hare RD. Manual for the Psychopathy Checklist: Screening Version (PCL:SV). Toronto: Multi-Health Systems; 1995.
[19] Hart SD. The role of psychopathy in assessing risk for violence: conceptual and methodological issues. Leg Criminol Psychol 1998;3:123–40.
[20] Kernberg PF, Weiner AS, Bardenstein KK. Personality disorders in children and adolescents. New York: Basic Books; 2000.
[21] Rutter M, Tuma AH, Lann IS, editors. Assessment and diagnosis of child psychopathology. New York: Guilford; 1988.
[22] Monahan J. Violence prediction: the last 20 years and the next 20 years. Crim Justice Behav 1996;23:107–20.
[23] Grisso T, Tomkins AJ. Communicating violence risk assessments. Am Psychol 1996;51: 928–30.
[24] Borum R. Improving the clinical practice of violence risk assessment: technology, guidelines, and training. Am Psychol 1996;51:945–56.
[25] Borum R, Douglas K. New directions in violence risk assessment. Psychiatric Times 2003; 20(3):102–3.
[26] Patterson GR, Forgatch MS, Voerger KL, et al. Variables that initiate and maintain an early-onset trajectory of offending. Dev Psychopathol 1998;10:531–47.
[27] Robins LN. Aetiological implications in studies of childhood histories relating to antisocial personality. In: Hare RD, Schalling D, editors. Psychopathic behavior: approaches to research. Chichester (UK): Wiley; 1978. p. 255–71.
[28] Moffitt TE, Caspi A. Childhood predictors differentiate life-course persistent and adolescence-limited antisocial pathways among males and females. Dev Psychopathol 2001;13:355–75.
[29] Cleckley H. The mask of sanity. St. Louis (MO): C. V. Mosbey Company; 1976.
[30] Hare RD. Psychopathy: theory and research. New York: Wiley; 1970.
[31] McCord W, McCord J. Psychopathy and delinquency. New York: Grune & Stratton; 1956.
[32] Forth AE, Kosson DS, Hare RD. Hare Psychopathy Checklist: Youth Version. Toronto: Multi-Health Systems; 2003.
[33] Forth AE, Hart SD, Hare RD. Assessment of psychopathy in male young offenders. Psychol Assess 1990;2:342–4.
[34] Kosson DS, Cyterski TD, Steuerwald BL, et al. The reliability and validity of the Psychopathy Checklist: Youth Version (PCL:YV) in nonincarcerated adolescent males. Psychol Assess 2003;14:97–109.
[35] Rogers R, Johansen J, Chang JJ, et al. Predictors of adolescent psychopathy: oppositional and conduct-disordered symptoms. J Am Acad Psychiatry Law 1997;25:261–71.
[36] Forth AE, Burke H. Psychopathy in adolescence: assessment, violence, and developmental precursors. In: Cooke DJ, Forth AE, Hare RD, editors. Psychopathy: theory, research and implications for society. Dodrecht (The Netherlands): Kluwer; 1998. p. 205–29.
[37] Mailloux DL, Forth AE, Kroner DG. Psychopathy and substance use in adolescent male offenders. Psychol Rep 1997;80:529–30.
[38] Roussy S, Toupin J. Behavioral inhibition deficits in juvenile psychopaths. Aggress Behav 2000;26:413–24.
[39] Frick PJ, Hare RD. The Antisocial Process Screening Device. Toronto: Multi-Health Systems; 2001.
[40] Frick PJ, Bodin SD, Barry CT. Psychopathic traits and conduct problems in community and

clinic-referred samples of children: further development of the Psychopathy Screening Device. Psychol Assess 2001;12:382–93.

[41] Frick PJ, Lilienfeld SO, Ellis ML, et al. The association between anxiety and psychopathy dimensions in children. J Abnorm Child Psychol 1999;27:383–92.

[42] Loney BR, Frick PJ, Ellis M, et al. Intelligence callous-unemotional traits, and antisocial behavior. J Psychopathol Behav Assess 1998;20:231–47.

[43] Frick PJ, Barry CT, Bodin SD. Applying the concept of psychopathy to children: implications for the assessment of antisocial youth. In: Gacono CB, editor. The clinical and forensic assessment of psychopathy: a practitioner's guide. Mahwah (NJ): Lawrence Erlbaum; 2000. p. 3–24.

[44] Frick PJ, O'Brien BS, Wootton JM, et al. Psychopathy and conduct problems in children. J Abnorm Psychol 1994;103:700–7.

[45] Frick PJ, Kimonis ER, Dandreaux D, et al. The 4 year stability of psychopathic traits in non-referred youth. Behav Sci Law 2003;21:713–36.

[46] Barry CT, Frick PJ, DeShazo TM, et al. The importance of callous-unemotional traits for extending the concept of psychopathy to children. J Abnorm Psychol 2000;109:335–40.

[47] Blair RJR. Responsiveness to distress cues in the child with psychopathic tendencies. Pers Individ Dif 1999;27:135–45.

[48] Blair RJR, Colledge E, Murray L, et al. A selective impairment in the processing of sad and fearful expressions in children with psychopathic tendencies. J Abnorm Child Psychol 2001;29:491–8.

[49] Pardini DA, Lochman JE, Frick PJ. Callous/unemotional traits and social cognitive processes in adjudicated youth. J Am Acad Child Adolesc Psychiatry 2003;42:364–71.

[50] Lynam DR. Pursuing the psychopath: capturing the fledgling psychopath in a nomological net. J Abnorm Psychol 1997;106:425–38.

[51] Lynam DR, Caspi A, Moffitt TE, et al. Adolescent psychopathy and the big five: results from two samples. J Abnorm Child Psychol 2005;33:431–43.

[52] Falkenbach DM, Poythress NG, Heide KM. Psychopathic features in a juvenile diversion population: reliability and predictive validity of two self-report measures. Behav Sci Law 2003;21:787–805.

[53] Fung MT, Raine A, Loeber R, et al. Reduced electrodermal activity in psychopathy-prone adolescents. J Abnorm Psychol 2005;114:187–96.

[54] Vitacco MJ, Rogers R, Neumann CS. The Antisocial Process Screening Device: an examination of its construct and criterion-related validity. Assessment 2003;10:143–50.

[55] Caputo AA, Frick PJ, Brodsky SL. Family violence and juvenile sex offending: the potential mediating role of psychopathic traits and negative attitudes toward women. Crim Justice Behav 1999;26:338–56.

[56] Silverthorn P, Frick PJ, Reynolds R. Timing of onset and correlates of severe conduct problems in adjudicated girls and boys. J Psychopathol Behav Assess 2001;23:171–81.

[57] Lee Z, Vincent GM, Hart SD, et al. The validity of the Antisocial Process Screening Device as a self-report measure of psychopathy in adolescent offenders. Behav Sci Law 2003;21: 771–86.

[58] Kruh IP, Frick PJ, Clements CB. Historical and personality correlates to the violence patterns of juveniles tried as adults. Crim Justice Behav 2003;32(1):69–96.

[59] Loney BR, Frick PJ, Clements CB, et al. Callous-unemotional traits, impulsivity, and emotional processing in adolescents with antisocial behavior problems. Journal of Clinical Child and Adolescent Psychiatry 2003;32:66–80.

[60] Murrie DC, Cornell DG. The Millon Adolescent Clinical Inventory and psychopathy. J Pers Assess 2000;7(1):110–25.

[61] Million T. Millon Adolescent Clinical Inventory: manual. Minneapolis (MN): National Computer Systems; 1993.

[62] Murrie DC, Cornell DG. Psychopathy screening of incarcerated juveniles: a comparison of measures. Psychol Assess 2002;14(4):390–6.

[63] Loper AB, Hoffschmidt SJ, Ash E. Personality features and characteristics of violent events committed by juvenile offenders. Behav Sci Law 2001;19:81–96.
[64] Lexcen F, Vincent GM, Grisso T. Validity of the Psychopathy Content Screening Scale. Behav Sci Law 2004;22:69–84.
[65] Andershed HA, Gustafson SB, Kerr M, et al. The usefulness of self-reported psychopathy-like traits in the study of antisocial behaviour among non-referred adolescents. Eur J Pers 2002; 16:383–402.
[66] Cooke DJ, Michie C. Refining the construct of psychopathy: towards a hierarchical model. Psychol Assess 2001;13:171–88.
[67] Skeem JL, Cauffman E. Views of the downward extension: comparing the youth version of the Psychopathy Checklist with the Youth Psychopathic Traits Inventory. Behav Sci Law 2003;21:737–70.
[68] Hemphill JF, Hart SD. Treatment of psychopathic personality disorder. In: Blauuw E, Sheridan L, editors. Psychopaths: current international perspectives. Amsterdam: Elsevier; 2002. p. 159–74.
[69] Bolt DM, Hare RD, Vitale JE, et al. A multigroup item response theory analysis of the Psychopathy Checklist–Revised. Psychol Assess 2004;16:155–68.
[70] Edens JF, Skeem JL, Cruise KR, et al. Assessment of "juvenile psychopathy" and its association with violence: a critical review. Behav Sci Law 2001;19:53–80.
[71] Hart SD, Watt KA, Vincent GM. Commentary on Seagrave and Grisso: impressions of the state of the art. Law Hum Behav 2002;26:241–5.
[72] Seagrave D, Grisso T. Adolescent development and the measurement of juvenile psychopathy. Law Hum Behav 2002;26:219–39.
[73] Mash EJ, Dozois DJA. Child psychopathology: a developmental-systems perspective. In: Mash EJ, Barkley RA, editors. Child psychopathology. 2nd edition. New York: Guilford; 2003. p. 3–71.
[74] Cicchetti D, Cohen DJ. Perspectives on developmental psychopathology. In: Cicchetti D, Cohen DJ, editors. Developmental psychopathology, vol. 1. New York: Wiley; 1995. p. 3–16.
[75] Achenbach TM, Edelbrock C. Diagnostic, taxonomic, and assessment issues. In: Ollendick TH, Herson M, editors. Handbook of child psychopathology. 2nd edition. New York: Plenum Press; 1989. p. 53–73.
[76] Cicchetti D, Rogosch FA. Equifinality and multifinality in developmental psychopathology. Dev Psychopathol 1996;8:597–600.
[77] Vincent GM, Hart SD. Psychopathy in childhood and adolescence: implications for the assessment and management of multi-problem youths. In: Corrado RR, Roesch R, Hart SD, et al, editors. Multi-problem violent youth: a foundation for comparative research on needs, interventions, and outcomes. Amsterdam: IOS Press; 2002. p. 150–62.
[78] Douglas K, Vincent GM, Edens J. Risk for criminal recidivism: The role of psychopathy. In: Patrick C, editor. Handbook of psychopathy. New York: Guilford Press; 2005. p. 533–54.
[79] Brandt JR, Wallace AK, Patrick CJ, et al. Assessment of psychopathy in a population of incarcerated adolescent offenders. Psychol Assess 1997;9:429–35.
[80] Toupin J, Mercier H, Déry M, et al. Validity of the PCL-R for adolescents. In: Cooke DJ, Forth AE, Newman JP, et al, editors. Issues in criminological and legal psychology: no. 24, international perspectives on psychopathy. Leicester (UK): British Psychological Society; 1996. p. 143–5.
[81] Hicks MM, Rogers R, Cashel M. Predictions of violent and total infractions among institutionalized male juvenile offenders. J Am Acad Psychiatry Law 2000;28:183–90.
[82] Gretton HM, McBride M, Hare RD, et al. Psychopathy and recidivism in adolescent sex offenders. Crim Justice Behav 2001;28:427–49.
[83] Catchpole R, Gretton M. The predictive validity of risk assessment with violent young offenders: a one-year examination of criminal outcome. Crim Justice Behav 2003;30:688–708.
[84] Vincent GM, Vitacco MJ, Grisso T, et al. Subtypes of adolescent offenders: affective traits and antisocial behavior patterns. Behav Sci Law 2003;21:695–712.
[85] Corrado RR, Vincent GM, Hart SD, et al. Predictive validity of the Psychopathy Checklist: Youth Version for general and violent recidivism. Behav Sci Law 2004;22:5–22.

[86] Ridenour TA, Marchant GJ, Dean RS. Is the revised Psychopathy Checklist clinically useful for adolescents? J Psychoed Assess 2001;19:227–38.
[87] Christian RE, Frick PJ, Hill NL, et al. Psychopathy and conduct problems in children: II. Implications for subtyping children with conduct problems. J Am Acad Child Adolesc Psychiatry 1997;6:233–41.
[88] Wootton JM, Frick PJ, Shelton KK, et al. Ineffective parenting and childhood conduct problems: the moderating role of callous unemotional traits. J Consult Clin Psychol 1997;65: 301–8.
[89] Frick PJ, Cornell AH, Barry CT, et al. Callous-unemotional traits and conduct problems in the prediction of conduct problem severity, aggression, and self-report of delinquency. J Abnorm Child Psychol 2003;31:457–70.
[90] Frick PJ, Stickle TR, Dandreaux DM, et al. Callous-unemotional traits in predicting the severity and stability of conduct problems and delinquency. J Abnorm Child Psychol 2005;33:471–87.
[91] Odgers CL, Moretti M, Reppucci ND. Examining the science and practice of violence risk assessment with female adolescents. Law Hum Behav 2005;29:7–27.
[92] Vitale JE, Newman JP. Response perseveration in psychopathic women. J Abnorm Psychol 2001;110(4):644–7.
[93] Forth AE. The Hare Psychopathy Checklist: Youth Version. In: Grisso T, Vincent GM, Seagrave D, editors. The handbook of screening and assessment tools for juvenile justice. New York: Guilford; 2005. p. 324–38.
[94] O'Neill ML, Lidz V, Heilbrun K. Adolescents with psychopathic characteristics in a substance abuse cohort: treatment process and outcomes. Law and Human Behavior 2003;27:299–313.
[95] Spain SE, Douglas KS, Poythress NG, et al. The relationship between psychopathic features, violence and treatment outcome: the comparison of three youth measures of psychopathic features. Behav Sci Law 2004;22:85–102.
[96] Blair J, Frith U. Neurocognitive explanations of the antisocial personality disorders. Crim Behav Ment Health 2000;10:S66–81.
[97] Frick PJ. Callous-unemotional traits and conduct problems: a two-factor model for psychopathy in children. In: Cooke DJ, Forth AE, Hare RD, editors. Psychopathy: theory, research and implications for society. Dodrecht (The Netherlands): Kluwer; 1998. p. 205–29.
[98] Andrews DA, Bonta J. The psychology of criminal conduct. 2nd edition. Cincinnati (OH): Anderson; 1998.
[99] Rogers R, Jackson R, Sewell KS, et al. Predictors of treatment outcome in dually-diagnosed antisocial youth: an initial study of forensic inpatients. Behav Sci Law 2004;22:215–24.
[100] Grisso T, Vincent GM, Seagrave D, editors. Mental health screening and assessment for juvenile justice. New York: Guilford Press; 2005.
[101] Levene KS, Augimeri LK, Pepler D, et al. Early assessment risk list for girls: EARL-21, version 1. Toronto: Earlscourt Child and Family Centre; 2001.
[102] Hoge RD, Andrews DA. Youth Level of Service/Case Management Inventory users guide. North Tonawanda (NY): Multi-Health Systems; 2002.
[103] Berlin FS, Galbreath NW, Geary B, et al. The use of actuarials at civil commitment hearings to predict the likelihood of future sexual violence. Sex Abuse 2003;15(4):377–82.
[104] Dvoskin JA, Heilbrun K. Risk assessment and release decision-making: toward resolving the great debate. J Am Acad Psychiatry Law 2001;29:6–10.
[105] Grisso T. Ethical issues in evaluations for sex offender re-offending. Presented at the Sex Offender Re-Offence Risk Prediction Training, Sinclair Seminars. Madison (WI), March 9–10, 2000.
[106] Grubin D, Wingate S. Sexual offence recidivism: prediction versus understanding. Crim Behav Ment Health 1996;6:349–59.
[107] Murrie DC, Cornell DG, McCoy WK. Psychopathy, conduct disorder, and stigma: does diagnostic labeling influence juvenile probation officer recommendations? Law Hum Behav 2005; 29:323–42.

ELSEVIER
SAUNDERS

Child Adolesc Psychiatric Clin N Am
15 (2006) 429–444

CHILD AND
ADOLESCENT
PSYCHIATRIC CLINICS
OF NORTH AMERICA

Will Future Forensic Assessment Be Neurobiologic?

Arne Popma, MD[a,*], Adrian Raine, DPhil[b]

[a]*Department of Child and Adolescent Psychiatry, VU University Medical Center, P/a De Bascule, Rijksstraatweg 145PB, 3031115 ZG Duivendrecht, Amsterdam, The Netherlands*
[b]*Department of Psychology, University of Southern California, Los Angeles, CA, USA*

During the past 2 decades, research on the role of biologic factors in antisocial behavior has made great progress. Delinquency, subtypes of aggressive behavior, and psychopathy are just a few of the behavioral constructs that have been associated with biologic parameters [1]. Moreover, some of the observed associations have now been investigated in longitudinal studies, uncovering biologic factors that predispose to antisocial behavior. Findings of these studies suggest that biologic factors are particularly involved in the shaping and development of behavior at a young age, that is, in children and adolescents. At the same time, biosocial models are being developed that incorporate both biologic and social factors, reflecting the assumption that both types of factors interact in a complex fashion to influence the development and persistence of antisocial behavior [2,3]. Current research and influential theories deriving from it shy away from biologic determinism but do stress the need to take into account and study biology as one of the important correlates of antisocial behavior.

The accumulating evidence for a link between biologic factors and antisocial behavior makes timely a discussion of the repercussions that these findings may have on future clinical practice. Such a discussion is relevant for the general juvenile mental health service, which spends a substantial percentage of its time and budget dealing with children and adolescents displaying antisocial behavior. The field of child and adolescent forensic psychiatry, in particular, deals primarily with a population whose psychiatric problems are both of an antisocial nature and still in development. The main purpose of this article is to relate findings from

* Corresponding author.
E-mail address: a.popma@debascule.com (A. Popma).

doi:10.1016/j.chc.2005.11.004

biologic research to the core activity of practitioners involved in forensic assessment in juvenile justice settings.

Forensic assessment has been conceptualized as consisting of four distinct components: (1) diagnostic identification, (2) providing treatment options, (3) assessing risk, and (4) evaluating treatment [4]. As discussed elsewhere in this issue, although psychosocial research has provided valuable tools for assessment, the specificity and effectiveness of all four of these aspects can be increased. This article discusses why improving the knowledge of the biologic underpinnings of antisocial behavior and implementing findings from biologic studies in assessment strategies may be one of the ways to accomplish this improvement [1,5]. Although it may be too early to draw definite conclusions on how neurobiologic insights will influence future forensic psychiatric assessment, the authors aim to initiate discussion and to develop ideas related to the provocative question posed in the title of this article.

First, the article briefly reviews the current literature, focusing on three important subfields of biologic research: genetics, psychophysiology/neuroendocrinology, and brain imaging. For each subfield, the authors discuss biologic correlates of antisocial behavior and specific interactions between biologic factors and social factors. Second, the authors evaluate how the reported findings from the reviewed literature may relate to each of the four specific aspects of forensic assessment. Third, the authors address some relevant philosophical, ethical, and political questions that inevitably arise when in a discussion of the biology of antisocial behavior. Finally, the authors discuss the agenda for the coming decade: what should be done to extend knowledge, to start implementing new knowledge in forensic assessment, and to adjust intervention strategies accordingly.

A brief review of the literature

Fig. 1 provides a basic model that can serve as a heuristic guide for the following review of some of the main subfields of biologic research. Although inevitably overly simplistic, the model highlights the key influences of genetic and environmental processes in giving rise to social and biologic risk factors that both individually and interactively predispose to antisocial behavior. In addition, it incorporates the idea that both biology and environment can constitute protective factors as well. Finally, the model suggests that, once antisocial behavior is subject to forensic assessment, all underlying factors may be of value in informing the clinical practitioner.

Genetics

Twin studies, adoptive studies, studies in twins reared apart, and molecular genetic studies clearly support the notion that there are genetic influences on antisocial and aggressive behavior [1,6,7]. Still, heritability estimates (ie, the

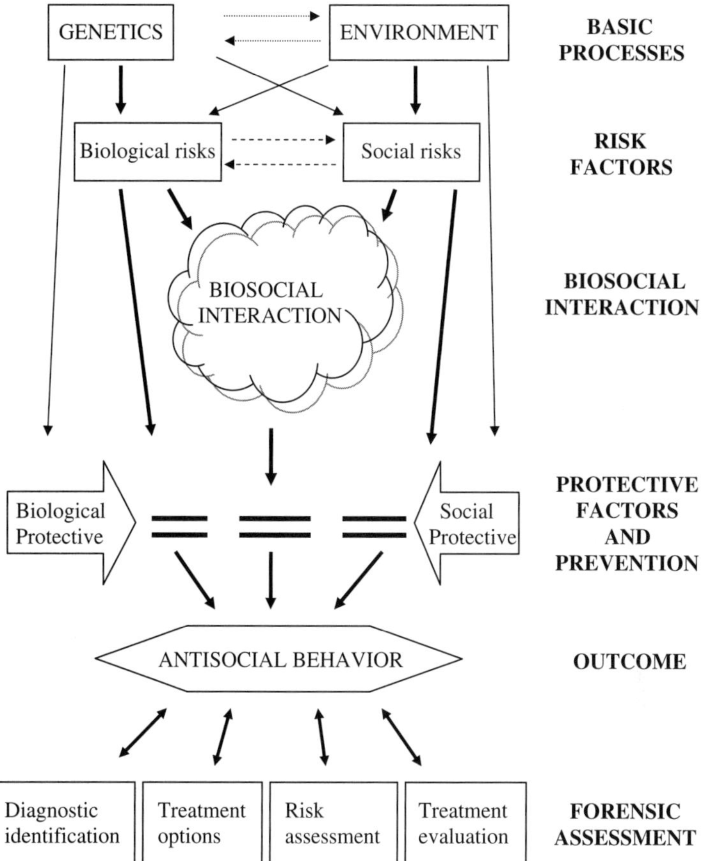

Fig. 1. Heuristic biosocial model of antisocial behavior as applied to forensic assessment. (*Adapted from* Raine A, Brennan P, Farrington DP. Biosocial bases of violence: conceptual and theoretical issues. In: Raine A, Brennan PA, Farrington DP, et al, editors. Biosocial bases of violence. New York: Plenum; 1997. p. 15; with permission.)

magnitude of genetic influences) vary largely among studies [8]. Significant progress in the understanding of these two issues and of the mechanisms through which genes exert their effect on antisocial behavior is likely to be made in the near future for three main reasons.

First, researchers have started to disentangle which distinct subtypes and aspects of antisocial behavior are particularly subject to genetic influence. For example, genetic influences were suggested to be greater for life-course–persistent antisocial behavior than for adolescence-limited antisocial behavior [9] and greater for aggressive antisocial behavior than for nonaggressive antisocial behavior [10].

Second, investigators have started to study associations between specific genes and antisocial behavior. As a result of technological advances, a large number of genetic markers are now available for studying DNA polymorphisms, and new laboratory techniques allow rapid genotyping, the process of identifying which alleles are present for any given marker for a particular person. In general medical research, an increasing number of genes are being identified for specific genetic syndromes. With respect to antisocial behavior, Brunner and colleagues [11] reported a single-gene mutation in the gene encoding the neurotransmitter-metabolizing enzyme monoamine oxidase A (MAOA) in an extended Dutch family in which multiple members exhibited violent criminal behavior. In psychiatric research such isolated mutations are rare, however [12], and it is clearly not plausible to consider them major determinants of multifactorial conditions such as antisocial behavior. Indeed, the precision of today's genetic research techniques makes it increasingly apparent that multiple genes are simultaneously involved in creating susceptibility for antisocial behavior.

Third, investigators have started to acknowledge the interplay between genetics and the environment; that is, whether genetic susceptibility leads to antisocial behavior may depend on the influence of environmental factors. Just as a genetic susceptibility for lung cancer may result in disease only after a person smokes cigarettes, a genetic susceptibility for antisocial behavior may remain latent in the absence of adverse environmental factors such as harsh parenting or living in a criminal neighborhood. For a person with both a genetic risk factor and an environmental risk factor for antisocial behavior, the actual risk for developing antisocial behavior may be far more than just the sum of the two risks [13,14].

An illustrative example, incorporating both the influence of a specific gene and its interaction with the environment in relation to antisocial behavior, is a recent, highly important and influential study by Caspi and colleagues [15]. A functional polymorphism in the gene encoding MAOA was studied in large sample of male children in New Zealand from birth to adulthood. Maltreated children who had a genotype conferring high levels of MAOA expression were found to be less likely to develop antisocial problems than maltreated children who had a genotype conferring low levels of MAOA expression. These findings provide evidence that specific genotypes can moderate children's sensitivity to environmental insults and may partly explain why not all victims of maltreatment grow up to victimize others. The recently increased interest in this kind of biosocial interaction is reflected in the fact that the findings of this study have already been replicated in humans [16] and in rhesus monkeys [17], although one human study did not find the same effect [18].

An interesting interaction effect of a different kind is imbedded in the social-push theory. Under this perspective, when an antisocial child lacks social factors that "push" or predispose him or her to antisocial behavior, biologic factors may more likely explain antisocial behavior [2,19]. In contrast, social causes of criminal behavior may be more important explanations of antisociality in those exposed to adverse early home conditions. This is not to say that antisocial children from adverse home backgrounds will never evidence biologic risk factors for antisocial and violent behavior, clearly, they will. Instead, the argument is that in such situations the link between antisocial behavior and biologic risk factors will be weaker than in antisocial children from benign social backgrounds, because the social causes of crime camouflage the biologic contribution. Conversely, in antisocial children from benign home backgrounds, the "noise" created by social influences on antisocial behavior is minimized, allowing the relationship between biology and antisocial behavior to shine through. Evidence supporting this theory comes from studies in various subfields of research. Within the field of genetic research, Christiansen [20] in a Danish sample of twins found heritability for crime was strikingly greater in those from high socioeconomic backgrounds and those who were rural born.

Exciting progress is being made in the knowledge concerning genetic contributions to antisocial behavior and the interplay of genetic factors with the environment. The exact mechanisms through which genetic factors lead to antisocial behavior, are not yet well understood, however. One probable important pathway is that genetic factors influence biologic factors, such as arousal and hormonal levels, as well as specific aspects of brain functioning, which in turn influence behavior. Therefore, studying such parameters is important to improve the understanding of the biologic mechanisms underlying antisocial behavior.

Psychophysiology and neuroendocrinology

A number of psychophysiologic and neuroendocrinologic correlates of aggressive, antisocial, and violent behavior have been reported [1,21–24]. For example antisocial behavior has been related to low serotonin [25], high testosterone [26], and low epinephrine [27], although findings have not always been consistent. To illustrate how studying biologic factors in this subfield may contribute to the understanding of which factors correlate with antisocial behavior and of the underlying mechanisms, a specific subgroup of psychophysiologic and neuroendocrinologic factors—those related to arousal—is discussed here.

The arousal theory postulates that low levels of arousal are related to antisocial behavior. Two explanations have been put forward for this assumption. First, the sensation-seeking theory argues that low arousal represents an unpleasant physiologic state. As such, antisocial behavior is viewed as a mode of sensation seeking, which is displayed to increase arousal levels to an optimal or normal level [28–30]. Second, the fearlessness theory argues that low levels of arousal (eg, as measured during mildly stressful psychophysiologic test sessions) are markers of low levels of fear [1,30]. For example, fearless individuals (such as bomb disposal experts who have been decorated for their bravery) were found to have particularly low heart rates and reactivity [31]. Antisocial and violent behavior (eg, fights and assaults) is considered to require a degree of fearlessness to execute, and a lack of fear of socializing punishments in early childhood may contribute to disturbed fear conditioning and lack of conscience development [1]. For a more extensive overview of the underlying theoretical framework see Raine [1,2].

The best-studied biologic parameter of arousal is heart rate, a measure of autonomic nervous system activity. Low heart rate is the most frequently replicated biologic correlate of antisocial behavior in children and adolescents [32]. Low heart rate has repeatedly been shown to predict antisocial behavior, opposing the notion that a delinquent way of life may have caused low heart rate [33]. For example, one study showed that a low resting heart rate as early as age 3 years relates to aggressive behavior at age 11 years [34]. An important feature of the relationship is its diagnostic specificity, because conduct disorder seems to be the only psychiatric disorder to have been linked consistently to low heart rate [32].

Although a low heart rate has been found to be a predictor of violence independent of other social risk factors [35], there is accumulating evidence a low heart rate, like the genetic susceptibility as described previously, interacts with social factors in relation to antisocial behavior. For example, boys who have low resting heart rates are more likely to become violent adult offenders if they also have a poor relationship with their parent and if they come from a large family [35]. Furthermore, boys who have a low heart rate are especially likely to be rated as aggressive by their teachers if their mother was a teenage parent, if they come from a family of low socioeconomic status, or if they were separated from a parent by age 10 years [35]. Studies of arousal also support the social-push perspective. Although the resting heart rate level is generally lower in antisocial individuals, a low resting heart rate is a particularly strong characteristic of antisocial individuals from higher social classes [34,36].

In line with findings from studies on heart rate, other direct and indirect parameters of arousal, including resting electroencephalogram [37] and skin conductance activity [38,39], have been related to antisocial behavior. An interesting and increasingly investigated neuroendocrinologic parameter related to arousal is cortisol, the final product of the hypothalamus-pituitary-adrenal (HPA) axis. Together, the autonomic nervous system and the HPA axis constitute the two most important arousal-regulating biologic systems. In line with the low-arousal theory, several studies have found low basal cortisol levels to be associated with antisocial behavior in clinically referred, at-risk, and general population samples of children and adolescents [40,41] Also, blunted cortisol responsivity to stress has been found in antisocial children and adolescents [42]. One study to date investigated the effect of cortisol levels on future antisocial behavior and found low cortisol levels at age 10 to 12 years to predict aggression at age 15 to 17 years [43]. So far, only one study has investigated how cortisol levels interact with social factors in relation to antisocial behavior. Scarpa and colleagues [44] found that high cortisol after a stressor was associated with aggression in victims of community violence but not in nonvictims.

In summary, this subfield of research is revealing biologic correlates of antisocial behavior and also aids the understanding of the underlying mechanisms. One other method of research, direct brain functioning, is likely to provide important additional information about the underlying mechanisms.

Brain imaging

Brain imaging is a growing and increasingly influential subarea of biologic research on antisocial behavior. Several imaging techniques (eg, MRI, functional MRI [fMRI], positron emission tomography, and single photon emission [CT]) are now in wide use. During the last decade, these techniques, particularly MRI and fMRI, have also been adjusted for use in children and adolescents. The predominant finding in neuroimaging studies of adults is that violent offenders have anatomic or functional deficits in the anterior regions of the brain, particularly the prefrontal region [45]. These studies have covered a substantial variety of samples (eg, murderers, violent schizophrenics, drug-abusing psychopaths, community samples of subjects who have antisocial personality disorder) and measures of frontal functioning (blood flow, glucose, *N*-acetyl aspartate), but sample sizes have generally been small. That most of them observe anterior frontal deficits in association with violent, aggressive, antisocial behavior suggests that frontal dysfunction may be related to generalized antisocial and violent behavior. Prefrontal deficits could lead to antisocial behavior through at least three routes: (1) through a disability to reason and to take appropriate decisions in risky situations [46]; (2) through poor fear conditioning and stress responsivity and thereby poor consciousness development [1,47]; or (3) by lowered arousal levels [48] which, as discussed earlier, can facilitate sensation-seeking and fearless forms of antisocial behavior.

The specific subregions of the prefrontal cortex that are structurally or functionally impaired in antisocial and aggressive individuals are still open to question. Findings from studies investigating damage to the prefrontal cortex in civilians [49] and in soldiers [50] implicate the ventromedial and orbitofrontal subregions. Alternatively, impairments to the dorsolateral region, which is critically involved in cognitive flexibility and response perseveration, cannot be ruled out, because recidivistic antisocial behavior can be conceptualized as perseverative, unmodifiable behavior in the face of a repeatedly punished response.

For long time, evidence for an association between prefrontal deficits and antisocial behavior in children and adolescents has been available from neuropsychologic studies revealing executive functioning deficits in antisocial children [51] and studies showing associations between prefrontal deficits and antisocial behavior after head injury [52,53]. In the twenty-first century imaging studies have started to provide the first, albeit preliminary, evidence for structural and functional brain abnormalities in antisocial children and adolescents. Preliminary studies using MRI [54] and fMRI [55] in small samples found deficits in children and adolescents who had conduct disorder similar to those in antisocial adults.

Again, the biologic correlates of antisocial behavior found in brain-imaging research are likely to be even more informative when interactions with environmental factors are taken into account [56]. For example, one fMRI study [57] showed that a biologic risk factor (initial right hemisphere dysfunction), when combined with a psychosocial risk factor (severe early physical abuse), predisposed to serious violence.

In conclusion, brain-imaging techniques have started to provide evidence linking brain deficits with antisocial behavior. More studies are needed to reveal which specific subtypes of antisocial behavior are related to which particular brain dysfunctions. Such research should include samples of juveniles and adults.

How do these findings relate to specific aspects of forensic assessment?

As mentioned previously, forensic assessment comprises (1) diagnostic identification, (2) providing treatment options, (3) assessing risk, and (4) evaluating treatment [4]. Some of the important current literature on the biologic factors of antisocial behavior have been reviewed. The question remains: how do findings from the literature relate to these four aspects of forensic assessment? Despite recent progress, major lacunae still exist in the knowledge of the relationship between biology and antisocial behavior. Moreover, the translation of knowledge from correlational and risk research to clinical practice must be undertaken with prudence and due circumspection. Nevertheless, it is important to start studying the future possibilities for biology to inform forensic child and adolescent psychiatry practice. As biosocial models begin to reveal the mechanisms by which biologic and social processes influence the development of antisocial behavior, both types of process may become of value for forensic assessment (see Fig. 1).

Diagnostic identification

Biologic factors may be useful in the process of diagnostic identification for several reasons. First, they may be important in extending the available range of diagnostic assessment possibilities. Currently, some psychiatric dysfunctions are extremely difficult to evaluate. For example, callous and unemotional traits have proven to be hard to assess in an interview or with pencil-and-paper questionnaires. Biologic parameters may be helpful in this respect; for example, callous and unemotional traits have been related to blunted heart rate reactivity [24]. Furthermore, brain-imaging research is beginning to identify the structural and functional correlates of pathologic lying and malingering that, at least in theory, could have implications for forensic assessment in this area [58,59]. Enlarging the range of current diagnostic possibilities by testing for neurobiologic functioning may help identify important psychobiologic deficits that are currently difficult to assess.

Second, specificity of diagnostic assessment may be enhanced when biologic factors are taken into account. It is widely accepted that psychiatric disorders in general, and hence externalizing disorders, are etiologically heterogeneous. Presently, the heterogeneity of patient groups hinders research, assessment, and treatment in psychiatry; all are likely to be more effective when based on a more homogeneous patient selection. Using biology to define subgroups of patients may be one of the ways to arrive at such homogeneity. For example, with respect to aggression, researchers in neurobiology are attempting to disentangle different subtypes of aggression (eg, reactive versus proactive) based on neurobiologic profiles. Eventually, uncovering underlying biologic mechanisms may even result in revisions of the diagnostic classification of some ranges of pathologic behavior.

Increasing the range of diagnostic tools and their specificity is not just an academic exercise but is likely to be of particular relevance for the three other aspects of forensic assessment also.

Providing treatment options

The improvements in diagnostic identification that may result from the increasing knowledge of the relationship between biology and behavior may simultaneously reveal means to enhance the specificity and effectiveness of current treatment options. Moreover, improved diagnostic identification may lead to new intervention approaches.

First, improving the knowledge about the biologic etiologic factors of antisocial behavior and incorporating these factors in forensic assessment may help direct specific interventions to specific subgroups of patients. In many subfields of somatic clinical practice, biologic markers already are standard determinants of intervention. For example, in cancer treatment, somatic markers are used to choose the most effective chemotherapeutic agent. In psychiatry, researchers have started to investigate biologic markers as predictors for treatment outcome. For example, in depressed patients, pretreatment baseline prolactine levels have been shown to predict response to antidepressant treatment [60], suggesting that subtyping specific patient groups based on this biologic profile can improve effectiveness of treatment.

Improved diagnostic identification may be relevant for other modes of treatment as well as for pharmacologic treatment programs. Preliminary evidence for this assumption comes from a study by Van de Wiel and colleagues [61], who studied cortisol responsivity during stress in 22 clinically referred behavior-disordered children before psychotherapeutic treatment. They found that low cortisol responsivity during stress predicted poor treatment outcome. The subgroup of children with this biologic profile might need different forms of treatment from those with a strong cortisol response to stress.

Second, new treatment possibilities may arise from biologic and biosocial studies. Influencing a biologic factor that is related to antisocial behavior may in turn modulate antisocial behavior. For example, as discussed earlier, low arousal has been related to antisocial behavior. There is evidence that stimulants (eg, methylphenidate) both increase arousal and reduce aggressive behavior [62]. Progress in pharmacologic treatment possibilities may be established by improving the knowledge about the actual underlying biologic deficits that may be targeted.

Taking biologic vulnerabilities into account in understanding juvenile antisocial behavior can also lead to new approaches for nonpharmacologic interventions. For example, there is some preliminary evidence for the possible efficacy of using biofeedback to increase physiologic arousal in hyperactive children [63]. With respect to HPA activity, preliminary evidence for the potential of nonpharmacologic programs to alter biologic vulnerability for antisocial behavior has been provided by Fisher and Stoolmiller [64] in a study evaluating a foster care intervention program. A group of aggressive juveniles were found to have a flattened diurnal pattern of cortisol levels before entering the program. After the intervention, diurnal cortisol patterns were found to be more normal, with high cortisol levels in the morning and a decrease during the day, and aggression levels had diminished. Additional indirect evidence for this assumption comes from prevention studies. For example, there is initial evidence that positive environmental manipulations are capable of both producing long-term shifts in arousal and psychophysiologic information processing as well as adult criminal behavior. In one study, children matched for early psychophysiologic functioning were randomly assigned to experimental and control conditions. The experimental condition consisted of a program in which physical exercise and nutritional and educational enrichment was provided from age 3 to 5 years. This program resulted in increased psychophysiologic arousal and orienting at age 11 years and reduced crime at age 23 years as compared with the control group [65,66].

In summary, incorporating components aimed at understanding and tackling the biologic basis of antisocial behavior in forensic assessment may extend the range of treatment options and improve their specificity and effectiveness.

Risk assessment

As with treatment options, risk taxation may be influenced by knowledge of biologic correlates of behavior. A certain biologic profile may be related to the risk of recidivism and predict treatment outcome. No studies to date have investigated this hypothesis, but indirect preliminary evidence can be found in the literature. For example, in a longitudinal study of the recurrence of depression after treatment, cortisol levels were measured after remittance of a depressive episode. Heightened cortisol levels were found to predict a new episode of depression. In another study, Prichep and colleagues [67] distinguished two separate subgroups of cocaine-dependent males on the basis of a qualitative electroencephalogram. By using this biologic typology, they were able to the predict relapse rate after treatment. In a similar fashion, biologic parameters may be useful in predicting reoccurrence of antisocial behavior. Still, studies investigating this hypothesis are currently lacking.

Treatment evaluation

The last aspect of forensic assessment that may be informed by biologic factors is treatment evaluation. When assessing a certain biologic profile that is correlated with behavioral problems before treatment, investigating this same biologic profile again after treatment may be useful as a measure of treatment outcome. As discussed previously, preliminary results of a study by Fisher and Stoolmiller [64] suggested that successfully diminishing aggressive behavior by means of a foster care intervention program coincided with normalization of diurnal cortisol patterns. Cortisol levels may be a parameter that could inform practitioners concerning treatment efficacy. Again, no studies to date have investigated the potential of biologic parameters to evaluate treatment outcome within forensic psychiatry.

In summary, although still largely hypothetical, the first evidence from studies in general medicine and other fields of psychiatry support the possibility that biologic parameters may also be useful for forensic psychiatric assessment. Obviously, this hypothesis requires further testing, and practical issues must be addressed when considering incorporating biologic factors in forensic assessment. For example, some of the biologic factors discussed here (eg, brain imaging) are clearly difficult and expensive to assess. Others are fairly simple, quick, and cost-efficient: most genetic tests only require a swab to obtain some cells from the mouth, heart rate can be measured by taking the pulse by hand or with a simple chronometer, and cortisol and several other hormones can be analyzed noninvasively and reliably from saliva. Although it is too early to reach firm conclusions, new studies that specifically test hypotheses concerning the mechanisms by which biologic factors are related to specific aspects of forensic assessment are both feasible and warranted.

Philosophical, ethical, and political considerations

Biologic research of antisocial behavior has a history of evoking passionate debate on philosophical, ethical, and political issues surrounding it. Although they are not the main focus of this article, the authors consider it important to address briefly a few relevant issues. New findings in the growing field of neurobiologic research challenge the current way of conceptualizing antisocial behavior and force consideration of some important questions. For example, now that prefrontal deficits are known to be related to aggression, how should society deal with the cold-blooded murderer who, years earlier, had a car accident damaging crucial parts of the frontal lobe? What repercussions should this knowledge of causality have on the concept of free will and judicial handling? In the future it may be possible to calculate a child's risk of becoming severely violent by adding up the child's gene profile, brain deficits caused by maternal smoking, low cortisol responsivity, and underactive prefrontal cortex—or by scanning the child's genes. Could such a person be forced into some kind of treatment program when this risk reaches a certain limit? If a juvenile in a psychiatric or justice facility has such a risk profile, does this profile influence decisions as to whether the child can return to the society?

Such questions, inspired by the increased interest and progress in biologic psychiatric research, have given rise to a lively philosophical debate. Although elaborating on philosophical theories is beyond the bounds of this article, the authors briefly discuss two issues. First, like scientific research models, philosophical models have been proposed for combining biologic and social perspectives in research. For example, Kendler [68] has advocated explanatory pluralism: hypothetically, by using multiple mutually informative perspectives differing in levels of abstraction, scientific research can provide complementary kinds of understanding. This author argues for a kind of explanatory pluralism, called "integrative pluralism" [69]; by building bridges between etiologic models but avoiding large theoretical frameworks, science may be most successful in uncovering mechanisms underlying mind and behavior. Such a philosophic structure is being provided by combining biologic factors and social factors within psychiatric research.

A philosophical issue that is more specifically linked with forensic psychiatry, and which has potential legal consequences, is related to the concept of free will. Although free will is a complex construct, for the present purposes free will is assumed to reflect the assumption that persons have control over their behavior and therefore can choose whether or not to do something. If biologic factors (eg, prefrontal damage) are causally involved in antisocial behavior, could such a biologic deficit constrain free will (eg, by causing impulsive behavior) and thereby reduce responsibility for a given crime? In this view, free will may be a continuous concept: the more severe the biologic deficit, the less free the will. Already there have been legal cases in which defense lawyers, sometimes successfully, have tried to reduce the charges against their clients by arguing that frontal damage, as revealed by brain imaging, caused the client to conduct the crime [70,71]. Still, such assumptions are currently hypothetical, because research on biosocial causal mechanisms of antisocial behavior is in its infancy; and firm conclusions as to whether a certain biologic factor caused a specific act of antisocial behavior cannot be drawn. Even if such mechanisms are further uncovered, there will be difficulties in moving from findings based on groups of offenders in research studies to conclusions about an individual criminal.

In addition to philosophical issues, this field of research has raised ethical questions, often overheard in political debates. Although ethical issues of biologic research have been discussed in a cautious and stimulating manner by researchers [71,72], this discussion has not prevented biologic research from being particularly unpopular with both right- and left-wing politicians. Conservatives worry that biologic research will be used to let vicious offenders go free. Liberals fret that biologic profiles may someday be used preventively to incarcerate an innocent person who has the profile of a violent offender. One important comment on such concerns is that the relationship between biology and complex constructs such as antisocial behavior will never be hardwired and one-directional. In contrast, it will always be probabilistic and reciprocal. A vast number of biologic and environmental factors interact together in relation to behavior, but it is unlikely that behavior can be predicted with 100% accuracy in the near future. Notably, the important discussion of how society and politics should deal with the knowledge of factors relating to antisocial behavior is as relevant for environmental predictors as for biologic ones.

Moreover, increased knowledge about the factors, including biologic factors, that cause antisocial behavior can help practitioners improve the tools for treatment and prevention of individual antisocial behavior as well as the tools for protecting society. More efficient prevention programs can reduce the number of children and adolescents who are currently being treated or simply incarcerated in costly residential settings, and more specific and effective treatment programs can contribute to handling their often serious psychiatric problems. Society as a whole can benefit, because improving and using the knowledge of biologic risk factors can be expected, at least to a certain degree, to help prevent the occurrence and severity of antisocial behavior. In contrast, ignoring the question of how juvenile antisocial behavior develops and persists will sacrifice the opportunity to decrease the vulnerability to crime and violence of both individuals and society.

Agenda for the coming decade

The answer to the question posed in the title of this article should probably be: no. It is highly unlikely that future forensic assessment will ever be completely neurobiologic. Nevertheless the authors hope they have shown that appreciating the contribution of both biologic and social factors in the shaping of behavior may prove fruitful. Biologic and biosocial research is starting to provide new insights into the backgrounds of antisocial behavior in children and adolescents. Further research is warranted to learn more about which distinct components of antisocial behavior are most strongly related to particular aspects of biology and the exact mechanisms by which biology interacts with the environment in relation to antisocial behavior. Researchers could help extend this knowledge by conducting new studies and remaining cautious and realistic when describing their results. In addition, the help of clinicians is of great importance in facilitating biologic research within their facilities and initiating the study of the possibilities of implementing the results of current and future biologic research in child and adolescent forensic clinical practice. Although provocative, new findings from this field of research may lead clinicians to rethink their approach to antisocial behavior of children and adolescents and help them find new answers to the causes and cures of their behavior while continuing to protect society.

References

[1] Raine A. The psychopathology of crime: criminal behavior as a clinical disorder. San Diego (CA): Academic Press, Inc; 1993.

[2] Raine A. Biosocial studies of antisocial and violent behavior in children and adults: a review. J Abnorm Child Psychol 2002;30:311–26.
[3] Cacioppo JT, Berntson GG, Sheridan JF, et al. Multilevel integrative analyses of human behavior: social neuroscience and the complementing nature of social and biological approaches. Psychol Bull 2000;126:829–43.
[4] Grisso T, Zimring FE. Double jeopardy: adolescent offenders with mental disorders. Chicago (IL): University of Chicago Press; 2004.
[5] Plomin R, McGuffin P. Psychopathology in the postgenomic era. Annu Rev Psychol 2003;54: 205–28.
[6] Rowe DC. Biology and crime. Los Angeles (CA): Roxbury Publishing; 2001.
[7] Rutter ML. The nature-nurture integration: the example of antisocial behavior. Am Psychol 1997;52:390–8.
[8] Rhee SH, Waldman ID. Genetic and environmental influences on antisocial behavior: a meta-analysis of twin and adoption studies. Psychol Bull 2002;128:490–529.
[9] Vermeiren R. Psychopathology and delinquency in adolescents: a descriptive and developmental perspective. Clin Psychol Rev 2003;23:277–318.
[10] Eley TC, Lichtenstein P, Moffitt TE. A longitudinal behavioral genetic analysis of the etiology of aggressive and nonaggressive antisocial behavior. Dev Psychopathol 2003;15:383–402.
[11] Brunner HG, Nelen M, Breakefield XO, et al. Abnormal behavior associated with a point mutation in the structural gene for monoamine oxidase A. Science 1993;262:578–80.
[12] Kendler KS. "A gene for...": the nature of gene action in psychiatric disorders. Am J Psychiatry 2005;162:1243–52.
[13] Button TM, Scourfield J, Martin N, et al. Family dysfunction interacts with genes in the causation of antisocial symptoms. Behav Genet 2005;35:115–20.
[14] Cloninger CR, Sigvardsson S, Bohman M, et al. Predisposition to petty criminality in Swedish adoptees. II. Cross-fostering analysis of gene-environment interaction. Arch Gen Psychiatry 1982;39:1242–7.
[15] Caspi A, McClay J, Moffitt TE, et al. Role of genotype in the cycle of violence in maltreated children. Science 2002;297:851–4.
[16] Foley DL, Eaves LJ, Wormley B, et al. Childhood adversity, monoamine oxidase a genotype, and risk for conduct disorder. Arch Gen Psychiatry 2004;61:738–44.
[17] Newman TK, Syagailo YV, Barr CS, et al. Monoamine oxidase A gene promoter variation and rearing experience influences aggressive behavior in rhesus monkeys. Biol Psychiatry 2005;57: 167–72.
[18] Haberstick BC, Lessem JM, Hopfer CJ, et al. Monoamine oxidase A (MAOA) and antisocial behaviors in the presence of childhood and adolescent maltreatment. Am J Med Genet B Neuropsychiatr Genet 2005;135:59–64.
[19] Mednick SA. A bio-social theory of the learning of law-abiding behavior. In: Mednick SA, Christiansen KO, editors. Biosocial bases of criminal behavior. New York: Gardner Press; 1977. p. 1–8.
[20] Cristiansen KO. A preliminary study of criminality among twins. In: Mednick SA, Christiansen KO, editors. Biosocial basis of criminal behavior. New York: Gardner Press; 1977. p. 89–108.
[21] Volavka J. The neurobiology of violence: an update. J Neuropsychiatry Clin Neurosci 1999; 11(3):307–14.
[22] Lahey BB, McBurnett K, Loeber R, et al. Psychobiology of conduct disorder. In: Sholevar G, editor. Conduct disorders in children and adolescents: assessments and interventions. Washington (DC): American Psychiatric Press; 1995.
[23] Susman EJ, Granger DA, Murowchick E, et al. Gonadal and adrenal hormones: developmental transitions and aggressive behavior. Ann N Y Acad Sci 1996;794:18–30.
[24] Lorber MF. Psychophysiology of aggression, psychopathy, and conduct problems: a meta-analysis. Psychol Bull 2004;130:531–52.
[25] Coccaro EF, Kavoussi RJ, Trestman RL, et al. Serotonin function in human subjects: intercorrelations among central 5-HT indices and aggressiveness. Psychiatry Res 1997;73:1–14.

[26] Archer J. The influence of testosterone on human aggression. Br J Psychol 1991;82:1–28.

[27] McBurnett K, Raine A, Stouthamer-Loeber M, et al. Mood and hormone responses to psychological challenge in adolescent males with conduct problems. Biol Psychiatry 2005;57: 1109–16.

[28] Eysenck H. Crime and personality. 3rd edition. St. Albans (UK): Paladin; 1977.

[29] Quay HC. Psychopathic personality as pathological stimulation-seeking. Am J Psychiatry 1965; 122:180–3.

[30] Raine A, Brennan PA, Farrington DP, et al. Biosocial bases of violence. New York: Plenum Press; 1997.

[31] O'Connor K, Hallam R, Rachman S. Fearlessness and courage: a replication experiment. Br J Psychol 1985;76:187–97.

[32] Ortiz J, Raine A. Heart rate level and antisocial behavior in children and adolescents: a meta-analysis. J Am Acad Child Adolesc Psychiatry 2004;43:154–62.

[33] Moffitt TE, Caspi A. Childhood predictors differentiate life-course persistent and adolescence-limited antisocial pathways among males and females. Dev Psychopathol 2001;13:355–75.

[34] Raine A, Venables PH, Mednick SA. Low resting heart rate at age 3 years predisposes to aggression at age 11 years: evidence from the Mauritius Child Health Project. J Am Acad Child Adolesc Psychiatry 1997;36:1457–64.

[35] Farrington DP. The relationship between low resting heart rate and violence. In: Raine A, Brennan PA, Farrington D, et al, editors. Biosocial bases of violence. New York: Plenum; 1997. p. 89–105.

[36] Raine A, Venables PH. Tonic heart rate level, social class and antisocial behaviour in adolescents. Biol Psychol 1984;18:123–32.

[37] Raine A, Venables PH. Evoked potential augmenting-reducing in psychopaths and criminals with impaired smooth-pursuit eye movements. Psychiatry Res 1990;31:85–98.

[38] Fowles DC. Electrodermal activity and antisocial behavior: empirical findings and theoretical issues. New York: Plenum; 1993.

[39] Raine A, Venables PH, Williams M. Autonomic orienting responses in 15-year-old male subjects and criminal behavior at age 24. Am J Psychiatry 1990;147:933–7.

[40] McBurnett K, Lahey BB, Rathouz PJ, et al. Low salivary cortisol and persistent aggression in boys referred for disruptive behavior. Arch Gen Psychiatry 2000;57:38–43.

[41] Shirtcliff EA, Granger DA, Booth A, et al. Low salivary cortisol levels and externalizing behavior problems in youth. Dev Psychopathol 2005;17:167–84.

[42] Van Goozen SH, Matthys W, Cohen-Kettenis PT, et al. Hypothalamic-pituitary-adrenal axis and autonomic nervous system activity in disruptive children and matched controls. J Am Acad Child Adolesc Psychiatry 2000;39:1438–45.

[43] Shoal GD, Giancola PR, Kirillova GP. Salivary cortisol, personality, and aggressive behavior in adolescent boys: a 5-year longitudinal study. J Am Acad Child Adolesc Psychiatry 2003;42: 1101–7.

[44] Scarpa A, Ollendick TH. Community violence exposure in a young adult sample: III. Psychophysiology and victimization interact to affect risk for aggression. Journal of Community Violence 2003;31:321–38.

[45] Ishikawa SS, Raine A. Prefrontal deficits and antisocial behavior: a causal model. In: Caspi A, Lahey BB, Moffit E, editors. Causes of conduct disorder and juvenile delinquency. New York: The Guilford Press; 2003. p. 79–104.

[46] Bechara A, Damasio H, Tranel D, et al. Deciding advantageously before knowing the advantageous strategy. Science 1997;275:1293–5.

[47] Hugdahl K. Cortical control of human classical conditioning: autonomic and positron emission tomography data. Psychophysiology 1998;35:170–8.

[48] Dahl RE. The regulation of sleep and arousal: development and psychopathology. In: Farber EA, Hertzig M, editors. Annual progress in child psychiatry and child development. Bristol (PA): Brunner/Mazel; 1998. p. 3–28.

[49] Damasio A. Descartes' error: emotion, reason, and the human brain. New York: Grosset/ Putnam; 1994.

[50] Grafman J, Schwab K, Warden D, et al. Frontal lobe injuries, violence, and aggression: a report of the Vietnam Head Injury Study. Neurology 1996;46:1231–8.
[51] Morgan AB, Lilienfeld SO. A meta-analytic review of the relation between antisocial behavior and neuropsychological measures of executive function. Clin Psychol Rev 2000;20:113–36.
[52] Hux K, Bond V, Skinner S, et al. Parental report of occurrences and consequences of traumatic brain injury among delinquent and non-delinquent youth. Brain Inj 1998;12:667–81.
[53] Max JE, Koele SL, Smith Jr WL, et al. Psychiatric disorders in children and adolescents after severe traumatic brain injury: a controlled study. J Am Acad Child Adolesc Psychiatry 1998;37: 832–40.
[54] Kruesi MJ, Casanova MF, Mannheim G, et al. Reduced temporal lobe volume in early onset conduct disorder. Psychiatry Res 2004;132:1–11.
[55] Sterzer P, Stadler C, Krebs A, et al. Abnormal neural responses to emotional visual stimuli in adolescents with conduct disorder. Biol Psychiatry 2005;57:7–15.
[56] Cacioppo JT, Berntson GG, Lorig TS, et al. Just because you're imaging the brain doesn't mean you can stop using your head: a primer and set of first principles. J Pers Soc Psychol 2003; 85:650–61.
[57] Raine A, Park S, Lencz T, et al. Reduced right hemisphere activation in severely abused violent offenders during a working memory task: an fMRI study. Aggress Behav 2001;27:111–29.
[58] Lee TM, Liu HL, Tan LH, et al. Lie detection by functional magnetic resonance imaging. Hum Brain Mapp 2002;15:157–64.
[59] Yang YL, Raine A, Lencz T, et al. Prefrontal structural abnormalities in liars. Br J Psychiatry 2005;187:320–5.
[60] Porter RJ, Mulder RT, Joyce PR. Baseline prolactin and L-tryptophan availability predict response to antidepressant treatment in major depression. Psychopharmacology (Berl) 2003;165: 216–21.
[61] Van de Wiel NM, Van Goozen SH, Matthys W, et al. Cortisol and treatment effect in children with disruptive behavior disorders: a preliminary study. J Am Acad Child Adolesc Psychiatry 2004;43:1011–8.
[62] Connor DF. Aggression and antisocial behavior in children and adolescents. New York: The Guilford Press; 2002.
[63] Monastra VJ, Lynn S, Linden M, et al. Electroencephalographic biofeedback in the treatment of attention-deficit/hyperactivity disorder. Appl Psychophysiol Biofeedback 2005;30:95–114.
[64] Fisher PA, Stoolmiller M. Investigating longitudinal trends in correlations between maltreated foster children's behavior and L-HPA axis activity. Presented at the International Conference of Infant Studies. Toronto (ON), April 18–21, 2002.
[65] Raine A, Venables PH, Dalais C, et al. Early educational and health enrichment at age 3–5 years is associated with increased autonomic and central nervous system arousal and orienting at age 11 years: evidence from the Mauritius Child Health Project. Psychophysiology 2001;38:254–66.
[66] Raine A, Mellingen K, Liu J, et al. Effects of environmental enrichment at ages 3–5 years on schizotypal personality and antisocial behavior at ages 17 and 23 years. Am J Psychiatry 2003; 160:1627–35.
[67] Prichep LS, Alper KR, Sverdlov L, et al. Outcome related electrophysiological subtypes of cocaine dependence. Clin Electroencephalogr 2002;33:8–20.
[68] Kendler KS. Toward a philosophical structure for psychiatry. Am J Psychiatry 2005;162: 433–40.
[69] Mitchell SD. Biological complexity and integrative pluralism. Cambridge (UK): Cambridge University Press; 2003.
[70] Sapolsky RM. The frontal cortex and the criminal justice system. Philos Trans R Soc Lond B Biol Sci 2004;359:1787–96.
[71] Raine A. Murderous minds: can we see the mark of Cain? Cerebrum 1999;1:15–30.
[72] Parker LS. Ethical concerns in the research and treatment of complex disease. Trends Genet 1995;11:520–3.

ELSEVIER
SAUNDERS

Child Adolesc Psychiatric Clin N Am
15 (2006) 445–458

CHILD AND ADOLESCENT PSYCHIATRIC CLINICS OF NORTH AMERICA

Mental Health Service Provision in Juvenile Justice Facilities: Pre- and Postrelease Psychiatric Care

John F. Chapman, PsyD[a,*], Rani A. Desai, PhD[b], Paul R. Falzer, PhD[b]

[a]*State of Connecticut–Judicial Branch, Court Support Services Division, 936 Silas Deane Highway, Wethersfield, CT 06516, USA*
[b]*Department of Psychiatry, Yale University School of Medicine, VA Connecticut Health System, West Haven, CT, USA*

Although many young people are referred to the juvenile justice system, only a small but significant number are incarcerated. Juvenile arrests in America are numerous, with 2.3 million juveniles arrested in 2002 [1]. The incarceration rate is lower. For the entire year of 1999 there were 371 juveniles per 100,000 in custody. Incarceration may take place either before a finding of guilt has been made by the court (preadjudication) or after a finding of guilt has been made (postadjudication). Incarceration can occur in a number of settings. Youth held in custody may be held in public locked detention centers and training schools or, more commonly, in locked or unlocked private facilities [2]. The type of services provided is generally related to the type of facility. Short-term facilities tend to offer less rehabilitation than long-term facilities [3].

This article introduces the mental health practitioner to certain concepts and challenges and to the satisfactions unique to practice in juvenile justice. It begins by describing the demographics of the youth incarcerated in the United States and the pathways in and out of the juvenile justice system and juvenile justice facilities with a focus on decision making. These pathways are surprisingly fluid because of multiple points of entry and re-arrest. For the underserved it is an entry point into the mental health care system. Common psychiatric problems in juvenile

* Corresponding author.
E-mail address: John.Chapman@jud.state.ct.us (J.F. Chapman).

1056-4993/06/$ – see front matter. Published by Elsevier Inc.
doi:10.1016/j.chc.2005.11.002

systems are discussed. Systems of mental health care delivery in juvenile justice are explored, including the relationship of these systems to the court and correctional custody structure. The possible contributions of social science to judicial and correctional decision making are described. Thoughts about evidence-based practice among this population are explored. The necessity of the interdisciplinary team and the role of the psychiatrist as part of that team are examined. Ultimately it is hoped that a multidisciplinary, multifaceted, and thoughtful approach will provide meaningful career choices for the psychiatrist and more seamless services to young people through the permeable walls of the juvenile justice system.

Characteristics of an incarcerated youth population

The majority of youth in juvenile facilities had property offenses as their most serious charge. Sixty percent of those held in custody are minority youth [2]. African American children are more likely to be placed in a juvenile justice facility than white youth, who are more likely to be hospitalized, despite little difference in presenting problems [4]. Juvenile justice is the gateway for many underprivileged youth to access mental health care. Children in the juvenile justice system have higher mortality rates from violence [5,6], problems with traumatic stress [7], comorbid anxiety, depression, substance use, other conditions [8], and suicide risk [9,10]. As many as 25% of adjudicated delinquents are placed out of the home [11].

Juvenile justice decision points

The juvenile justice system comprises a series of decision points and related processes. The most common entry point into the system is through arrest and a decision by a law enforcement officer to detain or refer to court. For juveniles who are in detention, a judicial hearing is held to determine whether they will be remanded or released pending adjudication of their charges. Those who are detained appear at a subsequent classification hearing that determines whether they will be housed in a secure or nonsecure faculty. In some states classification decisions require judicial approval. In other states, classification decisions are made by police, detention staff, or others. These decisions have direct consequences for the individuals involved because they affect a host of subsequent decisions and activities.

Later decision points include the detention or initial hearing, hearings on motions to transfer jurisdiction to criminal court, the trial or adjudication hearing, the disposition hearing, appeals hearings, and postdisposition review hearings for those placed in the home with services or for out-of-home placements (Fig. 1) [12].

These multiple decision points create a fluid juvenile justice system with permeable boundaries. There may be multiple readmissions, which are likely to

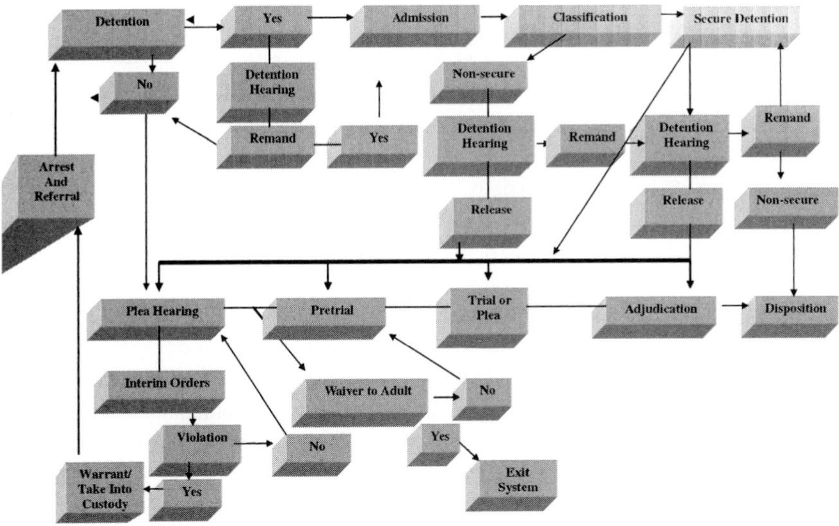

Fig. 1. Juvenile justice decision points.

interfere with existing or planned treatment interventions. These interruptions can be a major source of tension between legal and health care personnel. Frequent readmissions may indicate the need for more intensive mental health services. During evaluation by clinical staff, children admitted to a detention center more than once should be given particular consideration in an effort to identify any clinical factors associated with readmission.

Psychiatrists are frequently consulted at crucial decision points, and their clinical judgments inform the decisions of various juvenile justice system personnel, including judges, attorneys, and staff at detention facilities. Unfortunately, evidence from more than 50 years of investigation, beginning with Meehl's [13,14] studies comparing clinical findings with statistical predictions, leads to the incontrovertible conclusion that unaided decisions made by clinicians tend to be inaccurate, biased, and inconsistent, and similar problems may exist in judicial and administrative decision making. The sources of what is called "sub-optimal" decision making include attributional biases [15,16], illusory correlations [17,18], and cognitive illusions [19]. All of these biases may play a part in judicial decision making about confinement. Legal scholars suggest that persons trained as judicial decision makers have an inveterate distrust of the probabilistic reasoning and normative modeling that are intrinsic to traditional decision science [20–22]. After all, actuarial models express predictions about populations, but judges, police, and detention staff make judgments about individuals who present unique qualities and circumstances, and these judgments are made one at a time.

An alternative approach to unaided expert decision making involves the use of actuarial tools. For instance, Monahan and associates [23] developed an actuarial tool that has a 77% concurrence rate between future acts of violence committed by persons who have mental disorders and a statistical forecast of their behavior. Remarkably, the false-positive and false-negative rates for this instrument are almost equivalent, and it has been shown that such instruments are of substantial help in enhancing prediction.

Recently, a third approach to decision making has come to the fore that enables expert judgment to be informed by findings of empiric research and theories of decision science. The approach known as Structural Professional Judgment has been championed by a number of investigators [24–27]. Perhaps, as Swets and colleagues [28] suggest, decision science is well suited to healing the breach between clinical and judicial decision making. Significant progress has yet to be made in determining what criteria are actually used in making decisions concerning arrest, remand, and classification, and how these criteria are weighed and valued. Because of the focus on what ought to be done, inadequate attention has been given to what actually happens at the decision points shown in Fig. 1. The task is to find a way for juvenile justice policy makers and administrators to join with health staff and researchers to educate the courts about the importance of decision making.

One of the most critical decisions that can be made involves transfer or waiver to the adult system. Recent years have seen increases in jurisdiction transfers of cases from juvenile to adult court [29]. This situation also creates a major problem for practitioners who may be dealing with an adult population and who may be required to accommodate a much younger person, one who is developmentally unprepared for an adult facility. Further, specific accommodations may be necessary for the type of screenings and assessments, confidentiality issues, and behavioral outbursts that may be more common in adolescents. Health care practitioners, both medical and psychiatric, may find that staff education becomes a great responsibility [30].

Psychiatric disorders within juvenile facilities

Recently, high levels of psychopathology have been well documented among institutionalized youth [8,31]. Wierson and colleagues [32] found that in addition to conduct disorder, personality disorders, affective disorders (with 10%–30% prevalence), attention deficit disorder, substance abuse disorders, and mental retardation occur frequently in juvenile delinquent populations. Comparisons of the characteristics of psychopathology in adolescence-limited and life-course–persistent offenders emphasize the necessity of developing informed services in the juvenile justice system [33]. Desai and colleagues [34] note that there are few studies with sufficient rigor to calculate prevalence of mental health disorders in the juvenile justice system, but in the studies that do exist, a consistent finding is that almost two in three detained youths (65%) have such disorders. Additionally, children who have mental health problems are detained longer on average than those without such problems. Estimates suggest that 7% of detainees are waiting for community treatment, some as young as 7 years old. [35].

There is significant overlap between the criminal justice system and mental health system (Chapman JF, Wasilesky S, Zuccaro M. Assessment of the psychiatric needs of children in Connecticut's juvenile detention centers; unpublished manuscript.) [36,37]. Earlier onset of conduct problems is associated with greater degrees of psychopathology [38] and occurs in one half of boys who are eventually labeled persistent serious offenders [39]. Early-onset delinquency is complicated by earlier onset of substance-abusing behaviors and a more rapid escalation of problems than in later-onset delinquency [40]. Therefore, juvenile justice systems must consider developmental factors in juvenile justice youth.

Access to health care for those incarcerated is a constitutional right. The Supreme Court ruled that it has a duty to act when rights are in jeopardy [41]. Thus, the judicial system and system of care within correctional facilities are interconnected. The Federal government has used a 1980 law, the Civil Rights of Institutionalized Persons Act, in attempts to eliminate abuse, neglect, or problematic care within juvenile and adult facilities. This act allows investigation of civil rights violations involving those who have mental health or developmental disabilities [34,42].

The treatment plan and evidence-based considerations

A sensible first approach to treatment in facilities is development of an individualized treatment plan for those who have special needs such as the chronically mentally ill, the developmentally disabled, and those who have suicidal behaviors or functional impairments. The plan should address problems, symptoms, patient strengths, and risk management [43]. In many cases the plan will emanate from screening results. The treatment plan should include care in the facility and also include cross-system collaborations [44]. Treatments currently available may be modified for a locked setting. Hoagwood and colleagues [45] report several empirically supported outpatient treatments that may have portability into the juvenile facility. These include family-focused treatments with a cognitive behavioral or a structural basis and preparation for community-based treatments. Cognitive behavior therapy especially has shown great promise in decreasing violence and recidivism [46]. A number of studies point to the efficacy of multisystemic therapy [45,47–49], functional family therapy [50], multidimensional family therapy [51,52], and therapeutic foster care [53–55]. The clinician should consider such treatments in developing aftercare services. Therapies evaluated in jail settings include youth-focused operant treatment, youth-focused cognitive behavior therapy, social skills training, youth-focused relaxation training, youth-focused psychodynamic therapy, and others [56].

The effectiveness of treatments in terms of cost, applicability, and problem prevalence is an important consideration in determining which treatments to include and which to exclude. The dichotomy of evidence-based or non–evidence-based treatment should be replaced by a continuum of evaluation from not-evaluated, to evaluated, promising, well-established, and better or best treatments [57]. The process of moving efficacious treatments to other care settings requires changes in the service system and adaptations in the treatments themselves [58]. This process of residential treatment options moving from milieu to milieu has been described as "a tapestry of therapies" [59]. This tapestry is supported through multiple public and private initiatives, which the reader will find well summarized by Chambers and colleagues [60].

In a review of treatments, Burns and colleagues [61] noted the importance of parent management strategies. Families can be of considerable help in providing information necessary for in-facility treatment, and families can be enlisted in developing treatment aftercare plans, finding services for themselves or their child, and discussing possible barriers to treatment compliance. This family involvement may reduce the likelihood of readmission [62]. Facilitation of family intervention is not difficult and can be accomplished by such small efforts as establishing convenient and frequent opportunities for visitation, aiding families with transportation concerns, and developing family-focused activities such as meals shared with parents, siblings, and children. Factors that prevent parental involvement are rarely addressed in juvenile courts. Barriers exist between court personnel and parents in terms of communication, information sharing, and sanctions against nonresponsive parents [63]. Benefits of family involvement may be quite pronounced, however. A recent meta-analysis indicates that family and parenting interventions may decrease the amount of time juveniles spend in custody as well as decrease subsequent criminal behavior [64].

High rates of substance use are well documented among youth in custody [8,31]. In work with adults, Chandler and colleagues [65] found important benefits to integrating mental health and substance abuse service as well as growing support from a variety of public and private groups. Early initiation of treatment for both mental health and substance abuse problems is recommended by Koposov and colleagues [66], who found that adolescents who abuse alcohol are at high risk for a number of mental health problems.

The use of group treatment in juvenile justice programming is common but may have certain risks. Careful matching of treatment programming and client is of considerable importance. Benefits gained from group treatment may be diminished by deviant peer influences in group settings [67]. Delinquent peer associations are thought to carry risk for increasing delinquent behaviors [68,69]. Others support the group intervention model, noting that close supervision and effective behavior management can neutralize deleterious effects [70], an important consideration in juvenile justice facilities. Rohde and colleagues [71] reported success in treating major depression but not conduct disorder among a population of depressed juvenile justice youth who had comorbid conduct disorder. Dialectical behavior therapy has been used with varying success [72]. Dialectical behavior therapy is a comprehensive cognitive behavioral treatment that has shown success with suicidal and parasuicidal women who have borderline personality disorder, but integration of this program into both adult and juvenile systems is in its infancy [73].

Evidence-based treatment and juvenile justice research and practice

In a discussion of treatments for aggressive youth, Kazdin [74] points out that even well-studied interventions do not guarantee success under all circumstances. Also, treatments that do not address multiple domains may be unlikely to succeed in multiproblem, conduct-disturbed children. Parent Management Training is effective in allowing parents to engage differently with their children. Prosocial behavior is reinforced, rather than coercive behavior and unintentionally reinforced aggressive behaviors. Parent Management Training–type training for staff members has not been documented within juvenile justice facilities, but theoretically it is a worthwhile consideration, because staff members are not immune from similar unintentional reinforcements, and decreasing aggressive behavior and increasing prosocial interactions are goals within juvenile justice facilities. Programs involving close teacher consultation around behavioral issues have shown good outcomes [56].

Addressing skill deficits

Selection, design, and evaluation of treatment interventions are all functions of the clinical team. Treatments that address deficits in interpersonal skills, such as social skill training and aggression replacement training, are helpful with incarcerated juveniles. Also helpful are cognitive mediation training, stress inoculation, and multifaceted programs designed to treat academic, psychologic, and vocational needs. Successful outcomes of treatment programs are related primarily to the length of treatment and to the monitoring of programs to ensure that juveniles receive the prescribed treatment and that treatment is delivered by mental health staff rather than juvenile justice staff [46]. Continuing quality assurance and ongoing review of standards are important for successful outcomes. The ability to apply problem-solving skills to social situations becomes an important intervention for conduct-disturbed youth [74]. Programs that enhance social competency and conflict resolution programs improve outcomes with incarcerated children [75].

A number of case management approaches have met with success. Case management is an important consideration in bringing the youth to various services within the system [76]. Operating on the premise that a stay in custody is time limited and will result in eventual return to the community, case management strategies are critical for reducing recidivism and facilitating re-entry into society. Transitioning back to the community is an important task. Stewart and Trupin [77] found that children who score high for mental health needs are less likely to be eligible for transitional services and therefore would return directly to their communities without the benefit of transitional experiences in a less restrictive environment. This process leaves children who have mental health needs at a distinct disadvantage. Successful transitions back to the community can be made even when only limited community treatments are available [78].

Delivery of mental health care behind locked doors

The delivery of mental health care in locked facilities is unlike that in many other settings. Often population fluctuations require flexibility by providers who must be able to devote more or less time to individuals depending on the fluctuating population of the facility on any given day. Conditions and outcomes of confinement are affected by facility population size. Limits on facility sizes have been proposed to ensure appropriate standards of practice are met [79]. National accreditation of facilities can provide primary assurance of efficient organization and quality of care. National accrediting bodies include the American Correctional Association, the National Commission on Correctional Health Care (NCCHC), and others. The NCCHC is focused solely on health care provided by the medical and mental health system within correctional facilities and is identified as an important credentialing body by the American Academy of Child and Adolescent Psychiatry's (AACAP) report by the task force on juvenile justice reform [80]. The AACAP indicates that psychiatry can play a larger part in changing the system through the use of accreditation standards.

Provision of services within institutions is a challenge for health care administrators and practitioners, but a number of effective delivery strategies can be employed. Facilities may outsource their mental health care to ease bureaucratic inefficiencies inherent in many government systems. A sufficient allocation of funds for the outsourcing is vital to maintain quality of care [81].

A number of states and other jurisdictions are establishing collaborative relationships with local hospitals, universities, or treatment centers. There are mutual benefits to this arrangement, particularly for teaching hospitals or universities that may wish to use the sites for resident training. The collaboration can add needed training sites and enhance the status of justice administrators [82]. There is also strong continuity of care if the collaborating facility is local [83]. For the correctional institution, benefits include access to health care and advanced training opportunities. Medical students, residents, and child psychiatry fellows would benefit from education in juvenile correctional facilities [84]. Hospital- or university-based services can provide outreach and education to other hospitals or postrelease facilities that may accept a child upon discharge [85]. Time spent at a juvenile facility is an opportunity for both patient and doctor. Juvenile justice facilities can be an important part of resident training in systems of care [86].

Education in specific aspects of juvenile justice settings, such as policies and procedures, culture, and gang issues is important for care providers, as is an understanding of the roles and boundaries necessary for working within this system [84]. Issues of insurance and indemnification, rigid correctional rules, and students' fears must be considered, and an orientation program for all medical staff, faculty and students alike, is indicated [87].

Leadership in mental health care

A psychiatrist is particularly well suited for leadership of a treatment team within a juvenile facility [88]. The vast need for services necessitates a multidisciplinary team approach. Mutual respect, strong communication, and involvement of staff in training are sound investments that can lead to a better milieu and allow staff to make important contributions of observations and interventions [89].

Mental health staff must know the environment in which they will work and cannot restrict themselves to health care roles to avoid training in the system and operation of facilities. The relative inconvenience of necessary training in operations of the facility is essential, because proper clinical service cannot be provided without it and because there may be notable tension between the therapeutic best interests of the child and the legitimate custody goals of the institution [90].

Summary

Although in most cases it is preferable to avoid either public or private out-of-home placements within the juvenile justice system, the potential benefits from incarceration should be maximized. Without intervention during this important period, the best possible outcome is perhaps wasted time. Roush [91] states that detention centers are responsible for the care and custody of the children within them, but opinion differs as to which takes precedence.

Time spent in a juvenile justice facility should not be idle. Programming designed to address social skill deficits are an important component of any system. Programs designed to control anger, such as aggression replacement training, have shown success [92]. Cognitive behavioral interventions have clearly shown benefit, and case management can be used to bridge the time between preadmission services and planning for postdischarge treatment. Case management should begin at admission and proceed through the sanctions phase, removing barriers throughout and providing emotional support [93]. Benefits from time spent incarcerated can be enhanced by parental involvement. The type of facility may be unimportant. Outcomes of government-operated facilities are similar to those of alternative facilities [94].

To manage health care delivery effectively, the psychiatrist must hold a leadership position within a multidisciplinary team that includes other mental health disciplines, medical and nursing staff, education staff, custody staff, administration, and perhaps court personnel. High rates of complex psychopathology require sophistication and accuracy in assessment [33]. Efficient leadership will recognize potential in custody staff as well as health care. Most detention staff are moderately positive about their occupations and see themselves as effectively influencing the life of the children they encounter [95].

Finally, important information on correctional mental health care practice needs to be updated frequently. Continuous quality improvement requires feedback and a forum for health care practitioners to share information and demonstrate the quality of care they practice [96]. Accreditation by national bodies such as NCCHC is encouraged, and establishment of performance-based measures can gauge effective practice [91], making the experience of working in juvenile justice facilities a rewarding part of one's career.

References

[1] Snyder HN. Juvenile arrests 2002. Juvenile Justice Bulletin 2004. Office of Juvenile Justice and Delinquency Prevention. National Criminal Justice (NCJ) # 204608.

[2] Sickmund M. Juveniles in corrections. National Report Series Bulletin 2004. Office of Juvenile Justice and Delinquency Prevention. National Criminal Justice (NCJ) # 202885.

[3] Office of Juvenile Justice and Delinquency Prevention. Conditions of confinement: juvenile detention and corrections facilities. National Criminal Justice Reference Service (NCJRS) # 145793.

[4] Sheppard VB, Benjamin-Coleman R. Determinants of service placements for youth with serious emotional and behavioral disturbances. Community Ment Health J 2001;37(1):53–65.

[5] Coffey C, Veit F, Wolfe R, et al. Mortality in young offenders: retrospective cohort study. BMJ 2003;326:1064–7.

[6] Abram KM, Teplin LA, Charles DR, et al. Posttraumatic stress disorder and trauma in youth in juvenile detention. Arch Gen Psychiatry 2004;61(4):403–10.

[7] Ford JD. Treatment implications of altered neurobiology, affect regulation and information processing following child maltreatment. Psychiatr Ann 2005;35:410–9.

[8] Abram KM, Teplin LA, McClelland GM, et al. Comorbid psychiatric disorders in youth in juvenile detention. Arch Gen Psychiatry 2003;60(11):1097–108.

[9] Hayes L. Juvenile suicide in confinement: a national survey. Mansfield (MA): National Center on Institutions and Alternatives; 2004.

[10] DiFilippo JM, Esposito C, Overholser J, et al. High-risk populations. In: Spirito A, Overholser JC, editors. Evaluating and treating adolescent suicide attempters: from research to practice. San Diego (CA): Academic Press; 2003. p. 229–59.

[11] Puzzanchera CM. Juvenile court placement of adjudicated youth. Washington (DC): Office of Juvenile Justice and Delinquency Prevention (fact sheet #2); 2002.

[12] National Council of Juvenile and Family Court Judges. Juvenile delinquency guidelines: improving court practice in juvenile delinquency cases. Available at: http://www.ncjfcj.org. Accessed July 29, 2005.

[13] Meehl PE. Clinical versus statistical predictions: a theoretical analysis and revision of the literature. Minneapolis (MN): University of Minnesota Press; 1954.

[14] Meehl PE. Causes and effects of my disturbing little book. J Pers Assess 1986;50(3):370–5.

[15] Harari O, Hosey KR. Attributional biases among clinicians and nonclinicians. J Clin Psychol 1981;37(2):445–50.

[16] Jordan JS, Harvey JH, Weary G. Attributional biases in clinical decision making. In: Turk DC, Salovey P, editors. Reasoning, inference, and judgment in clinical psychology. New York: The Free Press; 1988. p. 90–106.

[17] Chapman LJ. Illusory correlation in observation report. Journal of Verbal Learning and Verbal Behavior 1967;6:151–5.

[18] Golding SL, Rorer LG. Illusory correlation and the learning of clinical judgment. Bulletin 11(10). Eugene (OR): Oregon Research Institute; 1971.
[19] Edwards W, von Winterfeldt D. On cognitive illusions and their implications. In: Connolly T, Arkes HR, Hammond KR, editors. Judgment and decision making: an interdisciplinary reader. 2nd edition. Cambridge (UK): Cambridge University Press; 2000. p. 592–620.
[20] Tribe LH. Trial by mathematics: precision and ritual in the legal process. Harv Law Rev 1971; 84(6):1329–93.
[21] Rostain T. Educating Homo economicus: cautionary notes on the new behavioral law and economics movement. Law Soc Rev 2000;34(4):973–1006.
[22] Melton GB, Monahan J, Saks MJ. Psychologists as law professors. Am Psychol 1987;42(5): 502–9.
[23] Monahan J, Steadman HJ, Robbins PC, et al. An actuarial model of violence risk assessment for persons with mental disorders. Psychiatr Serv 2005;56(7):810–5.
[24] Webster CD, Hucker SJ, Bloom H. Transcending the actuarial versus clinical polemic in assessing risk for violence. Crim Justice Behav 2002;29(5):659–65.
[25] Douglas KS, Kropp PR. A prevention-based paradigm for violence risk assessment: clinical and research applications. Crim Justice Behav 2002;29(5):617–58.
[26] Borum R. Improving the clinical practice of violence risk assessment: technology, guidelines, and training. Am Psychol 1996;51(9):945–56.
[27] Borum R, Otto R. Advances in forensic assessment and treatment: an overview and introduction to the special issue. Law Hum Behav 2000;24(1):1–7.
[28] Swets JA, Dawes RM, Monahan J. Psychological science can improve diagnostic decisions. Risk Anal 2000;1(1):1–26.
[29] Sickmund M. Juveniles in court. Juvenile Offenders and Victims National Report Series Bulletin. National Criminal Justice (NCJ) # 195420.
[30] National Commission on Correctional Health Care. Correctional mental health care: standards and guidelines for delivering services. Chicago: National Commission on Correctional Health Care; 2003.
[31] Teplin LA, Abram KM, McClelland GM, et al. Psychiatric disorders in youth in juvenile detention. Arch Gen Psychiatry 2002;59(12):1133–43.
[32] Wierson M, Forehand RL, Frame CL. Epidemiology and treatment of mental health problems in juvenile delinquents. Advances in Behavioral Research and Therapy 1992;14:93–120.
[33] Vermeiren R. Psychopathology and delinquency in adolescents: a descriptive and developmental perspective. Clin Psychol Rev 2003;23:277–318.
[34] Desai RA, Goulet JL, Robbins JR, et al. Mental health care in juvenile detention facilities: a review. Journal of the American Academy of Psychiatry and the Law, in press.
[35] Incarceration of youth who are waiting for community mental health services in the United States. Washington (DC): US House of Representatives Committee on Government Reform–Minority Staff, Special Investigations Division; 2004.
[36] Theriot MT, Segal SP. Involvement with the criminal justice system among new clients at outpatient mental health agencies. Psychiatr Serv 2005;56(2):179–85.
[37] Johnson TP, Cho YI, Fendrich M, et al. Treatment need and utilization among youth entering the juvenile corrections system. J Subst Abuse Treat 2004;26(2):117–28.
[38] Ruchkin V, Koposov R, Vermeiren R, et al. Psychopathology and age of onset of conduct problems in juvenile delinquents. J Clin Psychiatry 2003;64(8):913–20.
[39] Stouthamer-Loeber M, Loeber R. Lost opportunities for intervention: undetected markers for the development of serious juvenile delinquency. Crim Behav Ment Health 2002;12(1):69–82.
[40] Taylor J, Malone S, Iacono WG, et al. Development of substance dependence in two delinquency subgroups and nondelinquents from a male twin sample. J Am Acad Child Adolesc Psychiatry 2002;41(4):386–93.
[41] National Commission on Correctional Health Care. Correctional health care: guidelines for the management of an adequate delivery system. Chicago: National Commission on Correctional Health Care; 2001.

[42] Beyond the walls: improving conditions of confinement for youth in custody. Washington (DC): Office of Juvenile Justice and Delinquency Prevention; 1998.
[43] National Commission on Correctional Health Care. Correctional mental health care: standards and guidelines for delivering services. Chicago: National Commission on Correctional Health Care; 2003.
[44] Cocozza JJ, Skowyra K. Youth with mental health disorders: issues and emerging responses. Juvenile Justice 2000;7(1):3–13.
[45] Hoagwood K, Burns BJ, Kiser L, et al. Evidence-based practice in child and adolescent mental health services. Psychiatr Serv 2001;52:1179–89.
[46] Lipsey MW, Wilson DB, Cothern L. Effective intervention for serious juvenile offenders. Washington (DC): Office of Juvenile Justice and Delinquency Prevention; 2000.
[47] Henggeler SW, Rowland MD, Pickrel SG, et al. Investigating family-based alternatives to institution-based mental health services for youth: Lessons learned from the pilot study of a randomized field trial. J Clin Child Psychol 1997;26(3):226–33.
[48] Henggeler SW, Clingempeel WG, Brondino MJ, et al. Four-year follow-up of multisystemic therapy with substance-abusing and substance-dependent juvenile offenders. J Am Acad Child Adolesc Psychiatry 2002;41(7):868–74.
[49] Schoenwald SK, Ward DM, Heneggeler SW, et al. Multisystemic therapy versus hospitalization for crisis stabilization of youth: placement outcomes 4 months post referral. Ment Health Serv Res 2000;2(1):3–12.
[50] Robbins MS, Turner CW, Alexander JF, et al. Alliance and dropout in family therapy for adolescents with behavior problems. J Fam Psychol 2003;17(4):534–44.
[51] Liddle HA, Dakof GA, Parker K, et al. Multidimensional family therapy for adolescent drug abuse: results of a randomized clinical trial. Am J Drug Alcohol Abuse 2001;27(4):651–88.
[52] Liddle HA, Rowe CL, Quille TJ, et al. Transporting a research-based adolescent drug treatment into practice. J Subst Abuse Treat 2002;22(4):231–43.
[53] Murphy JW, Callahan KA. Therapeutic versus traditional foster care: theoretical and practical distinctions. Adolescence 1989;24:891–900.
[54] Stroul BA, Goldman SK. Study of community-based services for children who are severely emotionally disturbed. J Ment Health Adm 1990;17(1):61–77.
[55] Hahn RA, Lowy J, Bilukha O, et al. Therapeutic foster care for the prevention of violence: a report on recommendations on the Task Force on Community Preventive Services. MMWR Recomm Rep 2004;53(RR-10):1–8.
[56] Weisz JR, Hawley KM, Jensen Doss A. Empirically tested psychotherapies for youth internalizing and externalizing problems and disorders. Child Adolesc Psychiatr Clin N Am 2004; 13:729–815.
[57] Kazdin AE. Evidence-based treatments: challenges and priorities for practice and research. Child Adolesc Psychiatr Clin N Am 2004;13:923–40.
[58] Schoenwald SK, Hoagwood K. Effectiveness, transportability, and dissemination of interventions: what matters when? Psychiatr Serv 2001;52(9):1190–7.
[59] Epstein RA. Inpatient and residential treatment effects for children and adolescents: a review and critique. Child Adolesc Psychiatr Clin N Am 2004;13:411–28.
[60] Chambers DA, Ringeisen H, Hickman EE. Federal, state, and foundation initiatives around evidence-based practices for child and adolescent mental health. Child Adolesc Psychiatr Clin N Am 2005;14:307–27.
[61] Burns BJ, Hoagwood K, Mrazek PJ. Effective treatment for mental disorders in children and adolescents. Clin Child Fam Psychol Rev 1999;2(4):199–254.
[62] Osher T, Hunt P. Involving families of youth who are in contact with the juvenile justice system. National Center for Mental Health and Juvenile Justice Research and Program brief. Delmar (NY): National Center for Mental Health and Juvenile Justice Research and Program; 2002.
[63] Davies HJ, Davidson HA. Executive summary: parental involvement practices of juvenile courts. Report to the Office of Juvenile Justice and Delinquency Prevention. Washington (DC): American Bar Association; 2001.

[64] Woolfenden SR, Williams K, Peat JK. Family and parenting interventions for conduct disorder and delinquency: a meta-analysis of randomized control trials. Arch Dis Child 2002;86(4): 251–6.

[65] Chandler RK, Peters RH, Field G, et al. Challenges in implementing evidence-based treatment practices for co-occurring disorders in the criminal justice system. Behav Sci Law 2004; 22:431–48.

[66] Koposov RA, Ruchkin VV, Eisemann M, et al. Alcohol abuse in Russian delinquent adolescents: associations with co-morbid psychopathology, psychopathology, and parenting. Eur Child Adolesc Psychiatry 2005;14(5):254–61.

[67] Gifford-Smith M, Dodge KA, Dishion TJ, et al. Peer influence in children and adolescents: crossing the bridge from developmental to intervention science. J Abnorm Child Psychol 2005;33(3):255–65.

[68] Hanish LD, Martin CL, Fabes RA, et al. Exposure to externalizing peers in early childhood: homophily and peer contagion processes. J Abnorm Child Psychol 2005;33(3):267–81.

[69] Dishion TJ, McCord J, Poulin F. When interventions harm: peer group and problem behavior. Am Psychol 1999;54(9):755–64.

[70] Mager W, Milich R, Harris MJ, et al. Intervention groups for adolescents with conduct problems: is aggregation harmful or helpful? J Abnorm Child Psychol 2005;33(3):349–62.

[71] Rohde P, Clarke GN, Mace DE, et al. An efficacy/effectiveness study of cognitive-behavioral treatment for adolescents with comorbid major depression and conduct disorder. J Am Acad Child Adolesc Psychiatry 2004;43(6):660–8.

[72] Trupin EW, Stewart DG, Beach B, et al. Effectiveness of a dialectical behavior therapy program for incarcerated female juvenile offenders. Child Adolesc Ment Health 2002;7(3):121–7.

[73] Berzins LG, Trestman RL. The development and implementation of dialectical behavior therapy in forensic settings. International Journal of Forensic Mental Health 2004;3(1):93–103.

[74] Kazdin AE. Treatment for aggressive and antisocial children. Child Adolesc Psychiatr Clin N Am 2000;9(4):841–58.

[75] Roush DW. The importance of comprehensive skill-based programs in juvenile detention and corrections. In: Roberts AR, editor. Juvenile justice: policies, programs, and services. 2nd edition. Chicago: Nelson-Hall; 1998. p. 165–93.

[76] Terry YM, Van der Waal CJ, McBride DC, et al. Provision of drug treatment services in the juvenile justice system: a system reform. J Behav Health Serv Res 2000;27(2):194–214.

[77] Stewart DG, Trupin EW. Clinical utility and policy implications of a statewide mental health screening process for juvenile offenders. Psychiatr Serv 2003;54(3):377–82.

[78] Trupin EW, Turner AP, Stewart D, et al. Transition planning and recidivism among mentally ill juvenile offenders. Behav Sci Law 2004;22:599–610.

[79] Roush DW. The relationship between group size and outcomes in juvenile corrections: a partial review of the literature. Journal for Juvenile Justice and Detention Services 2002;17(1):1–18.

[80] Kraus LJ. Standards for juvenile detention and confinement facilities. Recommendations for juvenile justice reform. Washington (DC): American Academy of Child and Adolescent Psychiatry Task Force on Juvenile Justice Reform; 2001.

[81] Metzner JL. Trends in correctional mental health care. In: Moore J, editor. Management and administration of correctional health care. Kingston (NJ): Civic Research Institute, Inc.; 2003. p. 12-1–12-22.

[82] Appelbaum KL, Manning TD, Noonan JD. A university-state-corporation partnership for providing correctional mental health services. Psychiatr Serv 2002;53(2):185–9.

[83] Chapman JF, Coleman K, Davis J, et al. Contractual health services in juvenile detention centers. Correctional Health Care Report 2004;5(3):21, 34–6.

[84] Thomas CR, Penn JV. Juvenile justice mental health services. Child Adolesc Psychiatr Clin N Am 2002;11:731–48.

[85] Sanislow CA, Chapman JF, McGlashan TH. Crisis intervention services in juvenile detention centers. Psychiatr Serv 2003;54(1):107.

[86] McGinty KL. Training child and adolescent psychiatrists for systems of care. Psychiatr Serv 2003;54(1):29–30.

[87] Thomas DL, Silvagni AJ, Howell J. Developing a correctional medical rotation for medical students. Journal of Correctional Health Care 2004;10(4):557–62.
[88] Steiner H, Cauffman E. Juvenile justice, delinquency, and psychiatry. Child Adolesc Psychiatr Clin N Am 1998;7(3):653–72.
[89] Appelbaum KL, Hickey JM, Packer I. The role of correctional officers in multidisciplinary mental health care in prisons. Psychiatr Serv 2001;52(10):1343–7.
[90] American Academy of Child and Adolescent Psychiatry. Practice parameters for the assessment and treatment of youth in juvenile detention and correctional facilities. Available at: www.aacap.org. Accessed July 29, 2005.
[91] Roush DW. Juvenile detention: issues for the 21st century. In: Roberts AR, editor. Juvenile justice sourcebook. Oxford (UK): Oxford University Press; 2004. p. 218–46.
[92] Glick B. Aggression replacement training—a comprehensive intervention for aggressive youth. In: Schwartz B, editor. Correctional psychology practice programming and administration. Kingston (NJ): Civic Research Institute; 2003. p. 1-14–20.
[93] Cellini HR. Origins, case management, and treatment of the substance-abusing offender. In: Scwartz B, editor. Correctional psychology practice programming and administration. Kingston (NJ): Civic Research Institute; 2003. p. 11-1–30.
[94] Bowers DA. Juvenile corrections in the institution versus the community the experience of a sample of Alabama youth. Journal of Juvenile Justice and Detention Services 2002;17(2): 79–88.
[95] Wells JB, Minor KI, Woofter SL, et al. The social climates of juvenile institutions: staff perceptions of work environment and the relationship to demographic and other status characteristics. Journal for Juvenile Justice and Detention Services 2000;15(2):47–64.
[96] Rieger D. The elements of continuous quality improvement. In: Moore J, editor. Management and administration of correctional health care. Kingston (NJ): Civic Research Institute; 2003. p. 20-1–23.

ELSEVIER
SAUNDERS

Child Adolesc Psychiatric Clin N Am
15 (2006) 459–475

CHILD AND
ADOLESCENT
PSYCHIATRIC CLINICS
OF NORTH AMERICA

Forensic Psychiatric Inpatient Treatment: Creating a Therapeutic Milieu

Riittakerttu Kaltiala-Heino, MD, DrMedSci*,
Kristina Kahila, RN

Psychiatric Treatment and Research Unit for Adolescent Intensive Care (EVA), Tampere University Hospital, 33380 Pitkäniemi, Tampere, Finland

In different societies adolescent forensic psychiatric units may have different organizational status and belong to either health or prison services, but the overall tasks of such units are quite similar. All of them provide high-quality specialized psychiatric services, including assessment, treatment planning, and therapeutic activities, paying special attention to minimizing the risk of violence and other harm to the patients, staff, and society at large. Given the country- and state-specific differences in service structures, adolescents may enter forensic clinics by a variety of routes, from the juvenile justice or general justice system or through mental health or social services. Adolescent forensic psychiatric patients may be defined as adolescents who have severe mental disorder and a criminal background of any kind and also may include violent and noncompliant adolescent psychiatric patients who are involved with juvenile justice because of this behavior but who do not have an actual criminal background. They may also be severely delinquent youths under the age of criminal responsibility in their society who, despite the severity of their offenses, are not involved in the criminal justice system. Adolescent forensic units share the challenge of balancing the requirements of providing evidence-based intervention and controlling behavioral problems (ie, therapeutic goals and security). The authors perceive security not simply as a matter of control but as an integral part of the "fertile ground" that creates the therapeutic milieu of adolescent forensic care. This article discusses the principles of creating such a therapeutic milieu in adolescent forensic

* Corresponding author.
E-mail address: riittakerttu.kaltiala-heino@pshp.fi (R. Kaltiala-Heino).

1056-4993/06/$ – see front matter
doi:10.1016/j.chc.2005.11.007 **childpsych.theclinics.com**

inpatient care. A functional therapeutic milieu comprises far more elements than effective psychosocial treatments alone, ranging from physical environment to staffing, public relationships of the unit, work with adolescents' networks, aggression management, crisis management, and the challenges of leadership.

Planning

The planning of the service must be based on the needs of clients, which in turn are determined by the legal context, the position of the service in the health, social, and criminal services systems, the relation to other residential services available for juvenile offenders and behavior-disordered adolescent psychiatric patients, and, of course, the size of the population in the catchment area. Violent and persistent juvenile offenders, in particular, pose a challenge to all the services society may offer, and thus a newly created adolescent forensic unit may face expectations beyond the scope of psychiatric treatments. Even carefully conducted surveys in the planning phase among administrators, policymakers, and experts cannot completely predict the number of beds needed or the characteristics of the youth referred, although such surveys may be helpful in estimating expected patient flow, the security level required, and the required qualifications of the personnel. On the other hand, dialogue with administrators also gives the providers a chance to define the type of adolescent population the service is and is not designed to handle. In that way, unrealistic expectations can be avoided even in early planning stages.

Although incarcerated and hospitalized juvenile delinquents have been shown to be similar in terms of psychopathology [1], an adolescent forensic psychiatric unit cannot be simply a secure place for problematic youth, nor is its role one of meting out punishment for offenses. Many young offenders who have mental health needs can be adequately helped in correctional facilities [2–4]. Because of security needs, they often need detention rather than psychiatric admission. It is most important to communicate clearly the criteria for admission to the adolescent forensic psychiatric unit so it is not considered an alternative to detention. Processes for admission to forensic psychiatric inpatient treatment vary across jurisdictions [5]. Some adolescent forensic units may restrict their admission criteria to severe mental illness, primarily to conduct disorders or other nonpsychotic conditions, whereas others may offer treatment for mixed groups of varying psychiatric diagnoses (authors' personal observations in Belgium, Finland, the Netherlands and the United Kingdom). Therefore, defining clear criteria for admission may be intricate and definitely not generalizable cross-culturally. An additional complicating factor may be the high levels of comorbid psychiatric disorders in forensic populations, making it difficult to target only a specific kind of psychiatric problem.

One aspect of the planning phase that has implications for the therapeutic milieu is whether the unit will be for both girls and boys or for same-sex adolescents only. The authors have observed that several adolescent forensic units in Europe have chosen to focus on boys only. Female adolescents offend much less than male adolescents, but mental disorders and psychosocial risk factors are as common in offending female as in male juvenile offenders [6–9]. If both boys and girls are admitted, there are additional requirements for the physical environment and, especially, for supervision. There may also be specific reasons for not admitting both girls and boys to the same unit (eg, if the unit aims to offer treatment of young sexual offenders).

A safe physical environment as a prerequisite for therapeutic activities

A safe physical environment is of outmost importance for an adolescent forensic unit and liberates staff resources for therapeutic activities because they need not focus excessively on environmental safety issues.

The supervision of safety in an adolescent forensic unit should be based primarily on the personal presence of staff, because the simple presence of adults is likely to reduce destructive behavior in this age group. Both shared spaces and bedrooms and bathrooms must be supervised, and staff must be accessible for the youth should they be urgently needed while carrying out administrative tasks. Video camera monitoring, is a controversial issue. Although potentially useful for monitoring around corners and beyond the direct line of vision, it may create an illusion of control and safety in the staff and provoke paranoid ideation in the youth. The staff may feel less need for personal presence and observation when relying excessively on video camera supervision. Although staff presence is likely to prevent a number of destructive behaviors, video camera supervision may be too distant and abstract to encourage the youth to control their own behavior. Video monitoring merely reveals what is taking place, whereas the personal presence of staff is more likely to prevent incidents and to create learning situations by direct intervention. Staff may wish to trust video camera supervision because videotapes can be archived and can be used as evidence in case of accusations of sexual harassment or violence by staff. Although relevant as evidence, regulations may restrict the admission of video records so that they become meaningless in such situations. Video camera monitoring may, however, be useful at entrances, because it enables rapid identification of unwanted visitors such as gang members or people who have been forbidden access to a certain adolescent.

Although supervision is important for an adolescent forensic unit, an opposite and equally needed requirement is privacy. Adolescents admitted to forensic wards are likely to suffer from a number of deficiencies that hamper adequate functioning in peer groups, including social skills deficits, impulse control problems, low self-esteem, and paranoid ideation, among others. It is therefore necessary to offer privacy to allow an individual needed time and space to calm down and to teach adolescents to use self-administered time away when feelings are running out of control. Single rooms are a necessity for providing privacy and for reducing the risk of violent encounters.

The interiors of the ward, including all furniture, materials, doors, windows, locks, electricity, bathroom facilities, mirrors, and the like, should be constructed with specific attention to safety, using materials that do not burn and cannot easily be broken into sharp pieces or into blunt objects useful for violent assault on others or self-harm. At the same time, interiors should be made hospitable and pleasant, indicating respect for the adolescents. For example, in planning the interiors one must focus on minimizing the risks of using electricity for self-harm or fire setting and of using cutting sharp objects for self-harm or aggression against others. Access to equipment suitable for hanging or strangulation must be eliminated. Numerous everyday objects can be misused for self-harm or aggression against others and must not be placed or hung at random. When placed, they should be of materials that cannot harm or must be fixed so that they cannot be removed. The unit management and the staff must balance the needs of normal household activities and rehabilitation with those of safety.

For example, in the Psychiatric Treatment and Research Unit for Adolescent Intensive Care at Tampere University Hospital, there was discussion about whether, for safety reasons, plastic plates, glasses, forks, knives, and spoons should be used. It was decided not to do so because the patients need to practice everyday skills such as table manners and because the use of normal materials positively influenced the youths' self-respect and rehabilitation. Normal kitchen equipment is used, but functional solutions were established: access to the kitchen is supervised and for specified purposes only, forks, knives, and spoons are counted at all meals, and policies are in place for situations when a kitchen object is found missing.

It is advisable to create a list of objects and materials that are not allowed in the unit and to create comprehensive and strict policies for preventing access to such objects.

Sharp, cutting, exploding, and inflammable objects, as well as materials suitable for hiding substances, objects that can be used for suffocating or strangling, and "any other objects the staff considers weapon-like or dangerous" are not allowed in the authors' unit. The list is provided to the youth and their families in advance in an information package attached to the letter of invitation, is displayed at the unit entrance, and is available from the staff at any time. The youth's belongings can be checked for these objects at any time and are always checked at entrance and return from leave. Visitors are requested to leave such objects with the staff, and any visitor who does not comply with the routines may not enter the unit.

Safety precautions regarding forbidden materials should be based mainly on staff alertness and security routines. A metal detector can be helpful in preventing the entry of metal objects such as small knives, but no technology can ever replace staff adherence to security routines. Such routines need to be clear and explicit, easily available in written form for verification by all staff members, and integrated into staff training. In uneventful periods, which are likely to occur as the unit stabilizes and routines consolidate, there is a risk that staff will become less attentive to security routines. When the adolescents seem to be doing well, overly optimistic feelings of trust may be created, because the staff knows the youth, and confidence in them grows. In the absence of serious incidents, strict adherence to the rules and spending much time in checking may be perceived as unnecessary. A typical mistake is to allow an adolescent who is doing well to take liberties with regard to forbidden objects and security routines. When routines are loosened, they often are not tightened again when new adolescents enter the ward. The management must therefore remind staff that, even if a certain youth might indeed be reliable, others may not be. Loosening rules for one youth makes it easy for others to access forbidden objects: they may be passed to others or stolen, or their owners may be pressured or threatened into giving them away. Finally, when security routines are explicit and carefully followed without exceptions, the adolescents and their visitors accept them as a part of the unit's structure, and there is less risk of rules not being followed when they are most needed. Therefore regular review of security practices and the reasons for them is a necessity part of continuous education and supervision.

A part of a safe milieu is effective prevention of substance abuse in the facility. Routine testing for substance abuse on admission and on return from leave is useful in preventing undesirable behavior related to a youth's being under the influence of drugs or suffering withdrawal symptoms. Adolescents should be informed that routine and random testing will take place and of the policies for dealing with suspicion of drug trafficking or hiding drugs on the ward.

In the authors' unit the adolescents and their families are informed in advance of the drug-control policies that include routine testing for substance use on admission and on return from holidays or any unauthorized leave from the hospital. In addition, random testing may occur at any time. If a young person is suspected of hiding a substance, searches are organized, if necessary in cooperation with the police and a dog specially trained to detect drugs. Adolescents have the right to be present when their rooms and belongings are searched, but if an adolescent refuses to attend, the search is performed nevertheless. A substance found on the ward is removed and destroyed by the police. As for the offender, each situation is solved individually.

Staff

To maintain a therapeutic milieu, an adolescent forensic unit needs more staff per bed than general adolescent psychiatric units because of the increased risk of violence. The staff/patient ratio is influenced by the financial resources available, and legal, contextual, and cultural aspects also play a significant role. A variety of cultural and political issues that influence the labor market also affect staff attitudes as to what can be considered an acceptable risk. The number of nighttime staff needed may depend on the security assistance that is available from outside, which may be better in larger facilities. If nighttime security absorbs more staff, the total staff/patient ratio must be higher to ensure safe and therapeutic daytime activities.

Safety is often believed to require male staff whose physical strength is assumed to suppress patients' aggressive behavior or at least to ensure safe management of escalated situations. Some studies, however, have suggested that a greater proportion of female staff is associated with less use of seclusion and restraint [10], suggesting that male and female staff may differ not only in physical strength but also in communication and interpersonal styles, and that this difference may be important for ward atmosphere. The authors believe that, optimally, about half of the nursing staff should be males, not only because of physical strength but also because of the need for male role models. In practice this ratio is often difficult to achieve because of a shortage of males among nurses in general.

A staff-training course before the opening of a new unit is likely to facilitate the start. The training should provide a basic understanding of adolescent development, adolescent psychiatry, forensic psychiatry, behavioral management, de-escalation skills, team building, and relevant legislation. There is hardly any other period in the unit's development when the staff as a whole can attend training together. Although education can be given individually or in subgroups, meetings of the whole staff can be important for revealing the staff's interaction about specific topics, especially when staff members hold varying opinions. In the continuing professional education of each employee, the unit management should ensure that the entire clinical staff maintains updated basic knowledge of evidence-based approaches to the treatment of the problems the clients display. Staff members who do not actually conduct individual and group therapy also need knowledge of them so they can motivate adolescents and support them in behavioral change in everyday interactions on the ward according to the principles applied in therapy.

Giving the team a chance to work: public relations

An adolescent forensic psychiatric unit may encounter a great of prejudice and fear from the local residents and even from professionals. Adolescent forensic psychiatric patients are often stigmatized more than is appropriate for the offenses they have committed. The stigma may also influence the staff: when the patients they care for arouse ambivalent reactions, the staff may themselves feel rejected by other professionals. This sense of rejection generates stress, may create obstacles to the adolescent forensic unit staff's cooperation with other professional teams, and may influence their therapeutic relationship with the adolescents. It is therefore important to take an active approach to managing projections and negative fantasies. Doing so is primarily a task of the unit management and is an important part of assuring staff well being and thereby ensuring high-quality care.

Transparency and providing correct information are key approaches to integrating the unit with the larger setting or hospital where it is located and with society at large. Fears, mainly the idea that offending will increase, are likely to be more pronounced among those who live and work closest to the unit. The unit management should make every effort to reduce misinformation and to provide correct information. These efforts in turn improve staff morale and enhance the therapeutic milieu.

The reactions of society at large, reflected in part by media attention, are less predictable. An adolescent forensic unit may be portrayed in the media as a positive opportunity to establish a balance between the therapeutic needs of the youth and the safety of society. On the other hand, the media may present such a facility in a negative way, emphasizing the dangerousness of the youth, the excessive costs for the taxpayers, and the like. Agreement can usually be reached with the appropriate media on what and how to present information, especially when the unit explains why the interests of the youth require a certain approach.

Any unit that is likely to attract negative attention, such as a forensic psychiatric unit, should have clear policies for managing media relations, defining who can report to the media on behalf of the unit and how to respond if the staff is unexpectedly approached by media representatives. Rules for communicating with the media in case of undesirable events should be included in the unit's crisis management plan. The families of adolescent forensic patients may threaten the staff with negative publicity, and even during treatment the adolescents may do things that attract negative attention. Both the relatives' contacts with the media and the youth's activities outside the ward are beyond the unit's control. By assuming all responsibility for responding to media interest, the unit management needs to ensure that the threat of negative publicity does not disturb the staff's confidence in working according to agreed guidelines. On the contrary, the management should encourage the staff to work according to guidelines and evidence-based principles so that possible enquiries can be answered and remarks can be tackled appropriately.

Everyday routines with the adolescents

The therapeutic milieu of an adolescent forensic unit naturally requires that individual treatment plans be based on a thorough and structured assessment of the adolescents' psychiatric, social, and educational needs, including assessment of the immediate and longer-term risk of violence. Assessment and individual treatment planning is discussed in more detail elsewhere in this volume.

Offending, violent, and treatment-noncompliant youth are known to have numerous needs in a variety of domains covering daily living skills, education, social relationships, physical health, and psychologic symptoms [11]. Some of these needs are targets of individual and group therapies (see the article by Sukhodolsky and Ruchkin elsewhere in this issue), whereas others are not the core target of the forensic care itself (eg, treatment of somatic conditions, which can, however, be arranged during forensic psychiatric care, if necessary). Needs in areas such as self-care, personal hygiene, nutrition, household skills, appropriate handling of money and personal budget, or relevant daytime activities need to be met as part of a unit's day-to-day program. Motivation to acquire skills in these areas and to practice them can be provided in specific functional groups, as part of the primary nursing relationship, and by modeling in interactions with staff who guide the adolescents in these activities as a part of everyday ward routines. The importance of modeling is often not fully acknowledged by staff members. Therefore, it is important to stress that appropriate behavior cannot be expected from the youth if the staff does not demonstrate appropriate handling of social relationships.

Adolescent forensic patients often have unmet needs in school attendance and achievement [12]. Because the hospital school may be their only opportunity to complete basic education, ward structure and motivational work by all clinical staff should support schoolwork as much as possible.

Poor impulse control and aggressive and self-destructive behaviors are such essential problems of youth admitted to an adolescent forensic unit that creating a therapeutic milieu is inextricably linked with therapeutic aggression management. Specific aspects of anger control treatment are discussed in the article by Sudokholsky and Ruchkin elsewhere in this issue.

Structure is one of the most essential functional elements of a therapeutic milieu in an adolescent forensic unit. A predictable environment can be achieved by clear daily and weekly schedules, which reduce the patients' uncertainty and anxiety and thereby may also reduce tension likely to induce irritation and aggression. Predictable structures are helpful for handling a variety of problems typical of forensic psychiatric inpatients, such as paranoid ideation, poor impulse control, and poor executive functions [13–15]. The routines need not be rigid; in fact, rigid routines may evoke resistance because the adolescents feel restricted. When exceptions from day-to-day structures are needed, it is important to explain these exceptions in advance to reduce tension and aggressive reactions related to an inability to cope with changes. It is important to explain to the adolescents in advance what is going to take place, why, and who is responsible for it.

Appropriately scheduled days filled with relevant and adequately supervised activities may further help prevent undesirable and destructive activities. The more disturbed the adolescents are, and their poorer social skills, the less they can constructively organize their individual free time and benefit from spontaneous relating to peers. Instead, unsupervised and unstructured activities tend to create tension and lead to aggression. The staff needs to be aware of the of the adolescents' individual capacities to use possible free time constructively. When problems are expected, individual programs can be made in which the adolescent is instructed beforehand how he or she will use this time.

Appropriate limit setting is another crucial element of a therapeutic milieu in adolescent forensic units. Desirable and undesirable behaviors and the consequences of displaying undesirable behaviors must be explicitly defined. Focusing exclusively on negative behaviors and their consequences risks creating a punitive and custodial nursing style and is not likely to be effective in achieving long-term behavioral change that endures outside the inpatient setting. It is, however, appropriate to define explicitly the consequences of the most serious undesirable behaviors and to ensure that such consequences ensue consistently when the behavior occurs. Clear guidelines, particularly for the management of aggressive behaviors, are likely to improve staff morale, increase safety, and be therapeutic for the youth by increasing predictability.

A number of problems are likely to emerge in any case. The authors' unit has defined the routine consequences of violent behavior, threatening with violence, self-destructive behavior, and leaving without permission. There is always room for speculation whether an act committed by an adolescent actually falls into the category of one of these behaviors and whether the consequences are too harsh or too lenient for a particular young person. Some staff members may find the limits in general too permissive, others may find them too strict, and the youth are likely to find them unjustified on a number of occasions. It is, however, not detrimental for the therapeutic milieu when consequences in a specific situation turn out to be less than optimal. On the contrary, it is to be expected that consequences will have to be reviewed and even revised by the team and in community meetings [16,17]. For the staff to admit that their work was not perfect, to consider new aspects to be taken into account, and to make new agreements is in itself a therapeutic experience for the patients. Instead, it can be detrimental if defined rules and consequences remain suboptimal, because such a situation may lead to inconsistency and tension among staff members.

Positive reinforcement for adaptive prosocial behavior is an essential part of an efficacious behavioral management program for youth displaying aggressive and antisocial behavior [3]. This reinforcement is best individualized according to the needs of each adolescent and evaluated using behavior (functional) analysis techniques [18,19]. Reinforcers may be symbolic, material, or social-emotional. Privileges such as extra television or video game time, free time, extra individual staff attention, and the like are good examples of relevant reinforcers. In a token economy, a desired change is supported by rewarding predefined desired behavior by tokens that in themselves are not worth anything but can be exchanged to something of value to the patient [20–24]. Token systems should be individual, according the patient's cognitive level and capacity to wait for rewards. Preferably, parents should be consulted when defining reinforcers and rewards, because social reinforcers that are organized by parents may have substantial impact and be therapeutically relevant.

Community meetings, first introduced in the principles therapeutic community, are daily meetings of all the members of a community (for example, all the patients and staff of a ward). They offer an opportunity to practice shared responsibility, promote group cohesion, and practice social skills, as well as to ensure that everyone is receives attention every day [16,17]. One or two staff members assume the leadership of the group by rota. The goals of community meetings can vary from a forum for discussing primarily practical issues to an emotionally more challenging therapeutic process. It is essential that everyone participates, is noticed, and is encouraged to bring his or her views to the discussion. Once systematic use of community meetings has made this mode of communication familiar in everyday exchanges, community meetings are a good tool to emphasize shared responsibility when adolescents break rules and display undesirable behaviors. Difficult topics such as bullying, substance use, and threats of violence can be handled in community meetings only after community meetings have been established as a routine means of addressing safer topics. In community meetings, as well as in all other interactions between the youth and the staff, the staff promotes the social-relational skills and self-control the youth learn in their individual and group therapies by modeling and by reminding and supporting the adolescents to use the new techniques. Therefore it is important that all staff members have basic understanding of the individual and group therapy approaches that are in use in the unit.

Because poor impulse control and aggressive behavior are core problems of adolescents admitted to a forensic psychiatric unit, predictable structure, positive reinforcement, modeling, and community meetings should focus specifically on these aspects. A comprehensive aggression-management program extends from preventive measures such as physical environment, safe household routines, risk-reducing admission procedures, risk assessment, de-escalation procedures, drug policies, and the overall psychosocial organization of the therapeutic community to the actual management of serious physical aggressive behavior including physical intervention. The staff needs to be trained in all those aspects, with emphasis on the recognition of signs of aggression and effective management before loss of control occurs [25,26]. Through systematic monitoring and structured assessment of agitation, the staff is better able to use the methods appropriate to each situation and patient and to focus their efforts on situations that bear the greatest potential for dangerous behavior. The guiding principles of an active therapeutic aggression-management program should be that individuals can gain control over their own behavior when appropriate support is given and that patients should be engaged in planning strategies of how the staff can best help them in moments of escalation [26,27]. Also, making aggression-management programs clear to the adolescents enhances the predictability of the environment and therefore is likely to increase compliance.

Despite systematic limit setting, individual de-escalation schemes that take into account individual early-warning signs, and optimal interventions at each phase of an escalation, some adolescents will continue to display intolerable physical aggressive behavior. The regulatory context stipulates the conditions for using restraining methods such as physical restraint, seclusion, mechanical restraint, and medication in escalated situations. To manage these situations effectively in a way that respects the patient's dignity, a unit needs an explicit, written protocol for using coercive treatments and measures [28,29]. Indications for use and discontinuation of restraint should be explicit and also should specify situations in which their use is not justified. Any type of restraint should be used for as short a period as safely possible. A restrained young person should be repeatedly informed of the conditions for terminating the intervention as a part of the dialogue that aims at supporting the young person in regaining self-control [3,28–31].

Replacing the use of coercive control with de-escalation activities that focus on learning self-control skills is both a therapeutic and an ethical obligation. Reliance on coercive measures such as seclusion and restraint makes it unlikely that patients will develop the skills necessary for coping in difficult situations outside the hospital [32]. Physical interventions always risk violating civil rights and bear the risk of untherapeutic wielding of power. Therefore, systematic monitoring of the use of any kind of restraints is an important part of an adolescent forensic unit's continuous quality improvement [3,31,33]. All events of physical intervention need to be recorded in detail, discussed in the team meeting, and followed over time by the management, who give feedback to the team at intervals [28]. Careful monitoring of trends in using coercion, discussed with the whole team with emphasis on the patient's responsibility and ability for self-control and support for learning self-control skills, and staff training in de-escalation and therapeutic aggression management (so that the team truly has alternatives to using coercion) have proven effective in reducing the use of coercive measures in the treatment of patients who have a high risk of violent behavior [3,26,29,32,34].

The authors' unit primarily treats escalation by physical holding or physical restraint as part of a treatment approach that includes emphasis on maintaining self-control throughout ward activities, early intervention, constant dialogue with the patient in restraint situations, and gradual release as self-control increases. A routine part of aftercare is a debriefing with the young person that focuses on the patient's understanding the feelings, thoughts, and behavior in the situation that culminated in physical intervention and points out where the adolescent could choose to act differently next time [17,35–39].

Working with the youth's parents

An essential part of creating a therapeutic milieu in an adolescent forensic unit is winning the trust of the caregivers, particularly parents. Because the adolescents admitted to adolescent forensic unit are likely to have had difficulties in many domains for a long time, the parents probably have also experienced numerous failures in their role as parents and disappointments with agents offering help. Feelings of guilt and frustration are easily provoked in parents in this situation and can emerge as aggression toward treatment. Both the parents and the adolescents sometimes try to conceptualize that problems emerge as being the result of treatment, not that treatment is taking place because of the problems. Parental involvement in treatment is, however, significant for outcome, and effective parenting after discharge is a prerequisite for maintaining positive change [40]. Lewis and colleagues [41] reported placement in a family to be an important predictor of successful adjustment for juvenile delinquents after release into the community. Studies among suicidal adolescents [42] and general child and adolescent psychiatric patients [43] have indicated that parental problems such as family dysfunction, parental mental disorders, and abuse by parents negatively influence treatment compliance. Good parent–child relationships and parental support predict better outcomes in terms of less violent behavior in aggressive adolescents who have severe mental disorders [44]. Many adolescents admitted to an adolescent forensic psychiatric unit have a history of family dysfunction and parental psychosocial problems, and many may not have lived with their parents for several years. Nevertheless, consistent with the examples from the literature mentioned earlier, the authors have found parental attitude to treatment and parental support as expressed by parental participation in treatment planning and goal setting to be crucial for the adolescent's compliance. The authors also believe that overcoming parental resistance is even more important when the adolescent's and the parents' relationships are conflictual than when they are unproblematic. Therefore, motivating parents to become active partners in the treatment should be a continuous goal.

To win parental trust, parents should be involved in the treatment as much as possible [45]. From the preadmission information package to parents to parental involvement as informants in assessment after admission, to providing information, psychoeducation, participation in decision making in network meetings throughout treatment, and actual family therapy when appropriate, the value of parents as important sources of information and as influential persons in the adolescent's life should be emphasized. Research suggests that if parent–child relationships can be improved and parental support for the adolescent increased, compliance during inpatient care and behavioral outcomes in the short and long term can be expected to improve [41–45].

Sometimes the parents cannot actually support the adolescent, but a realistic picture of this situation is formed when they are involved in assessment and treatment planning. For some parents it is necessary to establish limit setting in the same way as with their adolescents (eg, regarding the adolescents' holidays, desire to gain special liberties for the adolescent, presents brought to the ward). There are always some parents who have great difficulty in accepting the ward rules and some who are quick to threaten official complaints and even media contacts. It is advisable to limit such parents' contacts to one or two team members, for example an assigned nurse and psychiatrist or social worker. For such parents, a system of predictable structure is required and preferably should be established before admission.

Crisis management

Any health care unit should have a written crisis management plan evaluating what kind of crises are most likely to occur and what measures must be taken in case of a particular crisis. Although certain crises are by no means confined to adolescent forensic units, some (eg, violent attacks and other offenses committed on the ward, arson, sexual harassment between the patients, accusations of abuse against the staff, and threats of assault by outsiders such as former patients, relatives, or gang members) may be more likely in adolescent forensic psychiatric units than in psychiatric units in general. For the crises reviewed, the crisis management plan gives clear instructions about what to do first, what to do as secondary measures, who is responsible for each action, whom to report to at what moment, and how to handle possible media attention. In an adolescent forensic unit's crisis management plan, a strategy for handling offending behavior occurring on the ward is a necessity.

The management of a crisis is completed by a structured evaluation that produces written documentation of the events for future review (eg, should the patient or parents press charges, or if questions emerge that require documentation, such as insurance reimbursement). The crisis management plan should be reviewed regularly and updated when new information emerges. Although a crisis management plan provides guidelines for acting in emergencies, the process of creating and maintaining it is also a valuable aspect of risk assessment and the prevention of undesirable events.

Leadership

Leadership is of the utmost importance for the therapeutic milieu in an adolescent forensic psychiatric unit. In part, the leadership requirements are the same as for any psychiatric unit, or for health services in general, but some aspects of an adolescent forensic psychiatric unit call for special attention by team leadership.

The attitudes of staff members in an adolescent forensic psychiatric unit are likely to vary from punitive-custodial, with a focus on discipline, to idealistic, advocating protection. Exploring these extremes of opinion while interviewing new applicants is advisable, but it is also necessary to be aware of the existence of this potential division as the unit develops. At the extreme ends of the opposing views, the therapeutic milieu is threatened by the risk of creating a custodial atmosphere and by the risk of jeopardizing appropriate limit setting and safety. When staff members hold different views, the result is inconsistency that may jeopardize the essential requirements of treatment, structure, and predictability. Openly conflicting views may also provide adolescent patients with opportunities to manipulate the personnel. It is an especially challenging task for the leadership to find an optimal balance between positive limit setting and structure on the one hand and a dynamic understanding of adolescent development on the other.

The fears, projections, and stigmatization related to adolescent forensic psychiatric patients may be stressful for the teams working with them, because the public often expresses negative attitudes and uninformed criticism both of failing to keep dangerous offenders under sufficient control and of depriving youth of their liberty and using unacceptable coercion. Another danger to be avoided is the idea that nothing works; this attitude may demotivate staff to invest in the treatment. It is an important task for the leaders to contain and work through the negative feelings provoked in the staff.

Adolescent forensic psychiatric patients have often experienced neglect and abuse [8,46–48]. Aggressive youth often have a history of poor parent–child relationships and poor support from family as well as foster care placement and frequent disruptions in care continuity [44,49]. Their ability to establish a therapeutic relationship is often hampered, and as a result even positive therapeutic practices, such as adult attention, adult presence, trust, modeling, and limit setting, may provoke negative, even destructive reactions. The youth in adolescent forensic units may also provoke contradictory feelings in staff members by being seriously disturbed, severely deprived, and victimized, but at the same time having committed offenses that may invoke fear, anger, or disgust. Such contradictory feelings may seem most pronounced with regard to young sex offenders. Denying the fact of past offenses would result in an unrealistic treatment approach, whereas focusing too much on past criminality may lead to an increasing use of custodial and punitive practices. A challenge for the leadership is to make these feelings a topic for open discussion in the team, to prevent their destructive potential, and to support staff members who experience frustration when the adolescents react destructively to positive approaches.

The importance of the day-to-day structure of ward activities is generally accepted by the team, but during stressful times there is a tendency to interrupt the structured activities, such as canceling group and individual meetings with assigned nurses, based on the notion that these activities can be performed only when the situation on the ward is normal. It is even more important to carry out the regular routines when the situation threatens to get out of control. Breaking the routines is upsetting for adolescents and may create an opportunity for their involvement in disruptive behavior and therefore is likely to exacerbate the situation. The staff may need additional support from the leaders to understand the importance of routines fully and to adhere to the routine activities even in exceptional situations.

The team also needs structured opportunities to discuss both everyday issues and crises. A routine procedure that is activated when threshold events occur is necessary to evaluate and defuse unexpected crises and to prepare for future incidents. Actual debriefing may be appreciated in the case of serious events (such as severe violence) in which staff members are at risk of being traumatized, even though routine debriefing of asymptomatic victims of traumatizing events has been severely criticized [50]. In this case the debriefing serves another role, not only handling the consequences of trauma but also maintaining a workable ward atmosphere and a motivated team. Although it is always good to listen informally to the staff's concerns on a variety of issues when they emerge, decision making is best postponed to the forum scheduled for discussion of the issue in question unless an emergency requires otherwise. Using both structured forums and less formal opportunities for discussion, the leadership should make an attempt to include all the staff in dialogue concerning the philosophy of care and the best practices to bring the chosen philosophy into action [29].

How to succeed in starting and running an adolescent forensic psychiatric unit

A successful therapeutic milieu is a matter of attitude and atmosphere. Good outcomes in residential treatment for juvenile delinquents have been associated with such factors as warmth, firmness, and high expectations [51]. The million-dollar question is how to maintain these factors in the everyday practice of an adolescent forensic psychiatric unit.

Adolescence is a positive period of life with much potential. In growth and development it is second only to the very first years of life. In the psychodynamic view adolescence has been described as "a second chance" to overcome difficulties created by maladaptive developments in early childhood [52,53]. There are greater opportunities to influence personality positively in the middle of adolescent development than at any point later in life. On the other hand, the needs of these patients and society's needs regarding these youth cannot be questioned. Adolescent forensic patients tend to have complex psychiatric, social, and educational needs that are difficult to meet and require specialized care in appropriate environments, not least to ensure the safety of all concerned. Finally, it is never boring to work with adolescents.

References

[1] Steiner H. Practice parameters for the assessment and treatment of children and adolescents with conduct disorder. J Am Acad Child Adol Psychiatry 1997;36S:122S–39S.

[2] Redding R, Lexcen F, Ryan E. Mental health treatment for juvenile offenders in residential psychiatric and juvenile justice settings. In: Heilburn K, Goldstein N, Redding R, editors. Juvenile delinquency. Prevention, assessment, and interventions. New York: Oxford University Press; 2005. p. 282–309.

[3] Friman P, Evans J, Lazerlere R, et al. Correspondence between child dysfunction and program intensiveness: evidence of continuum of care across five mental health programs. J Comm Psychology 1993;21:227–33.

[4] Lock J, Strauss G. Psychiatric hospitalization for adolescents with conduct disorder. Hosp Comm Psychiatry 1994;45:925–8.

[5] Salize HJ, Dressing H. Placement and treatment of mentally ill offenders—legislation and practice in EU member states. European Commission—Health and Consumer Protection Directorate–General. Lengerich (Germany): Pobst Science Publishers.

[6] Timmons-Mitchell J, Brown C, et al. Comparing the mental health needs of female and male incarcerated juvenile delinquents. Behav Sci Law 1997;15:195–202.

[7] Teplin L, Abram K, McClelland G, et al. Psychiatric disorders in youth in juvenile detention. Arch Gen Psychiatry 2002;59:1133–43.

[8] Vermeiren R. Psychopathology and delinquency in adolescents: a descriptive and developmental perspective. Clin Psychol Rev 2003;23:277–318.

[9] Domalanta D, Risser W, Roberts R, et al. Prevalence of depression and other psychiatric disorders among incarcerated youths. J Am Acad Child Adolesc Psychiatry 2003;42:477–84.

[10] Morrison P, Lehane M. Staffing levels and seclusion use. J Adv Nurs 1995;22:1193–202.

[11] Kroll L, Woodham A, Rothwell J, et al. Reliability of the Salford Needs Assessment Schedule for Adolescents. Psychol Med 1999;29:891–902.

[12] Nicol R, Stretch D, Whitney I, et al. Mental health needs and services for severely troubled

and troubling young people including young offenders in an N.H.S. region. J Adolesc 2002;23: 243–61.

[13] Moeller G, Barratt E, Dougherty D, et al. Psychiatric aspects of impulsivity. Am J Psychiatry 2001;158:1783–93.

[14] Epps K, Swaffer T. Cognitive-behavioural therapies. In: Bailey S, Dolan M, editors. Adolescent forensic psychiatry. London: Arnold; 2004. p. 265–85.

[15] Kazdin A, Weisz JR. Evidence-based psychotherapies for children and adolescents. New York: Guilford Press; 2003.

[16] Lanza ML. Community meeting: review, update and synthesis. Int J Group Psychother 2000; 50:473–85.

[17] Kennard D. The therapeutic community as an adaptable treatment modality across different settings. Psychiatr Q 2004;75:295–307.

[18] Miller LK. Principles of everyday behavior analyzes. 3rd edition. Pacific Grove (CA): Brooks/Cole; 1997.

[19] Sturmey P. Functional analysis in clinical psychology. In: Mark J, Williams G, editors. Clinical psychology. Chichester (UK): John Wiley & Sons; 2002. p. 53–143.

[20] Kazdin A. The token economy. New York: Plenum Press; 1977.

[21] Kazdin A. The token economy: a decade later. J Appl Behav Anal 1982;15:431–45.

[22] Liberman R. The token economy. Am J Psyhciatry 2000;157:1398.

[23] Field C, Nash H, Hanwerk M, et al. A modification of the token economy for nonresponsive youth in family-style residential care. Behav Modif 2004;28:438–57.

[24] McGonagle T, Sultana A. Token economy for schizophrenia. Cochrane Database Syst Rev 2005; 3:CD001473.

[25] D'Orio B, Purselle D, Stvens D, et al. Reduction of episodes of seclusion and restraint in a psychiatric emergency service. Psychiatr Serv 2004;55:581–3.

[26] Sullivan A, Bezmen J, Barron C, et al. Reducing restraints: alternatives to restraints in an inpatient psychiatric service—utilizing safe and effective methods to evaluate and treat the violent patient. Psychiatr Q 2005;76:51–65.

[27] Jonikas J, Cook J, Rosen D, et al. A program to reduce use of physical restraint in psychiatric inpatient facilities. Psychiatr Serv 2004;55:818–20.

[28] Barnett S, Dosreis S, Riddle M, and the Maryland Youth Practice Improvement Committee for Mental Health. Improving the management of acute aggression in state residential and inpatient psychiatric facilities for youths. J Am Acad Child Adol Psychiatry 2002;41:897–905.

[29] American Psychiatric Association, American Psychiatric Nursing Association, and National Association for Psychiatric Health Systems. Learning from each other. Success stories and ideas for reducing restraint/seclusion on behavioural health. Available at: http://www.naphs.org. Accessed July 30, 2005.

[30] Masters K, Bellonci C, and the Work Group on Quality Issues. Practice parameter for the prevention and management of aggressive behaviour in child and adolescent psychiatric institutions, with special reference to seclusion and restraint. J Am Acad Child Adol Psychiatry 2002; 41:4S–25S.

[31] Lebel J, Stromberg N, Duckworth K, et al. Child and adolescent inpatient restraint reduction: a state initiative to promote strength-based care. J Am Acad Child Adol Psychiatry 2004;43: 37–45.

[32] Donat D. An analysis of successful efforts to reduce the use of seclusion and restraint at a public psychiatric hospital. Psychiatr Serv 2003;54:1119–23.

[33] Shewhart WA. Economic control of quality of manufactures product. American Society for Quality Control 1980:30–5.

[34] Richmond I, Trujillo D, Schmelzer J, et al. Lest restrictive alternatives: do they really work? J Nurs Care Qual 1996;11:29–37.

[35] Miller D, Walker M, Friedmann D. Use of a holding technique to control the violent behaviour of seriously disturbed adolescents. Hosp Comm Psychiatry 1989;40:520–4.

[36] Barlow D. Therapeutic holding. Effective intervention with the aggressive child. J Psychosocial Nursing 1989;27:10–4.

[37] Stirling C, McHugh A. Developing a non-aversive intervention strategy in the management of aggression and violence for people with learning disabilities using natural therapeutic holding. J Adv Nurs 1998;27:503–9.

[38] Myeroff R, Mertlich G, Gross J. Comparative effectiveness of holding therapy with aggressive children. Child Psych Human Dev 1999;29:303–13.

[39] West M, Abolins D. Dealing with hostility. In: Forensic nursing and mental disorder in clinical practice. Oxford (UK): Butterford-Heinamann; 2001.

[40] Henggeler SW, Schoenwald SK, Borduin CM, et al. Multisystemic treatment of antisocial behaviour in children and adolescents. New York: Guilford Press; 1998.

[41] Lewis D, Yeager C, Lovely R, et al. A clinical follow-up of delinquent males: ignored vulnerabilities, unmet needs, and the perpetuation of violence. J Am Acad Child Adol Psychiatry 1994;33:518–28.

[42] King C, Hovey J, Brand E, et al. Suicidal adolescents after hospitalization: parent and family impacts on treatment follow-through. J Am Acad Child Adol Psychiatry 1997;36:85–93.

[43] Lau A, Weisz J. Reported maltreatment among clinic-referred children: implications for presenting problems, treatment attrition, and long-term outcomes. J Am Acad Child Adol Psychiatry 2003;42:1327–34.

[44] Vance JE, Bowen N, Fernandez G, et al. Risk and protective factors as predictors of outcome in adolescents with psychiatric disorder and aggression. J Am Acad Child Adol Psychiatry 2002;41:36–43.

[45] Cunnigham PB, Henggeler SW. Engaging multiproblem families in treatment: lessons learned throughout the development of multisystemic therapy. Fam Process 1999;38:281–6.

[46] Abram K, Teplin L, Devon C, et al. Posttraumatic stress disorder and trauma in youth in juvenile detention. Arch Gen Psychiatry 2004;61:403–10.

[47] Ruschkin V, Schwab-Stone M, Koposov R, et al. Violence exposure, posttraumatic stress, and personality in juvenile delinquents. J Am Acad Child Adol Psychiatry 2002;41:322–9.

[48] Steiner H, Garcia I, Matthews Z. Posttraumatic stress disorder in incarcerated juvenile delinquents. J Am Acad Child Adol Psychiatry 1997;36:357–65.

[49] Vivona J, Ecker B, Halgin R, et al. Self- and other-directed aggression in child and adolescent psychiatric inpatients. J Am Acad Child Adol Psychiatry 1995;34:434–44.

[50] Rose S, Bisson R, Churchill R, et al. Psychological debriefing for preventing post-traumatic stress disorder. Cochrane Database Syst Rev 2002;2:CD000560.

[51] Rutter M, Giller H. Juvenile delinquency. Trends and perspectives. New York: Guilford Press; 1984.

[52] Laufer M. Adolescent disturbance and breakdown. London: Penguin Books Ltd; 1975.

[53] Blos P. The adolescent passage. Developmental issues, 1979. New York: International Universities Press, Inc.; 1979.

ELSEVIER
SAUNDERS

Child Adolesc Psychiatric Clin N Am
15 (2006) 477–499

CHILD AND
ADOLESCENT
PSYCHIATRIC CLINICS
OF NORTH AMERICA

Psychopharmacologic Treatment in Juvenile Offenders

Marie V. Soller, BA[a], Niranjan S. Karnik, MD, PhD[a,b,*], Hans Steiner, Dr. med. univ., FAPA, FAACAP, FAPM[a]

[a]*Stanford University School of Medicine, Palo Alto, CA, USA*
[b]*University of California School of Medicine, San Francisco, CA, USA*

Psychopathology is substantially higher among juvenile offenders than in the general population, with some estimates finding between two thirds to three quarters of incarcerated youths meeting criteria for a psychiatric illness [1–3]. These estimates of psychiatric illness probably overestimate the prevalence of psychopathology across the spectrum of juvenile offenders, because incarcerated juveniles are more likely to have illness and to have greater morbidity than first-time offenders or those in diversion programs. Nevertheless, the high prevalence rates for psychopathology among juvenile offenders should be a cause of concern.

As an arm of the public welfare system, the juvenile justice system has an increasing burden placed on it. It is expected to house and sometimes rehabilitate juveniles who represent a danger to the public and also must address their often complex psychiatric illnesses that are increasingly seen as being intimately linked to their delinquency.

It is clear that the unique issues involved in treating confined juveniles make psychopharmacology difficult and ethically problematic. A recent consensus report recommends behavioral management and psychotherapy be used where indications clearly allow their use as first-line interventions. Only after these nonmedication approaches have failed should pharmacologic interventions be considered and tried as augmentation strategies [4,5]. For example, an acutely psychotic offender who presents with command auditory hallucinations and de-

* Corresponding author. Division of Child and Adolescent Psychiatry, Stanford University, 401 Quarry Road, Stanford, CA 94305.

E-mail address: nkarnik@stanford.edu (N.S. Karnik).

doi:10.1016/j.chc.2005.12.003

lusional thoughts would merit antipsychotic medications for stabilization followed by psychotherapy and medications if needed, whereas a young offender presenting with mild dysthymic symptoms might merit psychotherapy as initial treatment.

This article first reviews ways to assess children in the justice system who may benefit from psychopharmacologic treatments. Second, it summarizes the emerging understanding of the nature of aggression and violence and the utility of using the schema of reactive ("hot") and proactive ("cold") aggression as a way to consider pharmacologic options. Third, it summarizes the current published studies on the treatment of conduct disorder, which roughly corresponds to the population of children in the juvenile justice system. Finally, it examines the ways that different classes of medications might be considered when approaching juvenile delinquents and the ways that psychopharmacology could be used as part of an overall treatment plan.

Assessment and approach

The cornerstone of sound psychopharmacology is an accurate and detailed psychiatric assessment. The current nomenclature in the *Diagnostic and Statistical Manual of Mental Disorders*, *fourth edition* [6] is not necessarily well suited to the treatment of juvenile delinquents among whom comorbidities are the norm and multiple concurrent diagnoses may emerge. Although the International Classification of Diseases, tenth edition [7] uses similar criteria and syndrome-based classifications, it has a useful component that advocates making a principal diagnosis and moving to treat that illness first.

Maladaptive aggression has been found to complicate a wide array of diagnoses including posttraumatic stress disorder, depression, bipolar disorder, and attention deficit hyperactivity disorder (ADHD). The most conservative assumption would be to treat the principal diagnosis as specifically and comprehensively as possible. As the principal diagnosis responds, the expectation is that the maladaptive aggression will recede, as has been most clearly demonstrated in the case of ADHD [8]. Should this treatment prove ineffective, and residual symptoms remain, or should there be an inability to establish an initial principal diagnosis, it is wise to switch to a symptom-targeting approach and choose pharmacologic interventions based on the best estimate of risks and benefits for the individual. Because prominent aggression usually poses a danger to the patient and others, it may be necessary to stabilize the situation first while trying to minimize risk to the individual. It is expected that after the crisis has resolved the focus should return to establishing a primary diagnosis and targeting the treatment as specifically as possible.

Juvenile offenders present to authorities and clinicians at a variety of levels of care, from on-the-street encounters and local police stations to incarceration in a juvenile facility. The range of resources available at these various levels of care is wide. Because more medical resources are available at higher levels of care, the expectation is that greater care and time can be taken to complete a thorough assessment as a child progresses through the system (Fig. 1). The degree to which medications can be used as an intervention for juvenile offenders depends partially on the individual's location within the system and the resources available, as well as on the acuity of the psychiatric need.

Every assessment must have a thorough history and physical examination as a starting point. Assessment for neurologic findings is of primary importance, as is documentation of any visible evidence of abuse or neglect. It is common to find healed physical scars or wounds caused by recent or remote abuse. Baseline laboratory studies are also useful. Modern psychopharmacology requires that practitioners monitor height, weight, thyroid panels, diabetes measures, basic blood cell counts, electrolytes, and other parameters depending on the medication selected. EKGs could also be needed if certain atypical antipsychotics are used because of their propensity to cause QTc prolongation [9].

Practitioners working with problems of aggression should use standardized psychometric instruments as part of an initial assessment. As a first-line screening tool, many juvenile facilities make use of the Massachusetts Youth Screening Instrument, second version [10]. It is a relatively short instrument that can serve as an indicator for significant dysfunction and can be administered by most front-line personnel. More specialized psychometric or neuropsychologic testing may be performed as needed and depending on the circumstance, but in all cases such instruments should be used to track progress or lack thereof. A recent summary of a range of instruments is available [8].

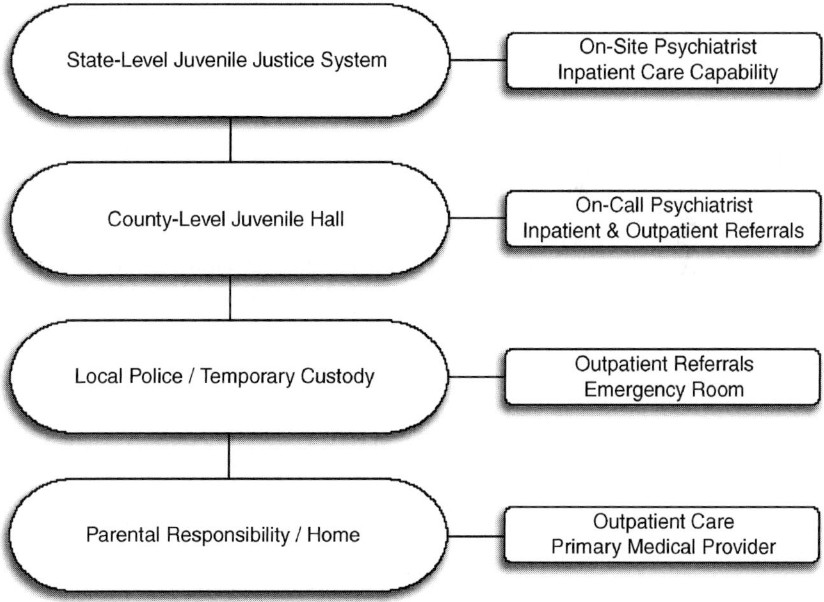

Fig. 1. Levels of juvenile justice and mental health care.

Children are dynamic beings, and behaviors exist along a developmental trajectory [11]. Behavior that is appropriate at one age may be inappropriate at another. Attention to the juvenile's psychologic development is important and must be included in any diagnostic work-up. After a diagnosis is made or, in an acute situation, after target symptoms are identified, it is appropriate to consider the potential use of a pharmacological agent.

During all assessments of children in the juvenile justice system, special attention needs to be paid to making a thorough and careful evaluation of suicidality. Juvenile offenders are at especially high risk for self-harm during detention or incarceration [12–16]. There probably is a multifactorial etiology to suicidality that may not be immediately evident, but prompt assessment is always necessary. Studies of in-patient populations have identified several risk factors for suicide attempts including prior suicide attempts, evidence of psychosis, and acuity of suicidal ideation. Fawcett and colleagues [17] suggest that adding severity of anxiety and agitation may be beneficial. Pharmacologic interventions can assist with acute anxiety and agitation including judicious and closely monitored use of benzodiazepines and second-generation hypnotics [18].

Subtypes of aggression as targets for psychopharmacology

Violence and aggression are often the precipitating factors that bring children into the juvenile justice system, and these problems plague the system before, during, and following incarceration. They also constitute one of the most common targets for psychopharmacology in the juvenile justice system. Functionally, there are two forms of violence—acute and chronic. Juvenile offenders often present as acutely aggressive or can be made so by interactions in the institutional environments. Care should be taken to use behavioral techniques, if possible, to reduce or de-escalate violence. In the event that de-escalation is impossible, and the juvenile poses a risk of harm to themselves or others, acute pharmacologic strategies can be employed as one component of an acute treatment plan. If the juvenile is able to cooperate sufficiently, oral medication can be given. Fast-acting benzodiazepines such as lorazepam or atypical antipsychotics such as olanzapine or risperidone can be used. Both olanzapine and risperidone come in formulations specifically designed for rapid oral delivery and to minimize the possibility of "cheeking" or other ways of avoiding medication dosing. Caution should be used when dosing benzodiazepines, because some children have paradoxical, disinhibited reactions to this class of medications.

If the situation requires immediate action to prevent harm, intramuscular preparations can be used. It is always better to have the juvenile in a secure environment when dosing with these formulations. It may be necessary to place the juvenile in physical restraints to avoid the possibility of harm during the delivery of the medication. Typical formulations used in these circumstances are haloperidol and lorazepam, often with diphenhydramine or benztropine given for prophylaxis against extrapyramidal symptoms (EPS). Thorazine has also historically been used but has lost some of its appeal because of its potential for significant side effects. More recently, intramuscular preparations of atypical antipsychotics such as olanzapine and ziprasidone have become available. Both of these are far less likely to cause EPS and tend to be less acutely sedating than the typical antipsychotics. One advantage of using less-sedating medications for juveniles is that behavioral control can be asserted while allowing the juvenile to communicate with staff and learn from the incident. Another reason to use these medications in juveniles is that they are easily converted from the intramuscular form to an oral form of the same agent. Children placed in restraints for safety and medication delivery should be released as soon as they are able to contract with staff for safety and after enough time has passed for the medications to take effect.

One of the challenging aspects of dealing with juvenile offenders is addressing the long-term control of chronic, repetitive aggression. Evidence from the neurobiology and psychology of aggression increasingly demonstrates that there are two major phenotypes of aggressive behavior. One phenotype has been termed "planned, instrumental, or proactive" (PIP), and the second is known as "reactive, affective, defensive or impulsive" (RADI). These two forms correspond to known differences in the psychobiology of aggression [19], and each most likely responds to very different interventions. PIP is often termed "cold" aggression and corresponds to what most investigators see as an early form of psychopathic violence. It is remorseless, calculated, and lacking in a moral decision-making structure. At the present time only limited evidence supports the use of medications in the treatment of this type of aggression. PIP aggression probably does not exist along a single neuronal architecture but instead emerges through multiple pathways at multiple sociopsychobiologic levels.

Conversely, RADI or "hot" aggression is an emotionally charged form of aggression that often is poorly thought out and highly reactive to situational stimuli [20]. It constitutes the prime target for psychopharmacology because of its strong links to specific targets and pathways in the frontal and prefrontal cortex. This form of aggression is known to have links to serotonin, dopamine, norepinephrine, and γ-aminobutyric systems. As much as the situation permits, attempts should be made to differentiate these forms of aggression, because understanding of the phenotype will guide treatment strategies and outcome expectations.

In trying to control chronic aggression, it is even more important to distinguish PIP and RADI subtypes. Compared with nondelinquent cohorts of equivalent age, both forms of aggression are more common in delinquent populations and co-occur in about 5% of youths who have clinically significant problems with aggression [21]. Clinically significant PIP aggression alone is quite rare in the community but is often concentrated in juvenile justice settings and most often is correlated with a history of substance abuse rather than other forms of psychopathology. Recent research shows that juveniles who have the RADI form of aggression respond well to mood stabilizers and specifically to the use of divalproex sodium [20,22–24]. The findings in this area of research are preliminary, and studies are underway to understand the nature of aggression and its responsiveness to pharmacologic interventions. At present, the response of PIP aggression to various treatments has not been well studied, but the emerging data suggest that this form of aggression may benefit from limited pharmacologic intervention in combination with psychotherapy and structured environments [25–27]. In studies of childhood aggression that did not subtype the behaviors into PIP or RADI forms, lithium was found to be moderately effective in addressing aggressive behavior [28–30].

Conduct disorder

Juvenile offenders have high rates of meeting diagnostic criteria for conduct disorder. The diagnostic criteria for conduct disorder are intended to distinguish normal childhood aggression from a repeated pattern of violating the rights of others or harming people, animals, or property [6]. Both PIP and RADI aggression partially overlap with conduct disorder. Control of conduct problems is difficult and often unpredictable. Fig. 2 shows these relationships schematically and highlights the functional overlaps of major classes of psychiatric illness and

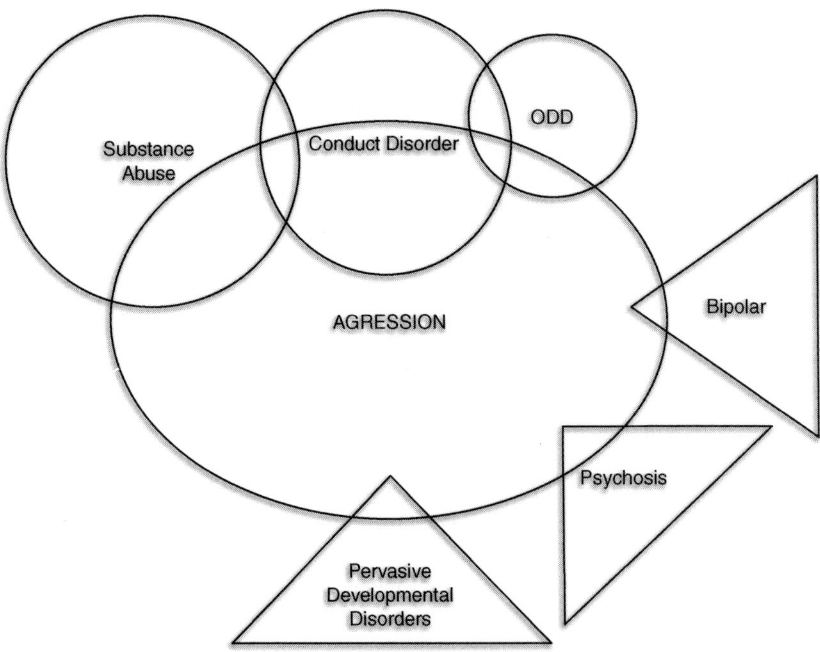

Fig. 2. Relationship of aggression to psychiatric illnesses.

aggression. Table 1 reviews all of the major studies that have examined the effects of major classes of medications on conduct disorder and its related symptomatology, which crudely overlaps with the aggressive patterns described previously. Most studies in juvenile offenders have taken place outside of detention facilities and have focused on outpatient presentations of conduct disorder, probably because of the difficulties involved in trying to organize controlled, clinical trials in incarcerated youth. (When research is being conducted, added layers of administrative, ethical, and clinical protections of incarcerated populations are in place.)

Evidence exists for the use of both atypical antipsychotics and mood stabilizers in the treatment of conduct disorder, especially when trying to target aggression, destructiveness, and impulsivity. Specifically, evidence from randomized, controlled clinical trials supports the use of valproate, lithium, carbamazepine, olanzapine, and risperidone (see Table 1). The choice of medication depends on the particular patient, weighing of risks and benefits, and the particular pharmacologic properties of each agent.

Both atypical antipsychotics and mood stabilizers require that the provider evaluate certain baseline factors and consistently monitor particular laboratory and physical indicators. For all of these medications, baseline weight and vital signs should be recorded. In addition, hemoglobin A1c and lipid panels should be drawn before initiating treatment with atypical antipsychotics because of the potential for the development of diabetes and related consequences. For mood stabilizers, basic chemistries and regular blood levels need to be drawn. Lithium can cause nephrotoxicity; valproate, divalproex, and carbamazepine can all be hepatotoxic. In addition, several of these agents have particular rare side effects that can be lethal, and patients need to be monitored closely for adverse events. Conducting thorough physical examinations is especially important among juvenile offenders who, as wards of the state, often lack the authority to make decisions about their care themselves. This state authority and the need to provide mental health care should be taken as a judicious responsibility, and risks and benefits should be documented before initiating pharmacotherapy.

Even excluding the high rates of conduct disorder, juvenile delinquent populations are faced with an extremely high burden of mental illness [31]. Several studies suggest that the majority of juveniles in detention suffer from illnesses such as depression, ADHD, substance-use disorders, and anxiety disorders [32,33]. Although many disorders seem to be more common in delinquents, this population is faced with the full spectrum of psychiatric illness, and thus individuals may benefit from the full spectrum of psychiatric medications. Because little research has been conducted on the majority of psychotropic medications in juvenile delinquents, the following sections briefly review only a selection of drug categories for a general child population, giving the common uses and any major side effects or other issues for each medication. Table 2 lists each medication and its Food and Drug Administration (FDA)–labeled indication, if applicable. For a more in-depth review of each medication, the reader is referred to a recent handbook by Martin and colleagues [34].

Table 1
Literature review by drug class for studies of conduct disorder

Study [reference]	Medication	Study design/ duration	Subjects	Scales used	Results
Typical antipsychotics					
Campbell 1984 [29]	Haloperidol and lithium	DB RCT/6 wk	N=61, hospitalized, 5–13 y, dx of CD	CPRS (b), CGI, CTQ, CPTQ, TORSA	Haloperidol and lithium better than placebo in reducing aggression and conduct problems; more "untoward effects" with haloperidol than with lithium
Aman 1991 [70]	Thioridazine and MPH	DB RCT with crossover/9 wk	N=30, 4–16 y, subaverage IQ; dx of CD or ADHD	CTQ, CTRS, DCB, GRTE, RBPC, RLRS	Thioridizine modestly effective on teacher ratings of conduct problems and hyperactivity; MPH very effective on all teacher ratings
Greenhill 1985 [71]	Thioridizine and molindone	DB RCT/8 wk	N=31, hospitalized, 6–11 y; dx of CD	CGI, CPRS, CRS, CTQ, DOTES	Thioridizine and molindone better than placebo in reducing aggression and conduct problems
Broche 1980 [72]	Pimozide	DB RCT with crossover/2 mo	N=10		Social integration improved
Joshi 1998 [73]	Droperidol	Case series/ emergency use	N=26, hospitalized, mean age 9.1 y; varied dx, DBD (N=17)	Subjective rating	Acute aggressive or violent behavior episode resolved such that all subjects returned to milieu in 2 hours after administration of droperidol
Hameer 2001 [74]	Droperidol	Case series/ emergency use over 20 wk	N=6, hospitalized, mean age 12 y; varied dx	Subjective rating	Hyperactive, violent, and/or combative subjects experienced "profound calming effect" with droperidol
Atypical antipsychotics					
Findling 2000 [75]	Risperidone	DB RCT/10 wk	N=20, 5–15 y; dx of CD	RAAPP; CGI, CBCL, CPRS (b)	Aggression on RAAPP significantly improved; no difference in parent rating
Snyder 2002 [76]	Risperidone	DB RCT/7 wk	N=110, 5–12 y, low IQ; dx of DBD, 80% dx of ADHD	ABC, BPI, CGI, CPT, CSI, CVLT, NCBRF	Aggression, hyperactivity, and self-injury significantly improved; no difference between ADHD and non-ADHD subjects

Findling 2004 [77]	Risperidone	Prospective open extension/48 wk	N=107, 5–12 y, low IQ; dx of DBD	Safety indicators, CGI, NCBRF	Safe and effective in reducing conduct problems
Aman 2005 [78]	Risperidone	Pooled analysis of two DB RCTs/6 wk	N=223 (pooled), 5–12 y, low IQ; dx of DBD	NCBRF	Improved social interaction, feelings of self-worth, and reintegration
Croonenberghs 2005 [79]	Risperidone	Open/1 y	N=504 (32 sites), 5–14 y, low IQ; dx of DBD	Safety indicators, CGI, NCBRF	Safe and effective in reducing conduct problems
Soderstrom 2002 [80]	Olanzapine	Case series	N=6, 14–19 y, male; "extremely aggressive"	Subjective rating	Suggests reduction in aggression
Stephens 2004 [81]	Olanzapine	Single-blind RCT/10 wk	N=10, 7–13 y; dx of Tourette's syndrome	CBCL	Aggression was significantly reduced
Anticonvulsants					
Kafantaris 1992 [82]	Carbamazepine	Open/4 wk	N=10, hospitalized, 5–10 y; dx of CD	CGI, CPRS, CPTQ, GCC	Aggression and explosiveness were significantly reduced
Mattes 1990 [83]	Carbamazepine and propanolol	RCT/varied duration	N=61, hospitalized, 16 y and older; dx of IED	Subjective evaluation	Temper outbursts modestly reduced; suggests carbamazepine as more effective for IED and propanolol for ADHD
Cueva 1996 [84]	Carbamazepine	DB RCT/9 wk	N=22, hospitalized, 5–12 y; dx of CD	CGI, CPRS, OAS	Not better than placebo in reducing aggression
Donovan 2000 [85]	Valproic acid	DB RCT with crossover/12 wk	N=20, 10–18 y; dx of DBD	DISC, M-OAS, SCID-V	Improved explosive temper and mood lability
Steiner 2003 [24]	Valproic acid	DB RCT/7 wk	N=71, mean age 15 y, males; dx of CD, in detention	CGI, WAI, YSR	Self-reported improvement in restraint and impulse control
Mood stabilizers					
Malone 1994 [30]	Lithium	Open/4 wk	N=8, hospitalized, 9–16 y; dx of CD	GCCR, OAS	Aggression significantly reduced
Campbell 1984 [29]	Haloperidol and lithium	DB RCT/6 wk	N=61, hospitalized, 5–13 y; dx of CD	CPRS (b), CGI, CTQ, CPTQ, TORSA	Halperidol and lithium better than placebo in reducing aggression and conduct problems; more "untoward effects" with haloperidol than with lithium

(continued on next page)

Table 1 (*continued*)

Study [reference]	Medication	Study design/ duration	Subjects	Scales used	Results
Campbell 1995 [28]	Lithium	DB RCT/8 wk	N=50, hospitalized, 5–12 y	CGI, CPRS (b), CTQ, GCJCS, POMS, PTQ	Lithium modestly better than placebo in reducing conduct problems, although difference not evident on POMS
Malone 2000 [86]	Lithium	DB RCT/6 wk	N=40, hospitalized, 10–17 y; dx of CD, severe and chronic aggression	CGI, GCJCS, OAS	Aggression was significantly reduced; more than 50% subjects experienced nausea, vomiting, and urinary frequency
Rifkin 1997 [87]	Lithium	DB RCT/3 wk	N=33, hospitalized, 12–17 y; dx of CD	BRS, CTRS, HRS-D, OAS	Lithium was not better than placebo in reducing overt aggression
Antidepressants					
Coccaro 1997 [88]	Fluoxetine	DB RCT/12 wk	N=15, hospitalized, mean age 39.4 y; IED, personality disorder	OAS	Aggression and irritability significantly reduced
Constantino 1997 [89]	Fluoxetine, paroxetine, and sertraline	Open/10+ wk	N=19, hospitalized	MOAS	Aggression not reduced by any of the SSRIs tested
Cherek 2002 [90]	Paroxetine	RCT/3 wk	N=12 adult males on felony parole	PSAP	Impulsivity significantly reduced; mixed reduction in aggression
Armenteros 2002 [91]	Citalopram	Open/7 wk	N=12, 7–15 y; 6+ mo aggression and impulsivity	CBCL, CGI, M-OAS	Impulsivity and aggression both significantly reduced
Zubieta 1992 [92]	Trazadone	Case series/ varied duration	N=22, hospitalized, 5–12 y impulsive and aggressive	CPTQ	Aggression, impulsivity, and hyperactivity all subjectively improved
Stimulants					
Klein 1997 [93]	MPH	DB RCT/5 wk	N=84, 6–16 y; dx of CD, two thirds also ADHD	CTRS, IAS, QRBPC	Antisocial behavior significantly reduced; no difference between ADHD and non-ADHD

Kaplan 1990 [94]	MPH	Mixed open and DB RCT/7 wk	N=9, 6 hospitalized, 13–16 y; dx of CD (N=8) or ODD (N=1), and ADHD (N=7)	AABC, CTRS, DICA	Aggression on the AABC significantly reduced; overall pattern of reduced aggression and hyperactivity
Hazell 2003 [95]	MPH and clonidine	DB RCT/6 wk	N=67, 6–14 y, white; dx of ADHD and CD or ODD	CBCL, CPRS, CTRS	Adding clonidine to MPH significantly improved conduct symptoms and had no effect on ADHD symptoms
Alpha-agonists					
Kemph 1993 [96]	Clonidine	Open/1–18 mo	N=17, 5–17 y; dx of CD or ODD	CBCL, RAAPP	Aggression significantly reduced
Schvehla 1994 [97]	Clonidine	Retrospective/ average 21 d	N=18, hospitalized, 6–12 y, male; dx of ADHD and CD or ODD	GAF, CGI	Anger, aggression, hyperactivity, and impulsivity all significantly reduced
Beta-blockers					
Silver 1999 [98]	Propranolol	Mixed open and DB RCT/varied duration	N=20, 18+ y; chronic aggression; serious psychiatric dx or mental retardation	CGI, OAS	Aggression significantly reduced in seven subjects
Kuperman 1987 [99]	Propranolol	Open/3+ mo	N=16, 4–24 y; physically aggressive	Subjective rating	Frequency and intensity of aggressive outbursts reduced in 10 subjects
Mattes 1990 [83]	Carbamazepine and propanolol	RCT/varied duration	N=61, hospitalized, 16 y and older; dx of IED	Subjective rating	Temper outbursts modestly reduced; suggests carbamazepine more effective for IED and propanolol for ADHD
Connor 1997 [100]	Nadolol	Open/5 mo	N=12, 9–24 y, male; developmentally delayed	CGI, Iowa CTRS, OAS	Aggression was significantly reduced
Buitelaar 1996 [101]	Pindolol	DB RCT/4 wk	N=52, 7–13 y; dx of ADHD	ACRS	Pindolol and MPH reduced conduct problems and hyperactivity at home equally, but pindolol was less effective than MPH at school and according to psychologic testing; significant side effects

(continued on next page)

Table 1 (*continued*)

Study [reference]	Medication	Study design/ duration	Subjects	Scales used	Results
Other					
Pfeffer 1997 [102]	Buspirone	Open/9 wk	N=25, hospitalized; anxiety and aggression	CGAS, MAVRIC	Aggression was not significantly reduced
Stanislav 1994 [103]	Buspirone	Retrospective/ varied duration	N=20, hospitalized, 15–55 y; varied dx	Subjective rating	Overt aggression was significantly improved for 9/10 subjects given buspirone for 3+ mo
Vitiello 1991 [104]	Diphenhydramine	DB RCT/ emergency use	N=21, hospitalized, 5–13 y; varied dx	CGI, CTRS	Diphenhydramine and placebo improved aggression equally
King 2001 [105]	Amantadine	Open/5–14 d	N=8, hospitalized, 4–12 y, males; neurodevelopmental disorder (N=7)	Subjective rating	Impulse control improved in all subjects (four with marked response, four with moderate response)

Abbreviations: AABC, Adolescent Antisocial Behavior Checklist; ABC, Aberrant Behavior Checklist; ACRS, Abbreviated Conners Rating Scale; ADHD, attention deficit hyperactivity disorder; BPI, Behavior Problems Inventory; BRS, Behavior Rating Scale; CBC(L), Child Behavior Checklist; CD, conduct disorder; CGAS, Clinical Global Assessment Score; CGI, Clinical Global Impression scale; CPRS, Conners Parent Rating Scale; CPRS (b), Chidren's Psychiatric Rating Scate; CPT, Continuous Performance Task; C(P)TQ, Conners (Parent) Teacher Questionnaire; CSI, Childhood Symptom Inventory; CTRS, Conners Teacher Rating Scale; CVLT, California Verbal Learning Test for Children; DB, double-blind; DBD, Disruptive Behavior Disorder; DCB, Devereux Child Behavior Rating Scale; DICA, Diagnostic Interview for Children and Adolescents; DISC, Diagnostic Interview Schedule for Children; DOTES, Dosage Order Treatment Emergent Symptoms Scale; dx, diagnosis; GAF, Global Assessment of Functioning; GCC(R), Global Clinical Consensus Ratings; GCJCS, Global Clinical Judgments Consensus Scale; GRTE, Global Rating of Treatment Effectiveness; HRS-D, Hamilton Rating Scale for Depression; IAS – Iowa Aggression Scale; IED, Intermittent Explosive Disorder; MAVRIC, Measure of Aggression, Violence, and Rage in Children; MPH, methylphenidate; (M)OAS, (Modified) Overt Aggression Scale; NCBRF, Nisonger Child Behavior Rating Form; ODD, oppositional deviant disorder; POMS, Profile of Mood States; PSAP, Point Subtraction Aggression Paradigm; PTQ, Parent-Teacher Questionnaire; QRBPC, Quay Revised Behavior Problem Checklist; RAAPP, Rating of Aggression Against People and/or Property; RBPC, Revised Behavior Problem Checklist; RCT, randomized, controlled trial; RLRS, Ritvo-Freeman Real Life Rating Scale for Autism; SCID-V, Structured Clinical Interview for DSM-V; SSRI, selective serotonin reuptake inhibitor; TORSA, Timed Objective Rating Scale for Aggression; WAI, Weinberger Adjustment Inventory; YSR, Youth Self Report.

Table 2
Selected pediatric psychiatric medications approved by the Food and Drug Administration

Medication	FDA approval in pediatrics
Antidepressants	
Citalopram	None
Fluoxetine	Depression and OCD 7 y and older
Fluvoxamine	OCD 8 y and older
Paroxetine	None
Sertraline	OCD 6 y and older
Clomipramine	OCD 10 y and older
Wellbutrin	None
Typical antipsychotics	
Chlorpromazine	Hyperactivity (short-term treatment) and severe behavior problems 1 y and older
Fluphenazine	Schizophrenia 12 y and older
Haloperidol	Hyperactivity (short-term treatment), psychotic disorders, severe behavior problems, and Tourette's disorder 3 y and older
Loxapine	Schizophrenia 16 y and older
Mesoridazine	None
Molindone	Schizophrenia 12 y and older
Perphenazine	None
Pimozide	Tourette's syndrome 2 y and older
Thioridazine	Schizophrenia 2 y and older
Thiothixene	Schizophrenia 12 y and older
Trifluoperazine	Schizophrenia and anxiety 6 y and older
Atypical antipsychotics	
Clozapine	None
Olanzapine	None
Quetiapine	None
Risperidone	None
Ziprasidone	None
Benzodiazepines	
Alprazolam	None
Chlordiazepoxide	Anxiety 6 y and older
Clonazepam	None
Diazepam	Anxiety, muscle spasm, seizure 6 mo and older Premedication 30 d and older
Lorazepam	Anxiety 12 y and older
Second-generation hypnotics	
Eszopiclone	None
Zaleplon	None
Zolpidem	None
Mood stabilizers	
Anticonvulsants	
Carbamazepine	Epilepsy
Divalproex sodium	Epilepsy; migraine 16 y and older
Lithium	Bipolar disorder 12 y and older
Stimulants and atomoxetine	
Dextroamphetamine	ADHD and narcolepsy
Methylphenidate	ADHD and narcolepsy 6 y and older
Pemoline	ADHD 6 y and older
Atomoxetine	ADHD

Abbreviations: ADHD, attention deficit hyperactivity disorder; OCD, obsessive-compulsive disorder.

Specific classes of medication

Antidepressants

Selective serotonin reuptake inhibitors (SSRIs) are commonly used in pediatric populations in the treatment of depression, obsessive-compulsive disorder (OCD), and anxiety, in addition to other disorders. Among the SSRIs, fluoxetine, fluvoxamine, and sertraline have FDA approval in pediatrics for OCD. Only fluoxetine is labeled for use in pediatric depression and has been the subject of a small clinical investigation in juvenile delinquents. This study suggested that fluoxetine was useful in treating eight adolescent substance-dependent males who had conduct disorder and who suffered from major depression that persisted or emerged after 4 weeks of abstinence [35]. Another commonly used SSRI, paroxetine, has demonstrated efficacy in treating social anxiety disorder [36], OCD [37], and depression [38]. Citalopram likewise has been effective in treating childhood depression [39]. A recent review of the efficacy of all classes of antidepressants in children concludes that only citalopram, fluoxetine, and sertraline have adequately demonstrated superiority to placebo [40].

Clomipramine, a tricyclic antidepressant, has FDA approval for treating pediatric OCD. Buproprion, which inhibits norepinephrine and dopamine reuptake, has also been used to treat depression, ADHD, and tobacco addiction in children, although no randomized, controlled trials have been conducted to confirm its efficacy in juveniles [40].

Common adverse effects of SSRIs in both adults and children include sexual dysfunction, nausea, drowsiness, constipation, nervousness, and fatigue [38,41,42]. Following a review of 24 trials that included 4400 depressed children who evidenced an increased risk of suicidality from 2% among the placebo group to 4% among children on antidepressants, the FDA issued a public health advisory in October 2004 [43]. The issue of increased suicide risk remains controversial, because other authors suggest that antidepressants decrease overall suicide rates [44]. SSRIs have also been shown to have effectiveness in treating posttraumatic stress disorder [45,46]. Given the high rates of posttraumatic stress disorder in this population [47], the use of SSRIs may be beneficial by enabling providers to address multiple core symptoms with a single agent.

Antipsychotics

Antipsychotics have been used in childhood psychosis, bipolar disorder, conduct disorder, and aggression, among other disorders. Typical antipsychotics with FDA approval for pediatric schizophrenia include fluphenazine, haloperidol, loxapine, molindone, thiothixene, thioridazine, and trifluoperazine. Chlorpromazine and haloperidol have FDA approval for short-term treatment of hyperactivity and severe behavior problems. Pimozide has FDA approval only for pediatric Tourette's syndrome. Adverse effects associated with typical antipsychotics are significant and include EPS (ie, akathisia, acute dystonia, and drug-induced parkinsonism), seizure, weight gain, liver dysfunction, sedation, and cardiovascular and hematologic effects. Younger individuals may be at an increased risk of developing EPS [48]. Given these findings, consideration should always be given to using diphenhydramine or benztropine as prophylaxis against EPS, especially when these medications are used in high doses or emergency situations. EPS and neuroleptic malignant syndrome can occur at any dose, but there is a dose-related relationship to the likelihood of developing EPS and neuroleptic malignant syndrome [34,49].

Atypical antipsychotics have less risk of EPS and have the potential to combat schizophrenia resistant to treatment with typical antipsychotics, which is a particular concern among adolescents with early onset of the disease [50]. Probably for these reasons and because of the milder side-effect profile in general, atypical antipsychotics are used more commonly than the older class of antipsychotics in pediatric patients, even though the research literature is lacking on this subject. None of the atypical antipsychotics have FDA approval in pediatrics, although off-label usage of olanzapine, quetiapine, ziprasidone, and particularly risperidone is fairly common. One recent review of atypical antipsychotic use in children suggests that they are efficacious in treating psychosis, bipolar disorder, pervasive developmental disorder, and Tourette's syndrome and are probably efficacious in severe ADHD, conduct disorder, and mental retardation; however, the authors state that more rigorous clinical investigation is warranted [51]. The most common side effects (which varied by drug) uncovered by this review were cardiovascular effects, weight gain, sedation, sialorrhea, EPS, and hyperprolactinemia. Clozapine notably requires hematologic monitoring because of its risk of leukopenia and agranulocytosis and is thus a second-line agent. Specific treatment recommendations and guidelines exist for the use of atypical antipsychotics to treat aggressive behavior, and these guidelines should be consulted before initiating the use of these compounds [4,5].

Benzodiazepines

Chlordiazepoxide, diazepam, and lorazepam are among the commonly used benzodiazepines that are FDA approved in children for anxiety. Alprazolam and clonazepam are not labeled for pediatric usage, but both have a long history of use in pediatric populations. Sedation is a common side effect of benzodiazepines, although this class of medications is generally well tolerated for short-term therapy [52]. Careful consideration must be given to the use of these medications, because they can be extremely habituating. Habituation is especially significant in populations like juvenile offenders who have high rates of substance-use disorders.

Second-generation hypnotics

Zolpidem is a nonbenzodiazepine sedative hypnotic with side effects that include dizziness, lightheadedness, somnolence, headache, and gastrointestinal upset. Zaleplon and eszopiclone are nonbenzodiazepine hypnotics similar to zolpidem that have been more recently developed. None of these have been studied extensively in children, nor do they have pediatric FDA indications.

Mood stabilizers

The anticonvulsant agents carbamazepine and divalproex sodium are used as mood stabilizers in pediatric illnesses such as bipolar disorder, ADHD, and conduct disorder. Although both drugs have FDA approval for pediatric epilepsy, neither is approved to treat pediatric psychiatric disorders. Nevertheless, increasing evidence has become available on the use of divalproex sodium for the treatment of disruptive behavior disorders [23,24] and an array of other pediatric psychiatric illnesses [22].

Lithium has traditionally been a favored treatment for bipolar disorder in adults and adolescents. Although much has been learned about the drug in the last 50 years, the precise mechanisms by which lithium treats acute mania and diminishes recurrence remain largely unknown [53]. Lithium is approved by the FDA to treat bipolar disorder in children older than 12 years but has been used in younger patients. It also has mixed efficacy in treating aggression and irritability, as described in Table 1. Side effects of lithium may be significant and include tremor, varied gastrointestinal symptoms, polyuria, hypothyroidism, reversible T-wave depression on EKG, and neutrophilia [34].

Stimulants and atomoxetine

ADHD is among the most common psychiatric diagnoses in the United States, and stimulants are the most common medication used to treat the disorder. Stimulants have a long history and have generated an extremely large treatment literature [34]. Methylphenidate (MPH) is the most commonly studied and prescribed of the stimulants. Dextroamphetamine is a longer-acting stimulant than MPH, although longer-duration and once-daily formulations of MPH have been created (ie, MPH-SR). Pemoline is considered second-line stimulant therapy for ADHD because of its associated risk of hepatic failure. Common side effects of stimulants in general include insomnia, decreased appetite, headache, and jitteriness. As with benzodiazepines consideration must be given to the possible abuse potential of stimulants in youthful offenders.

A recent meta-analysis by Connor and colleagues [54] found that stimulant medications were as effective for ADHD-related aggressive behaviors as they are for the core symptoms of ADHD. They also found, however, that the effect size diminished if there was co-morbid conduct disorder.

Given the growing black-market trade and illegal use of stimulants among children and adolescents [55–57], it may be preferable to use nonstimulant medications for the treatment of ADHD. Atomoxetine selectively inhibits the reuptake of norepinephrine but was not successfully used in depression. Instead, it now has FDA labeling for ADHD in children. Unlike the stimulants, atomoxetine is not a federally controlled substance. Atomoxetine was successful in treating ADHD in two studies of children who had oppositional deviant disorder [58,59] but improved symptoms of oppositional deviant disorder in only one [59]. It is generally well tolerated and has a side-effect profile similar to that of stimulants [60], although liver injury is a small risk as well. Atomoxetine now has the same black-box warning that exists for SSRIs for increased suicidal ideation among children and adolescents.

Integrated treatment planning

Sound psychopharmacology requires integrated treatment. Increasing evidence suggests that using psychotherapy in combination with pharmacology has the best outcomes [61]. In a long-term study of depressed adults, Nemeroff and colleagues [62] have found that those who had significant histories of trauma were more likely to respond to structured cognitive-behavioral therapy with or without medications than to medications alone. This finding is an important consideration, given the high rates of trauma that exist in delinquent populations [47,63,64]. In a related vein, the MTA (NIMH Collaborative Multisite Multimodal Treatment Study of Children with Attention-Deficit/Hyperactivity Disorder) study found that medications alone or medications plus behavioral therapy yielded better outcomes than behavioral therapy alone or standard community care in the treatment of ADHD and oppositional defiant disorder [65]. Although the effect of the use of medication plus therapy did not differ from that of the use of medication alone, the authors believe that combination treatment holds the best promise for juvenile offenders because of adherence issues.

Williams and colleagues [66] reported that more than half of their sample of female adolescents in juvenile detention were skeptical about the benefits of pharmacotherapy and that those who had positive prior experiences in psychiatric treatment were more likely to view medication therapy as positive.

As part of integrated treatment, it is important to try to involve juveniles in long-term treatment planning. Although minors typically do not have the full authority to refuse treatment, and this authority traditionally resides with their parents or guardians, juvenile offenders are in a unique situation whereby the state usually has authority to determine medical treatment. In some states, parental consent may be required for psychopharmacologic treatment [67]. Unless the situation is acute or an emergency, consideration should be given to involving the youth and his or her family in treatment decisions, because there is evidence from outpatient studies that family therapy can help in reducing aggression [68]. In addition, it is clear that although compelling treatment while the youth is incarcerated or detained may be legally and even pragmatically possible, the benefits of long-term treatment are likely to be lost when the youth is released from custody unless a good therapeutic alliance is established. The period of time in detention or incarceration might then be seen as a starting point for care with an aim of reducing psychiatric morbidity to reduce recidivism. Psychopharmacology can play an important role in this process, especially when the young offender and his or her family is part of the process and is engaged with care in a meaningful way.

Summary

Juvenile offenders face an array of psychiatric problems that can be consequent to their incarceration or detention and also may contribute to the factors that result in juvenile detention. Prompt assessment and evaluation by trained professionals is an essential component to providing care for juvenile offenders [69]. Psychopharmacologic interventions hold some promise for improving the lives of young offenders and also have the potential to help reduce recidivism by enabling young people gain better control of their lives. Nevertheless, all medications have risks, and these risks need to be weighed against the potential benefits in each individual case. Identifying the reasons for using medications and the specific targets for treatment can allow more prudent and better use of pharmacologic interventions. Integrating psychopharmacologic treatment with psychotherapy and family therapy is also a vital component, especially if these interventions are intended to be lasting parts of the treatment plan for the young offender.

References

[1] Teplin LA, Abram KM, McClelland GM, et al. Psychiatric disorders in youth in juvenile detention. Arch Gen Psychiatry 2002;59(12):1133–43.

[2] Vermeiren R. Psychopathology and delinquency in adolescents: a descriptive and developmental perspective. Clin Psychol Rev 2003;23(2):277–318.

[3] Wasserman GA, McReynolds LS, Fisher P, et al. Psychiatric disorders in incarcerated youths. J Am Acad Child Adolesc Psychiatry 2003;42(9):1011.

[4] Pappadopulos E, Macintyre II JC, Crismon ML, et al. Treatment recommendations for the use of antipsychotics for aggressive youth (TRAAY). Part II. J Am Acad Child Adolesc Psychiatry 2003;42(2):145–61.

[5] Schur SB, Sikich L, Findling RL, et al. Treatment recommendations for the use of antipsychotics for aggressive youth (TRAAY). Part I: a review. J Am Acad Child Adolesc Psychiatry 2003;42(2):132–44.

[6] American Psychiatric Association Task Force on DSM-IV. Diagnostic and statistical manual of mental disorders: DSM-IV-TR. Washington (DC): American Psychiatric Association; 2000.

[7] World Health Organization. The ICD-10 classification of mental and behavioural disorders: clinical descriptions and diagnostic guidelines. Geneva (Switzerland): World Health Organization; 1992.

[8] Connor DF. Aggression and antisocial behavior in children and adolescents: research and treatment. New York: Guilford Press; 2002.

[9] Blair J, Taggart B, Martin A. Electrocardiographic safety profile and monitoring guidelines in pediatric psychopharmacology. J Neural Transm 2004;111(7):791–815.

[10] Grisso T, Barnum R, Fletcher KE, et al. Massachusetts Youth Screening Instrument for mental health needs of juvenile justice youths. J Am Acad Child Adolesc Psychiatry 2001;40(5):541–8.

[11] Steiner H. The scientific basis of mental health interventions in children and adolescents: an overview. In: Steiner H, editor. Handbook of mental health interventions in children and adolescents: an integrated developmental approach. San Francisco (CA): Jossey-Bass Publishers; 2004. p. 11–34.
[12] Battle AO, Battle MV, Tolley EA. Potential for suicide and aggression in delinquents at juvenile court in a southern city. Suicide Life Threat Behav 1993;23(3):230–44.
[13] Farand L, Chagnon F, Renaud J, et al. Completed suicides among Quebec adolescents involved with juvenile justice and child welfare services. Suicide Life Threat Behav 2004;34(1): 24–35.
[14] Kempton T, Forehand R. Suicide attempts among juvenile delinquents; the contribution of mental health factors. Behav Res Ther 1992;30(5):537–41.
[15] Ruchkin VV, Schwab-Stone M, Koposov RA, et al. Suicidal ideations and attempts in juvenile delinquents. J Child Psychol Psychiatry 2003;44(7):1058–66.
[16] Thomas CR, Penn JV. Juvenile justice mental health services. Child Adolesc Psychiatr Clin N Am 2002;11(4):731–48.
[17] Busch KA, Fawcett J, Jacobs DG. Clinical correlates of inpatient suicide. J Clin Psychiatry 2003;64(1):14–9.
[18] Fawcett J. Treating impulsivity and anxiety in the suicidal patient. Ann N Y Acad Sci 2001;932:94–102 [discussion 102–5].
[19] Blair RJ, Coccaro EF, Connor DF, and members of the Workgroup on Juvenile Impulsivity and Aggression. The neuroscience of maladaptive aggression. J Am Acad Child Adolesc Psychiatry, in press.
[20] Steiner H, Saxena K, Chang K. Psychopharmacologic strategies for the treatment of aggression in juveniles. CNS Spectr 2003;8(4):298–308.
[21] Steiner H, Delizonna L, Saxena K, et al. Does the two-factor model of aggression hold incarcerated delinquents? In: Proceedings of the annual meeting of the American Psychiatric Association. Atlanta (GA): American Psychiatric Association; 2005. Available at: http://www.psych.org.
[22] Rana M, Khanzode L, Karnik N, et al. Divalproex sodium in the treatment of pediatric psychiatric disorders. Expert Rev Neurother 2005;5(2):165–76.
[23] Saxena K, Delizonna L, Durkin A, et al. Divalproex sodium in outpatients with disruptive behavior disorders. In: Proceedings of the annual meeting of the American Psychiatric Association. Atlanta (GA): American Psychiatric Association; 2005. Available at: http://www.psych.org.
[24] Steiner H, Petersen ML, Saxena K, et al. Divalproex sodium for the treatment of conduct disorder: a randomized controlled clinical trial. J Clin Psychiatry 2003;64(10):1183–91.
[25] McDougle CJ, Stigler KA, Posey DJ. Treatment of aggression in children and adolescents with autism and conduct disorder. J Clin Psychiatry 2003;64(Suppl 4):16–25.
[26] Vitiello B, Behar D, Hunt J, et al. Subtyping aggression in children and adolescents. J Neuropsychiatry Clin Neurosci 1990;2(2):189–92.
[27] Vitiello B, Stoff DM. Subtypes of aggression and their relevance to child psychiatry. J Am Acad Child Adolesc Psychiatry 1997;36(3):307–15.
[28] Campbell M, Adams PB, Small AM, et al. Lithium in hospitalized aggressive children with conduct disorder: a double-blind and placebo-controlled study. J Am Acad Child Adolesc Psychiatry 1995;34(4):445–53.
[29] Campbell M, Small AM, Green WH, et al. Behavioral efficacy of haloperidol and lithium carbonate. A comparison in hospitalized aggressive children with conduct disorder. Arch Gen Psychiatry 1984;41(7):650–6.
[30] Malone RP, Luebbert J, Pena-Ariet M, et al. The Overt Aggression Scale in a study of lithium in aggressive conduct disorder. Psychopharmacol Bull 1994;30(2):215–8.
[31] American Academy of Pediatrics. Health care for children and adolescents in the juvenile correctional care system. Pediatrics 2001;107(4):799–803.
[32] Abram KM, Teplin LA, McClelland GM, et al. Comorbid psychiatric disorders in youth in juvenile detention. Arch Gen Psychiatry 2003;60(11):1097–108.

[33] Feinstein RA, Lampkin A, Lorish CD, et al. Medical status of adolescents at time of admission to a juvenile detention center. J Adolesc Health 1998;22(3):190–6.
[34] Martin A. Pediatric psychopharmacology: principles and practice. Oxford (UK): Oxford University Press; 2003.
[35] Riggs PD, Mikulich SK, Coffman LM, et al. Fluoxetine in drug-dependent delinquents with major depression: an open trial. J Child Adolesc Psychopharmacol 1997;7(2):87–95.
[36] Wagner KD, Berard R, Stein MB, et al. A multicenter, randomized, double-blind, placebo-controlled trial of paroxetine in children and adolescents with social anxiety disorder. Arch Gen Psychiatry 2004;61(11):1153–62.
[37] Geller DA, Wagner KD, Emslie G, et al. Paroxetine treatment in children and adolescents with obsessive-compulsive disorder: a randomized, multicenter, double-blind, placebo-controlled trial. J Am Acad Child Adolesc Psychiatry 2004;43(11):1387–96.
[38] Keller MB, Ryan ND, Strober M, et al. Efficacy of paroxetine in the treatment of adolescent major depression: a randomized, controlled trial. J Am Acad Child Adolesc Psychiatry 2001; 40(7):762–72.
[39] Wagner KD, Robb AS, Findling RL, et al. A randomized, placebo-controlled trial of citalopram for the treatment of major depression in children and adolescents. Am J Psychiatry 2004; 161(6):1079–83.
[40] Wagner KD. Pharmacotherapy for major depression in children and adolescents. Prog Neuropsychopharmacol Biol Psychiatry 2005;29(5):819–26.
[41] Emslie GJ, Rush AJ, Weinberg WA, et al. A double-blind, randomized, placebo-controlled trial of fluoxetine in children and adolescents with depression. Arch Gen Psychiatry 1997;54(11): 1031–7.
[42] March JS, Biederman J, Wolkow R, et al. Sertraline in children and adolescents with obsessive-compulsive disorder: a multicenter randomized controlled trial. JAMA 1998;280(20): 1752–6.
[43] US Food and Drug Administration. FDA public health advisory: suicidality in children and adolescents being treated with antidepressant medications. Washington (DC): US Food and Drug Administration; 2004.
[44] Gibbons RD, Hur K, Bhaumik DK, et al. The relationship between antidepressant medication use and rate of suicide. Arch Gen Psychiatry 2005;62(2):165–72.
[45] Donnelly CL. Pharmacologic treatment approaches for children and adolescents with posttraumatic stress disorder. Child Adolesc Psychiatr Clin N Am 2003;12(2):251–69.
[46] Putnam FW, Hulsmann JE. Pharmacotherapy for survivors of childhood trauma. Semin Clin Neuropsychiatry 2002;7(2):129–36.
[47] Plattner B, Silvermann MA, Redlich AD, et al. Pathways to dissociation: intrafamilial versus extrafamilial trauma in juvenile delinquents. J Nerv Ment Dis 2003;191(12):781–8.
[48] Keepers GA, Clappison VJ, Casey DE. Initial anticholinergic prophylaxis for neuroleptic-induced extrapyramidal syndromes. Arch Gen Psychiatry 1983;40(10):1113–7.
[49] Schatzberg AF, Nemeroff CB, editors. Textbook of psychopharmacology. Arlington (VA): American Psychiatric Publishing; 2004.
[50] Meltzer HY, Rabinowitz J, Lee MA, et al. Age at onset and gender of schizophrenic patients in relation to neuroleptic resistance. Am J Psychiatry 1997;154(4):475–82.
[51] Cheng-Shannon J, McGough JJ, Pataki C, et al. Second-generation antipsychotic medications in children and adolescents. J Child Adolesc Psychopharmacol 2004;14(3):372–94.
[52] Bernstein GA, Shaw K. Practice parameters for the assessment and treatment of children and adolescents with anxiety disorders. J Am Acad Child Adolesc Psychiatry 1997;36(10 Suppl): 69S–84S.
[53] Lenox RH, Hahn CG. Overview of the mechanism of action of lithium in the brain: fifty-year update. J Clin Psychiatry 2000;61(Suppl 9):5–15.
[54] Connor DF, Glatt SJ, Lopez ID, et al. Psychopharmacology and aggression. I: a meta-analysis of stimulant effects on overt/covert aggression-related behaviors in ADHD. J Am Acad Child Adolesc Psychiatry 2002;41(3):253–61.
[55] McCabe SE, Knight JR, Teter CJ, et al. Non-medical use of prescription stimulants among

US college students: prevalence and correlates from a national survey. Addiction 2005;100(1): 96–106.

[56] McCabe SE, Teter CJ, Boyd CJ, et al. Prevalence and correlates of illicit methylphenidate use among 8th, 10th, and 12th grade students in the United States, 2001. J Adolesc Health 2004;35(6):501–4.

[57] Teter CJ, McCabe SE, Boyd CJ, et al. Illicit methylphenidate use in an undergraduate student sample: prevalence and risk factors. Pharmacotherapy 2003;23(5):609–17.

[58] Kaplan S, Heiligenstein J, West S, et al. Efficacy and safety of atomoxetine in childhood attention-deficit/hyperactivity disorder with comorbid oppositional defiant disorder. J Atten Disord 2004;8(2):45–52.

[59] Newcorn JH, Spencer TJ, Biederman J, et al. Atomoxetine treatment in children and adolescents with attention-deficit/hyperactivity disorder and comorbid oppositional defiant disorder. J Am Acad Child Adolesc Psychiatry 2005;44(3):240–8.

[60] Michelson D, Faries D, Wernicke J, et al. Atomoxetine in the treatment of children and adolescents with attention-deficit/hyperactivity disorder: a randomized, placebo-controlled, dose-response study. Pediatrics 2001;108(5):E83.

[61] Steiner H. Handbook of mental health interventions in children and adolescents: an integrated developmental approach. San Francisco (CA): Jossey-Bass Publishers; 2004.

[62] Nemeroff CB, Heim CM, Thase ME, et al. Differential responses to psychotherapy versus pharmacotherapy in patients with chronic forms of major depression and childhood trauma. Proc Natl Acad Sci U S A 2003;100(24):14293–6.

[63] Carrion VG, Steiner H. Trauma and dissociation in delinquent adolescents. J Am Acad Child Adolesc Psychiatry 2000;39(3):353–9.

[64] Cauffman E, Feldman SS, Waterman J, et al. Posttraumatic stress disorder among female juvenile offenders. J Am Acad Child Adolesc Psychiatry 1998;37(11):1209–16.

[65] Arnold LE, Chuang S, Davies M, et al. Nine months of multicomponent behavioral treatment for ADHD and effectiveness of MTA fading procedures. J Abnorm Child Psychol 2004;32(1): 39–51.

[66] Williams RA, Hollis HM, Benoit K. Attitudes toward psychiatric medications among incarcerated female adolescents. J Am Acad Child Adolesc Psychiatry 1998;37(12):1301–7.

[67] Arroyo W. Children, adolescents, and families. In: Ethics primer of the American Psychiatric Association. Washington (DC): American Psychiatric Publishing, Inc.; 2001. p. 11–22.

[68] Nickel MK, Nickel C, Leiberich P, et al. Aggressive female youth benefit from outpatient family therapy: a randomized, prospective, controlled trial. Pediatr Int 2005;47(2):167–71.

[69] Arroyo W, Buzogany W, Hanson G, et al. Recommendations for juvenile justice reform. Washington (DC): American Academy of Child and Adolescent Psychiatry; 2001.

[70] Aman MG, Marks RE, Turbott SH, et al. Clinical effects of methylphenidate and thioridazine in intellectually subaverage children. J Am Acad Child Adolesc Psychiatry 1991;30(2):246–56.

[71] Greenhill LL, Solomon M, Pleak R, et al. Molindone hydrochloride treatment of hospitalized children with conduct disorder. J Clin Psychiatry 1985;46(8 Pt 2):20–5.

[72] Broche JP. [Use of pimozide (ORAP) in child psychiatry (author's transl)]. Acta Psychiatr Belg 1980;80(3):341–6.

[73] Joshi PT, Hamel L, Joshi AR, et al. Use of droperidol in hospitalized children. J Am Acad Child Adolesc Psychiatry 1998;37(2):228–30.

[74] Hameer O, Collin K, Ensom MH, et al. Evaluation of droperidol in the acutely agitated child or adolescent. Can J Psychiatry 2001;46(9):864–5.

[75] Findling RL, McNamara NK, Branicky LA, et al. A double-blind pilot study of risperidone in the treatment of conduct disorder. J Am Acad Child Adolesc Psychiatry 2000;39(4):509–16.

[76] Snyder R, Turgay A, Aman M, et al. Effects of risperidone on conduct and disruptive behavior disorders in children with subaverage IQs. J Am Acad Child Adolesc Psychiatry 2002;41(9): 1026–36.

[77] Findling RL, Aman MG, Eerdekens M, et al. Long-term, open-label study of risperidone in children with severe disruptive behaviors and below-average IQ. Am J Psychiatry 2004;161(4): 677–84.

[78] Aman M, Buitelaar J, Smedt GD, et al. Pharmacotherapy of disruptive behavior and item changes on a standardized rating scale: pooled analysis of risperidone effects in children with subaverage IQ. J Child Adolesc Psychopharmacol 2005;15(2):220–32.
[79] Croonenberghs J, Fegert JM, Findling RL, et al. Risperidone in children with disruptive behavior disorders and subaverage intelligence: a 1-year, open-label study of 504 patients. J Am Acad Child Adolesc Psychiatry 2005;44(1):64–72.
[80] Soderstrom H, Rastam M, Gillberg C. A clinical case series of six extremely aggressive youths treated with olanzapine. Eur Child Adolesc Psychiatry 2002;11(3):138–41.
[81] Stephens RJ, Bassel C, Sandor P. Olanzapine in the treatment of aggression and tics in children with Tourette's syndrome – a pilot study. J Child Adolesc Psychopharmacol 2004;14(2):255–66.
[82] Kafantaris V, Campbell M, Padron-Gayol MV, et al. Carbamazepine in hospitalized aggressive conduct disorder children: an open pilot study. Psychopharmacol Bull 1992;28(2):193–9.
[83] Mattes JA. Comparative effectiveness of carbamazepine and propranolol for rage outbursts. J Neuropsychiatry Clin Neurosci 1990;2(2):159–64.
[84] Cueva JE, Overall JE, Small AM, et al. Carbamazepine in aggressive children with conduct disorder: a double-blind and placebo-controlled study. J Am Acad Child Adolesc Psychiatry 1996;35(4):480–90.
[85] Donovan SJ, Stewart JW, Nunes EV, et al. Divalproex treatment for youth with explosive temper and mood lability: a double-blind, placebo-controlled crossover design. Am J Psychiatry 2000;157(5):818–20.
[86] Malone RP, Delaney MA, Luebbert JF, et al. A double-blind placebo-controlled study of lithium in hospitalized aggressive children and adolescents with conduct disorder. Arch Gen Psychiatry 2000;57(7):649–54.
[87] Rifkin A, Karajgi B, Dicker R, et al. Lithium treatment of conduct disorders in adolescents. Am J Psychiatry 1997;154(4):554–5.
[88] Coccaro EF, Kavoussi RJ, Hauger RL. Serotonin function and antiaggressive response to fluoxetine: a pilot study. Biol Psychiatry 1997;42(7):546–52.
[89] Constantino JN, Liberman M, Kincaid M. Effects of serotonin reuptake inhibitors on aggressive behavior in psychiatrically hospitalized adolescents: results of an open trial. J Child Adolesc Psychopharmacol 1997;7(1):31–44.
[90] Cherek DR, Lane SD, Pietras CJ, et al. Effects of chronic paroxetine administration on measures of aggressive and impulsive responses of adult males with a history of conduct disorder. Psychopharmacology (Berl) 2002;159(3):266–74.
[91] Armenteros JL, Lewis JE. Citalopram treatment for impulsive aggression in children and adolescents: an open pilot study. J Am Acad Child Adolesc Psychiatry 2002;41(5):522–9.
[92] Zubieta JK, Alessi NE. Acute and chronic administration of trazodone in the treatment of disruptive behavior disorders in children. J Clin Psychopharmacol 1992;12(5):346–51.
[93] Klein RG, Abikoff H, Klass E, et al. Clinical efficacy of methylphenidate in conduct disorder with and without attention deficit hyperactivity disorder. Arch Gen Psychiatry 1997;54(12): 1073–80.
[94] Kaplan SL, Busner J, Kupietz S, et al. Effects of methylphenidate on adolescents with aggressive conduct disorder and ADDH: a preliminary report. J Am Acad Child Adolesc Psychiatry 1990;29(5):719–23.
[95] Hazell PL, Stuart JE. A randomized controlled trial of clonidine added to psychostimulant medication for hyperactive and aggressive children. J Am Acad Child Adolesc Psychiatry 2003;42(8):886–94.
[96] Kemph JP, DeVane CL, Levin GM, et al. Treatment of aggressive children with clonidine: results of an open pilot study. J Am Acad Child Adolesc Psychiatry 1993;32(3):577–81.
[97] Schvehla TJ, Mandoki MW, Sumner GS. Clonidine therapy for comorbid attention deficit hyperactivity disorder and conduct disorder: preliminary findings in a children's inpatient unit. South Med J 1994;87(7):692–5.
[98] Silver JM, Yudofsky SC, Slater JA, et al. Propranolol treatment of chronically hospitalized aggressive patients. J Neuropsychiatry Clin Neurosci 1999;11(3):328–35.

[99] Kuperman S, Stewart MA. Use of propranolol to decrease aggressive outbursts in younger patients. Open study reveals potentially favorable outcome. Psychosomatics 1987;28(6):315–9.

[100] Connor DF, Ozbayrak KR, Benjamin S, et al. A pilot study of nadolol for overt aggression in developmentally delayed individuals. J Am Acad Child Adolesc Psychiatry 1997;36(6): 826–34.

[101] Buitelaar JK, van der Gaag RJ, Swaab-Barneveld H, et al. Pindolol and methylphenidate in children with attention-deficit hyperactivity disorder. Clinical efficacy and side-effects. J Child Psychol Psychiatry 1996;37(5):587–95.

[102] Pfeffer CR, Jiang H, Domeshek LJ. Buspirone treatment of psychiatrically hospitalized prepubertal children with symptoms of anxiety and moderately severe aggression. J Child Adolesc Psychopharmacol 1997;7(3):145–55.

[103] Stanislav SW, Fabre T, Crismon ML, et al. Buspirone's efficacy in organic-induced aggression. J Clin Psychopharmacol 1994;14(2):126–30.

[104] Vitiello B, Hill JL, Elia J, et al. P.r.n. medications in child psychiatric patients: a pilot placebo-controlled study. J Clin Psychiatry 1991;52(12):499–501.

[105] King BH, Wright DM, Snape M, et al. Case series: amantadine open-label treatment of impulsive and aggressive behavior in hospitalized children with developmental disabilities. J Am Acad Child Adolesc Psychiatry 2001;40(6):654–7.

ELSEVIER
SAUNDERS

Child Adolesc Psychiatric Clin N Am
15 (2006) 501–516

CHILD AND
ADOLESCENT
PSYCHIATRIC CLINICS
OF NORTH AMERICA

Evidence-Based Psychosocial Treatments in the Juvenile Justice System

Denis G. Sukhodolsky, PhD[a,*],
Vladislav Ruchkin, MD, PhD[a,b,c]

[a]*Child Study Center, Yale University School of Medicine, New Haven, CT, USA*
[b]*Center for Violence Prevention, Karolinska Institute, Stockholm, Sweden*
[c]*Skonviks Psychiatric Clinic, Center for Forensic Psychiatry, Säter, Sweden*

Juvenile crime and delinquency represent a significant social and public health concern. Nearly 2.3 million juvenile arrests are reported annually in the United States; a much larger number of delinquent acts are undetected or unreported [1]. The scope of the problem of juvenile delinquency is matched by the complexity of factors that contribute to the development and maintenance of delinquency [2,3]. During the past 3 decades, considerable progress has been made in the development, implementation, and evaluation of psychosocial treatments focused on alleviation of risk factors of delinquency, reduction of juvenile crime, and prevention of recidivism. Psychosocial treatments that target multiple risk factors for delinquency, such as multisystemic therapy (MST) and multidimensional treatment foster care (MTFC), have been tested in randomized, controlled studies and shown to have significant effects on reduction of criminal behavior [4,5]. Quantitative reviews also documented the effectiveness of psychosocial treatments in juvenile justice, specifically those based on cognitive-behavioral principles [6,7].

Prevention of criminal behavior is not the only goal of psychosocial treatments in juvenile justice. Most youth in the juvenile justice system are likely to meet criteria for a psychiatric disorder, substance use disorder, or both [8]. Depression and posttraumatic stress disorder (PTSD) are among the most frequent internalizing conditions co-occurring with juvenile delinquency. Psychiatric disorders in

* Corresponding author. Child Study Center, Yale University School of Medicine, 230 South Frontage Road, New Haven, CT 06520.

E-mail address: Denis.Sukhodolsky@yale.edu (D.G. Sukhodolsky).

1056-4993/06/$ – see front matter
doi:10.1016/j.chc.2005.11.005

delinquent youth are related to substantial psychosocial impairment, may be predictive of subsequent involvement in antisocial activities, and are related to higher rates of recidivism [9]. The juvenile justice system is often the only source of mental health services for many youths who have serious emotional and behavioral disturbances [10]. High rates of psychiatric disorders and substance abuse in juvenile offenders require that these problems also be addressed in treatments provided through juvenile justice services. Opportunities for delivery of mental health services including psychotherapy and counseling are available during mandated residential treatment, during aftercare, or as part of services alternative to incarceration.

Despite advances in the development of psychosocial treatments for criminal behavior and increasing awareness of the mental health needs of juvenile offenders, little is known about the application of evidence-based child psychotherapies in the juvenile justice system. Hundreds of randomized, controlled studies have been conducted to examine the effects of child psychotherapy for psychiatric disorders, and excellent reviews of these studies and evidence-based interventions are available [11]. Only a handful of these studies have been conducted in juvenile correctional facilities, however [12]. Furthermore, there is an acknowledged gap between psychotherapy research and application of evidence-based treatments across various systems of mental health care. Implementation of evidence-based practices in juvenile justice shares the challenges of transporting treatments from research settings into real-world contexts and adds its own unique practical considerations. Although a plethora of treatment manuals, clinical resources, and therapy guides are commercially available, the principles of effective implementation of these resources in juvenile justice are not well examined.

The goals of this article are threefold. First, it reviews selected youth-, family-, and community-based psychosocial treatments for delinquent behavior that are likely to be used in the juvenile justice system. Youth- and family-based interventions are often embedded in broader systems of care, whereas community-based, multicomponent interventions may be used as alternatives to residential treatments. Second, it reviews psychosocial treatments for internalizing disorders that have been evaluated with juvenile offenders. Finally, it discusses issues in dissemination and implementation of evidence-based psychosocial treatments in the juvenile justice system.

Treatments for delinquent behavior

Youth-focused treatments

Historically, traditional approaches to individual psychotherapy and counseling have been part of services for juvenile delinquents [13]. With advances in child and adolescent psychotherapy research, certain interventions for specific disorders and behavioral problems have been identified as empirically supported or as evidence-based treatments [14]. As a result, policy makers, administrators, and practitioners across various sectors of care, including the juvenile justice system, have become increasingly interested in implementing evidence-based treatments. Youth-focused treatments such as anger control training and problem-solving skills training (PSST) have demonstrated efficacy for reducing relatively mild forms of antisocial behavior and improving a child's psychosocial functioning [15]. Other treatment modalities such as social skills training (SST) often have been used either as stand-alone interventions or as parts of multi-component treatments. This article briefly reviews the theoretical background, clinical features, and research support for psychosocial treatments that are likely to be components of comprehensive services in the juvenile justice system.

Anger control training is a cognitive-behavioral treatment that aims to improve emotion regulation and ameliorate associated social-cognitive deficits in aggressive children. Children are taught to monitor their emotional arousal and to use cognitive and behavioral coping skills for modulating elevated levels of anger. As part of the training, children also practice socially appropriate responses to potentially anger-provoking situations such as being teased by peers or reprimanded by adults. Excessive levels of anger and poor regulation of emotion have been found to be associated with aggression in juvenile delinquents [16–19]. Numerous studies have demonstrated that deficits in social information processing are related to aggressive behavior in children and adolescents [20,21]. The purported mechanism of anger control training is that improvement in the ability to regulate frustration would also result in reduction of aggressive and disruptive behavior. Anger control training was first developed for adults by Novaco [22], based on Meichenbaum's [23] stress inoculation model. Several programs of research have evaluated versions of anger control training in children [24,25], adolescents [26,27], juvenile offenders [28], and adults [29–31].

PSST addresses cognitive processes, such as perception and decision making, that are involved in social interaction. For example, hostile attribution bias or inability to generate alternative solutions may contribute to aggressive behavior. Beginning from research on social information processing [21] and problem solving in children [32], hundreds of studies have examined the association between thinking about social situations and aggressive behavior [33]. Over the past 3 decades, several PSST approaches have been developed for use by mental health and education specialists to help adolescents cope better with conflicts. Modifications of this treatment approach are available for young children [34], incarcerated juveniles [35], and adults [36]. Participants of PSST are taught to analyze interpersonal conflicts, to develop nonaggressive solutions, and to think about the consequences of their actions in problematic situations. The efficacy of PSST has been demonstrated in several controlled studies [37–39], including one study in incarcerated delinquents [40]. There is initial evidence that the effects of PSST on conduct problems may be mediated by change in the targeted deficits in social information processing [41]. Based on the review of empiric support for PSST, this treatment modality has been recommended as one of the likely efficacious treatments for child conduct problems [42,43].

SST has been used as part of the treatment for various disorders including schizophrenia and autism, as well as for conduct problems in children. As a result, the actual skills taught during a particular program can vary depending on the population in which it is used, but the training techniques in SST treatments are similar. These techniques involve modeling, role-play, corrective feedback, and reinforcement for appropriate performance [44,45]. SST programs are based on the assumption that prosocial behavior can be enhanced through these training procedures. The theoretical background of SST can be traced to behavioral and social-learning theories [46] as well as to early behavioral approaches to psychotherapy [47]. Aggressive youth have been shown to have weak verbal skills, poor conflict resolution skills, and deficits in skills that facilitate friendships [48,49]. The goal of SST with aggressive youth is to enhance or develop specific social behaviors that can be deployed instead of aggression as well as behaviors that can be used to develop friendships with nondelinquent peers [50,51]. Several narrative and meta-analytic reviews of SST with children and adolescents are available; the estimated effect on reduction of SST on antisocial behavior is moderate [52].

Overall, the beneficial effects of monomodal youth-focused treatments on mild forms of delinquency, as well as on the psychologic characteristics that may be associated with more serious delinquent acts, have been well documented. Serious and chronic delinquency, however, is likely to be caused by multiple factors that may be uniquely combined for each individual. Treatments that address only a narrow set of risk factors may be insufficient for addressing the scope of the problem if used as isolated interventions [53]. Also, iatrogenic effects of aggregating delinquent youth in groups for treatment, attributed to deviancy training, were reported [54] but not well understood [55]. Furthermore, little is known about how to match psychosocial treatments to the risk factors of a particular youth. Most treatments are time-limited, with the number of sessions averaging between 8 and 18, and little is known about the relative effects of different youth-focused treatments [56]. Further research is needed to identify the active ingredients of youth-focused treatments and the principles of successful integration of these ingredients in comprehensive treatment programs for juvenile delinquents [57].

Family- and community-focused treatments

Family-based programs target family risk factors for delinquency including inconsistent or harsh discipline and poor supervision [58]. Parent management training (PMT) is a psychosocial treatment in which parents are taught skills for managing their children's disruptive behavior [59,60]. The broad goals of PMT are to improve parental competence in dealing with child behavioral problems and to improve the child's adaptive behavior. Parenting skills taught include using frequent praise for appropriate behavior, communicating directions effectively, and using consistent consequences for disruptive behaviors. The interactions between the therapist and the parent during PMT sessions emphasize active training. New parenting skills are developed through modeling, practice, role-playing, and feedback. PMT techniques stem from the fundamental principle of operant conditioning, which states that the likelihood that behavior will reoccur is increased or weakened by the events that follow the behavior [61]. For example, a child is more likely to have another tantrum if previous tantrums have led to getting his or her way. Furthermore, PMT targets parent–child interactions that have been shown to foster disruptive behaviors. Behaviors such as noncompliance, whining, or bickering can be reinforced if they result in escape or avoidance of situations such as homework or room-cleaning that could be aversive to the child [62]. Harsh and inconsistent discipline, such as excessive scolding and corporal punishment, has also been shown to increase a child's aggression [63]. PMT has been evaluated in numerous randomized, controlled studies, and several programs of research in different centers continue to investigate this treatment [37,59,64]. There is some evidence that the improvements in child behavior are stable over time and can be generalized to other areas such as reduction in family stress [65].

Functional family therapy (FFT) combines social learning and family systems approaches for treatment of disruptive behavior disorders and delinquency [66]. The treatment goals are to improve the clarity of family communication, expression of feelings, presentation of demands, and discussion of alternative solutions. FFT is commonly conducted in homes with parent and child seen together. Case management is also provided to enhance generalization of change to community settings relevant to each youth. Treatment duration varies from 8 to 26 hours. Trained and supervised mental health practitioners provide the therapy. Several studies of adolescents referred by the juvenile courts showed significant reduction in status offenses following FFT, as compared with other forms of family therapy [66,67]. FFT has not been well studied with chronic or violent offenders, however. There is evidence that this model of treatment can be effectively delivered by trained paraprofessionals [68].

MST is based on socioecologic [69] and family systems models of behavior [70] and targets multiple individual, family, peer, school, and community risk factors for delinquency. MST shares common characteristics with traditional family therapies but also includes problem-focused interventions that address specific areas within peer, school, and other systems as needed. Treatment is usually delivered over a period of 3 to 5 months by a team of master-level counselors who are trained and supervised in MST techniques. Most sessions are conducted in the family's home at a convenient time, but a few meetings are held in other locations, such as schools or community mental health centers. Because treatment is highly individualized, the frequency and number of sessions may vary among participants. For example, in the two primary outcome studies of MST [71,72], the duration of direct contact was 33 (SD, 29) and 24 (SD, 8) hours. Treatment manuals and procedures for training, supervision, and monitoring of treatment fidelity are well described and allow individualized and flexible delivery of treatment in settings relevant for each participant. The effects of MST on delinquent behavior have been evaluated in several randomized, controlled studies [71–74]. A long-term follow-up demonstrated that delinquent youth who received MST had lower re-arrest rates and shorter incarceration periods than youth receiving the usual treatment [75].

MTFC is a treatment alternative to placement in group care centers or secure facilities for adolescents referred from juvenile justice departments. MTFC is based on social learning principles [76] and involves placing delinquent youth in a foster family trained in PMT techniques, including providing a structured daily routine, clear rules, and supervision [5]. The program was developed in the early 1980s and has been evaluated in several randomized studies [77–79]. MTFS has been found more effective than usual services as measured by police-reported offenses and self-reported delinquency. These effects were mediated by adult supervision, consistent discipline, a positive relationship with a mentoring adult, and a lower level of association with delinquent peers [80]. During treatment, youth also participate in weekly individual therapy focused on problem solving and other coping skills, and biologic parents receive family counseling. MTFC staff provides ongoing consultation, supervision, and crisis management support for the foster families. The placement lasts 6 to 9 months, and only one child at a time is placed in the foster home.

Treatments for internalizing problems

The treatment of internalizing problems in juvenile offenders has been much less studied than the treatment of delinquent behavior. Indeed, as stated by the Office of Juvenile Justice and Delinquency Prevention [81], the main focus in the treatment of juvenile offenders is to reduce the risks for future delinquent behavior while enhancing protective factors that will help the youth reintegrate successfully in their communities. It is possible, however, that alleviation of internalizing problems may lead to improved psychosocial functioning and potentially reduce recidivism rates. Given the growing awareness of high rates of mental disorders in the juvenile justice system and the custodial treatment obligation, it is crucial to identify evidence-based interventions for internalizing problems relevant to juvenile offenders.

Psychosocial treatments for depression

Depression is a common disorder among juvenile offenders, with prevalence estimates in juvenile justice settings ranging between 11% and 33% [9]. Psychosocial treatments such as cognitive-behavioral therapy (CBT) [82–84] and interpersonal psychotherapy [85] have been evaluated in depressed youth from the general population [86,87]. CBT for depression has also been shown to have some effect, at least in the short term, in juvenile offenders [88] and in adolescents with co-occurring depression and conduct disorder [89]. It was also suggested that cognitive-behavior approaches in general may be particularly applicable to youth in the juvenile justice system because of the structured format and relevance to both internalizing and externalizing behaviors [7].

CBT for depression stems from Beck's model [90,91], in which depression is viewed as a consequence of automatic maladaptive thoughts, underlying negative assumptions, and core beliefs regarding oneself, the world, and the future. The goal of the therapy is to learn how to recognize these dysfunctional thoughts and replace them with more adaptive thoughts, which subsequently will lead to more appropriate and beneficial behaviors. Rohde and colleagues [89] evaluated CBT in a sample of 93 adolescents who had major depression and conduct disorder referred from a juvenile justice setting. Participants were randomly assigned to a group CBT intervention or a life-skills/tutoring condition. The CBT intervention was characterized by a focus on current actions and cognitions as targets for change, structured sessions, repeated practice of skills, use of rewards and contracts, homework assignments, and a relatively small number of sessions. Youth were taught coping skills such as mood monitoring, behavioral activation, relaxation, cognitive restructuring, communication, and conflict resolution. The study demonstrated greater recovery rates for depression (39% versus 19%), greater reductions in self-reported depressive symptoms, and improvement in social functioning in the CBT condition at immediate posttest but not at the 6- and 12-months follow-up evaluations. The effects of CBT on the reduction of depression in juveniles were mediated by the change in automatic negative cognitions [92]. A version of CBT, modified to address broader strategies to cope with distress, was tested in a randomized, controlled study of 76 incarcerated adolescents whose selection was not based on depression or other psychiatric disorder [88]. Compared with youths receiving treatment as usual, youths in the CBT condition showed significant reduction in self-reported externalizing behaviors and improvement in self-esteem.

Psychosocial treatments for suicidality risk factors

Interventions that may reduce risk of suicidal behavior are relevant to the juvenile justice system [93]. The number of youth at increased risk for suicide tends to be particularly high in juvenile justice settings, with the history of suicide attempts ranging between 14% and 30% and reports of suicidal ideation ranging between 22% and 34% [9]. Because managing life-threatening and aggressive behaviors is critical to the safe operation of a correctional environment, the potential for suicidal behavior must always be taken into account when treating youth who have major depression and other mood disorders. Trupin and colleagues [94] evaluated the effects of dialectical behavior therapy in 45 incarcerated adolescent females. Dialectical behavior therapy was originally developed for the treatment of borderline personality disorder and associated challenging behaviors [95,96]. The treatment consists of reframing an adolescent's thinking about problem behaviors and developing more effective skills of emotion regulation. Dialectical behavior therapy was offered on a mental health treatment unit and a general population unit of the correctional facility in a format of 60- to 90-minute sessions conducted once or twice per week over a period of 4 weeks. A significant reduction in suicidal acts, aggressive behavior, and class disruption was observed from pretest to the end of the treatment. Te levels of these problem behaviors at posttreatment did not differ significantly from the previous year average, however.

Psychosocial treatments for posttraumatic stress disorder

The prevalence of PTSD in juvenile offenders varies between 2% and 13% for males and between 14% and 36% for females. Because posttraumatic stress may have an effect on the development of delinquent behavior [97,98], treatments that reduce PTSD symptoms may indirectly influence the trajectories of delinquent behavior. Several controlled studies evaluated psychosocial interventions for PTSD in children and adolescents from the general population [99–101]. Psychosocial treatments for trauma commonly include coping skills training and direct therapeutic exposure [102]. Treatment approaches using direct therapeutic exposure consider PTSD to be a learned response to a conditioned stimulus that is associated with negative emotional, cognitive, and physiologic reactions and thus becomes avoided [103]. To extinguish the negative response, this treatment modality involves repeated exposure to traumatic cues and memories within a supportive therapeutic environment. Training in coping skills aims at improving the individual's ability to manage emotional reactions related to traumatic events [104]. Psychosocial interventions for PTSD may also include relaxation techniques, role playing, and cognitive restructuring.

The initial evaluations of CBT-based treatment for PTSD in juvenile offenders offer promising results. McMackin and colleagues [104] reported a qualitative study of a group intervention with 24 juvenile offenders who had PTSD symptoms. Qualitative analysis and individual case reports were used to infer generally positive effects of the intervention. Ahrens and Rexford [103] evaluated an eight-session group intervention based on cognitive processing therapy [105] in 19 incarcerated adolescents who had PTSD compared with a waiting-list control condition. The intervention led to significant reduction of symptoms of depression and posttraumatic stress assessed 4 weeks after the treatment.

Clearly, there is a paucity of studies evaluating psychosocial treatment for internalizing problems in juvenile offenders. CBT-based interventions are good candidates for implementation and dissemination treatment studies in juvenile delinquents who have co-occurring internalizing disorders such as depression and PTSD. CBT for internalizing disorders is likely to share many techniques and procedures with CBT for aggression and delinquent behaviors [57]. On the one hand, this overlap may benefit the development of treatment approaches for multiproblem youths [88]. On the other hand, limitations of treatments for delinquent behavior, such as the possibility of harmful effects of aggregation for therapy [54], may be applicable to psychosocial treatments of internalizing conditions.

Implementation of evidence-based treatments in juvenile justice

There is a considerable lag between science and service in health care [106]. In psychotherapy and mental health services research, the issue is often addressed in the context of efficacy versus effectiveness of interventions. On the one hand, a growing number of randomized, controlled studies, the criterion of efficacy research, have demonstrated positive effects of psychotherapy in well-controlled laboratory conditions. On the other hand, in real-world settings the effectiveness of psychotherapy has often been found to be limited. The disparity between the implementation of psychosocial treatments in the research settings versus the real-world settings may stem from the differences in client, therapist, and organization characteristics. For example, clients in the real-world settings are likely to be more heterogeneous and to present with high rates of comorbid disorders; therapists are likely to have large caseloads; and organizations may have no resources for training and supervision in new interventions [107]. In the juvenile justice system these differences may be compounded by the contrasting goals of rehabilitation and punishment, the high rates of staff turnover, lack of acceptance by the administration, and malingering or secondary gains by the juveniles [108,109].

A number of recent reviews addressed the issue of dissemination and implementation of evidence-based practices in the real-world settings [57,110,111]. The first step in this process is the selection of an evidence-based treatment, a task that involves review of the efficacy studies as well as the actual treatment procedures tested in these trials. Virtually all psychosocial treatments for children that have achieved the status of evidence-based interventions include detailed manuals [11]. From the methodology standpoint, the use of manuals in psychotherapy research is a prerequisite for being able to confirm that the treatment was delivered as planned. From the clinical standpoint, the manuals describe clinical procedures including therapeutic techniques, in-session activities, homework assignments, handouts, and other therapy resources. Although sometimes perceived as unduly obstructing clinical ingenuity [112], treatment manuals can be individualized and used in a flexible manner [113]. The application of treatment manuals in mental health services provided in juvenile correctional facilities should be guided by knowledge of administrative rules and operations of the facility [114].

The availability of a manual does not guarantee that the treatment will be delivered properly. Training and supervision of therapists, as well as continuous monitoring of the therapy process, are essential steps in assuring that evidence-based treatments are adequately implemented [115]. In contrast to the development of manuals, the training and supervision of therapists in administration of manualized treatments have been relatively neglected in the research literature. One study reported an association between the quality of the therapists' training in a particular intervention and the outcomes of the clinical trial [116], and another study reported that therapists in a large clinical trail perceived having continuous supervision to be more important than having a manual [117]. Adequate implementation of treatment is usually documented by evaluating various aspects of treatment fidelity, most notably a therapist's adherence to the treatment manual [118]. There is emerging evidence that greater treatment fidelity can be related to better clinical outcomes [119,120]. The effectiveness of psychosocial treatments in juvenile justice can be evaluated either as part of routine monitoring or in the context of effectiveness research.

A discussion of measurement issues in psychotherapy research is beyond the scope of this article. However, the authors note that the evaluation of the effects of particular psychosocial intervention should be informed by the guidelines for mental health assessment in the juvenile justice system [121].

Summary

Mental health services in the juvenile justice system need to be comprehensive; that is, they need to address multiple risk factors and involve environmental domains that influence the development and perpetuation of juvenile criminal behavior. This article has reviewed evidence-based psychosocial treatments for delinquent behavior and internalizing disorders that have a potential for being successfully implemented in the juvenile justice system. It has been suggested that the recent shift from a rehabilitative policy toward one based on retribution occurred in the juvenile justice, mostly in response to a general disillusionment with the ability of existing treatment strategies to rehabilitate juvenile offenders successfully and to control their behavior adequately [122]. Interventions may be ineffective for many reasons, including failure to address relevant risk factors, insufficient dose or duration, or failure to address the unique needs of individual juveniles. Recent research demonstrates that there are effective psychosocial treatments for juvenile delinquency, including even chronic, serious, or violent offenders. Future studies should examine the means of transferring psychosocial treatments from the research settings to the mental health services in the juvenile justice system.

References

[1] Roberts AR. An overview of juvenile justice and juvenile delinquency: cases, definitions, trends, and intervention strategies. In: Roberts AR, editor. Juvenile justice sourcebook: past present, and future. New York: Oxford University Press; 2004. p. 5–40.

[2] Moffitt TE. The new look of behavioral genetics in developmental psychopathology: gene-environment interplay in antisocial behaviors. Psychol Bull 2005;131(4):533–54.

[3] Loeber R, Green SM, Kalb L, et al. Physical fighting in childhood as a risk factor for later mental health problems. J Am Acad Child Adolesc Psychiatry 2000;39(4):421–8.

[4] Henggeler SW, Schoenwald SK, Borduin CM, et al. Multisystemic treatment of antisocial behavior in children and adolescents. New York: Guilford Press; 1998.

[5] Chamberlain P. Treating chronic juvenile offenders: advances made through the Oregon

multidimensional treatment foster care model. Washington (DC): American Psychological Association; 2003.

[6] Grietens H, Hellinckx W. Evaluating effects of residential treatment for juvenile offenders by statistical metaanalysis: a review. Aggress Violent Behav 2004;9(4):401–15.

[7] Lipsey MW, Wilson DB. Effective intervention for serious juvenile offenders: a synthesis of research. In: Loeber R, Farrington DP, editors. Serious and violent juvenile offenders: risk factors and successful interventions. Thousand Oaks (CA): Sage; 1998. p. 86–105.

[8] Teplin LA, Abram KM, McClelland GM, et al. Psychiatric disorders in youth in juvenile detention. Arch Gen Psychiatry 2002;59(12):1133–43.

[9] Vermeiren R. Psychopathology and delinquency in adolescents: a descriptive and developmental perspective. Clin Psychol Rev 2003;23(2):277–318.

[10] Burns BJ, Costello EJ, Angold A, et al. Children's mental health service use across service sectors. Health Aff (Millwood) 1995;14(3):147–59.

[11] Kazdin AE, Weisz JR, editors. Evidence-based psychotherapies for children and adolescents. New York: Guilford Press; 2003.

[12] Weisz JR, Doss AJ, Hawley KM. Youth psychotherapy outcome research: a review and critique of the evidence base. Annu Rev Psychol 2005;56:337–63.

[13] Borduin CM. Innovative models of treatment and service delivery in the juvenile justice system. J Clin Child Psychol 1994;23(Suppl):19–25.

[14] Chambless DL, Ollendick TH. Empirically supported psychological interventions: controversies and evidence. Annu Rev Psychol 2001;52:685–716.

[15] Brestan EV, Eyberg SM. Effective psychosocial treatments of conduct-disordered children and adolescents: 29 years, 82 studies, and 5,272 kids. J Clin Child Psychol 1998;27(2):180–9.

[16] Cornell DG, Peterson CS, Richards H. Anger as a predictor of aggression among incarcerated adolescents. J Consult Clin Psychol 1999;67(1):108–15.

[17] Zeman J, Suveg C, Zeman J, et al. Anger and sadness regulation: predictions to internalizing and externalizing symptoms in children. J Clin Child Adolesc Psychol 2002;31(3):393–8.

[18] Davidson RJ, Putnam KM, Larson CL. Dysfunction in the neural circuitry of emotion regulation—a possible prelude to violence. Science 2000;289(5479):591–4.

[19] Sukhodolsky DG, Ruchkin VV. Association of normative beliefs and anger with aggression and antisocial behavior in Russian male juvenile offenders and high school students. J Abnorm Child Psychol 2004;32(2):225–36.

[20] Lochman JE, Dodge KA. Social-cognitive processes of severely violent, moderately aggressive, and nonaggressive boys. J Consult Clin Psychol 1994;62(2):366–74.

[21] Dodge KA, Bates JE, Pettit GS. Mechanisms in the cycle of violence. Science 1990;250(4988):1678–83.

[22] Novaco RW. Anger control: the development and evaluation of experimental treatment. Lexington (MA): D. C. Health; 1975.

[23] Meichenbaum D, Cameron R. Stress inoculation: a skills training approach to anxiety management. Waterloo (Ontario, Canada): University of Waterloo; 1973.

[24] Lochman JE, Barry TD, Pardini DA. Anger control training for aggressive youth. In: Kazdin AE, Weisz JR, editors. Evidence-based psychotherapies for children and adolescents. New York: Guilford Press; 2003. p. 263–81.

[25] Sukhodolsky DG, Solomon RM, Perine J. Cognitive-behavioral, anger control intervention for elementary school children: a treatment outcome study. J Child Adolesc Group Ther 2000;10(3):159–70.

[26] Feindler EL, Ecton RB. Adolescent anger control: cognitive-behavioral techniques. New York: Pergamon Press; 1986.

[27] Deffenbacher JL, Lynch RS, Oetting ER, et al. Anger reduction in early adolescents. J Counsel Psychol 1996;43(2):149–57.

[28] Schlichter KJ, Horan JJ. Effects of stress inoculation on the anger and aggression management skills of institutionalized juvenile delinquents. Cognit Ther Res 1981;5(4):359–65.

[29] Tafrate RC, Kassinove H. Anger control in men: barb exposure with rational, irrational, and irrelevant self-statements. Journal of Cognitive Psychotherapy 1998;12(3):187–211.
[30] Kassinove H, Tafrate RC. Anger management: the complete treatment guidebook for practitioners. Atascadero (CA): Impact Publishers Inc.; 2002.
[31] DiGuiseppe R, Tafrate RC. Anger treatment for adults: a meta-analytic review. Clinical Psychology: Science and Practice 2003;10(1):70–84.
[32] Shure MB, Spivack G. Means-ends thinking, adjustment, and social class among elementary-school-aged children. J Consult Clin Psychol 1972;38(3):348–53.
[33] Dodge KA. Do social information-processing patterns mediate aggressive behavior? In: Lahey BB, Moffitt TE, Caspi A, editors. Causes of conduct disorder and juvenile delinquency. New York: Guilford Press; 2003. p. 254–74.
[34] Shure MB. I can problem solve (ICPS): interpersonal cognitive problem solving for young children. Early Child Dev Care 1993;96:49–64.
[35] Bourke ML, Van Hasselt VB. Social problem-solving skills training for incarcerated offenders: a treatment manual. Behav Modif 2001;25(2):163–88.
[36] D'Zurilla TJ, Goldfried MR. Problem solving and behavior modification. J Abnorm Psychol 1971;78(1):107–26.
[37] Kazdin AE, Siegel TC, Bass D. Cognitive problem-solving skills training and parent management training in the treatment of antisocial behavior in children. J Consult Clin Psychol 1992;60(5):733–47.
[38] Hudley C, Graham S. An attributional intervention to reduce peer-directed aggression among African-American boys. Child Dev 1993;64(1):124–38.
[39] Camp BW, Blom GE, Hebert F, et al. "Think aloud": a program for developing self control in young aggressive boys. J Abnorm Child Psychol 1977;5(2):157–69.
[40] Guerra NG, Slaby RG. Cognitive mediators of aggression in adolescent offenders: 2. Intervention. Dev Psychol 1990;26(2):269–77.
[41] Sukhodolsky DG, Golub A, Stone EC, et al. Dismantling anger control training for children: a randomized pilot study of social problem-solving versus social skills training components. Behav Ther 2005;36(1):15–23.
[42] Chambless DL, Ollendick TH. Empirically supported psychological interventions: controversies and evidence. Annu Rev Psychol 2001;52:685–716.
[43] Eyberg SM, Boggs SR, Algina J. Parent-child interaction therapy: a psychosocial model for the treatment of young children with conduct problem behavior and their families. Psychopharmacol Bull 1995;31(1):83–91.
[44] Merrell KW, Gimpel GA. Social skills of children and adolescents: conceptualization, assessment, treatment. Mahwah (NJ): Lawrence Erlbaum Associates; 1998.
[45] Spence SH. Social skills training with children and young people: theory, evidence and practice. Child Adoles Mental Health 2003;8(2):84–96.
[46] Bandura A. Aggression: asocial learning analysis. Oxford (UK): Prentice-Hall; 1973.
[47] Wolpe J. Psychotherapy by reciprocal inhibition. Stanford (CA): Stanford University Press; 1958.
[48] Barratt ES, Kent TA, Felthous A, et al. Neuropsychological and cognitive psychophysiological substrates of impulsive aggression. Biol Psychiatry 1997;41(10):1045–61.
[49] Deater-Deckard K. Annotation: recent research examining the role of peer relationships in the development of psychopathology. J Child Psychol Psychiatry 2001;42(5):565–79.
[50] Hawkins JD, Jenson JM, Catalano RF, et al. Effects of a skills training intervention with juvenile delinquents. Res Soc Work Pract 1991;1(2):107–21.
[51] Spence SH, Marzillier JS. Social skills training with adolescent male offenders. II. Short-term, long-term and generalized effects. Behav Res Ther 1981;19(4):349–68.
[52] Losel F, Beelmann A. Effects of child skills training in preventing antisocial behavior: a systematic review of randomized evaluations. Ann Am Acad Pol Soc Sci 2003;587:84–109.
[53] Taylor TK, Biglan A, Eddy JM. Interpersonal skills training to reduce aggressive and delinquent behavior: limited evidence and the need for an evidence-based system of care. Clin Child Fam Psychol Rev 1999;2(3):169–82.

[54] Dishion TJ, Poulin F, McCord J. When interventions harm: peer groups and problem behavior. Am Psychol 1999;54(9):755–64.
[55] Mager W, Milich R, Harris MJ, et al. Intervention groups for adolescents with conduct problems: is aggregation harmful or helpful? J Abnorm Child Psychol 2005;33(3):349–62.
[56] Sukhodolsky DG, Kassinove H, Gorman BS. Cognitive-behavioral therapy for anger in children and adolescents: a meta-analysis. Aggress Violent Behav 2004;9(3):247–69.
[57] Chorpita BF, Daleiden EL, Weisz JR. Identifying and selecting the common elements of evidence based Interventions: a distillation and matching model. Ment Health Serv Res 2005;7(1):5–20.
[58] Farrington DP, Welsh BC. Family-based prevention of offending: a meta-analysis. Australian and New Zealand Journal of Criminology 2003;36(2):127–51.
[59] Patterson GR, Chamberlain P, Reid JB. A comparative evaluation of a parent-training program. Behav Ther 1982;13(5):638–50.
[60] Kazdin AE. Parent management training: treatment for oppositional, aggressive, and antisocial behavior in children and adolescents. New York: Oxford University Press; 2005.
[61] Skinner BF. The behavior of organisms: an experimental analysis. New York: Free Press; 1938.
[62] Patterson GR, DeBaryshe BD, Ramsey E. A developmental perspective on antisocial behavior. Am Psychol 1989;44(2):329–35.
[63] Gershoff ET. Corporal punishment by parents and associated child behaviors and experiences: a meta-analytic and theoretical review. Psychol Bull 2002;128(4):539–79.
[64] Bank L, Marlowe JH, Reid JB, et al. A comparative evaluation of parent-training interventions for families of chronic delinquents. J Abnorm Child Psychol 1991;19(1):15–33.
[65] Webster-Stratton C, Hollinsworth T, Kolpacoff M. The long-term effectiveness and clinical significance of three cost-effective training programs for families with conduct-problem children. J Consult Clin Psychol 1989;57(4):550–3.
[66] Alexander JF, Parsons BV. Short term behavioral intervention with delinquent families: impact on family process and recidivism. J Abnorm Psychol 1973;81(3):219–25.
[67] Gordon DA, Graves K, Arbuthnot J. The effect of functional family therapy for delinquents on adult criminal behavior. Crim Justice Behav 1995;22:60–73.
[68] Gordon DA, Arbuthnot J. The use of paraprofessionals to deliver home-based family therapy to juvenile delinquents. Crim Justice Behav 1988;15(3):364–78.
[69] Bronfenbrenner U. Contexts of child rearing: problems and prospects. Am Psychol 1979;34(10):844–50.
[70] Minuchin S. Families and family therapy. Oxford (UK): Harvard University Press; 1974.
[71] Henggeler SW, Melton GB, Smith LA. Family preservation using multisystemic therapy: an effective alternative to incarcerating serious juvenile offenders. J Consult Clin Psychol 1992;60(6):953–61.
[72] Borduin CM, Mann BJ, Cone LT, et al. Multisystemic treatment of serious juvenile offenders: long-term prevention of criminality and violence. J Consult Clin Psychol 1995;63(4):569–78.
[73] Henggeler SW, Pickrel SG, Brondino MJ. Multisystemic treatment of substance-abusing and dependent delinquents: outcomes, treatment fidelity, and transportability. Ment Health Serv Res 1999;1(3):171–84.
[74] Henggeler SW, Rowland MD, Randall J, et al. Home-based multisystemic therapy as an alternative to the hospitalization of youths in psychiatric crisis: clinical outcomes. J Am Acad Child Adolesc Psychiatry 1999;38(11):1331–9.
[75] Schaeffer CM, Borduin CM. Long-term follow-up to a randomized clinical trial of multisystemic therapy with serious and violent juvenile offenders. J Consult Clin Psychol 2005;73(3):445–53.
[76] Patterson GR, Reid JB, Dishion TJ. A social learning approach: IV. Antisocial boys. Eugene (OR): Castalia; 1992.
[77] Chamberlain P, Reid JB. Using a specialized foster care community treatment model for children and adolescents leaving the state mental hospital. J Community Psychol 1991;19(3):266–76.

[78] Chamberlain P, Moore K. A clinical model for parenting juvenile offenders: a comparison of group care versus family care. Clin Child Psychol Psychiatry 1998;3(3):375–86.
[79] Chamberlain P, Reid JB. Comparison of two community alternatives to incarceration for chronic juvenile offenders. J Consult Clin Psychol 1998;66(4):624–33.
[80] Chamberlain P, Ray J, Moore KJ. Characteristics of residential care for adolescent offenders: a comparison of assumptions and practices in two models. J Child Fam Stud 1996;5: 259–71.
[81] Bazemore G, Pranis K, Umbreit MS. Balanced and restorative justice for juveniles: a framework for juvenile justice in the 21st century. Washington (DC): US Department of Justice, Office of Justice Programs, Office of Juvenile Justice and Delinquency Prevention; 1997.
[82] Lewinsohn PM, Clarke GN, Hops H, et al. Cognitive-behavioral treatment for depressed adolescents. Behav Ther 1990;21(4):385–401.
[83] Compton SN, March JS, Curry J, et al. Cognitive-behavioral psychotherapy for anxiety and depressive disorders in children and adolescents: an evidence-based medicine review. J Am Acad Child Adolesc Psychiatry 2004;43(8):930–59.
[84] March JS. Fluoxetine, cognitive-behavioral therapy, and their combination for adolescents with depression: Treatment for Adolescents with Depression Study (TADS) randomized controlled trial. JAMA 2004;292(7):807–20.
[85] Mufson L, Moreau D, Weissman MM, et al. Interpersonal psychotherapy for depressed adolescents. New York: Guilford; 1993.
[86] Ryan ND. Treatment of depression in children and adolescents. Lancet 2005;366(9489): 933–40.
[87] DuBois DL, Reinecke MA, Ryan NE. Cognitive-behavioral therapy of depression and depressive symptoms during adolescence: a review and meta-analysis. J Am Acad Child Adolesc Psychiatry 1998;37(1):26–34.
[88] Rohde P, Jorgensen JS, Seeley JR, et al. Pilot evaluation of the coping course: a cognitive-behavioral intervention to enhance coping skills in incarcerated youth. J Am Acad Child Adolesc Psychiatry 2004;43(6):669–76.
[89] Rohde P, Jorgensen JS, Seeley JR, et al. An efficacy/effectiveness study of cognitive-behavioral treatment for adolescents with comorbid major depression and conduct disorder. J Am Acad Child Adolesc Psychiatry 2004;43(6):660–8.
[90] Beck AT. The current state of cognitive therapy: a 40-year retrospective. Arch Gen Psychiatry 2005;62(9):953–9.
[91] Beck AT, Rush AJ, Shaw BF, et al. Cognitive therapy of depression. New York: Guilford Press; 1979.
[92] Kaufman NK, Rohde P, Seeley JR, et al. Potential mediators of cognitive-behavioral therapy for adolescents with comorbid major depression and conduct disorder. J Consult Clin Psychol 2005;73(1):38–46.
[93] Ruchkin VV, Schwab-Stone M, Vermeiren R, et al. Suicidal ideations and attempts in juvenile delinquents. J Child Psychol Psychiatry 2003;44(7):1058–66.
[94] Trupin EW, Stewart DG, Beach B, et al. Effectiveness of dialectical behaviour therapy program for incarcerated female juvenile offenders. Child Adoles Mental Health 2002;7(3):121–7.
[95] Linehan MM. Behavioral treatments of suicidal behaviors: definitional obfuscation and treatment outcomes. In: Maris RW, Canetto SS, McIntosh J, et al, editors. Review of suicidology. New York: Guilford Press; 2000. p. 84–111.
[96] Linehan MM. Cognitive-behavioral treatment of borderline personality disorder. New York: Guilford Press; 1993.
[97] Widom CS. The cycle of violence. Science 1989;244(4901):160–6.
[98] Steiner H, Garcia IG, Matthews Z. Posttraumatic stress disorder in incarcerated juvenile delinquents. J Am Acad Child Adolesc Psychiatry 1997;36(3):357–65.
[99] Chemtob CM, Nakashima JP, Hamada RS. Psychosocial intervention for postdisaster trauma symptoms in elementary school children: a controlled community field study. Arch Pediatr Adolesc Med 2002;156(3):211–6.

[100] Cohen JA, Mannarino AP, Deblinger E, et al. A multisite, randomized controlled trial for children with sexual abuse-related PTSD symptoms. J Am Acad Child Adolesc Psychiatry 2004;43(4):393–402.

[101] March JS, Amaya-Jackson L, Murray MC, et al. Cognitive-behavioral psychotherapy for children and adolescents with posttraumatic stress disorder after a single-incident stressor. J Am Acad Child Adolesc Psychiatry 1998;37(6):585–93.

[102] Cohen JA, Bernet W, Dunne JE, et al. Practice parameters for the assessment and treatment of children and adolescents with posttraumatic stress disorder. J Am Acad Child Adolesc Psychiatry 1998;37(10 Suppl):4S–26S.

[103] Ahrens J, Rexford L. Cognitive processing therapy for incarcerated adolescents with PTSD. J Aggress Maltreat Trauma 2002;6(1):201–16.

[104] McMackin RA, Leisen MB, Sattler L, et al. Preliminary development of trauma-focused treatment groups for incarcerated juvenile offenders. J Aggress Maltreat Trauma 2002;6(1): 175–99.

[105] Resick PA, Schnicke MK. Cognitive processing therapy for sexual assault victims. J Consult Clin Psychol 1992;60(5):748–56.

[106] Lenfant C. Shattuck lecture: clinical research to clinical practice—lost in translation? N Engl J Med 2003;349(9):868–74.

[107] Weisz JR, Donenberg GR, Weiss B, et al. Bridging the gap between laboratory and clinic in child and adolescent psychotherapy. J Consult Clin Psychol 1995;63(5):688–701.

[108] US Department of Justice. Guide for implementing the comprehensive strategy for serious, violent, and chronic juvenile offenders. Washington (DC): US Department of Justice; 1995.

[109] Chandler RK, Peters RH, Field G, et al. Challenges in implementing evidence-based treatment practices for co-occurring disorders in the criminal justice system. Behav Sci Law 2004; 22(4):431–48.

[110] Addis ME. Methods for disseminating research products and increasing evidence-based practice: promises, obstacles, and future directions. Clinical Psychology: Science and Practice 2002; 9(4):367–78.

[111] Herschell AD, McNeil CB, McNeil DW. Clinical child psychology's progress in disseminating empirically supported treatments. Clinical Psychology: Science and Practice 2004;11(3): 267–88.

[112] Strupp HH, Anderson T. On the limitations of therapy manuals. Clinical Psychology: Science and Practice 1997;4(1):76–82.

[113] Kendall PC, Chu B, Gifford A, et al. Breathing life into a manual: flexibility and creativity with manual- based treatments. Cognitive and Behavioral Practice 1998;5(2):177–98.

[114] Penn JV, Thomas C. Practice parameter for the assessment and treatment of youth in juvenile detention and correctional facilities. J Am Acad Child Adolesc Psychiatry 2005;44(10): 1085–98.

[115] Sholomskas DE, Syracuse-Siewert G, Rounsaville BJ, et al. We don't train in vain: a dissemination trial of three strategies of training clinicians in cognitive-behavioral therapy. J Consult Clin Psychol 2005;73(1):106–15.

[116] Crits-Christoph P, Siqueland L, Chittams J, et al. Training in cognitive, supportive-expressive, and drug counseling therapies for cocaine dependence. J Consult Clin Psychol 1998;66(3): 484–92.

[117] Najavits LM, Weiss RD, Thase ME, et al. Therapist satisfaction with four manual-based treatments on a national multisite trial: an exploratory study. Psychotherapy 2004;41(1):26–37.

[118] Moncher FJ, Prinz RJ. Treatment fidelity in outcome studies. Clin Psychol Rev 1991;11(3): 247–66.

[119] Henggeler SW, Brondino MJ, Melton GB, et al. Multisystemic therapy with violent and chronic juvenile offenders and their families: the role of treatment fidelity in successful dissemination. J Consult Clin Psychol 1997;65(5):821–33.

[120] Frank E, Kupfer DJ, Wagner EF, et al. Efficacy of interpersonal psychotherapy as a maintenance treatment of recurrent depression: contributing factors. Arch Gen Psychiatry 1991; 48(12):1053–9.

[121] Wasserman GA, Jensen PS, Ko SJ, et al. Mental health assessments in juvenile justice: report on the consensus conference. J Am Acad Child Adolesc Psychiatry 2003;42(7):752–61.

[122] Harris PW, Welsh WN, Butler F. A century of juvenile justice. In: LaFree G, editor. Criminal justice 2000, vol. I: The nature of crime: continuity and change. Washington (DC): National Institute of Justice; 2000. p. 359–425.

ELSEVIER
SAUNDERS

Child Adolesc Psychiatric Clin N Am
15 (2006) 517–537

CHILD AND
ADOLESCENT
PSYCHIATRIC CLINICS
OF NORTH AMERICA

Providing Effective Substance Abuse Treatment for Young-Offender Populations: What Works!

Craig Dowden, PhD[a,*], Jeff Latimer[b]

[a]Carleton University, Ottawa, ON, Canada
[b]Research and Statistics Division, Department of Justice, Ottawa, ON, Canada

The prevention of criminal behavior, especially in young-offender populations, has become an increasingly important enterprise for criminal justice professionals. Considerable research attention has been devoted to identifying and documenting the factors that place an adolescent at risk for engaging in delinquent behavior. Previous research has consistently demonstrated that both static and dynamic risk factors are linked with criminal activity. Because static risk factors such as criminal history remain constant and do not change as a function of intervention, the primary thrust of correctional research has been to identify dynamic risk factors that are linked with criminal behavior, also termed criminogenic needs.[1] Several researchers have noted the importance of emphasizing dynamic rather than static risk factors in both risk assessment and treatment delivery [1–3]. One of the most prominent consistently identified dynamic risk factors has been substance abuse.

Several terms are used interchangeably in the extant literature to designate problematic substance involvement, including "substance use," "substance abuse," "dependence," and "addiction" [4]. Despite this range of terms, only substance abuse and dependence have officially recognized diagnostic criteria outlined in the *Diagnostic and Statistical Manual of Mental Disorders* [5]. A substance abuser is characterized as a person who encounters negative social or

The opinions expressed herein are those of the authors and not necessarily those of the Department of Justice, Canada.

* Corresponding author. 276 Presland Road, Apartment #2, Ottawa, ON K1K 2B8, Canada.

E-mail address: cdowden@rogers.com (C. Dowden).

[1] Changes in dynamic factors that do not necessarily reduce recidivism but may nonetheless generate some benefit, for example, enhanced self-worth, are known as noncriminogenic needs [1].

1056-4993/06/$ – see front matter
doi:10.1016/j.chc.2005.12.002 *childpsych.theclinics.com*

interpersonal consequences as a result of substance abuse. Substance dependence is a more extreme diagnosis, because an individual must exhibit signs of addiction, such as increased tolerance to the substance or symptoms of withdrawal once use is terminated, and, as a result, be constantly preoccupied with "feeding" the addiction. This article considers both substance-abusing and substance-dependent youth.

Antecedents and consequences of substance abuse

Substance abuse, delinquency, and other problem behaviors in young offenders

Strong linkages between substance abuse and delinquent activity have been documented among young offenders [2,6–10], similar to findings reported in the adult literature [1,11,12]. (A caveat should be mentioned here: currently, there is no universally accepted definition of what constitutes a young offender in the criminological literature, because the age range differs depending on the country of origin. For example, in Canada a young offender is classified as someone who is between 12 and 17 years of age at the time of his or her offence. Thus, studies involving young offenders in this article may represent a broad range of age groups.) Past research has demonstrated that there is also a clear link between alcohol or drug abuse and violent crime [7,10], including homicide [13]. This latter trend is consistent with findings from studies of nondelinquent populations in which increased alcohol consumption has been associated with more aggressive behavior [14–16].

Watts and Wright [10] provided several compelling explanations that may account for the strong relationship between substance abuse and criminal behavior among young offenders. First, the young offender may see the use and abuse of substances as an integral part of the "tough guy" image required for acceptance within a peer group that is predominantly antisocial. Second, the adolescent may engage in excessive substance use to obtain greater parental attention or, conversely, to act defiantly toward parental authority. In addition, as has been suggested elsewhere, abusing substances provides an escape from the real world. Their final explanation is biologically based and argues that young offenders suffer from a chronic state of underarousal and so turn to substance abuse as a means to enhance stimulation, a tenet related to the disease model of alcoholism or addiction.

The relationship between alcohol/drug abuse and delinquent activity has been maintained across various demographic categories, including racial and ethnic minorities such as Mexican-American and African American youth [10,17,18]. This relationship has been observed among both male and female adolescents [7,18].

Criminal justice agencies have dedicated enormous fiscal and human resources to this important problem, but the impact of substance abuse on the lives of adolescents is not restricted solely to delinquent behavior [19]. Substance abuse has been linked to poor school performance, physical and mental health problems, problematic peer involvement, and poor family relations [4,7,18,19]. Based on this plethora of evidence, Huizinga and Jacob-Chien [8] emphatically asserted that the linkage of substance abuse with various problem behaviors, including delinquency, is irrefutable.

Concomitantly, these findings highlight that the appropriate treatment of adolescent substance-abusing offenders is important for the criminal justice system. This need is even more pronounced when one considers the robust relationship between delinquency and substance abuse across various demographic categories such as gender, race, and age. The next section of this article reviews the literature on the treatment of substance abuse for the past 25 years and provides some overall recommendations based on these findings.

Substance abuse treatment for youthful offenders: what works!

Unfortunately, there has been a paucity of research examining the effective provision of substance-abuse treatment services in the adolescent literature [4,20], a problem that is further exacerbated in the literature on young offenders [9]. Consequently, it was necessary to review other sources of information to extract information pertinent to the treatment of adolescent-offender populations. More specifically, articles were reviewed within the literature on the treatment of general offenders (including both youth and adult samples) and, to a lesser extent, within the literature on the treatment of adolescent substance abuse.

Approach

Catalano and colleagues [21] suggested that researchers should examine pretreatment, in-treatment, and posttreatment variables when exploring the effectiveness of substance-abuse treatment. This method is an elegant way of representing the multiple influences that may operate on a correctional program at any given time. This format has been adopted for the present article.

Pretreatment variables

Catalano and colleagues [21] noted several characteristics of program participants that may be important in determining successful client outcomes. Some of the more commonly discussed characteristics in the research literature include age, age of onset, gender, history of substance use (eg, risk level), and psychopathology.

Age

The findings related to the age of the participant are quite contradictory: some studies have reported that younger participants do better, but others have documented that older individuals experience enhanced programmatic effects [22,23].

Still others have concluded that age does not have an impact on treatment outcomes [24]. In a slightly different vein, a recent study by D'Amico [25] reported that younger youth were more likely and willing to engage in alcohol-related treatment services than older youth. Most of these studies were conducted on nonoffender populations, however, and it may be valuable to examine what relationships, if any, have been found between the age of the participant and programmatic effects in research on young offenders. The findings of two meta-analyses that have been conducted on the literature concerning correctional treatment may provide some preliminary insight into this question.

Latimer [26] conducted a meta-analytic review of the family intervention literature for young offenders and reported that programs that engaged participants who were younger than 15 years of age yielded significantly higher mean reductions in reoffending than programs that engaged older clients. More related to the present review, Dowden conducted a meta-analysis of the entire literature on correctional treatment of both adult and juvenile offenders (Craig Dowden, unpublished Master's thesis, 1998). In a preliminary analysis of programs that addressed substance abuse as a program target, the findings were similar to those reported by Latimer, in that age had an inverse correlation with program success. These findings complement the fervent arguments made by other researchers regarding the importance of early identification and treatment of substance-abuse problems in adolescent populations [27]. Thus, the preliminary correctional-based evidence that is available suggests that, unlike the literature on the treatment of adolescent substance abuse, the age of the client may have an impact on treatment success.

Age of onset

Perhaps the most influential variable affecting the substance abuse–delinquency relationship is age of onset, with several studies documenting that earlier involvement in substance abuse is associated with increased criminal activity [7,13,28]. Furthermore, earlier abusers are also much more likely to develop a substance-abuse problem as adults [29]. The strength of this relationship is further enhanced when offenders become engaged in substance use/abuse during their formative years, a result that has been found in both Canadian [29] and American studies [30].

Past research has found that age of onset of substance use is related not only to involvement in delinquent activities but also to success in treatment. More specifically, several studies have reported that the earlier the age of substance-abuse onset reported by adolescents, the poorer the treatment outcome [22,31,32]. Unfortunately, these studies did not examine young-offender populations, so caution should be exercised when considering the external generalizability of the results, especially considering the important age-related differences that seemed to emerge in the previous discussion of delinquent as opposed to nondelinquent populations. Another reason for exercising caution is that these studies reported substance-use problems retrospectively, and thus the reliability of these data may be questioned.

Gender

It may be assumed, based on past evidence, that because substance abuse and juvenile delinquency co-occur among both male and female young offenders [33], targeting this criminogenic need for intervention would yield positive programmatic effects for both genders. Once again, Dowden's meta-analysis was consulted to explore this question (Craig Dowden, unpublished Master's thesis, 1998). Although there were too few cases to examine the differential effectiveness of treatment for both male and female adolescent offenders, when adult and juvenile offenders in substance-abuse treatment were combined, similar positive programmatic impacts were found for both genders.

Despite the positive findings reported for the effectiveness of substance-abuse treatment programs for both genders, this analysis does not address issues related to program delivery (a point that could be extended to other demographic characteristics such as age and ethnicity). More specifically, it does not indicate whether delivering the program in a particular way or focusing on specific material may make it more relevant or therapeutically meaningful for one gender over another. For example, several advocates for gender-specific treatment have argued for the importance of attending to relationship-oriented issues when treating female offenders [34,35], but unfortunately this recommendation has not yet been tested. Therefore, future evaluations should explore gender-specific responses to treatment and identify those related to positive program delivery.

Psychopathology

Psychopathology has been noted as one of the most persistent indicators of negative program outcome, and thus several researchers have stressed the need to address this issue within treatment. As discussed by Randall and colleagues [36], symptoms classified as either externalizing or internalizing can be strongly related to unsuccessful program completion in both correctional [37] and non-correctional samples [20,38]. It has been recommended that, for treatment programs to be more effective, more attention must be paid to the psychopathology of adolescent substance abusers [20,21,38,39]. In particular, those who have externalizing problems must be appropriately identified to ensure that their motivation for program participation is addressed [4,21]. Several recommendations have been forwarded, including ensuring the treatment plan is maximally personalized so that the youth can see how the program will meet their goals and helping the adolescents overcome social and personal deficits or problems which may be hampering their involvement in treatment [9,21].

Identifying and distinguishing substance abusers who exhibit different types of psychopathology at intake is also important, because each of these populations has unique treatment needs [20,36,38]. For example, Randall and colleagues [36] documented that substance abusers who have externalizing disorders also have poorer familial environments; therefore, engaging the parents and other family members in treatment may have a positive impact on the youth. In particular, emphasis could be placed on assisting the parents in more effectively structuring, monitoring, and supervising the behavior of the adolescent. For those who have internalizing disorders (such as anxiety or depression), programs could be tailored so that the youth are taught coping skills to help deal with these emotional difficulties [36]. Although these preliminary suggestions admittedly need to be validated through additional empiric study, the value of these recommendations is evident, given the reviewed findings on the negative impacts of psychopathology on program success. (For example, a recent study by Pagnin [40] found adolescents who had more self-reported symptoms of anxiety/depression yielded better initial adherence, more regular attendance, and longer lengths of stay in treatment.)

Risk

Although the variable of risk has not received any attention within the general literature on the treatment of adolescent substance abuse, the risk principle of case classification has been lauded as an integral component in the delivery of effective correctional treatment for offenders [1,41,42]. The risk principle states that the amount of intervention an offender receives must be appropriately matched to the likelihood that he or she will reoffend. More specifically, higher-risk offenders should receive more intensive and extensive services, whereas lower-risk clients should receive minimal or no intervention.

Meta-analytic reviews of the literature concerning the correctional treatment of young offenders have provided strong empirical evidence for this principle. Programs that target high-risk cases exhibit more positive programmatic effects than those that target low-risk cases [42–45]. The clinical utility of this principle has also been demonstrated with female offenders [46] and minority offenders [47]. Furthermore, indirect support for this principle has been found in the literature concerning adolescent substance abuse. For example, Breda and Heflinger [39] reported that poly-substance–abusing youth (who could be considered high-risk substance abusers) demonstrated more incentive to change than youth who used only alcohol or marijuana. Therefore, administrators of substance-abuse interventions should ensure that program clients undergo appropriate risk assessments and that high-risk cases are prioritized for treatment involvement and receive more intensive exposure to treatment.

In-treatment variables

Several researchers have highlighted the critical importance of exploring the "black box" of treatment. Process evaluations, in which researchers examine program and policy-delivery issues that accompany an intervention, are the primary method for achieving this goal [48–50]. If these process issues are ignored, it is virtually impossible to determine whether a treatment program is truly responsible for the observed results and, more importantly, how it actually works [51,52]. Despite the beneficial contributions such studies make to the literature on correctional treatment, this evaluative approach has been essentially ignored in the mainstream criminological literature [52,53]. This unfortunate situation is compounded in that most evaluations examine programmatic impacts on only a short list of outcome variables such as recidivism, resulting in a limited and arguably incomplete perspective of program success [54].

Although outcome evaluations of programs are of paramount importance in ascertaining the effectiveness of a particular intervention, not knowing how the participant performed in the treatment (eg, was there a decrease in a treatment-related outcome variable such as attitudes favorable to substance abuse), makes it difficult, if not impossible, to tie the effects of program participation directly to the outcome achieved. Linking changes in intermediate measures to program outcome data is the most comprehensive and reliable way to assess the effectiveness of a correctional program [1]. As summarized nicely by Prendergast and colleagues [52], if programs possessing a certain combination of characteristics are responsible for significant differences in the observed therapeutic impact, then agencies responsible for delivering such programs can improve the effectiveness of their treatment services by focusing on these characteristics. Several variables that fall within this broad category of program factors include program setting, organizational characteristics, program length, program targets, relapse prevention, client-treatment matching, and style and mode of program delivery.

Program setting

The literature on correctional treatment has emphasized the importance of the site of the program delivery on client outcomes. More specifically, several researchers have argued that ideally programs should be delivered within community rather than residential settings [1,41,55]. This issue has also been debated in the literature on the treatment of substance abuse, although the terminology is somewhat different, with inpatient and outpatient programs corresponding to community and residential programs, respectively.

Several studies have explored the impact of inpatient versus outpatient programs for treatment of substance abuse on client outcomes. To date, the evidence supporting the differential effectiveness of one over the other is lacking (Dowden et al, manuscript in preparation, 2006) [21,55]. More specifically, some evaluations have reported both settings yield equally positive results, whereas others have found greater improvements within one at the exclusion of the other. The difficulty in interpreting these findings appropriately is compounded because these studies have used different outcome measures and follow-up periods [21]. Furthermore, and arguably more important, the applicability of these findings to substance-abusing young offenders is questionable, given that the results were generated from the literature on the treatment of adolescent substance abuse. Some of the findings from the literature on correctional treatment are reviewed here to supplement this discussion.

Previous meta-analyses of the literature on correctional treatment have found that the program setting significantly impacts program outcomes for young offenders. More specifically, programs delivered in community settings have achieved significantly higher mean reductions in recidivism than those conducted within institutional settings (Craig Dowden, unpublished Master's thesis, 1998) [55]. A more recent meta-analytic review of the substance abuse treatment literature by Dowden and colleagues (Dowden et al, manuscript in preparation, 2006) provides some additional preliminary evidence. These authors report that young offender substance-abuse programs yielded more positive client outcomes (as measured by reduced recidivism) when delivered in a community than in a residential setting.

Program length

Another variable that may be related to program effectiveness is program length. Although preliminary evidence from both correctional [50] and non-correctional populations [23,32,57,58] suggests that the length of exposure to treatment is positively related to program outcomes, its contribution to overall program effectiveness is minimal [21]. A recent study by Latimer and colleagues [56] may help explain this discrepancy. Their results indicate that, although length of exposure to treatment was positively associated with client outcome for inpatient and outpatient settings, this effect was evident only at 6 months following program termination. The authors suggest that previous contradictory findings and the limited magnitude of the observed effects may result from insufficient follow-up of program graduates to capture the therapeutic impacts of the program. Clearly, replication of these findings in noncorrectional and, more importantly for the present article, correctional samples of adolescents is key.

The findings for program duration (or dosage) have been examined explicitly only in populations of nonoffender substance-abusing adolescents. In the literature concerning correctional treatment, Dowden reported that program exposure (measured in treatment hours) was associated with significantly improved client outcomes for young offenders (Craig Dowden, unpublished Master's thesis, 1998). Further explorations of the impact of program length on client outcome are warranted, because the preliminary evidence suggests this variable is an important programmatic consideration.

Program targets

Several recent meta-analyses of the literature concerning correctional treatment have made a concerted effort to determine the effects of the programmatic targets of the intervention on client outcomes. Although some studies have categorized these factors as criminogenic versus noncriminogenic needs [43,46,59], others have followed a more generic approach [44,45,60,61]. Regardless of the perspective taken, each of these meta-analyses has demonstrated that program targets, including but not limited to substance abuse, have significant effects on program outcomes. Although an analysis of all of the possible additional treatment targets is clearly beyond the scope of this article, those that have been mentioned most frequently within the literature on adolescent substance abuse are discussed. (Readers who are interested in meta-analytic summaries of the most effective treatment targets for correctional interventions with young offenders are referred to the works of Lipsey [43], Lipsey and Wilson [44], and Dowden and Andrews [42].)

Among additional promising areas to target, Wright and Fitzpatrick [61] suggest efforts to reduce substance-abuse behaviors should focus on academic achievement and building positive teacher–student interactions. A recent meta-analysis of the literature concerning treatment of young offenders found that treatment gains were made when educators were directly involved in the treatment program and school attendance/performance were targeted [63,64].

Other researchers have suggested that for substance abuse programs to be effective, additional areas should be addressed. For example, in their synthesis of the literature concerning prevention of drug use in vulnerable young people, Roe and Becker [63] found that interventions that targeted life-skills training had positive effects on participants, even among the groups at highest risk. Sambrano and colleagues [57] also reported the positive effects of targeting life skills with adolescent substance abusers. Building on this perspective, Dowden and Latimer (manuscript under review, 2006) examined the value of vocational-skills programming for young-offender populations. Overall, the results revealed that this form of correctional intervention is promising, although targeting specific vocational skills (eg, automobile mechanics or carpentry) was far more effective in reducing recidivism than targeting general vocational skills (eg, resume writing).

Several researchers have emphasized the necessity of adopting a multimodal approach to substance-abuse treatment. Based on the findings from their meta-analytic review of school-based alcohol/drug prevention programs, Wilson and colleagues [65] concluded that it is highly unlikely that any single type of strategy, implemented in isolation, will have a large impact on client alcohol or drug abuse. This conclusion suggests that a more meaningful way to explore "what works" is to focus on which combinations or sequences of program types work best. Past research essentially has ignored issues surrounding the potential additive and multiplicative effects of combining different programs. The importance of the concurrent or sequential delivery of programming is even more evident when considering the co-occurrence of substance abuse with various other forms of problem behavior. As a result, Wilson and colleagues [65] urged researchers to explore the relative effectiveness of different sets and combinations of interventions so that a knowledge base can be developed that will aid in the selection of the most appropriate constellation of programs for a particular treatment population.

Several other researchers have forwarded Wilson and colleagues' suggestion (Dowden et al, manuscript in preparation, 2006) [18,66]. As these authors note, research has generally found that a constellation of factors (including substance abuse and delinquent behavior) operates concurrently. The significance for intervention is that program deliverers should ensure that these multiple problem areas (eg, academics, family, antisocial peer group membership) are targeted to make the intervention as effective as possible.

One potential avenue of investigation for enhancing program effectiveness centers on involving the family in treatment programs [62,67]. Dobkin and colleagues [20] found that treatment completion was far better in cases in which the parents were actively involved in the program than in cases in which parents were not involved. Further confirmatory evidence for the importance of familial variables was found in a recent evaluation of a substance-abuse program offered to youthful offenders. In this evaluation, program staff identified family issues as one of the key barriers to successful program completion [51]. Finally, several researchers have lauded the utility of involving other family members in preventative efforts aimed at keeping adolescents from developing substance-abuse problems [68,69].

The importance of family treatment for young offenders has also been demonstrated in various meta-analyses of the literature on correctional treatment [26,43,44,60,70]. Dowden and Andrews [69], however, noted that not necessarily all forms of family intervention are effective. Programs that focused on increasing family affection and monitoring/supervision practices yielded significant mean reductions in reoffending compared with control groups. More generic family intervention programs (eg, those that did not discuss their family-oriented treatment targets) were associated with negative client outcomes. In addition, and arguably more important for the present article, a recent meta-analysis conducted by Dowden and colleagues [70] reported that family intervention programs that involved parents in treatment yielded a significantly higher effect size than those that did not. Thus, program administrators should ensure that they are explicit regarding their program targets and address familial factors important for reducing criminal behavior in adolescents while encouraging the participation of family members in treatment.

Relapse prevention

Although it could be argued that relapse prevention should be considered a program target, given its popularity within the literature on the treatment of substance abuse and the more recent expansion of this concept into a complete programmatic framework, it was decided to address this topic separately. The necessity of incorporating some form of relapse prevention into a substance-abuse treatment program is illustrated in previous work that has reported relapse rates as high as 85% among both adult and adolescent substance abusers [21]. Thus, it is not surprising that relapse prevention has been viewed as an integral component of delivering effective treatment (Dowden et al, manuscript in preparation, 2006) [21].

Despite the widespread attention given to this approach within the mainstream literature, few controlled outcome studies have formally evaluated its effectiveness within correctional [71] or noncorrectional samples [21,72,73]. A recent meta-analysis of the correctional treatment literature by Dowden and colleagues [70] consolidated the findings of correctional interventions that identified relapse prevention as one of their program targets. The authors found relapse-prevention programs as a whole to be effective, resulting in an average decrease in recidivism of 15% compared with programs without a relapse-prevention component. More importantly, using relapse prevention with youthful offenders yielded significantly stronger programmatic effects in terms of recidivism reduction than when it was used with adult offenders. Thus, the critical importance of incorporating elements of relapse prevention in a treatment protocol for young offenders seems evident.

Client–treatment matching

Several researchers have noted that one of the most critical aspects of effective programming involves appropriate client identification, assessment, and referral [37,74]. A technique adopted in the field of substance-abuse treatment to deal with this concern has been labeled client–treatment matching, otherwise known as the matching hypothesis (Dowden et al, manuscript in preparation, 2006). The fundamental principle underlying this approach is that a client with a certain set of factors may respond more favorably to a particular kind of treatment program or setting than to another. To maximize the therapeutic benefits of program participation, due diligence must be exercised to ensure appropriate matching of client to treatment. Despite the relative newness of the concept, Annis [55] found empiric support for this hypothesis in her review of the literature concerning the treatment of substance abuse: she reported 15 studies had documented positive programmatic effects from client–treatment matching.

Client–treatment matching has also received support in the correctional literature. Dowden's recent meta-analytic review reported that programs that assessed the offender's needs at intake and subsequently assigned the offender to an appropriate treatment program based on this assessment yielded significantly higher mean reductions in reoffending compared with programs that did not employ this practice (Craig Dowden, unpublished Master's thesis, 1998). This trend has also been found in evaluations of correctional programs that involved juvenile offenders [43] and female offenders [46].

Overall, these studies provide convincing empiric evidence for the clinical utility of this approach when delivering correctional treatment to substance-abusing young offenders. This practice has a great deal of intuitive appeal as well, because one would expect that individuals assigned to programs that target an identified "personal" need area would be much more likely to obtain positive effects from program participation.

Style and mode of program delivery

Considerable research attention has focused on the style and mode of program delivery, with particular emphasis placed on determining whether cognitive-behavioral/behavioral methods (such as modeling, graduated practice, rehearsal, and role playing) or nonbehavioral methods (eg, didactic, client-focused) are equally effective when delivering substance-abuse treatment to adolescent populations. Most of the evidence to date suggests that cognitive-behavioral/behavioral methods are far superior, and this superiority has been demonstrated within school-based substance-abuse programs [65], substance-abusing adolescents [58,67,75], young offenders [43,44], and substance-abusing offenders [61]. Clearly, the plethora of research evidence supports a behavioral or cognitive-behavioral framework for delivering substance-abuse treatment to youthful offenders.

Organizational variables

Recently, correctional investigators have begun to explore the role of organizational-level variables (eg, staff turnover, staff training, organizational support for the rehabilitative ideal) in the delivery of effective correctional treatment. This shift in focus has been motivated by the substantial variations in program effectiveness that have been documented within programs, even within those following the same treatment modality [53]. Although little research to date has focused on these issues, the preliminary empiric evidence suggests that organizational factors may be one of the most important determinants for successful programs because of their strong influence on program implementation and delivery [48,52,74,76].

One such organizational variable that may affect the therapeutic potential of a program is staff turnover [52,74]. Several intuitively appealing explanations for the link between increased staff turnover and poorer program performance have been forwarded by Mears and Kelly [50]. First, youth may be attached to the officers who leave their positions, may subsequently feel abandoned, and therefore may not put as much effort into the program. Furthermore, hiring new staff who require extensive training may impinge on the effectiveness of the program, because these new employees will not be as effective with program clients. Finally, several other correctional investigators have noted, maintaining and nurturing a therapeutic milieu for program clients is a colossal task when there is a constant turnover of staff, because replacement staff members have limited knowledge of the program and its participants [54,74].

Another organizational variable that has received preliminary support in the extant literature is the age of the program. For example, Mears and colleagues [51] found that newer programs evidenced stronger programmatic effects, presumably because of the enthusiasm and sustainable human and fiscal resources surrounding the venture. This finding has also been found in the literature on correctional treatment (Craig Dowden, unpublished Master's thesis, 1998). Thus, more seasoned programs should give attention to maintaining both their enthusiasm and funding so they continue to provide positive impact for their clients.

A recent meta-analysis of the literature on correctional treatment provided strong empiric evidence for the clinical utility of a cluster of organizational-level variables termed "program integrity" [76]. Program integrity refers to a program that is conducted in practice as intended in theory and design [76–78]. In the meta-analysis by Andrews and Dowden [76], programs were evaluated on their adherence to certain indicators of program integrity: whether the program followed a specific model; whether the staff were appropriately selected, trained and supervised; whether printed materials (eg, program goals and content) were available; and whether changes in intermediate outcome measures were monitored. The results indicated that each of these aspects of program integrity was associated with enhanced program effectiveness. All these indicators, except for monitoring in-program changes, were linked with significant programmatic improvements in terms of client outcomes (eg, programs that incorporated these elements of program integrity yielded significantly higher mean reductions in reoffending than programs that did not use these elements).

Posttreatment factors

Aftercare

Aftercare is defined as the provision of therapeutic activities and support to the substance-abusing client following program completion, to help ensure the gains made during treatment are maintained afterwards [50,79,80]. This transference of treatment gains is necessary because one of the major criticisms lodged against substance-abuse treatment is that, because of the complexity of the problem, it is naive to expect that changes observed within a residential setting will transfer successfully to the community setting [52].

One of the reasons aftercare has been viewed as a critical factor in effective substance-abuse treatment programs is that past research has demonstrated that roughly 50% of the variation in postrelease failure in adult populations can be attributed to posttreatment factors (eg, family support) [81]. Studies that have examined the effects of aftercare intervention have consistently found that increased participation in aftercare is associated with a reduced risk of relapse [81]. Aftercare has also been related to the maintenance of proximal gains made in treatment [82].

A dearth of comparable data in the literature on adolescent substance abuse marks a significant knowledge gap [57]. Only one existing study was identified that tested the effects of aftercare with youth [83]. Preliminary results from a study using individual brief therapeutic telephone contacts during aftercare have shown promise [84]. Therapists and patients both report finding the approach acceptable, feasible, and useful.

Despite the intuitive appeal of this form of programming, few studies involving correctional populations have examined aftercare impacts [50]. A recent meta-analysis of the literature on correctional treatment provides preliminary evidence: it demonstrated that programs that incorporate elements of aftercare sessions into their program model yield moderate programmatic improvements [70].

Additional considerations

Protective factors

Past research has demonstrated that there is considerable individual variability in how adolescents respond to the same risk factors. Accordingly, experts in the field have attempted to identify protective or strength factors that contribute to the resilience of these juveniles. These studies mark a relatively new line of scientific inquiry within the field of adolescent substance-abuse treatment.

Protective factors are separate from risk factors and should not be viewed as the absence of risk factors [4]. In addition, it is premature to assume that protective and risk factors operate at opposite ends of the same continuum, because this claim has yet to be verified [85,86]. More precisely, these factors may moderate the risk of substance misuse, or in the ideal scenario, make the youth more resilient when faced with potentially harmful situations [85,87].

Gilvarry [4] listed several of the preeminent protective factors in the literature on adolescent substance abuse: a positive temperament; a family environment supportive to the youth; a functional, caring relationship with at least one adult; and an external support system that values and rewards prosocial values. Fergusson and colleagues [7] also found a series of protective factors including high intelligence, nonengagement in novelty-seeking behavior, and the absence of friendships with antisocial peers. Cooper and colleagues [88] examined protective factors among adolescents and found that parent–child communication, behavioral control (ie, how families express and maintain standards of behavior), and general family functioning were associated with lower levels of drug use. Additional protective factors include positive coping skills, self-efficacy, problem-solving ability, educational achievement, affect regulation, positive self-esteem, and positive response to authority [89,90].

Unfortunately, none of the studies examined in this article explored protective factors and their role in providing effective treatment to a young-offender population. The significance of protective factors for both the prediction and treatment of criminal behavior tied to substance abuse has several obvious implications. For example, treatment programs could be built around these strength factors to enhance preexisting positive conditions in the lives of young offenders. This approach has been adopted successfully in the family intervention, functional family therapy [91–93]. This approach has received strong empiric support for its therapeutic potential in populations of young offenders [91,94–96]. Therefore, in the future considerable resources should be dedicated to explore this topic in the treatment of substance abuse treatment in young offenders.

Dropout rates

A major problem that has plagued the field of substance-abuse treatment is the high dropout rates [37,97], a concern that has been noted in the literature on the treatment of nonoffenders as well [20]. This problem is a major consideration for program administrators. Individuals who drop out of treatment waste valuable and scarce program resources, because the costs expended during intake and initial treatment are not recovered through the reduction of problematic client behaviors such as recidivism or substance use/abuse [37]. Several variables associated with program attrition in adult probationers include unemployment and high levels of depression, anxiety, and hostility [37]. Psychopathology is a key client variable related to program attrition.

Given the importance of program attrition in the field of substance-abuse treatment, researchers should devote considerable energy to uncovering the factors that are predictive of this critical negative treatment outcome. Some intuitively appealing variables that may be expected to be reasonably linked with client attrition but require further empiric validation include the satisfaction of the client with the program [98], client expectations of the treatment process [99], and the quality of the relationship between the counselor and the client [100,101].

Directions for future research

This article has drawn together disparate lines of evidence examining the relationship between substance use and abuse and criminal activity and the variables that may affect the delivery of successful substance-abuse treatment for young offenders. Although much additional research is required across each of these areas, several key points are presented here to conclude the discussion.

More research needs to explore the specific relationships between the type of substance abuse and the corresponding type of criminal behavior. More specifically, several researchers have documented that certain types of substance abuse have strong influences on certain types of criminal activity but not on others [6,18]. Therefore, in designing a treatment protocol for individual offenders, knowledge of the type and magnitude of these specific relationships is imperative to ensure maximal therapeutic impact.

An additional area for future research may be exploring the personal motivations behind substance-abusing behavior in adolescents. Such research may provide a more direct understanding of why certain individuals are drawn to certain types of deviant activity [102]. For example, offenders who engage in substance-abusing behavior to self-medicate require a different intervention protocol from those who use substances to self-stimulate. Thus, understanding and appreciating the mechanisms underlying these differences in motivation will enhance the therapeutic effectiveness of substance-abuse program for young offenders.

As several correctional researchers have noted, some suggestions have been forwarded to deal with the problems related to client attrition from substance-abuse treatment programs [36], but future research must explore various mechanisms to address this important treatment issue [37,50,97]. One particular avenue would be to collect qualitative information, such as through a focus group format in which youthful offenders have the opportunity to explain what factors negatively affected their motivation for engaging in the program.

Summary

Although much research has been conducted on substance abuse and crime in general, much less has been aimed at exploring effective treatment strategies for young offenders. Despite these concerns, the available literature suggests that some programs are effective when delivered under certain conditions [37,50,80]. Practitioners can incorporate several strategies into their program delivery protocol that will enhance the therapeutic potential of the intervention. Box 1 provides list of issues that program administrators should consider when developing

Box 1. Checklist for delivering effective substance abuse treatment with young offenders

Client characteristics

- Ensure high-risk individuals receive the most intensive treatment services.
- Ensure program content and delivery style take into consideration the demographics of the treatment group including gender, age, and race/ethnicity.
- Assess the psychopathology of program clients and address this psychopathology before or, at the very least, during treatment.
- Assess client motivation and develop strategies to minimize the probability of program attrition by linking program participation with clear and observable rewards.
- Identify and target substance abuse problems for intervention as early as possible.

Program development

- Target multiple areas of need within the treatment strategy including familial relationships (eg, affection, communication), structural familial variables (eg, monitoring and supervision practices of the parents), academic and vocational performance, life skills, and antisocial peer group involvement.
- Deliver programs as much as possible within community settings to ensure maximum skill transfer. If residential treatment is the only available option, ensure that aftercare and advocacy/brokerage services are used.
- Deliver programs in financially supported correctional settings with low staff turnover and an atmosphere supportive of rehabilitation.
- Ensure attention is paid to program integrity (ie, ensure that the program is based on a specific, theoretical model, workers are trained in program delivery and are supervised by a trained supervisor, printed program materials are available describing program goals and content, in-program monitoring of key performance behaviors is conducted, and staff are selected on key interpersonal or skill factors).
- Identify and target protective or strength factors.
- Design program services for an extended period to ensure penetration of program content.
- Incorporate elements of relapse prevention into the treatment protocol.
- Ensure clients are matched to the appropriate program.

programs for treating adolescent substance abuse. This list is based on the most robust findings reviewed in the literature to date.

Acknowledgments

The authors thank Drs. Vladislav Ruchkin and Robert Vermeiren for their guidance during the editorial process. Their helpful comments greatly improved the quality of the final product, and the authors sincerely appreciate their input.

References

[1] Andrews DA, Bonta J. The psychology of criminal conduct. 3rd edition. Cincinnati (OH): Anderson Publishing; 2002.
[2] Farabee D, Shen H, Hser Y, et al. The effect of drug treatment on criminal behavior among adolescents in DATOS-A. J Adolesc Res 2001;16:679–96.
[3] Gendreau P. The principles of effective intervention with offenders. In: Harland A, editor. Choosing correctional options that work. Thousand Oaks (CA): Sage; 1996. p. 117–30.
[4] Gilvarry E. Substance abuse in young people. J Child Psychol Psychiatry 2000;41:55–80.
[5] Diagnostic and statistical manual of mental disorders. 4th edition. Washington (DC): American Psychiatric Association; 1994.
[6] Dawkins MP. Drug use and violent crime among adolescents. Adolescence 1997;32:395–405.
[7] Fergusson DM, Lynskey MT, Horwood LJ. Alcohol misuse and juvenile offending in adolescence. Addiction 1996;91:483–94.
[8] Huizinga D, Jakob-Chien C. The contemporaneous co-occurrence of serious and violent juvenile offending and other problem behaviors. In: Loeber R, Farrington DP, editors. Serious and violent juvenile offenders: risk factors and successful interventions. Thousand Oaks (CA): Sage; 1998. p. 47–67.
[9] Pickrel SG, Henggeler SW. Multisystemic therapy for adolescent substance abuse and dependence. Child Adolesc Psychiatr Clin N Am 1996;5:201–11.
[10] Watts WD, Wright LS. The relationship of alcohol, tobacco, marijuana, and other illegal drug use to delinquency among Mexican-American, black, and white adolescent males. Adolescence 1990;25:171–81.
[11] Pelissier B, Gaes G. United States federal prisons: drug users, drug testing, and drug treatment. Forum on Corrections Research 2001;13:15–7.
[12] Weekes JR, Moser AE, Langevin CM. Assessing substance abusing offenders for treatment. In: Latessa EJ, editor. What works—strategic solutions: the International Community Corrections Association examines substance abuse. Arlington (VA): Kirby Lithographic Company; 1998. p. 1–41.
[13] Yu J, Williford W. Alcohol, other drugs, and criminality: a structural analysis. Am J Drug Alcohol Abuse 1994;20:373–93.
[14] Bushman BJ, Cooper HM. Effects of alcohol on human aggression: an integrative research review. Psychol Bull 1990;107:341–54.
[15] Gustafson R. What do experimental paradigms tell us about alcohol-related aggressive responding? J Stud Alcohol 1993;11:20–9.
[16] Taylor SP, Chermack ST. Alcohol, drugs, and human physical aggression. J Stud Alcohol 1993;11:78–88.
[17] Dawkins R, Dawkins MP. Alcohol use and delinquency among black, white, and Hispanic adolescent offenders. Adolescence 1983;18:799–809.

[18] Farrell AD, Danish SJ, Howard CW. Relationship between drug use and other problem behaviors in urban adolescents. J Consult Clin Psychol 1992;60:705–12.
[19] Crowe AH. Drug identification and testing in the juvenile justice system. Washington (DC): Office of Juvenile Justice and Delinquency Prevention; 1998.
[20] Dobkin PL, Chabot L, Maliantovitch K, et al. Predictors of outcome in drug treatment of adolescent inpatients. Psychol Rep 1998;83:175–86.
[21] Catalano RF, Hawkins JD, Wells EA, et al. Evaluation of the effectiveness of adolescent drug abuse treatment, assessment of risks for relapse, and promising approaches for relapse prevention. Int J Addict 1990;25:1085–140.
[22] Feigelman W. Day-care treatment for multiple drug abusing adolescents: social factors linked with completing treatment. J Psychoactive Drugs 1987;19:335–44.
[23] Hubbard RL, Cavanaugh ER, Craddock SG, et al. Characteristics, behaviors, and outcomes for youth in the TOPS. In: Friedman AS, Beschner GM, editors. Treatment services for adolescent substance abusers. Washington (DC): National Institute on Drug Abuse, US Department of Health and Human Services; 1985.
[24] Sells SB, Simpson DD. Predicting treatment outcomes for juvenile and young adult clients in the Pennsylvania substance-abuse system. In: Breschner GM, Friedman AS, editors. Youth drug abuse: problems, issues, and treatment. Lexington (MA): D.C. Heath; 1979. p. 629–56.
[25] D'Amico EJ. Factors that impact adolescents' intentions to utilize alcohol-related prevention services. J Behav Health Serv Res 2005;32(3):332–41.
[26] Latimer JW. A meta-analytic examination of youth delinquency, family treatment, and recidivism. Can J Criminol 2001;43:237–54.
[27] Webster-Stratton C, Taylor T. Nipping early risk factors in the bud: preventing substance abuse, delinquency, and violence in adolescence through interventions targeted at young children (0–8 years). Prev Sci 2001;2:165–92.
[28] Gordon MS, Kinlock TW, Battjes RJ. Correlates of early substance use and crime among adolescents entering outpatient substance abuse treatment. Am J Drug Alcohol Abuse 2004; 30(1):39–60.
[29] Vanderburg SA, Weekes JR, Millson WA. Early substance use and its impact on adult offender alcohol and drug problems. Forum on Corrections Research 1995;7(1):14–6.
[30] Van Kammen WB, Loeber R, Stouthamer-Loeber M. Substance use and its relationship to antisocial and delinquent behavior in young boys. J Youth Adolesc 1991;20:399–414.
[31] De Angelis GG, Koon M, Golstein E. Treatment of adolescent phencyclidine (PCP) abusers. J Psychoactive Drugs 1980;12:279–86.
[32] Friedman AS, Glickman NW, Morrissey MR. Prediction of successful treatment outcome by client characteristics and retention in adolescent drug treatment programs: a large-scale cross validation study. J Drug Educ 1986;16:149–65.
[33] Simourd L, Andrews DA. Correlates of delinquency : a look at gender differences. Forum on Corrections Research 1994;6:26–31.
[34] Bloom B. Gender-responsive programming for women offenders: guiding principles and practices. Forum on Corrections Research 1999;11:22–7.
[35] Covington S. Creating gender-specific treatment for substance-abusing women and girls in community correctional settings. The International Community Corrections Association Journal 1998:24–9.
[36] Randall J, Henggeler SW, Pickrel SG, et al. Psychiatric comorbidity and the 16-month trajectory of substance-abusing and substance-dependent juvenile offenders. J Am Acad Child Adolesc Psychiatry 1999;38:1118–24.
[37] Hiller ML, Knight K, Simpson DD. Risk factors that predict drop-out from corrections-based treatment for drug abuse. Prison J 1999;79:411–30.
[38] Kaminer Y, Tarter RE, Bukstein OG, et al. Comparison between treatment completers and noncompleters among dually diagnosed substance-abusing adolescents. J Am Acad Child Adolesc Psychiatry 1992;31:1046–9.
[39] Breda C, Heflinger CA. Predicting incentives to change among adolescents with substance abuse disorder. Am J Drug Alcohol Abuse 2004;30(2):251–68.

[40] Pagnin D, de Queiroz V, Saggese E. Predictors of attrition from day treatment of adolescents with substance-related disorders. Addictive Behaviors 2005;30(5):1065–9.

[41] Andrews DA, Bonta J, Hoge RD. Classification for effective rehabilitation: rediscovering psychology. Crim Justice Behav 1990;17:19–52.

[42] Dowden C, Andrews DA. What works in young offender treatment: a meta-analysis. Forum on Corrections Research 1999;11(2):21–4.

[43] Lipsey MW. What do we learn from 400 research studies on the effectiveness of treatment with juvenile delinquents? In: McGuire J, editor. What works: reducing reoffending—guidelines from research and practice. Chichester (UK): John Wiley & Sons; 1995. p. 63–78.

[44] Lipsey MW, Wilson DB. Effective intervention for serious juvenile offenders: a synthesis of research. In: Loeber R, Farrington DP, editors. Serious and violent offenders: risk factors and successful interventions. Thousand Oaks (CA): Sage; 1998. p. 313–45.

[45] Dowden C, Andrews DA. What works for female offenders: a meta-analytic review. Crime Delinq 1999;45:438–52.

[46] Andrews DA, Dowden C, Rettinger JL. Special populations. In: Winterdyk J, editor. Corrections in Canada. Toronto (Canada): Prentice Hall Allyn & Bacon; 2001. p. 170–212.

[47] Cullen FT, Gendreau P. Assessing correctional rehabilitation: policy, practice, and prospects. In: Horney J, editor. Criminal justice, vol. 3. Washington (DC): National Institute of Justice, Department of Justice; 2000. p. 109–75.

[48] Rossi PH, Freeman HE, Lipsey MW. Evaluation: a systematic approach. 6th edition. Thousand Oaks (CA): Sage; 1999.

[49] Sealock MD, Gottfredson DC, Gallagher CA. Drug treatment for juvenile offenders: some good and bad news. J Res Crime Delinq 1997;34:210–36.

[50] Mears DP, Kelly WR. Linking process and outcomes in evaluating a statewide drug treatment program for youthful offenders. Crime Delinq 2002;48:99–115.

[51] Mears DP, Kelly WR, Durden ED. Findings from a process evaluation of a statewide residential substance abuse treatment program for youthful offenders. Prison J 2001;81:246–70.

[52] Prendergast ML, Podus D, Chang E. Program factors and treatment outcomes in drug dependence treatment: an examination using meta-analysis. Subst Use Misuse 2000;35:1931–65.

[53] Harachi TW, Abbott RD, Catalano RF, et al. Opening the black box: using process evaluation measures to assess implementation and theory building. Am J Psychol 1999;27:711–31.

[54] Hill JK, Andrews DA, Hoge RD. Meta-analysis of treatment programs for young offenders: the effect of clinically relevant treatment on recidivism, with controls introduced for various methodological variables. Can J Program Eval 1991;6:97–109.

[55] Annis HM. Effective treatment for drug and alcohol problems: what do we know? Forum on Corrections Research 1990;2(4). Available at: http://www.csc-scc.gc.ca/text/pblct/forum/e024/e024j.shtml. Accessed January 21, 2005.

[56] Latimer WW, Newcomb M, Winters KC, et al. Adolescent substance abuse treatment outcome: the role of substance abuse severity, psychosocial, and treatment factors. J Consult Clin Psychol 2000;68:684–96.

[57] Sambrano S, Springer JF, Sale E, et al. Understanding prevention effectiveness in real-world settings: the national cross-site evaluation of high risk youth programs. Am J Drug Alcohol Abuse 2005;31(3):491–515.

[58] Dowden C, Antonowicz DH, Andrews DA. The effectiveness of relapse prevention with offenders: a meta-analysis. Int J Offender Ther Comp Criminol 2003;47:516–28.

[59] Garrett CJ. Effects of residential treatment on adjudicated delinquents: a meta-analysis. J Res Crime Delinq 1985;22:287–308.

[60] Pearson FS, Lipton DS. A meta-analytic review of the effectiveness of corrections-based treatments for drug abuse. Prison J 1999;79:384–410.

[61] Wright DR, Fitzpatrick KM. Psychosocial correlates of substance use behaviors among African American youth. Adolescence 2004;39(156):653–68.

[62] Latimer J, Dowden C, Morton-Bourgon KE. Treating youth in conflict with the law: a new meta-analysis. Ottawa (Canada): Research and Statistics Division, Department of Justice Canada; 2003.

[63] Roe S, Becker J. Drug prevention with vulnerable young people. Drugs Educ Prev Policy 2005;12(2):85–100.
[64] Greenwood PW. Substance abuse problems among high-risk youth and potential interventions. Crime Delinq 1992;38:444–58.
[65] Wilson DB, Gottfredson DC, Najaka SS. School-based prevention of problem behaviors: a meta-analysis. J Quant Criminol 2001;17:247–72.
[66] Vaughn MG, Howard MO. Adolescent substance abuse treatment: a synthesis of controlled evaluations. Res Soc Work Pract 2004;14(5):325–35.
[67] DeMarsh J, Kumpfer KL. Family-oriented interventions for the prevention of chemical dependency in children and adolescents. Journal of Children in Contemporary Society 1985; 18:117–52.
[68] Kumpfer KL, Turner CW. The social ecology model of adolescent substance abuse: implications for prevention. Int J Addict 1990;25:435–63.
[69] Dowden C, Andrews DA. Does family intervention work for delinquents? Results of a meta-analysis. Canadian Journal of Criminology and Criminal Justice 2003;45:327–42.
[70] Dowden C, Medveduke D, Andrews DA. The importance of treatment targets and program design for the delivery of effective family treatment to juvenile delinquents: a meta-analysis. Poster presented at the annual meeting of the Canadian Psychological Association. Montreal (Canada), June 10, 2005.
[71] Laws DR. Relapse prevention: the state of the art. J Interpers Violence 1999;14:285–302.
[72] Stephens RS, Roffman RA, Simpson EE. Treating adult marijuana dependence: a test of the relapse prevention model. J Consult Clin Psychol 1994;62:92–9.
[73] Farabee D, Prendergast M, Cartier J, et al. Barriers to implementing effective correctional drug treatment programs. Prison J 1999;79:150–62.
[74] Waldron HB, Kaminer Y. On the learning curve: the emerging evidence supporting cognitive-behavioral therapies for adolescent substance abuse. Addiction 2004;99(93):93–106.
[75] McBride DC, VanderWaal CJ, Terry YM, et al. Breaking the cycle of drug use among juvenile offenders. Washington (DC): National Institute of Justice, Department of Justice; 1999.
[76] Andrews DA, Dowden C. Managing correctional treatment for reduced recidivism: a meta-analytic review of program integrity. Leg Criminol Psychol 2005;10(2):173–87.
[77] Hollin C. The meaning and implications of "programme integrity". In: McGuire J, editor. What works: reducing reoffending: guidelines from research and practice. Chichester (UK): John Wiley & Sons; 1995. p. 193–206.
[78] Correctional Service Canada. Literature review: substance abuse treatment modalities 1996. Available at: http://www.cscscc.gc.ca/text/pblct/litrev/treatmod/toce.shtml. Accessed January 21, 2005.
[79] Lurigio AJ. Drug treatment availability and effectiveness: studies of the general and criminal justice populations. Crim Justice Behav 2000;27:495–528.
[80] Stein SL, Garrett CJ, Christiansen D. Treatment strategies for juvenile delinquents to decrease substance abuse and prevent adult drug and alcohol dependence. In: Milkman HB, Sederer LI, editors. Treatment choices for alcoholism and substance abuse. Lexington (MA): D.C. Heath and Co.; 1990. p. 225–33.
[81] Moos RH, Finney JW, Cronkite RC. Alcoholism treatment: context, process, and outcome. New York: Oxford University Press; 1990.
[82] Godley SH, Godley MD, Dennis ML. The Assertive Aftercare Protocol for adolescent substance abusers. In: Wagner EF, Waldron HB, editors. Innovations in adolescent substance abuse interventions. Amsterdam: Pergamon/Elsevier Science Inc; 2001. p. 313–31.
[83] Kaminer Y. Dial for therapy: aftercare for adolescent substance use disorders. J Am Acad Child Adolesc Psychiatry 2004;43(9):1171–4.
[84] Newcomb MD, Felix-Ortiz M. Multiple protective and risk factors for drug use and abuse: cross-sectional and prospective findings. J Pers Soc Psychol 1992;63:280–96.
[85] Rutter M. Protective factors: independent or interactive? J Am Acad Child Adolesc Psychiatry 1991;30:151–2.

[86] Newcomb MD, Bentler PM. Consequences of adolescent drug use: impact on the lives of young adults. Newbury Park (CA): Sage; 1988.
[87] Graves KL. Risky sexual behavior and alcohol use among young adults: results from a national survey. Am J Health Promot 1995;10:27–36.
[88] Cooper M, Agocha V, Sheldon M. A motivational perspective on risky behaviors: the role of personality and affect regulatory processes. J Pers 2000;68(6):1059–88.
[89] Glantz DM, Sloboda Z. Analysis and reconceptualization of resilience. Resilience and development: positive life adaptations. New York: Kluwer Academic/Plenum Publishers; 1999. p. 109–28.
[90] Alexander JF, Parsons BV. Short-term family intervention: a therapy outcome study. J Consult Clin Psychol 1973;2:195–201.
[91] Alexander JF, Pugh C, Parsons BV, et al. Functional family therapy. In: Elliott DS, editor. Blueprints for violence prevention, book 3. 2nd edition. Boulder (CO): Center for the Study and Prevention of Violence, Institute of Behavioral Science, University of Colorado; 2000. p. 1–8.
[92] Alexander JF, Sexton TL, Robbins MS. The developmental status of family therapy in family psychology intervention science. In: Liddle H, Santisteban D, Leavant R, et al, editors. Family psychology intervention science. Washington (DC): American Psychological Association; 2000. p. 17–40.
[93] Barton C, Alexander JF, Waldron H, et al. Generalizing treatment effects of functional family therapy: three replications. Am J Fam Ther 1985;13:16–26.
[94] Gordon DA, Graves K, Arbuthnot J. The effect of functional family therapy for delinquents on adult criminal behavior. Crim Justice Behav 1995;22:60–73.
[95] Klein NC, Alexander JF, Parsons BV. Impact of family systems intervention on recidivism and sibling delinquency: a model of primary prevention and program evaluation. J Consult Clin Psychol 1977;3:469–74.
[96] Henggeler SW, Pickrel SG, Brondino, et al. Eliminating (almost) treatment dropout of substance abusing or dependent delinquents through home-based multisystemic therapy. Am J Psychiatry 1996;153:427–8.
[97] Hiller ML, Knight K, Simpson DD. Prison-based substance abuse treatment, residential aftercare, and recidivism. Addiction 1999;94:833–42.
[98] McCorkel J, Harrison LD, Inciardi JA. How treatment is constructed among graduates and dropouts in a prison therapeutic community. J Offender Rehabil 1998;27:37–59.
[99] Broome KM, Knight DK, Hiller ML, et al. Drug treatment process indicators for probationers and prediction of recidivism. J Subst Abuse Treat 1996;13:487–91.
[100] Broome KM, Knight DK, Knight K, et al. Peer, family and motivational influences on drug treatment process and recidivism for probationers. J Clin Psychol 1997;53:387–97.
[101] White HR. Marijuana use and delinquency: a test of the "independent cause" hypothesis. J Drug Issues 1991;21:231–56.
[102] Anglin MD, Hser Y. Treatment of drug abuse. In: Tonry M, Wilson JQ, editors. Drugs and crime. Chicago: University of Chicago Press; 1990. p. 393–460.

ELSEVIER
SAUNDERS

Child Adolesc Psychiatric Clin N Am
15 (2006) 539–556

CHILD AND
ADOLESCENT
PSYCHIATRIC CLINICS
OF NORTH AMERICA

Treatment and Postrelease Rehabilitative Programs for Juvenile Offenders

Lee A. Underwood, PsyD[a,b,*], Pamela Knight, MA[a]

[a]*Regent University, School of Psychology and Counseling, Virginia Beach, VA, USA*
[b]*National Center for Mental Health and Juvenile Justice, Delmar, NY, USA*

One of the critical changes in juvenile justice during the past decade is the increasing use of treatment interventions (mental health, substance use, skill development, and others) for juvenile offenders. Whereas treatment was previously handled on a case-by-case basis, most juveniles are now required to be treated [1–5]. The recommended treatment of youths forces juvenile justice administrators to expand their principle tenet (emphasis on rehabilitation, control, and custody) to include the implementation of best-practice and evidence-based treatment interventions. In reality, however, juveniles are often involved in juvenile justice programs that are not necessarily designed to provide effective postrelease programs [5,6]. Many juvenile justice systems are not equipped to handle the acute needs of youths [5,7]. Juvenile corrections professionals are hindered by the lack of research, questionable models of care, insufficient policy development, ineffective experience and training of direct-care staff members, and inadequate practices for successfully treating these youths and their families [2,8–11]. Although juvenile justice organizations have not historically provided standardized and best-practice treatment services for its youths, they have nonetheless begun to address this area [12,13].

The growing need for juvenile justice organizations to address the treatment needs of youths is further complicated by the increasing numbers of these youths entering the juvenile justice system. Each year, more than 2 million youths under the age of 18 years are arrested. More than 100,000 are placed in youth cor-

* Corresponding author. Regent University, School of Psychology and Counseling, 1000 University Drive, CRB 215, Virginia Beach, VA 23463.

E-mail address: leeunde@regent.edu (L.A. Underwood).

doi:10.1016/j.chc.2005.11.009

rections facilities [14]. At the same time, there has been a significant increase in the number of juveniles who have been diagnosed as having mental health and substance use disorders [14–16]. Studies of juvenile offenders who have mental health disorders indicate that 20% to 30% of all juveniles who enter the justice system present serious mental disorders and other service needs [5,6,17–20].

Juvenile justice plays a key role in coordinating systems of care for the provision of treatment for youths involved in postrelease programs. Juvenile justice and treatment providers must develop the capacity to provide effective post-release treatment. Providers working with youths involved in postrelease programs must understand the pertinent issues that are unique to juveniles who have treatment needs [13,21,22].

Effective postrelease rehabilitation programs must simultaneously balance three major goals: (1) ensuring public community safety, (2) holding youths accountable for their actions, and (3) providing an environment in which youths can develop into capable, productive, and responsible citizens [23]. To address these goals adequately, attention must be paid to the reinforcement of effective programs.

This article summarizes a body of literature on systematic postrelease rehabilitative approaches to juvenile offenders. The principles of cognitive-behavioral theoretical models and core postrelease treatment strategies are described. The necessity of focusing on postrelease rehabilitative programs that center on problem behaviors within the context of schools, family, peers, culture, and socioeconomic level is discussed. A review of youths who have specialized needs in light of postrelease practices is provided. Last, several model postrelease rehabilitation programs, their treatment targets, and their outcomes are discussed.

Cognitive-behavioral treatment models

The treatment literature indicates that cognitive-behavioral treatment models are most effectively used to treat juvenile offenders involved in postrelease programs [24–27]. In developing cognitive-behavioral treatment models, researchers should rely on research models that are empirically based, multidimensional, and focus on a causal modeling approach [28]. Results of causal modeling studies show that serious mental illness and delinquent behavior in juveniles are multidetermined and that postrelease treatment interventions should be flexible enough to address multiple known and unknown determinants [29–31].

Cognitive-behavior therapies provide a framework for multiple and integrated postrelease programs and interventions based on a rational approach to change. For example, treatment interventions used from functional family therapy aim at improving the psychosocial functioning of youths and their families and promoting the parents' ability to monitor youths [32]. Providers rely on motivational enhancement techniques to engage youths and their families effectively in therapeutic dialogue [33]. Youth and family members are taught about high-risk situations and recovery techniques to prevent and recover from relapse.

The next section provides information on core postrelease treatment strategies. These strategies may be tailored, depending on the nature of the postrelease rehabilitation program and the characteristics of the youth.

Core postrelease treatment strategies

Core postrelease treatment strategies, in part, focus on skill building with the ultimate goal of reducing recidivism and delinquent behaviors that lead to contact with the juvenile justice system. These strategies range from mental health screens and assessments to the provision of applicable case-management services.

Initial mental health screening

Before youths enter postrelease programs, an initial mental health screening should be provided. The mental health screening should be designed to identify youths who are at increased risk of having learning disorders, mental health, substance abuse, and delinquency needs that warrant immediate attention, intervention, or a more comprehensive review. Screening is a triage process and should be conducted on the first day of a youth's admittance to the program with follow-up screenings throughout the stay in the program [34].

Follow-up assessment and diagnoses

Follow-up assessment and diagnoses should be conducted on youths whose initial mental health screening is elevated. The assessment is designed to be a more comprehensive and individualized examination of the psychosocial needs and problems identified during the initial screening. The assessment includes the type and extent of mental health problems, substance abuse, delinquency needs, community adjustment, and recommendations for treatment intervention.

Generally, following an assessment, diagnoses may be provided. The diagnoses provide the juvenile justice and mental health providers with critical information that leads to the implementation of proven and evidence-based treatment principles. Like screening, assessment serves different purposes at different stages in the juvenile justice process. For example, at postrelease intake, assessment results may be used to streamline services, resulting in more appropriate and individualized postrelease service plans.

Treatment planning

Before a youth is released from a youth corrections facility, a discharge plan should be developed. The discharge plan provides critical information for the transition into the postrelease program. Based on the need, interdisciplinary team members of the postrelease program should recommend and oversee the implementation of treatment/case-management services. The purpose of the treatment plan is to integrate observations and findings from paraprofessional and professional staff members regarding the youth and to transfer that knowledge to the treatment plan. Treatment plans address issues in education, community adjustment, life skills, medical, mental health, community life activities, and other critical areas of care. Treatment plans serve as a contract between the youth, the family, the juvenile justice staff, and the treatment provider. Treatment plans should be consistently updated, generally on a monthly basis, with a formal meeting of professional staff with the youth, his or her parent, and members of the interdisciplinary treatment team. Treatment plans should be clearly spelled out with measurable goals and objectives and shared with all members of the interdisciplinary treatment team. All youths should review and sign their treatment plans.

Treatment stage models

When measuring treatment progress of youths involved in postrelease programs, it is important to recognize the impact of treatment-stage models. These models are designed to evaluate the progress of the youth by integrating manifested behaviors with treatment outcomes. Treatment-stage models should be implemented in ways that target internalized and externalized behaviors. The stages of treatment should be hierarchical and should build upon the knowledge obtained in the previous stage. For example, each stage should emphasize a major step toward treatment mastery and may be divided as follows:

Level I: Develop readiness for treatment
Level II: Understand behavior change
Level III: Achieve behavior change
Level IV: Implement the relapse prevention plan

The treatment-stage system should include specific treatment and behavioral criteria for attainment, and promotion should depend on the youth's demonstration of appropriate thinking, behavior, and progress in treatment.

Transition planning

Transition planning involves bidirectional responsibilities and requires collaboration among multiple community providers. It is understood that some youths will be fully released from postrelease program services, whereas others may be stepped down to less restrictive programs. Efforts in the past to help youths transition from more highly to less restrictive programs have only been as good as the program's partnerships in the community. To transition youths effectively, the provider should rely upon an integrated case-management system to ensure that key individuals in all the relevant systems are involved. A significant role of postrelease programs is to coordinate the timing and delivery of services and assist each youth and his or her family in obtaining services upon release from the program.

Ongoing treatment/case-management services

Based on the program needs of youths involved in postrelease programs, specific treatment interventions should be implemented to address a wide variety of problems and solutions. The case-management services should target behavior symptoms and the provision of skills training for specific behavioral deficits. The treatment and case-management interventions should rely on best-practice and evidence-based procedures including positive reinforcement, behavioral monitoring, goal monitoring, behavioral shaping, coaching, modeling, role-play practice, and constructive feedback. These procedures may be administered in small groups of individuals and during individual counseling sessions. The provision of skill training should target a variety of symptoms by using the following techniques: staying on topic, focusing attention, avoiding problem situations, identifying emotional triggers, accurately identifying their and others' emotions, improving interpersonal behavior, and learning coping skills. Skills training for families should include improving their understanding of mental health and substance-abuse disorders, recognizing and decreasing stresses that may lead to relapse, and teaching effective communication skills [22].

Structured counseling services

Structured individual and crisis counseling

Structured individual and crisis counseling services should be used with youths based upon their level of risk for recidivism and psychosocial need. These services can be rendered by a paraprofessional or graduate prepared provider [12]. As treatment progresses, the frequency of individual counseling may be changed. Individual counseling should focus on aspects of the youth's mental health, substance use, delinquency, community adjustment, and family needs. Individual counseling should also focus on daily issues that arise that are pertinent to the youth's behavior symptoms. Crisis intervention services should be provided to alleviate negative emotional symptoms (eg, depression, anxiety, guilt) experienced by some youths. These services should be designed to encourage youths to use effective coping strategies.

Structured group counseling

Structured group counseling should be used with youths to improve their coping and problem-solving skills. Group counseling should occur in process and psychoeducational group modules, which should be short term and relatively structured. A group-counseling schedule should be used, and the group sessions should be scheduled sequentially, beginning with basic skills and advancing to intermediate and higher level skills. During the group sessions, each youth's interactions should be observed, and immediate feedback should be provided to help offset the development of negative peer groups [35].

Family interventions

Current studies support the need to shift away from the individual intrapsychic view of services to one that encompasses the family [29]. An examination of all key factors influencing the youth should be involved in family interventions (ie, school, peers, culture, and socioeconomic level). Family interventions should provide a variety of services consisting of live face-to-face sessions, telephone sessions, family group sessions, or a combination of these methods. According to Underwood and colleagues [22], those applying interventions with families should consider the following assumptions:

1. Every youth enters treatment with a "family," whether distant, functional, or dysfunctional, and the involvement of their family is a critical component in ensuring compliance and developing skills necessary to build and support productive lifestyle changes.
2. The family should be seen as the primary socializing unit and in most cases as the most influential system to which the youth belongs. The focus of family interventions should be on the family strengths.
3. The youth cannot be considered as separate from the social context from which he or she resides.
4. The family remains a family, whether reunited or not, and family members often will continue to have relationships throughout their lives.

The relationship between youths who have special needs and postrelease practices

From a community safety perspective, it is important to identify youths who have specialized needs to address those needs adequately with the purpose of rehabilitation. The behaviors of these youths may or may not develop along the same pathways as other youths [30], potentially increasing their risk to the community. Youths who have special needs, including those who have histories of being traumatized, of significant substance use problems, of severe family dysfunctions, and ethnic minority youths, require specialized postrelease intervention and treatment services. Specialized and culturally competent interventions must be integrated into the treatment plan for these youths. Collaboration with care systems and providers is especially relevant with these youths to manage them effectively in postrelease programs [36].

Traumatized youths

Many youths have been exposed to traumatic events. Whether these events have consequences depends on internal and external resources and the nature and the extent of the event. Juveniles vary considerably in their responses to traumatic events. Some youths may experience devastating, horrific events and have few effects, whereas others may experience minor events and have significant long-term reactions. It is important to understand that many normal experiences (eg, an illness or death in the family) may be traumatic [37,38]. Certain types of experiences increase the likelihood of psychologic damage, including being taken by surprise, trapped, or exposed to the point of exhaustion (eg, experiencing lack of sleep, hunger, heat, or cold), experiencing physical violation or injury, being exposed to extreme violence, and witnessing grotesque death [38]. The degree of psychologic damage is indeed related to treatment outcomes for youths in both residential and postrelease rehabilitative programs. Traumatized youths tend to be more emotionally vulnerable in their communities and present histories of aggression [38].

The approach in postrelease rehabilitative treatment programs may need to be adapted for these youths. Treatment expectations and curricula should be consistent with the empiric literature for these youths.

Substance-abusing youths

Youths placed in residential facilities are much more likely than youths in public schools to report the use of alcohol, drugs, and illegal substances, and they are more likely to initiate substance use at an earlier age. In recent years, it has been concluded that youths who abuse substances present with higher rates of comorbid psychiatric problems, such as depression and conduct disorder [39–41], and that youths who abuse substances are especially at high risk of co-occurring mental health and substance-use disorders [14,42]. A 1999 study reported that psychiatric comorbidity of substance use with internalizing disorders may have a different outcome than comorbidity of substance use with externalizing disorders [43,44]. For example, adolescent substance abuse combined with comorbid externalizing disorders predicted a high rate of school dropout [45] and inpatient treatment failure, [46] whereas comorbid internalizing disorders predicted completion of inpatient treatment for substance-abusing adolescents [47].

Family and environmental difficulties

The profiles of juveniles in postrelease rehabilitative programs vividly illustrate the scope of family and environmental risk factors. Family factors that have been consistently implicated in juvenile justice include poor parent–child relationships, neglect, coercive child rearing [29], lack of warmth and affection, inconsistent parenting, violence, sexual abuse, disrupted attachments, and parental substance abuse [31].

Various studies have linked delinquent behavior and emotional distress with many different aspects of family functioning that may very well impact the youths while in the community. Factors described in literature that may contribute to poor adjustment while involved in postrelease programs are familial antisocial behavior or values, including delinquent behavior as part of the family history, harsh parental discipline, and family conflict [49]. Several studies across a range of populations related delinquent and poorly controlled emotional regulation to a lack of parental monitoring, neglect, poor discipline methods, and conflict about discipline [48,50–52]. Similarly associated are low levels of parental warmth, acceptance, and affection, low cohesion, high conflict and hostility, divorce, parental absence, and parental loss [51,53,54].

Incorporating the findings of the aforementioned literature into postrelease rehabilitative treatment programs may require program adaptations. Treatment expectations and curricula should be consistent with the empiric literature for these youths.

Ethnic minority youths

Ethnic minorities, specifically African Americans and Latinos, are increasingly at risk for entry in the juvenile justice systems rather than treatment systems [55–58]. Delinquent behavior and emotional disorders in youths of color stem from complicated social, medical, and psychologic factors [55,59]. Their clinical profiles are characteristic of a young, undereducated, truant from school living in a single-family household headed by mother who is likely to be unemployed and on welfare [60–62].

Correlations with delinquency among youths of color include lack of legitimate job opportunities, increasing social isolation, poor schools, and weak community organizations [63]. Urban poverty, homelessness, and social disorganization yield maternal and child risk factors that include low birth weight, cognitive impairment, and child abuse/neglect, each of which constitutes a risk factor for crime and violence in adolescence and young adulthood [63].

Additionally, substantial evidence indicates that ethnic minority youths involved in postrelease programs should have their individualized needs addressed by integrating procedures that influence youths' decision making [60,61,64]. Providers involved in postrelease programs should continually review their goals and objectives to ensure that the needs of ethnic minority youths are addressed. Providers should be trained in motivational enhancement techniques, stages of change, and engagement strategies.

Promising postrelease rehabilitation programs

Postrelease rehabilitation programs may consist of system diversion, non–system diversion, and residential community corrections. According to Whitehead and Lab [65], system-diversion programs are those services that fully divert youths from the juvenile justice system. Examples of these programs may include family counseling, crisis counseling, vocational training, and Big Brother/Big Sister–related organizations. Conversely, non–system-diversion programs are services that are formally part of the juvenile justice system. These services may include court-ordered family counseling, skills training, and informal probation. Community corrections programs are alternatives to incarceration, such as independent living, work programs, probation, parole, and other programs designed to manage adolescents in the community [66].

In determining the effectiveness of postrelease programs and their impact on recidivism, the individual characteristics of youths must be considered. For example, certain treatments may be more effective with certain subgroups of youths. In general, cognitive-behavioral programs tend to produce the best results [29].

Postrelease treatment programs should rely on the following:

1. Use of clear-cut and objective diagnostic indicators to ensure a high level of services
2. Use of family intervention services that are inclusive and culturally relevant
3. Use of treatment interventions that are empowering for youths and their families
4. Implementation of ongoing reliability and validity studies
5. Use of reliable and accurate treatment protocols that have sound empiric research with demonstrated effectiveness
6. Use of multiple interventions that address a variety of risk factors (eg, family, school, peer, school, community)
7. Use of mental health providers, not correctional staff, as primary treatment providers
8. Collaboration between juvenile justice, mental health, substance abuse, and education systems

Many innovative, promising, best-practice and evidence-based postrelease rehabilitation programs are available to practitioners in the field. The promising programs described in this section were selected because they adhere to the values and principles of empiricism and have demonstrated their effectiveness [67]. Many programs are designed to address the multiple determinants of problem behavior. The authors have selected postrelease rehabilitation programs with at least some documented use in juvenile justice or clinical settings and some evidence of effectiveness and practical use.

Multisystemic therapy

When multisystemic therapy (MST) was first established in the early 1980s, Henggeler and Bourdin [68] described it as "a family-ecological systems approach" [69]. MST is now considered to be an intensive family- and community-based treatment for youths who display antisocial behaviors that put them at risk for out-of-home placement. MST has been applied to youths who have a variety of clinical problems: (1) chronic and violent juvenile offenders, (2) substance-abusing juvenile offenders, (3) adolescent sexual offenders, (4) youths in psychiatric crisis (homicidal, suicidal, and psychotic youths), and (5) youths who have maltreating families [44]. In treating these particular populations, the ultimate goals of MST programs are to reduce the rates of antisocial behavior, enhance the youth's functioning, and decrease the use of out-of-home placements (incarceration and residential treatment). MST's focal point is on the juvenile's surrounding environment (eg, neighborhood, family, peers, school) and how it contributes to the juvenile's well being. Service delivery occurs within the home environment and the community. Cortes [70] posited that many authors believe in the effectiveness of home-based family therapy because it reduces the attrition rate of families who may not trust the mental health field or may not possess transportation. Home-based services may also benefit the juvenile and his or her family because the family is more at ease, and therefore is able to develop a better relationship with the therapist while maintaining some type of control. Home-based services provide more accessible services for low-income families [29].

Multisystemic services are provided for male and female juveniles between 12 and 17 years of age. Because of their chronic antisocial behaviors, these juveniles are at risk of being placed outside their home environment. The duration of MST services is usually based on the needs of the juvenile and the family, but the general estimate of MST service duration is 4 months.

A body of research supports the effectiveness of MST for juveniles involved in postrelease programs, with reductions up to 70% in long-term rates of re-arrest, reductions up to 64% in out-of-home placements, and improvements in family functioning [31,44].

Functional family therapy

Functional family therapy is a family-based intervention. Functional family therapy services involve four different phases, namely impression, motivation, behavior change, and generalization, and include assessments of the family, specific interventions used throughout the treatment, and the goals of the therapist. The phases allow a systematized approach to the care of youths and families. Functional family therapy's ultimate goal is to enhance the family's pattern of communication and help family members address the positive aspects of each family member rather than dwelling on the negative. Additional goals include enhancing parenting and problem-solving skills [32].

Functional family therapy renders services for youths between the ages of 6 and 18 years. A positive aspect of functional family therapy is that it recently incorporated multiethnic and multicultural components into its program. This program addresses delinquent behavior, substance abuse, and commonly seen mental health disorders among juveniles, including conduct disorder and oppositional defiant disorder.

Functional family therapy has displayed several positive outcomes. With less serious juvenile offenders, there has been a 50% to 75% reduction in recidivism rates; a 35% reduction in recidivism rates has been reported for more severe juvenile offenders [32].

Multidimensional treatment foster care

Multidimensional treatment foster care (MTFC) is an alternative to placing juvenile offenders in group homes or residential facilities. Smith [71] posited that MTFC is designed to take advantage of the socializing role of the family by using MTFC-trained foster parents, who provide behavior management techniques on a daily basis to youths placed in their home. One of the most popular behavior management techniques is the point-and-level system. As described by Rimm and Masters [72], earning points reinforces behavior, and losing points discourages undesirable behavior. Eddy and Chamberlain [73] discussed four key components, supervision, discipline, positive adult-youth relationship, and decreased association with delinquent peers, which contribute to MTFC's effectiveness. The ultimate goal of this program is for the juvenile offender to be reunited with the family in the natural home environment. Intensive parental training is provided to give parents/guardians more effective methods of parenting the juvenile when reunited. This program relies on the use of behavioral management methods to elicit change.

MTFC renders services to juvenile delinquents who need assistance in addressing familial difficulties. The expected duration of the MTFC program is 6 to 9 months. During this time, the program focuses on reducing criminal behavior, improving school attendance, establishing positive peer relationships, and improving familial relationships. Following the termination of services, the 12 months of intensive parental training continue.

At 6 months and 2 years follow-up after treatment, Chamberlain [74] demonstrated significantly lower rates of violent incidents in children who received MTFC than seen in those who received services in group home care. Also these juveniles ran away from placements three times less often than they did before receiving the MTFC treatment [74].

Intensive aftercare program

Altschuler and Armstrong [75] developed the intensive aftercare program model in 1988 as a program specifically designed to meet the needs of juvenile offenders and to assist them with transitioning from youth corrections facilities back into the community. Services are initiated when the juvenile first enters residential placement and continue after the juvenile's release to the community. The duration of services depends on the progress of the juveniles, who are monitored on a regular basis to assess their interactions with their surrounding environment.

The concept of the intensive aftercare program model was based on five main principles [75]:

1. Preparing juveniles for increased responsibility and freedom
2. Facilitating interaction between the youth and the community
3. Assisting both the offender and community support systems
4. Developing new resources and supports
5. Monitoring whether the youth and community facilities can effectively work together

Mixed results have been reported for the intensive aftercare program, which may result in part from criteria not being followed appropriately [9]. More research is needed.

Big Brothers/Big Sisters of America

Big Brothers/Big Sisters of America (BBBSA) is a community-based organization that provides a mentoring relationship for delinquent youths, ages 6 to 18 years, mostly with the help of volunteers. The purpose of BBBSA is to provide these youths with role models, "who will provide them with positive experiences, teach them to make healthy decisions, and help them to strive for the best in life" [76]. BBBSA is one of the most rigorous mentoring programs because of its strict guidelines [76]. All participants undergo a background check, an extensive interview, and a home assessment. There is also a psychosocial assessment conducted on the youth. The guidelines allow the volunteer to learn more about the youth whom he or she will be mentoring. Matching is essential to the effectiveness of this program and is based on the youth's needs, the parent's preference, and the availability of the volunteer. Roberts [77] posited that BBBSA is more effective when paired with other intensive interventions, such as MST.

Tierney and colleagues [78] have demonstrated the effectiveness of BBBSA services (as compared with youths on the waiting list) with respect to the levels of violence, teenaged pregnancy, and inappropriate behaviors. Frecknall and Luks [79] evaluated parental assessments of BBBSA effectiveness and found that 63% of the youths were rated as greatly improved and another 14% as exhibiting some improvement. Parents reported an overall improvement in school attendance, academic achievement, and ability to get along with family members and with peers, enhanced self-esteem, and greater levels of responsibility [79]. Youth who participated in BBBSA presented a more positive attitude toward their academic behavior and performance. The youths also reported that they had more positive relationships with friends and family [80].

Wrap-around Milwaukee

The Wrap-around Milwaukee program relies on community services and natural supports for youths and families to achieve positive outcomes [81]. The wraparound approach ensures that youths and families use a single, individualized treatment plan that connects a youth's strengths and needs with specific services from within the home, school, and the community. This program uses wraparound services for youths with the goal of reducing out of home placements. The Wrap-around Milwaukee approach has been effective in reducing out-of-home placements as well as improving the social functioning of youths [81].

Effectiveness studies, as measured by the Child and Adolescent Functional Assessment Scale [82], have demonstrated promising trends. For a group of 300 delinquent youths enrolled in Wrap-around Milwaukee, the average score of psychosocial impairment decreased from a high level at the time of enrollment to a moderate level at 6 months and 1 year after enrollment in the program. Goldman and Faw [83] have also described positive effects.

Summary

Even though youths are returning to the community from youth corrections facilities at high rates, and aftercare services are limited, several promising postrelease treatment strategies are available upon their return to the community. These programs have demonstrated promising results in reducing recidivism, improving family functioning, and improving the quality of life for youths [84]. Promising postrelease programs are generally described as multidimensional, action-oriented, culturally competent, remedial, and systemic in nature.

Postrelease programs using cognitive-behavior principles are reported to have the best results. The reviewed postrelease programs are consistent with the direction in which the field of juvenile justice is taking—namely, decreasing the number of youths in secure corrections facilities and increasing the number of youths involved in postrelease programs. Before postrelease programs can be considered truly effective, they must address certain issues (eg, the youth's neighborhood, cultural aspects, and family communication) and individual characteristics (eg, trauma and substance use). Promising and evidence-based practices must fit to the population being treated.

In light of the advances made in the area of promising practices and evidence-based practices and postrelease programs, the authors have argued that juveniles in postrelease programs should receive the same level of services as youths involved in the mental health, substance abuse, and child welfare systems.

The emergence of postrelease rehabilitation programs as a relevant research topic in the study of juvenile delinquents has encouraged careful analyses of the development of newly emerging treatment strategies. Short- and long-term outcome studies are needed to capture pertinent information for the months after discharge from community programs. The focus of these studies should measure technical violations (re-arrests and other incidents) and positive outcomes (school attendance, freedom from substance use, peer association, and community involvement). Future longitudinal studies should determine if there are critical characteristics in these youths that would improve the ability of researchers to determine the most salient targets for change. Aggression and its mediating impact on the psychosocial adjustment of delinquent youths is a critical area for further exploration.

References

[1] American Academy of Child and Adolescent Psychiatry Task Force on Juvenile Justice Reform. Washington (DC): American Academy of Child and Adolescent Psychiatry; 2001.
[2] Butterfield F. Prisons replace hospitals for the nation's mentally ill. New York Times March 5, 1998;A1:1–6.
[3] Cocozza J, Skowyra K. Youth with mental health disorders: issues and emerging responses. Juvenile Justice 2000;7(1):1–13.
[4] Grisso T. Double jeopardy: adolescent offenders with mental disorders. Chicago (IL): University of Chicago Press; 2004.
[5] Teplin L, Abram K, McClelland G, et al. Psychiatric disorders in youth in juvenile detention. Arch Gen Psychiatry 2002;59:1133–43.
[6] Timmons-Mitchell J, Brown C, Schulz S, et al. Comparing the mental health needs of female and male incarcerated juvenile delinquents. Behav Sci Law 1997;15:195–202.
[7] Trupin E, Boesky L. Working together for change: co-occurring mental health and substance use disorders among youth involved in the juvenile justice system: cross training, juvenile justice, mental health, substance abuse. Delmar (NY): The National GAINS (Gathering, Assessing Information, Networking Systems) Center; 1999.
[8] ABT (Association of Behavioral Therapy) Associates Inc. Conditions of confinement: juvenile detention and corrections facilities. Washington (DC): Office of Juvenile Justice and Delinquency Prevention; 1994.
[9] Altschuler D. Trends and issues in the adultification of juvenile justice. In: Harris P, editor. Research to results: effective community corrections. Lanham (MD): American Correctional Association; 1999. p. 6–16.
[10] Burns BJ, Hoagwood K, Mrazek P. Effective treatment for mental disorders in children and adolescents. Clin Child Fam Psychol Rev 1999;2(4):199–254.
[11] Hartman L. Children are left out. Psychiatr Serv 1997;48(7):953–4.
[12] Boesky L. Juvenile offenders with mental illness. Lanham (MD): American Correctional Association; 2002.
[13] Stewart DG, Trupin EW. Clinical utility and policy implications of a statewide mental health screening process for juvenile offenders. Psychiatr Serv 2003;54(3):377–82.
[14] Cocozza J. Identifying the needs of juveniles with co-occurring disorders. Corrections Today 1997;6:147–9.
[15] Faenza M, Siegfried C. Responding to the mental health treatment needs of juveniles. Juvenile Justice Update 1998;15:3–4.
[16] Villani S. Responding to the challenges of violence. The New Psychiatric Preview 1999;2(1): 2–4.
[17] Davis D, Bean G, Schumacher J, et al. Prevalence of emotional disorders in a juvenile justice institution population. Am J Forensic Psychol 1991;9:1–13.
[18] Ruchkin VV, Schwab-Stone M, Koposov R, et al. Violence exposure, posttraumatic stress, and personality in juvenile delinquents. J Am Acad Child Adolesc Psychiatry 2002;41(3): 322–9.
[19] Vermeiren R, Ruchkin V, Leckman P, et al. Exposure to violence and suicide risk in adolescents: a community study. J Abnorm Child Psychol 2002;30(5):529–37.
[20] Vermeiren R, Schwab-Stone M, Ruchkin V, et al. Predicting recidivism in delinquent adolescents from psychological and psychiatric assessment. Compr Psychiatry 2002;43(2):142–9.

[21] Henggeler S, Schoenwald S, Borduin C, et al. Multisystemic treatment of antisocial behavior in children and adolescents. New York: Guildford Press; 1988.

[22] Underwood LA, Barretti L, Storms TL, et al. A review of clinical characteristics and residential treatments for adolescent males with mental health disorders: a promising program. Journal of Trauma, Violence and Abuse 2004;5(3):199–242.

[23] Altschuler D, Armstrong T. Juvenile corrections and continuity of care in a community context: the evidence and promising directions. Fed Probat 2002;6:72–7.

[24] Andrews DA, Bonta J, Hoge RD. Classification for effective rehabilitation: rediscover psychology. Crim Justice Behav 1990;17:19–52.

[25] Gendreau P, Goggin C. The principles of effective intervention with offenders. In: Harland AJ, editor. Choosing correctional options that work: defining the demand and evaluating the supply. Thousand Oaks (CA): Sage Publications; 1995.

[26] Kazdin A. Conduct disorders in childhood and adolescence. Beverly Hills (CA): Sage Publications; 1987.

[27] Lipsey MW, Derzon JH. Predictors of violence and serious delinquency in adolescence and early adulthood: a synthesis of longitudinal research. In: Loeber R, Farrington DP, editors. Serious and violent juvenile offenders: risk factors and successful interventions. Thousand Oaks (CA): Sage Publications; 1998. p. 86–105.

[28] Bourdin C. Multisystemic treatment of criminality and violence in adolescents. J Am Acad Child Adolesc Psychiatry 1999;38(3):242–9.

[29] Henggeler S, Mihalic S, Rone L, et al. Blueprints for violence prevention, vol. 6: Multisystemic therapy. Boulder (CO): Center for the Study and Prevention of Violence; 1998.

[30] Melton GB, Pagliocca PM. Treatment in the juvenile justice system: directions for policy and practice. In: Cocozza JJ, editor. Responding to the mental health needs of youth and the juvenile justice system. Seattle (WA): National Coalition for the Mentally Ill in the Criminal Justice System; 1993. p. 107–39.

[31] Mulvey E, Arthur M, Reppucci N. The prevention and treatment of juvenile delinquency: a review of the research. Clin Psychol Rev 1993;13:133–67.

[32] Alexander J, Pugh C, Parsons B. Functional family therapy. In: Elliot DS, editor. Blueprints for violence prevention, vol. 3. Golden (CO): Venture; 2002.

[33] Miller W, Zweben A, Diclemente C, et al. Motivational enhancement therapy manual: a clinical resource guide for therapist treating individuals with alcohol abuse and dependence. The National Institute on Alcohol Abuse and Alcoholism Project MATCH Monograph series, vol. 2. Washington (DC): US Department of Health and Human Services; 1995.

[34] Grisso T, Underwood LA. Screening and assessing co-occurring disorders in the juvenile justice system. Washington (DC): The Federal Office of Juvenile Justice Delinquency Prevention (OJJDP) and The National GAINS (Gathering, Assessing Information, Networking Systems) Center for People with Co-Occurring Disorders in the Justice System; 2005.

[35] Dishion TJ, McCord J, Poulin F. When interventions harm: peer groups and problem behavior. Am Psychol 1999;54(9):755–64.

[36] Underwood L, Mullan W, Walter C. We built them and they came: new insights for managing Ohio's aggressive juvenile offenders with mental illness. Corrections Management Quarterly 1997;1(4):19–27.

[37] Prescot L. Adolescent girls with co-occurring disorders in the juvenile justice system. Delmar (NY): The National GAINS (Gathering, Assessing Information, Networking Systems) Center; 1997.

[38] Veysey B. Recommendations for assessing trauma in youth with histories of sexual and other abuse. New Orleans (LA): The Louisiana State University Health Sciences Center, Juvenile Corrections Program; 2003.

[39] Greenbaum P, Foster-Johnson L, Petrilla A. Co-occurring addictive and mental disorders among adolescents: prevalence research and future directions. Washington (DC): American Orthopsychiatry Association; 1996.

[40] Waldron H, Slesnick N, Peterson T, et al. Treatment outcomes for adolescent substance abuse at 4- and 7-month assessments. J Consult Clin Psychol 2001;69(5):802–18.

[41] Weinberg N, Rahdert E, Colliver J, et al. Adolescent substance abuse: a review of the past 10 years. J Am Acad Child Adolesc Psychiatry 1998;37:252–61.
[42] Thompson L, Riggs P, Mikulich S, et al. Contribution of ADHD symptoms to substance problems and delinquency in conduct-disordered adolescents. J Abnorm Child Psychol 1996; 24:325–47.
[43] Drake R, Mueser K, Clark R, et al. The course, treatment and outcomes of substance disorder in persons with severe mental illness. Am J Orthopsychiatry 1999;66(1):42–51.
[44] Randall J, Henggeler SW, Pickrel SG, et al. Psychiatric comorbidity and the 16-month trajectory of substance-abusing and substance-dependent juvenile offenders. J Am Acad Child Adolesc Psychiatry 1999;38(9):1118–24.
[45] Kessler R, Foster C, Saunder W, et al. Social consequences of psychiatric disorders. Am J Psychiatry 1995;152:1026–32.
[46] Abram K, Teplin L. Co-occurring disorders among mentally ill jail detainees: implications for public policy. Am Psychol 1991;46(10):1036–45.
[47] Kaminer Y, Frances R. Inpatient treatment of adolescents with psychiatric and substance abuse disorders. Hosp Community Psychiatry 1991;42:894–6.
[48] Patterson G, Reid J, Dishion T. Antisocial boys: a social interactional approach, vol. 4. Eugene (OR): Castalia; 1992.
[49] Loeber R, Farrington DP. Young children who commit crime: epidemiology, developmental origins, risk factors, early interventions, and policy implications. Dev Psychopathol 2000; 12:737–62.
[50] Capaldi D, Patterson G. Can violent offenders be distinguished from frequent offenders? Prediction from childhood to adolescence. Journal of Research Crime and Delinquency 1996; 33:206–31.
[51] Farrington D. Childhood, adolescent, and adult features of violent males. In: Aggressive behavior: current perspectives. New York: Plenum Press; 1994. p. 215–40.
[52] Gorman-Smith D, Tolan P, Loeber R, et al. Relation of family problems to patterns of delinquent involvement among urban youth. J Abnorm Child Psychol 1998;26(5):319–33.
[53] Henggeler S, Melton G, Smith L. Family preservation using multisystemic therapy: an effective alternative to incarcerating serious juvenile offenders. J Consult Clin Psychol 1992;60:953–61.
[54] McCord J. A longitudinal study of the link between broken homes and criminality. In: Abnormal offender's delinquency and the criminal justice system. London: Wiley; 1982.
[55] Bilchik S. Minorities in the juvenile justice system. 1999 National Report Series. Juvenile Justice Bulletin. Washington (DC): Department of Justice, Office of Juvenile Justice and Delinquency Prevention; 1999. p. 1–15.
[56] Elliot D. Serious violent offenders: onset, developmental course, and termination: The American Society of Criminology 1993 presidential address. Criminology 1994;32:1–21.
[57] Elliot DS, Huizinga D, Menard S. Multiple problem youth: delinquency, substance use and mental health problems. New York: Springer-Verlag; 1989.
[58] Tolan PH, Guerra NG. What works in reducing adolescent violence: an empirical review of the field. Monograph prepared for the Center for the Study of Prevention of Youth Violence. Boulder (CO): University of Colorado Press; 1994.
[59] Canino I, Spurlock J. Culturally diverse children and adolescents. New York: Guilford Press; 1994.
[60] Boyd-Franklin N. Culturally sensitive treatment of the inner-city African-American adolescent: multi-systemic model. In: Snyder W, Ooms T, editors. Empowering families, helping adolescents: family-centered treatment of adolescents with alcohol, drug abuse and mental health problems. Washington (DC): US Department of Health and Human Services; 1991.
[61] Isaacs M. Assessing the mental health needs of children and adolescents of color in the juvenile justice system. Overcoming institutionalized perceptions and barriers. In: Cocozza J, editor. Responding to the mental health needs of youth in the juvenile justice system. Seattle (WA): National Coalition for the Mentally Ill in the Criminal Justice System; 1992. p. 141–63.
[62] Osher F, Steadman H, Barr H. A best practice approach to community re-entry from jails for

inmates with co-occurring disorders: the APIC model. Delmar (NY): The National GAINS (Gathering, Assessing Information, Networking Systems) Center; 2002.

[63] Group for the Advancement of Psychiatry, Committee on Preventive Psychiatry. Violent behavior in children and youth: preventive intervention from a psychiatric perspective. J Am Acad Child Adolesc Psychiatry 1999;38(3):235–41.

[64] Underwood L, Rawles P. Screening and assessing African-American youth involved in the juvenile justice system: practical considerations. Juvenile Correctional Mental Health Report 2002;2(4):1–84.

[65] Whitehead J, Lab S. A meta-analysis of juvenile correctional treatment. Journal of Research Crime and Delinquency 1998;26(3):276–95.

[66] Petersilia J, Travis J. From prison to society: managing the challenges of prisoner reentry. Crime Delinq 2001;47(3):291–305.

[67] National Mental Health Association. Mental health treatment for youth in the juvenile justice system: a compendium of promising practicing. Washington (DC): National Mental Health Association; 2004.

[68] Henggeler S, Bourdin C. Family therapy and beyond: a multisystemic approach to treating the behavior problems of children and adolescents. Pacific Grove (CA): Brooks/Cole; 1990.

[69] Sheidow AJ, Woodford MS. Multisystemic therapy: an empirically supported, home-based family therapy approach. The Family Journal: Counseling and Therapy for Couples and Families 2003;11(3):257–63.

[70] Cortes L. Home-based family therapy: a misunderstanding of the role and a new challenge for therapists. The Family Journal: Counseling and Therapy for Couples and Families 2004; 12(2):184–8.

[71] Smith D. Risk, reinforcement, retention in treatment, and reoffending for boys and girls in multidimensional treatment foster care. Journal of Emotional and Behavioral Disorders 2004; 12(1):38–48.

[72] Rimm D, Masters J. Behavior therapy: techniques and empirical findings. New York: Academic Press; 1974.

[73] Eddy J, Chamberlain P. Family management and deviant peer association as mediators of the impact of treatment condition on youth antisocial behavior. J Consult Clin Psychol 2000;5: 857–63.

[74] Chamberlain P. The prevention of violent behavior by chronic and serious male juvenile offenders: a 2-year follow-up of a randomized clinical trial. Journal of Emotional and Behavioral Disorders 2004;12(1):2–8.

[75] Altschuler D, Armstrong T. Issues and challenges in the community supervision of juvenile offenders. South Ill Univ Law J 1998;23:469–83.

[76] Fashola O. Developing the talent of African American male students during the nonschool hours. Urban Educ 2003;38(4):398–430.

[77] Roberts C. Effective practice and service delivery: what works; reducing reoffending: guidelines from research and practice. Chichester (UK): Wiley; 1995.

[78] Tierney J, Grossman J, Resch N. Making a difference: an impact study of Big Brothers/Big Sisters. Philadelphia: Public/Private Ventures; 1995.

[79] Frecknall P, Luks A. An evaluation of parental assessment of the Big Brothers/Big Sisters program in New York City. Adolescence 1992;27(107):715–8.

[80] McGill D, Mihalic S, Grotpeter J. Blueprints for violence prevention, book two: Big Brothers Big Sisters of America. Boulder (CO): Center for the Study and Prevention of Violence; 1998.

[81] Burns BJ, Goldman SK. Promising practices in wraparound for children with serious emotional disturbance and their families. Systems of care: promising practices in children's mental health, 1998 series, vol. IV. Washington (DC): Center for Effective Collaboration and Practice, American Institutes for Research; 1999.

[82] Hodges K. CAFAS self-training manual and blank scoring forms. Ypsilanti (MI): Eastern Michigan University Psychology Department; 1995.

[83] Goldman SK, Faw L. Three wraparound models as promising approaches. In: Burns BJ, Goldman S, editors. Promising practices in wraparound for children with serious emotional

disturbance and their families. Systems of care: promising practices in children's mental health, 1998 series, volume IV. Washington (DC): Center for Effective Collaboration and Practice, American Institutes for Research; 1999. p. 17–60.

[84] Kumpfer KL, Alvardo R. Effective family strengthening interventions. Juvenile Justice Bulletin 1998;4:1–15.

ELSEVIER SAUNDERS

Child Adolesc Psychiatric Clin N Am 15 (2006) 557–566

CHILD AND ADOLESCENT PSYCHIATRIC CLINICS OF NORTH AMERICA

Index

Note: Page numbers of article titles are in **boldface** type.

1056-4993/06/$ – see front matter
doi:10.1016/S1056-4993(06)00019-8

childpsych.theclinics.com

Changing Your Address?

Make sure your subscription changes too! When you notify us of your new address, you can help make our job easier by including an exact copy of your Clinics label number with your old address (see illustration below.) This number identifies you to our computer system and will speed the processing of your address change. Please be sure this label number accompanies your old address and your corrected address—you can send an old Clinics label with your number on it or just copy it exactly and send it to the address listed below.

We appreciate your help in our attempt to give you continuous coverage. Thank you.

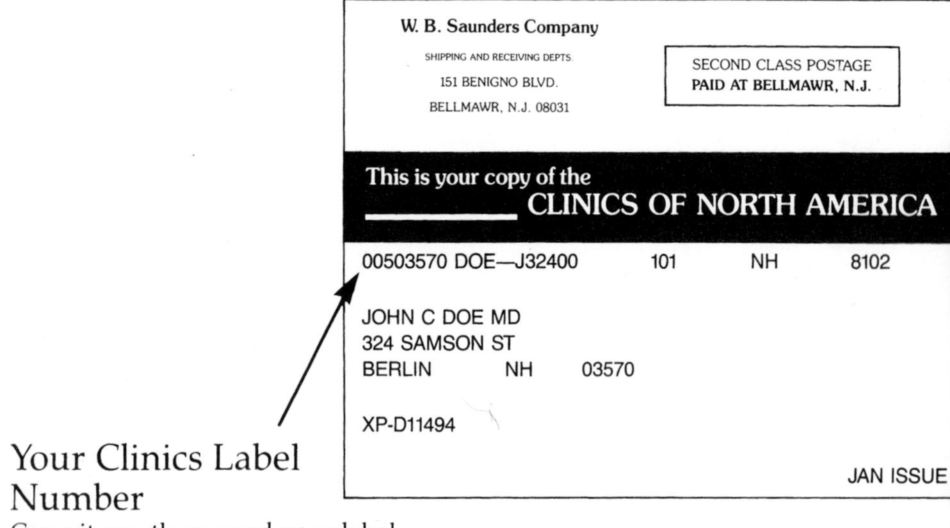

Copy it exactly or send your label along with your address to:
W.B. Saunders Company, Customer Service
Orlando, FL 32887-4800
Call Toll Free 1-800-654-2452

Please allow four to six weeks for delivery of new subscriptions and for processing address changes.